Secessionism and Separatism in Europe and Asia

The boundaries between secessionism and separatism are often blurred and, in many cases, the study of secessionism encompasses that of separatism and vice versa. Recognizing this inherent relationship, this book provides a comparative survey of recent attempts at secession and separatist movements from across Europe and Asia, and assesses the responses of the respective host governments. The chapters address two main questions that arise from the relationship between state governments and secessionist movements: first, how secessionist or separatist movements gather support and mobilize their target populations and, second, how central political authorities respond to the challenges that secessionist or separatist movements pose to their capacity to control the country. With political analysis of recent cases ranging from the Balkans, the USSR, the UK and the Basque Country to Sri Lanka, Burma, China, Tibet and Taiwan, the authors identify both similarities and differences in the processes and outcomes of secessionist and separatist movements across the two distinct regions.

This volume will be an invaluable resource for those who wish to understand the dynamics of secessionist movements, and as such will appeal to students and scholars of Asian and European politics, comparative politics, international relations and conflict studies. It will also be helpful to practitioners and policy-makers who wish to understand and contribute to the resolution of such conflicts.

Jean-Pierre Cabestan is Professor and Head of the Department of Government and International Studies at Hong Kong Baptist University. He is also associate researcher at the Asia Centre at Sciences Po, Paris, France.

Aleksandar Pavković is Associate Professor of Politics at Macquarie University, Sydney, Australia.

Politics in Asia series

Formerly edited by Michael Leifer
London School of Economics

ASEAN and the Security of South-East Asia
Michael Leifer

China's Policy towards Territorial Disputes
The case of the South China Sea islands
Chi-kin Lo

India and Southeast Asia
Indian perceptions and policies
Mohammed Ayoob

Gorbachev and Southeast Asia
Leszek Buszynski

Indonesian Politics under Suharto
Order, development and pressure for change
Michael R.J. Vatikiotis

The State and Ethnic Politics in Southeast Asia
David Brown

The Politics of Nation Building and Citizenship in Singapore
Michael Hill and Lian Kwen Fee

Politics in Indonesia
Democracy, Islam and the ideology of tolerance
Douglas E. Ramage

Communitarian Ideology and Democracy in Singapore
Beng-Huat Chua

The Challenge of Democracy in Nepal
Louise Brown

Japan's Asia Policy
Wolf Mendl

The International Politics of the Asia-Pacific, 1945–1995
Michael Yahuda

Political Change in Southeast Asia
Trimming the banyan tree
Michael R.J. Vatikiotis

Hong Kong
China's challenge
Michael Yahuda

Korea versus Korea
A case of contested legitimacy
B.K. Gills

Taiwan and Chinese Nationalism
National identity and status in international society
Christopher Hughes

Managing Political Change in Singapore
The elected presidency
Kevin Y.L. Tan and Lam Peng Er

Islam in Malaysian Foreign Policy
Shanti Nair

Political Change in Thailand
Democracy and participation
Kevin Hewison

The Politics of NGOs in Southeast Asia
Participation and protest in the Philippines
Gerard Clarke

Malaysian Politics Under Mahathir
R.S. Milne and Diane K. Mauzy

Indonesia and China
The politics of a troubled relationship
Rizal Sukma

Arming the Two Koreas
State, capital and military power
Taik-young Hamm

Engaging China
The management of an emerging power
Edited by Alastair Iain Johnston and Robert S. Ross

Singapore's Foreign Policy
Coping with vulnerability
Michael Leifer

Philippine Politics and Society in the Twentieth Century
Colonial legacies, post-colonial trajectories
Eva-Lotta E. Hedman and John T. Sidel

Constructing a Security Community in Southeast Asia
ASEAN and the problem of regional order
Amitav Acharya

Monarchy in South East Asia
The faces of tradition in transition
Roger Kershaw

Korea after the Crash
The politics of economic recovery
Brian Bridges

The Future of North Korea
Edited by Tsuneo Akaha

The International Relations of Japan and South East Asia
Forging a new regionalism
Sueo Sudo

Power and Change in Central Asia
Edited by Sally N. Cummings

The Politics of Human Rights in Southeast Asia
Philip Eldridge

Political Business in East Asia
Edited by Edmund Terence Gomez

Singapore Politics under the People's Action Party
Diane K. Mauzy and R.S. Milne

Media and Politics in Pacific Asia
Duncan McCargo

Japanese Governance
Beyond Japan Inc.
Edited by Jennifer Amyx and Peter Drysdale

China and the Internet
Politics of the digital leap forward
Edited by Christopher R. Hughes and Gudrun Wacker

Challenging Authoritarianism in Southeast Asia
Comparing Indonesia and Malaysia
Edited by Ariel Heryanto and Sumit K. Mandal

Cooperative Security and the Balance of Power in ASEAN and the ARF
Ralf Emmers

Islam in Indonesian Foreign Policy
Rizal Sukma

Media, War and Terrorism
Responses from the Middle East and Asia
Edited by Peter Van der Veer and Shoma Munshi

China, Arms Control and Nonproliferation
Wendy Frieman

Communitarian Politics in Asia
Edited by Chua Beng Huat

East Timor, Australia and Regional Order
Intervention and its aftermath in Southeast Asia
James Cotton

Domestic Politics, International Bargaining and China's Territorial Disputes
Chien-peng Chung

Democratic Development in East Asia
Becky Shelley

International Politics of the Asia-Pacific since 1945
Michael Yahuda

Asian States
Beyond the developmental perspective
Edited by Richard Boyd and Tak-Wing Ngo

Civil Life, Globalization, and Political Change in Asia
Organizing between family and state
Edited by Robert P. Weller

Realism and Interdependence in Singapore's Foreign Policy
Narayanan Ganesan

Party Politics in Taiwan
Party change and the democratic evolution of Taiwan, 1991–2004
Dafydd Fell

State Terrorism and Political Identity in Indonesia
Fatally belonging
Ariel Heryanto

China's Rise, Taiwan's Dilemmas and International Peace
Edited by Edward Friedman

Japan and China in the World Political Economy
Edited by Saadia M. Pekkanen and Kellee S. Tsai

Order and Security in Southeast Asia
Essays in memory of Michael Leifer
Edited by Joseph Chinyong Liow and Ralf Emmers

State Making in Asia
Edited by Richard Boyd and Tak-Wing Ngo

US–China Relations in the 21st Century
Power transition and peace
Zhiqun Zhu

Empire and Neoliberalism in Asia
Edited by Vedi R. Hadiz

South Korean Engagement Policies and North Korea
Identities, norms and the sunshine policy
Son Key-young

Chinese Nationalism in the Global Era
Christopher R. Hughes

Indonesia's War over Aceh
Last stand on Mecca's porch
Matthew N. Davies

Advancing East Asian Regionalism
Edited by Melissa G. Curley and Nicholas Thomas

Political Cultures in Asia and Europe
Citizens, states and societal values
Jean Blondel and Takashi Inoguchi

Rethinking Injustice and Reconciliation in Northeast Asia
The Korean experience
Edited by Gi-Wook Shin, Soon-Won Park and Daqing Yang

Foreign Policy Making in Taiwan
From principle to pragmatism
Dennis Van Vranken Hickey

The Balance of Power in Asia-Pacific Security
US–China policies on regional order
Liselotte Odgaard

Taiwan in the 21st Century
Aspects and limitations of a development model
Edited by Robert Ash and J. Megan Green

Elections as Popular Culture in Asia
Edited by Chua Beng Huat

Security and Migration in Asia
The dynamics of securitisation
Edited by Melissa G. Curley and Wong Siu-lun

Political Transitions in Dominant Party Systems
Learning to lose
Edited by Edward Friedman and Joseph Wong

Torture, Truth and Justice
The case of Timor-Leste
Elizabeth Stanley

A Rising China and Security in East Asia
Identity construction and security discourse
Rex Li

Rise of China
Beijing's strategies and implications for the Asia-Pacific
Edited by Hsin-Huang Michael Hsiao and Cheng-yi Lin

Governance and Regionalism in Asia
Edited by Nicholas Thomas

Constructing a Security Community in Southeast Asia
ASEAN and the problem of regional order
Second edition
Amitav Acharya

East Asia's New Democracies
Deepening, reversal, non-liberal alternatives
Yin-wah Chu and Siu-lun Wong

China's Multilateral Cooperation in Asia and the Pacific
Institutionalizing Beijing's 'Good Neighbour Policy'
Chien-peng Chung

The International Politics of the Asia-Pacific
Third edition
Michael Yahuda

Asia-Pacific Security Dynamics in the Obama Era
A new world emerging
S. Mahmud Ali

New Thinking about the Taiwan Issue
Theoretical insights into its origins, dynamics and prospects
Jean-Marc F. Blanchard and Dennis V. Hickey

Votes, Party Systems and Democracy in Asia
Jungug Choi

Security Cooperation in Northeast Asia
Architecture and beyond
Edited by T.J. Pempel and Chung-Min Lee

Japan and Germany as Regional Actors
Evaluating change and continuity after the Cold War
Alexandra Sakaki

Japan's Relations with Southeast Asia
The Fukuda Doctrine and beyond
Edited by Peng Er Lam

Secessionism and Separatism in Europe and Asia
To have a state of one's own
Edited by Jean-Pierre Cabestan and Aleksandar Pavković

Secessionism and Separatism in Europe and Asia

To have a state of one's own

Edited by
Jean-Pierre Cabestan and
Aleksandar Pavković

LONDON AND NEW YORK

First published 2013
by Routledge
2 Park Square, Milton Park, Abingdon, Oxon OX14 4RN

Simultaneously published in the USA and Canada
by Routledge
711 Third Avenue, New York, NY 10017

Routledge is an imprint of the Taylor & Francis Group, an informa business

© 2013 Jean-Pierre Cabestan and Aleksandar Pavković

The right of the editor to be identified as the author of the editorial
material, and of the authors for their individual chapters, has been asserted
in accordance with sections 77 and 78 of the Copyright, Designs and
Patents Act 1988.

All rights reserved. No part of this book may be reprinted or reproduced or
utilised in any form or by any electronic, mechanical, or other means, now
known or hereafter invented, including photocopying and recording, or in
any information storage or retrieval system, without permission in writing
from the publishers.

Trademark notice: Product or corporate names may be trademarks or
registered trademarks, and are used only for identification and explanation
without intent to infringe.

British Library Cataloguing in Publication Data
A catalogue record for this book is available from the British Library

Library of Congress Cataloging in Publication Data
Secessionism and separatism in Europe and Asia : to have a state of one's
own / edited by Jean-Pierre Cabestan and Aleksandar Pavković.
   p. cm. – (Politics in Asia series)
   Includes bibliographical references and index.
   1. Secession–History. 2. Separatist movements–History.
   3. Secession–Europe–History. 4. Separatist movements–Europe–
History. 5. Secession–Asia–History. 6. Separatist movements–Asia–
History. I. Cabestan, Jean-Pierre. II. Pavkovic, Aleksandar.
   JC327.S465 2012
   320.54095–dc23
                2012012973

ISBN: 978-0-415-66774-6 (hbk)
ISBN: 978-0-203-09426-6 (ebk)

Typeset in Times New Roman
by Taylor & Francis Books

Contents

List of illustrations	xi
Notes on contributors	xii
Secession and separatism from a comparative perspective: an introduction	1
ALEKSANDAR PAVKOVIĆ AND JEAN-PIERRE CABESTAN	
1 Sovereignty, national self-determination and secession: reflections on state-making and breaking in Asia and Europe	20
JAMES MAYALL	

PART I
Europe

35

2 Paradise lost: autonomy and separatism in the South Caucasus and beyond	37
JOHN CUFFE AND DAVID S. SIROKY	
3 Patterns of secession and disintegration in the USSR	53
RICHARD SAKWA	
4 From Yugoslavia to the western Balkans	66
RADMILA NAKARADA	
5 Host state responses to ethnic rebellion: Serbia and Macedonia in comparison	82
KEIICHI KUBO	
6 Seceding by the force of arms: Chechnya and Kosovo	99
ALEKSANDAR PAVKOVIĆ	

x *Contents*

7 Secession and liberal democracy: the case of the Basque Country 110
FERRAN REQUEJO AND MARC SANJAUME I CALVET

8 Nationalism, unionism and secession in Scotland 127
MICHAEL KEATING

PART II
Asia 145

9 Secessionism in independent India: failed attempts,
irredentism, and accommodation 147
JEAN-LUC RACINE

10 Separatism in Sri Lanka 164
DAVID FEITH

11 Separatism, ethnocracy, and the future of ethnic politics in
Burma (Myanmar) 178
RENAUD EGRETEAU

12 Language practices and protracted conflict: the Tibet–China
dispute 196
ROBERT BARNETT

13 Separatism in China: the case of the Xinjiang Uyghur
Autonomous Region 220
DRU C. GLADNEY

14 The case of Taiwan: independence without secession? 237
JEAN-PIERRE CABESTAN

Index 254

Illustrations

Figures

2.1	Separatism and current autonomy status	41
2.2	Relationship between separatism and autonomy status	41
7.1	Map of Spain	112
7.2	Map of the Basque Country	114
7.A1	Basque elections (1980–2009)	122
7.A2	General elections: results from the Basque Country (1977–2008)	122
8.1	Scottish GDP as a percentage of the UK figure (1924–2006)	132
8.2	Support for independence in Scotland (1999–2010)	137
8.3	National identity in Scotland (1992–2006)	138
9.1	Population map of India (2011)	151
10.1	Sri Lanka – Tamil majority areas (left) and area claimed as a Tamil homeland by the LTTE (right)	165
11.1	States and regions of Burma (Myanmar) since 2008	179

Tables

2.1	Theoretical expectations of ethnic mobilization	39
2.2	Bivariate relationship between separatism and current autonomy status	40
2.3	Relationship between separatism and autonomy status	42
7.1	A summary of Basque political parties	115
9.1	Religions in India (2001) as a percentage of the population and in millions	149

Contributors

Robert Barnett is the Director of the Modern Tibetan Studies Program, an Associate Research Scholar and an Adjunct Professor at Columbia University in New York. He directs development and educational projects in Tibet and ran an annual summer course for foreign students at Tibet University from 2000 to 2006. His latest books are *Tibetan Modernities: Notes from the Field* (with Ronald Schwartz, 2008) and *Lhasa: Streets with Memories* (2006). His recent publications include studies of modern Tibetan history, post-1950 leaders in Tibet, Tibetan cinema and TV, women and politics in Tibet, and contemporary exorcism rituals.

Jean-Pierre Cabestan is Professor and Head of the Department of Government and International Studies at Hong Kong Baptist University. He is also associate researcher at the Asia Centre at Sciences Po, Paris and at the French Centre for Research on Contemporary China, Hong Kong. His main themes of research are Chinese politics and law, China's foreign and security policies, China–Taiwan relations and Taiwanese politics. His most recent publications include *La politique internationale de la Chine. Entre intégration et volonté de puissance* (Paris: Presses de Sciences Po, 2011).

John Cuffe is a PhD candidate in the Department of Political Science at the University of California, Irvine, USA. He is interested in models of party formation and competition, mass political behaviour, ethnic conflict and political methodology.

Renaud Egreteau is a Research Assistant Professor with the Hong Kong Institute for the Humanities and Social Sciences (including the Centre of Asian Studies) at The University of Hong Kong. A political scientist, he wrote *Wooing the Generals: India's New Burma Policy* (Delhi: Authorspress, 2003) and *Histoire de la Birmanie contemporaine: le pays des prétoriens* (Paris: Fayard, 2010). His research focuses on interstate relations in Asia, democratization processes in Burma as well as on the contemporary trajectories and transnational networks of various Indian and Burmese diasporic communities.

David Feith has been involved in observing, researching, interpreting and writing about the ethnic conflict in Sri Lanka since 1983. Since 2003, he has taught at Monash College, Melbourne, Australia. He has written numerous articles on Sri Lanka. Recent publications include the chapter 'Tamil Nationalism in Sri Lanka' in *Sri Lanka: 60 Years of 'Independence' and Beyond?* ed. A. Pararajasingham (2009) and 'Tamil and Sinhala Relations in Sri Lanka: A Historical and Contemporary Perspective' in *Global Change, Peace and Security* Vol. 22, No. 3 (October 2010).

Dru C. Gladney is Professor of Anthropology at Pomona College in Claremont, California, USA. Previously, he was President of the Pacific Basin Institute at Pomona (from 2006–2010), and prior to that was Professor of Asian Studies at the University of Hawai'i at Manoa (1993–2006), as well as Senior Research Fellow at the East–West Center (1993–1998) and inaugural Dean of the Asia-Pacific Center in Honolulu, Hawai'i (1998–2000). He is the author of the award-winning book *Muslim Chinese: Ethnic Nationalism in the People's Republic* (Harvard University Press, 1996, 1st edn 1991), as well as *Ethnic Identity in China: The Making of a Muslim Minority Nationality* (Cengage, 1998). He edited *Making Majorities: Constituting the Nation in Japan, China, Korea, Malaysia, Fiji, Turkey, and the U.S.* (Stanford University Press, 1998) and *Dislocating China: Muslims, Minorities, and Other Sub-Altern Subjects* (Chicago: University of Chicago Press, 2004).

Michael Keating is Professor of Politics at the University of Aberdeen and has previously held faculty appointments at the European University Institute, University of Western Ontario, University of Strathclyde and North Staffordshire Polytechnic. He has published widely on nationalism and territorial politics. His most recent books are *The Independence of Scotland* (Oxford University Press, 2009), *Political Autonomy and Divided Societies* (edited with Alain-G. Gagnon; Palgrave 2012) and *The Crisis of Social Democracy in Europe* (edited with David McCrone; Edinburgh University Press, 2012). He is currently writing a book on *Rescaling Europe*, to be published by Oxford University Press.

Keiichi Kubo is Associate Professor at Waseda University, Japan. He has published a monograph on ex-Yugoslavia (in Japanese), entitled *The State Torn Apart: Democratization and Ethnic Problems in the Former Yugoslavia* (Tokyo: Yushindo-Kobunsya, 2003) as well as various journal articles written in Japanese and English. His recent publications include two chapters in *The Ashgate Research Companion to Secession*, eds A. Pavković and P. Radan (Ashgate, 2011) and 'Why Kosovar Albanians Took Up Arms against the Serbian Regime: The Genesis and Expansion of the UÇK in Kosovo', *Europe–Asia Studies*, Vol. 62, No. 7 (2010).

James Mayall is Emeritus Professor of International Relations at the University of Cambridge, a fellow of Sidney Sussex College and of the British Academy and Academic Adviser to the Royal College of Defence Studies.

He has written widely on the impact of nationalism on international politics and on the theory and practice of international society. Among his recent publications are *Towards the New Horizon: World Order in the 21st Century* (with Krishnan Srinivasan, 2009) and *The New Protectorates, International Tutelage and the Making of Liberal States* (with Ricardo Soares de Oliveira, 2011).

Radmila Nakarada is a Professor of Peace Studies and the Director of the Peace Studies Center at the Faculty of Political Sciences, University of Beograd, Serbia. She was the first spokesperson for the Yugoslav Truth and Reconciliation Commission (established in 2001). Recent publications include the book *Disintegration of Yugoslavia, Problems of Diagnosing, Confronting, Transcending* (in Serbian, Beograd, 2008) and essays 'The Normative Paradoxes of Globalization' (*Security Dialogues*, 2, 2010), 'Serbia and NATO – the Sources of Dilemmas' (in *Integration of Western Balkans in the Global Security Network*, Beograd, 2011) and 'Globalization and the New Normative Standards' (*State and Democracy*, FPS, Beograd, 2011).

Aleksandar Pavković is Associate Professor of Politics at Macquarie University, Sydney, Australia. He previously taught at the universities of Beograd, Melbourne and Macau (China). Apart from the theory and practice of secession, his research interests include the idea of the World State and comparative study of national anthems. He is the author (with Peter Radan) of *Creating New States: Theory and Practice of Secession* (Ashgate, 2007). He edited (with Peter Radan) *On the Way to Statehood* (Ashgate, 2007), the *Ashgate Research Companion to Secession* (Ashgate, 2011) and (with Igor Primoratz) *Patriotism* (Ashgate, 2008).

Jean-Luc Racine is Senior CNRS (French National Centre for Scientific Research) Fellow at the Centre for South Asian Studies of the Ecole des Hautes Etudes en Sciences Sociales (EHESS) and Vice-President of Asia Centre, Paris. His last volumes edited in French have focused on India's Asia relationship (CNRS Editions, 2009) and the geopolitics of Pakistan (*Hérodote* Special Issue, No. 139, 2010).

Ferran Requejo is Professor of Political Science at the Universidad Pompeu Fabra, Barcelona, Spain. He was awarded the *Rudolf Wildenmann Prize* (ECPR, 1999), the *Ramon Trias Fargas* Prize (2002) and the *Spanish Political Science Association Prize* (2006). He was a member of the Spanish Electoral Board (2004–2008). Recent works include *Federalism, Plurinationality and Democratic Constitutionalism* (Routledge, 2012), *Federalism beyond Federations* (Ashgate, 2011), *Federalism and Plurinationality. Theory and Case Analysis* (Routledge, 2011), *Political Liberalism and Multinational Democracies* (Routledge, 2010), *Foreign Policy of Constituent Units at the Beginning of 21st Century* (IEA, 2010) and *Multinational Federalism and Value Pluralism* (Routledge, 2005).

Richard Sakwa is Professor of Russian and European Politics at the University of Kent and an Associate Fellow of the Russia and Eurasia Programme at the Royal Institute of International Affairs, Chatham House, UK. He has published widely on Soviet, Russian and post-Communist affairs. Recent books include *Russian Politics and Society* (London and New York, Routledge, 4th edn, 2008), *Putin: Russia's Choice* (Routledge, 2nd edn, 2008), *The Quality of Freedom: Khodorkovsky, Putin and the Yukos Affair* (Oxford University Press, 2009) and *The Crisis of Russian Democracy: The Dual State, Factionalism, and the Medvedev Succession* (Cambridge University Press, 2011).

Marc Sanjaume i Calvet is a Teaching Assistant in the Political and Social Sciences Department of Universidad Pompeu Fabra, Barcelona, Spain. He is a member of the Political Theory Research Group. His recent publications include 'Basque Secession: From Bullets to Ballots?' in *The Ashgate Research Companion to Secession*, eds A. Pavković and P. Radan (Ashgate, 2011) and (with Jaume López and Ivan Serrano) 'Estat de la qüestió en la literatura académica' in *Noves estatalitats i processos de sobirania*, ed. A. Bosch, Idees, 33, 2010.

David S. Siroky is Assistant Professor of Political Science in the School of Politics and Global Studies at Arizona State University, and faculty affiliate of the Center for the Study of Religion and Conflict as well as the Melikian Center for Russian, Eurasian and East European Studies, USA. Before taking up his current position, he was Henry Hart Rice Fellow at Yale University. His research has appeared in *Comparative Sociology, Defence and Peace Economics, Democratization, Ethnopolitics, Nationalities Papers, Statistics Surveys*; he also wrote a chapter in *The Ashgate Research Companion to Secession* eds. A. Pavković and P. Radan (Ashgate, 2011).

Secession and separatism from a comparative perspective

An introduction

Aleksandar Pavković and Jean-Pierre Cabestan[1]

Secession is a contested concept, at least among jurists and political scientists. The subject of contention is not the outcome of secession: almost everyone agrees that its outcome is a new state formed on a territory that was governed by another, already existing state prior to secession. Scholars appear to differ primarily in how they view the process of secession and the type of sovereignty (colonial or non-colonial) that was exercised by the previous state over the territory on which the new state is created. Thus, Crawford's and Radan's definitions stand at the opposite ends of the spectrum of definitions of secession: the former defines secession as " ... the creation of a State by the use or threat of force without the consent of the former sovereign" (Crawford 2006: 375), whereas the latter defines it as the creation of a new state "upon territory previously forming part of, or being a colonial entity of, an existing State" (Radan 2008: 218). According to Crawford's narrow definition, there are very few cases of secession (in fact only one, that of Bangladesh in 1971) partly because, in the cases of federations—USSR, Yugoslavia, Czechoslovakia—at some point, there was no effective "former sovereign" to withhold consent and, in many cases of decolonization, there was no use or threat of force. In contrast, according to Radan's definition, there have been many secessions as all cases of decolonization, dissolution of federations, and partition of states into new states count as secession. This book's contributors appear to accept neither Radan's nor Crawford's definition: they do not regard decolonization or all cases of dissolution of federations as secession, and nor do they assume that the use or threat of force is necessary for a secession. They assume that secession can be achieved by peaceful means but that it requires an *intentional* act or acts of political and legal withdrawal of a territory from an existing state, a territory which is not, in the United Nations (UN) jargon, classified as non-self-governing territory, that is, as a colony.

There are no such scholarly disagreements regarding separatism. Separatism is based on a political objective that aims to reduce the political and other powers of the central government of a state over a particular territory and to transfer those powers to the population or elites representing the population of the territory in question. As Wood succinctly puts it, separatism " ... [covers] all instances of political alienation which feature a desire for the reduction of control by a central authority in a specific area" (Wood 1981: 110).

There has been no attempt to narrow this definition by restricting separatism to the use of particular means (e.g., force or the threat of the use of force) or to a particular kind of territory or power. As Wood (1981: 110) notes, some separatist movements develop in a secessionist direction: they aim to remove not some powers but all the powers, including sovereign powers, from the central governments. In this sense, secessionism is the end point of separatism: it is a separatism that aims to remove all the sovereign powers of an existing state. And some secessionist movements—such as those of Aceh in Indonesia or of Tibet in China—become merely separatist by publicly abandoning their previous secessionist objectives. As some political movements oscillate between separatist and secessionist goals as well (Wood 1981: 110), in practice, the distinction between secessionism and separatism may become rather blurred. In theory, there is no obstacle for a movement to shift from merely separatist to secessionist political goals. The obstacles to the move to secessionism are more of a practical nature: populations supportive of some form of (for example cultural) separatism may not be supportive of secessionism, and host states may tolerate or accommodate certain forms of separatism while suppressing any form of secessionism. Cases of the latter kind discussed in this volume include India, Spain and, to some extent, China/Taiwan. China's Xinjiang, which is also discussed in this book, presents similar difficulties: a divided society made up of around 43 percent Uighurs, mostly in favor at least of meaningful political autonomy (and some—whose number is hard to estimate—who favor independence) and nearly as many Han Chinese (between 40 and 42 percent) strongly attached to the current arrangement—a formal but superficial autonomy contradicted by the Communist Party of China's (CCP) complete control of the region.

In view of these blurred boundaries between secessionism and separatism, in many cases, the study of secessionism in fact encompasses that of separatism and vice versa. This is why both appear in the title of this volume. It should be added here that neither secessionism nor separatism has been used by the contributors of this book in a derogatory way; they have been understood as political phenomena subject to scholarly study.

The present volume includes studies of secessionism/separatism in Europe—the United Kingdom (UK)'s Scotland, Spain's Basque Country, former Yugoslavia, Serbia, Macedonia as well as in the periphery of Europe—the former USSR and the Caucasus. In Asia, the studies include India, Sri Lanka, Burma (Myanmar), Tibet, Xinjiang and China/Taiwan. In the first chapter, James Mayall provides a general overview of the global impact of secessionism on international relations.

Although the chapters do not follow the same methodological model or framework, they all explore separatism/secessionism within the triadic nexus of secessionist/separatist movements, the central government of the host state, and outside states or organizations. Most studies of this phenomenon have explored a variety of aspects of this basic nexus (Wood 1981; Siroky 2011). Most of the chapters in the volume deal with secessionist movements and the

Introduction   3

central authorities: apart from the introductory chapter, a few explore in some detail the role of external factors—outside states and international organizations—in the dynamic relations between host states' governments and secessionist movements.

This volume's contributions mainly address two types of questions arising from this dynamic: first, in what way secessionist/separatist movements gather support and mobilize their target populations and, second, how central political authorities respond to the challenges that secessionist/separatist movements pose to their capacity to control the country. The exploration of the first set of issues leads our authors to examine the social, ethnic, and identity cleavages of which these movements make use, as well as the grievances which they exploit or voice. The exploration of the second leads to inquiry into the responses that the secessionist/separatist movements face. Apart from the two basic types of response—accommodation of separatist demands and suppression of the separatist/secessionist movements—and the frequent oscillation or combination of the two, our contributors also explore a third, relatively unusual response—that of indifference. As we shall see in Chapter 8, the English general public and the UK central government seemed at times to meet the Scottish secessionist demands with polite indifference.

In Chapter 1, James Mayall analyzes the present and possible future responses to the secessionist creation of new states and briefly compares contemporary responses to secession by the states in Europe and Asia. Prior to the American and French revolutions, conquest, dynastic marriage, and sometimes purchase or exchange were considered legitimate means of ceding territory; it was the will of the rulers, and not of the ruled, that mattered. The idea of popular sovereignty gradually delegitimized all these means, and the will of the "people"—inhabitants of the territory—came to be viewed as the only factor that determined the "belonging" of a contested or disputed territory. However, the purchase of territory—in particular, colonial territory—remained a legitimate means of acquisition of territory well into the nineteenth century and, with the currently rising sea levels threatening the existence of a few established island states, the idea has recently been revived. With the spread of nation-states and nationalisms in Europe in the nineteenth century, Mayall notes, the territory of a nation-state became sacralized: the loss of national territory to another state or to a new state came to be viewed as unacceptable. The dissolution of empires—the Ottoman and the Austrian ones—was, however, not regarded as the loss of territory of any particular nation and, after 1919, was sanctioned by the principle of self-determination of peoples. The principle, Mayall notes, does not determine who the people or peoples are, and we have not found, as yet, any effective normative principle that can determine this. During the age of decolonization from 1947 until the 1970s, the principle of *uti possidetis juris* was used to determine the territory that is the subject of self-determination—this in effect kept the existing colonial borders. The UN organization, which advanced and regulated the decolonization project, refused to give countenance to the application of this principle

4   A. Pavković and J.-P. Cabestan

outside the colonial context. Unilateral secession—secession without the consent of the host state—is still banned from the realm of legitimacy, and only in a few cases have states that gained independence through unilateral secession (Bangladesh, for example) gained wide international recognition (see also Geldenhuys 2011; Radan 2011). But Mayall notes that some democratic states of Europe—as well as Canada—agreed to secession from their territory: Slovakia seceded peacefully from Czechoslovakia in 1993 and Montenegro from the Union of Serbia and Montenegro in 2006. Provided that there is enough popular support for secession, Scotland and Quebec would also be able to secede with the consent of their respective host states (see also Chapter 8). No democratic state in Asia, Mayall notes, appears to be ready to countenance secession from its territory: the cases of India and Sri Lanka are obvious examples of the suppression of secessionist attempts by force by democratic states (see also Chapters 9 and 10). But not all democratic states in Europe are so permissive: Spain, for example, rules out any secession of the Basque region. In general, however, after the end of the Cold War, states in Europe and North America have shown a more relaxed or tolerant attitude to secession than have states in Asia. Whether the shift of global power to Asia—to India and China in particular—will see a retreat from this attitude and the renewed rejection of secession is, in Mayall's opinion, uncertain. Further modernization of these emergent powers, according to Mayall, may involve a shift to a more permissive stance toward secession and a relaxation of their insistence on the sacredness and inviolability of states' territories.

In contrast to Mayall's chapter, which deals with the response of the states and the international community to secession, Cuffe and Siroky in Chapter 2 explore one set of institutional or historical factors that influence or foster separatism and secession. In recent decades, social scientists have debated the impact of institutional autonomy on secessionism: some have argued that it gives rise to secessionism whereas others have argued that it "dampens" secessionist inclinations. Cuffe and Siroky believe that the category of "non-autonomous" groups in these debates has conflated two distinct types of groups—those that never enjoyed autonomy and those that had autonomy but lost it. The principal hypothesis, put forward and tested in this chapter, is that the groups that had autonomy and lost it display more separatist and secessionist tendencies than the groups that never had autonomy or the groups that had not lost the autonomy they currently possess. Cuffe and Siroky thus argue that lost autonomy fosters ethnic resentment, reduces the viability of using non-violent strategies, and significantly weakens the central government's ability to make credible commitments to the group that lost autonomy. Their first test, on 115 ethnic groups in Europe and Asia, shows that 89 percent of the groups that lost autonomy have launched secessionist campaigns in contrast to only 2 percent of groups that were never autonomous. The second test involves the survey of autonomous republics and other regions (but not the highest federal units, union republics) in the former

USSR: the great majority of these autonomous regions were not secessionist in any way, and the great majority of autonomous regions in west European states (Italy and Portugal) are not secessionist either (for the secessionism of the Soviet Union republic, see Chapter 3). Current autonomous status does not, according to Cuffe and Siroky, indicate the likelihood of secessionist tendencies. Finally, their hypothesis is tested in the case of Georgia. Of the five regions with secessionist potential in Georgia—Abkhazia, South Ossetia, Adjara, Javakheti, and Kvemo-Kartli—only two—Abkhazia and South Ossetia—seceded from Georgia whereas the other three regions showed few if any, separatist tendencies. These two regions had suffered from the retraction or withdrawal of their previous autonomy in the USSR and, in Cuffe's and Siroky's view, this is the principal factor that contributed their secession. The two authors do not claim that retraction or loss of autonomy is always the principal cause of or motivator for secession, but only that it can in some cases explain secession better than other factors cited in literature. Although their hypothesis needs further confirmation, it does identify an important and neglected factor in the explanation of secessions or secession claims. Some cases discussed in this book—in particular Kosovo, Tibet, and Xinjiang—appear to provide further evidence for their hypothesis.

In his chapter on the disintegration of the USSR in Chapter 3, Richard Sakwa adopts another explanatory model: that of the impact of democratization on federations that were not based on democratic foundations. Democratization in such federations challenged their very foundations, leading either to further decentralization or disintegration or to centralization. In the case of the USSR, Sakwa maintains, "[T]he latent powers of the republics now came to life, and were exploited by entrepreneurial elites to advance their own agendas." Partly as a result of confused and contradictory responses of the central government to secessionist demands, this led to the disintegration of the federation. In contrast to scholars who emphasize the role of nationalism, Sakwa argues that, at the start of Gorbachev's reforms in 1985, there was relatively little "separatist sentiment" in the USSR and that popular mobilization was initially aimed not at secession but at the removal of the Communist mono-party monopoly and the political system that it dominated. The "entrepreneurial elites" mobilized their target national groups first in support of Gorbachev's democratizing reforms and, then, starting with the Baltic republics, for secession from the Soviet Union. In view of this, he writes, "nationalism as such … was a product rather than the cause of the Soviet disintegration."

In the process of disintegration, Sakwa notes different timing and different models of secessionist mobilization. First, the "decolonization" model of the union republics—Latvia, Lithuania, Estonia, and Moldova—which were forcibly incorporated into the USSR during World War Two and which aimed to reverse their "colonization" by secession. Second, the "affirmation" model in the largest union republics—Russia and Ukraine—aimed to affirm their perceived national interests, which the Soviet federal model ignored or suppressed. In Russia, there was a widespread perception that it was subsidizing

6   *A. Pavković and J.-P. Cabestan*

other parts of the USSR while being the object of the opprobrium of non-Russian national groups. Under the presidency of Yeltsin, Russia joined the Baltic "early seceders" in proclaiming its sovereignty in June 1990, followed by other union republics. Finally, there was the "secession by default" of the union republics such as Belarus and the Central Asian republics, which had secession thrust upon them where there were no secessionist movements and, in most cases, the Communist elites were taken by surprise by the disintegration of the Soviet Union and managed to stay in power only in "re-branding" themselves as nationalists.

The disintegration of the USSR, culminating in the mutually agreed dissolution in December 1991, was accompanied by relatively little violence. This was not so with attempts at secession from the states formed out of former union republics—Moldova (Transnistria), Georgia (Abkhazia, South Ossetia), Russia (Chechnya), and Azerbaijan (Nagorno-Karabakh). All of those attempts led to large-scale violent conflicts. Sakwa notes that there is no accepted international mechanism to adjudicate these competing claims to statehood, and that the rhetoric justifying secession in those cases was not of self-determination but of just cause or remedies to restore justice. The violent secessions of small, often non-viable entities, in his opinion, draw our attention to the need to find solutions to competing claims to statehood in ethnically mixed areas other than that of nation-state formation by the use of force, the method that is still predominant in the post-Soviet space and in other parts of the world.

In Chapter 4, Radmila Nakarada explores some features of Yugoslavia's dissolution that distinguish it from the dissolutions of Czechoslovakia and the USSR. Yugoslavia initiated a form of socialism "with a human face," well-known for its promotion of self-management and a non-aligned international position, which included a high degree of cooperation with the European Community (EC). Yet many of the features that distinguished Yugoslavia from other Communist-ruled countries also involved a potential for disintegration: for example, its open market and heavily indebted economy were more exposed to global economic downturns; as a result, the credit crunch that Yugoslavia witnessed in the early 1980s led to a sudden decrease in the standard of living and consequent widespread industrial unrest. Nakarada also argues that Slovene and Croat separatism/secessionism was not a response to rising Serb nationalism and nationalist mobilization in Serbia, but has roots in autochthonous separatist and nationalist political movements in the late 1960s and 1970s. She suggests that, in the Yugoslav case, democratization—the introduction of multi-party elections—favored the separatist political movements that had been suppressed before. In this respect, the democratization model employed by Sakwa in the previous chapter is of some relevance to the Yugoslav case. Croatia and Slovenia were, in her view, the initiators of the chain of secessions involving Bosnia and Herzegovina (and several attempted secessions from this emerging state), Kosovo, Macedonia, and finally, Montenegro. This classification has some parallel in Sakwa's classification of the secessionist units of the USSR into "early seceders," "affirmation seceders," and "seceders by default." In Bosnia and Herzegovina, as well as in Kosovo, the civil wars, resulting from the armed rebellions of secessionist populations, were ended only by the North Atlantic Treaty Organization's (NATO) military intervention. This kind of conflict and intervention has no clear parallel in the disintegration of the USSR, although some parallels could be found with violent secessionist conflicts in post-Soviet space that are discussed by Sakwa as well as by Cuffe and Siroky (Chapter 2) and Pavković (Chapter 6). In contrast, the secessions of Macedonia and of Montenegro were "collateral" but peaceful secessions resulting from the earlier secessions. In conclusion, Nakarada suggests the following possible explanations for the extreme violence that characterized some of the Yugoslav secessions: extreme violence and wars were possibly a continuation or replica of the extreme violence to which the region was exposed in the past two centuries; violence was perhaps an instrument through which the narcissism of small differences (which reigns in this region) was translated into irreconcilable differences; and extreme violence was perhaps a consequence of an overload of simultaneous challenges that the dissolution of the Yugoslav community presented for many members of that community—an overload that "denaturalized" or "dehumanized" them to the extent that enabled them to act with blind hatred toward each other.

In Chapter 5, Keiichi Kubo examines the responses of two states to Albanian ethnic separatist armed rebellion: that of Serbia in 1998 and Macedonia in 2001. In Serbia, President Milošević's authoritarian regime launched a combined police attack on the family compound of Adem Jashari, a militant leader of the Kosovo Liberation Army which was at the time pursuing a low-intensity violent campaign against Serbian rule in Kosovo. The resulting massacre of 58 family members (including women and children) sparked a mass armed rebellion in this part of Kosovo. This transformed a low-intensity conflict into a major insurgency, which the Serbian/Yugoslav authorities confronted with the deployment of armored units, heavy weaponry, and air strikes. In contrast, the Macedonian authorities responded to the low-intensity campaign started in January 2001 by the Macedonian Albanian National Liberation Army (NLA) with systematic attempts to negotiate a peaceful solution to the conflict. As a result, the conflict was ended in August 2001 with the signing of the Ohrid Framework Agreement, which instituted constitutional power-sharing provisions between the Macedonian majority and the Albanian minority. Kubo argues that there are two sets of factors that explain the difference in the two states' responses to armed rebellion. First, the electoral incentives were hugely different in these two cases. Facing a rapidly declining legitimacy, the Serbian President Milošević sought to widen his support by creating a coalition with the nationalist parties that advocated repression of Kosovo rebel activities. The defense of "Serbian Kosovo" was a central plank of his political platform from the beginning of his ascent to power, and reasserting this platform through the repression of the Kosovo

8   *A. Pavković and J.-P. Cabestan*

rebellion was an instrument in consolidating the legitimacy of his rule. In contrast, the Macedonian President Trajkovski's election to the presidency resulted from large Macedonian Albanian support, and he was, from the very start, committed to cooperation and reconciliation with the Albanian minority. Second, in these two cases, the United States (US) and the European Union (EU) member states took a different stand toward the rebellion. Prior to the attack on the Jashari compound, US officials were publicly describing the KLA (of which Jashari was a leader) as a terrorist organization. This was interpreted as a signal that its repression by force would be acceptable to the US government. In contrast, the EU and US actively supported and were directly engaged in the negotiations with the NLA leading to the Ohrid Agreement. Although Kubo notes that there were other salient differences between these two cases—in particular, that the Serbian regime was authoritarian whereas the Macedonian was not—these two factors, he believes, explain best the different responses in the armed separatist rebellion. Only future research will tell whether these two factors play a similar role in other cases of armed separatist or ethnic rebellion.

Whereas Kubo's chapter examines the state response to separatist rebellions, Pavković's contribution (Chapter 6) analyzes the separatist/secessionist movements' response to the central government's rejection of their secessionist demands and its attempts to suppress the secessionist movement. Once again, two different types of response are examined: the violent and the non-violent response. The economic, social, and political conditions in Chechnya and Kosovo prior to the outbreak of violent conflict showed remarkable similarities: both regions were located on the outer periphery of the state, with mountainous terrain; both had the lowest standard of living and the highest level of unemployment in the host state; both had populations with a different religion (Islam), culture, and language from that of the majority in the host state; both had a functioning and politically salient clan social system; and its members had been exposed to widespread discrimination and negative prejudices in the host state. All these common factors are conducive to mobilizing the population for a violent confrontation with the oppressive host state and its agents. And this is what in fact happened in Chechnya, but not in Kosovo. Prior to the declaration of secession, the principal secessionist party in Chechnya, the Chechen National Congress, organized an armed militia which it deployed against its political opponents in Chechnya. This armed militia was further used, with extraordinary effect, against both the Russian-supported Chechen militias and the Russian army in 1994. In contrast, the Democratic League of Kosovo, from its very beginning in 1989, publicly denounced the use of violence in pursuit of its political goals and did not organize an armed force. Unlike the former, the latter was a mass secessionist party modeled on the Polish Solidarnosc' movement, which had wide support among all segments of Kosovo Albanian society. The reliance of the Chechen National Congress on military force may be, Pavković suggests, a tactic of a party appealing primarily to rural populations in the southern areas of

Chechnya while facing stiff political competition for power from other parties. The organization and arming of its militia occurred during a power vacuum resulting from the failure of the Soviet or Russian central authorities to establish effective control over the region after the failed Moscow coup in August 1991. No such power vacuum occurred in Kosovo until the armed rebellion was led by another organization, the Kosovo Liberation Army, in 1998. Finally, the personal history, educational and professional background of the two secessionist leaders, General Dudaev and Dr Rugova, differed hugely: brought up in exile outside Chechnya and trained as a military pilot, with a poor command of the Chechen language and customs, General Dudaev used his military credentials and martial image to gain and maintain power. Dr Rugova, a postmodernist literary scholar, who had studied in Paris, had no faith in military solutions, in part because he believed that they would cause widespread suffering and death among his own people. According to Pavković, it is these three quite disparate factors that may, perhaps, explain the difference between the tactics used by these two secessionist parties.

In contrast to the previous chapters, Chapters 7 and 8 examine separatism and secessionism in two established liberal democracies—Spain and the UK—which are both members of the EU and NATO. In spite of similar political systems and international alliances, there are significant differences between the two states both in the responses of their central governments to secessionist demands and in the strategies and tactics of their secessionist parties.

Unlike the previous chapters, which primarily approach separatism and secessionism from an explanatory point of view, in Chapter 7, Ferran Requejo and Marc Sanjaume i Calvet analyze Basque separatism/secessionism from the point of view of normative theories of secession and state organization. Their starting point is a multidimensional normative theory whose principal elements are: "individual and collective minority rights; the politics of recognition; constitutional accommodation through liberal group protections and partnership agreements; and the democratic vote." This theory incorporates the right of secession of minority groups—the right that is at present denied by the Spanish state (as well as many others). By referring to the 1998 opinion of the Supreme Court of Canada, regarding the secession of Quebec, Requejo and Sanjaume maintain, in effect, that the Basque Country would, under certain constitutional and democratic conditions, have a right to secede from Spain.

Their chapter examines the political and legal context in which this right has been denied so far. After 1974, Spain evolved from a centralized state to a state with seventeen autonomous communities. Although the latter (and their legislatures and executive bodies) have significant autonomy, they have no representation in the central state representative institution, nor is there any institution for the coordination of autonomous communities at the central state level. Political parties in the Basque Autonomous Community are highly

10   *A. Pavković and J.-P. Cabestan*

polarized: there are four secessionist parties while the other five advocate various degrees of autonomy and federalism. In addition, there is a secessionist organization ETA which, from 1959 until recently, has engaged in systematic acts of violence against the agents of the Spanish state. The Spanish state has actively suppressed this organization while engaging at times in (so far) unsuccessful negotiations. In 2011, ETA publicly abandoned the use of violence and called for political negotiations with the Spanish government. In the past few years, other Basque political leaders have attempted to negotiate conditions for eventual secession from Spain including a plebiscite on secession in the Basque Country. However, in September 2008, the Spanish Constitutional Court rejected the latest proposal for the plebiscite in the Basque Country, reasserting the indivisibility and unity of the will of the Spanish nation as the only repository of sovereignty in the Spanish state.

In Requejo's and Sanjaume's opinion, the repeated rejection of these political proposals for a negotiated separation/secession of the Basque Country underscores both the failure to accommodate national pluralism within the Spanish state and the maintenance of a "tyranny of majority" over minorities. They argue that their multidimensional normative approach would provide a much better theoretical framework for the accommodation of national pluralism.

In contrast to the normative approach to the issue of secession in the Basque region, in Chapter 8, Michael Keating notes that such normative approaches— in particular, the discourse of self-determination—have no role in the political debate on the potential secession of Scotland from the UK. This may be a result of the lack of opposition to the secession among the principal political parties and leaders in the UK. In contrast to the major Spanish political parties, no political party in the UK opposes or questions the legality of the secession of Scotland. Scotland has a legal and political status similar to that of the Basque region in so far as it has its own legislature and executive government with wide powers. Like the Basque region, it has no separate representation in the UK Parliament and there is no federal-type body to coordinate the three "regions" of the UK that have these autonomous powers. But unlike the Basque region, Scotland has a separate judicial system and a system of law that is different from that of the UK. Most importantly, Scotland has a long history of independent statehood, which came to an end with its voluntary union with England in 1707. The secessionist—home rule—parties emerged in Scotland only in the 1930s, and the distinction between anti-secessionist (unionist) and secessionist (home rule) positions was at the time not all that clear because the unionist side supported devolution and the decentralization of power to Scotland. The Labour government won a large majority in its 1997 referendum in support of the restoration of the Scottish Parliament and devolution of powers to it. But the main secessionist—pro-independence—party, the Scottish National Party (SNP), started to gain support again in the early 2000s, and in 2007 was able for the first time to form a government in Scotland. In 2011, it won an absolute majority in the

Scottish Parliament and announced that it will hold a referendum on independence by 2014. Paradoxically, the SNP's victory was achieved while opinion polls started to show a decrease in public support for independence, a support that has never been more than 30 percent of the electorate. Keating argues that those who are voting for the SNP do not, necessarily, support the independence of Scotland, but support its social democratic and devolutionary platform. Moreover, the support for independence does not appear to increase in times of economic crisis or hardship, but in times of relative economic prosperity.

In Keating's view, although there are no serious political or legal obstacles to Scotland's independence, there are serious practical difficulties such as: no capacity to fund the present social democratic policies without the current subsidies from the UK; the division of the UK debt; monetary policies and the currency (Euro or British pound?); EU membership; and the question of the borders and shared governmental agencies with the rump UK. Keating argues, in some detail, that support for independence in Scotland is limited and that there is much greater support for further devolution of powers to the Scottish Parliament and government. All this, however, he claims, does not mean that, in the long run, Scotland's union with the UK will survive in the present form: some time in the future, Scotland may indeed secede or establish some form of confederal or federal relationship with the UK.

What are the specific features of secessionism/separatism in Europe? The above chapters can hardly offer any conclusive or even indicative answers to this question. Yet, Chapters 5, 7, and 8 indicate that, in European liberal democratic states, governments are capable of accommodating separatist and even secessionist demands without embarking on violent suppression of the separatist/secessionist movements. Even in a post-Communist state without a consolidated liberal democratic regime, such as Macedonia, the government (or, in the case of Macedonia, its president) was able to accommodate the demands of an armed separatist group that had engaged in an insurgency against the government. While rejecting the secessionist demands, the Spanish government has not used force against those secessionist groups or individuals who have not engaged in violence and was also able to accommodate a wide range of separatist demands by transferring significant powers to the political authorities in the Basque region. The response of the UK political parties to the possible secession of Scotland is quite similar to the response of the Czech political parties to the secessionist demands and mobilization of the Slovak political parties prior to the dissolution of Czechoslovakia in 1993. These chapters present some evidence in support of Mayall's hypothesis in Chapter 1 that liberal democratic regimes in Europe appear to be more inclined to accommodate or tolerate separatism and secessionism than those in Asia. They also show that, in European liberal democratic states, the principal grievance of many secessionists—domination and oppression by a foreign regime—has been largely absent or ineffective in secessionist mobilization.

But apart from that, the chapters on Europe reveal little if any general common features of secessionist/separatist movements in Europe. Secessionist movements have used violent means to further their aims both in the post-Communist states of the USSR and former Yugoslavia and in liberal democratic states such as Spain and France (Corsica). As shown in Chapters 2, 3, and 4, many post-Communist states, which gained their independence by peaceful secession, have not only rejected the secessionist demands on their territory, but have also extensively used force against secessionist movements. And yet even under the post-Communist authoritarian regime, such as Milošević's in Serbia, a secessionist movement committed to peaceful means of achieving statehood—Rugova's Democratic League of Kosovo—could develop and even flourish (Chapters 5 and 6). In addition to the issues of violence and repression, there are many other significant differences, especially in terms of political context, mobilizational strategies, and political ideologies. As a result, one can only conclude that there is no single model that could explain the emergence of secessionist movements in Europe.

What about Asia? Although the number of cases included in this volume is more limited, some useful conclusions can also be drawn from their comparison, both among themselves and with the European examples just discussed.

Three of the six Asian cases presented in this book—India, Sri Lanka, and Burma—are former British colonies. In view of the principles indicated above and applied to most decolonized countries, territorial integrity has been perceived by the governments of these three states as sacrosanct. Of course, the establishment of independent India was marred by the tragic partition that gave birth to Pakistan in 1947. But the democratic Indian Union has always claimed that it could manage and accommodate the large diversity of peoples, cultures, languages, and religions of the country in introducing a federal system, parliamentary democracy, and secularism. In Chapter 9, Jean-Luc Racine shows that this has globally been true, but also that not every separatist/autonomy claim could be efficiently addressed, the best-known exception being Muslim-dominated Kashmir. Indeed, Kashmir's separatist tendencies have offered India's neighbor, Pakistan, the opportunity to influence or try to influence the future of Kashmir, a province of which it occupies the northern half and where it supports separatist Kashmiri movements (both pro-Pakistani and pro-independence), with the continued help of Pakistani jihadi forces. And as Racine shows, New Delhi has clearly not always adopted the most appropriate strategy and the most democratic means to address the Kashmiri political requests. But important geo-political considerations also explain the Indian government's attitude, especially its rivalry with Pakistan, in both South Asia and Afghanistan: a strategic competition that has acquired a nuclear dimension since 1998. Moreover, since 2001, the US-led global war on terror has both weakened and divided the Kashmiri movements supporting self-determination. Nevertheless, the Kashmir and

Introduction 13

other separatist causes underscore the limits of the Indian Union's capacity to tolerate and manage such forces.

As David Feith demonstrates in Chapter 10, such limits have been much more obvious and constraining in the case of the Tamils' quest for independence in northern Sri Lanka. Sri Lanka's Sinhalese Buddhist majority and domination of the political system have directly contributed to alienating the significant Tamil Hindu minority concentrated in the northern part of the island and also dominating India's Tamil Nadu state. Although the international dimension of the Tamil issue has always played a role, India intervened only once in the late 1980s, but not really decisively, leaving Colombo to decide how to solve this issue, and actually tacitly accepting the fierce and uncompromising armed suppression of the violent Liberation Tigers of Tamil Eelam (LTTE) movement, a deeply contested task completed in 2009. Since then, both sides have had to learn to live together again. However, as Feith indicates, it remains to be seen whether the Buddhist majority will be able to grant more meaningful political and economic rights to the Tamil minority and whether the latter will accept Sri Lanka's democratic institutions, electoral processes, and the rule of the majority.

Burma's separatist movements have received less attention but can be traced back to this country's declaration of independence in 1948. In Chapter 11, Renaud Egreteau convincingly argues that, after six decades of creeping civil war, these movements (Karen, Shan, etc.) are in decline, in particular because of the increasing capacity of the central government to control border areas. However, as he also shows, non-Burman ethnic identities have not weakened. And to date, neither Burman-dominated parliamentary democracy (1948–1962) nor the successive military regimes have been able to satisfactorily address the ethnic minorities' autonomous claims. Thus, in spite of the political reform process currently taking place, the game is far from being over: although secessionist trends have no chance of prevailing, separatism and de facto armed control of portions of the territory by ethnic minorities will remain a force to be reckoned with in the foreseeable future, with the risk of complicating Burma's relations with its neighbors, especially China.

Any study of secession and separatism in Asia cannot ignore China. Although this country has never been formally colonized (Hong Kong and Macau excepted), in the past two centuries, it was subject to multiple foreign encroachments (both western and Japanese), particularly the establishment of concessions and zones of influence up to the end of World War Two. This recent history explains to a large extent the nervousness of Chinese nationalist and later Communist authorities vis-à-vis any secessionist or separatist force. Heirs of an immense empire after the collapse of the Manchu dynasty in 1911, the Kuomintang (KMT or Nationalist Party)'s Sun Yat-sen and other leaders rapidly opted to keep the totality of the territory which this dynasty had conquered and administered. However, this non-Chinese (or non-Han) dynasty controlled an empire that was much larger than those ruled by any previous dynasty (e.g., the Han, the Tang, the Song, and the Ming)—with the exception of the other non-Chinese Yuan dynasty established by Kublai Khan, Genghis Khan's grandson, which for a short time linked Tibet with China (in the thirteenth and fourteenth centuries). For instance, contrary to the Ming, the Manchu empire included Mongolia, Manchuria (today, China's three northeastern provinces), East Turkestan, which it named Xinjiang ("new border area" or "new dominion" to use Dru Gladney's terminology), and Tibet. As we know, the only territory of this multi-ethnic empire that managed to secede was the part of Mongolia—called "Outer Mongolia"—whose leaders were loosely connected (and actually often in conflict with) the Manchu Court. This country became independent in the early 1920s thanks to the support of the recently established and Communist-ruled USSR. The Tibetan rulers of the first half of the twentieth century were tempted to imitate their Mongolian brothers (a society that shares with Tibet the same type of Buddhism). However, attempts to gain full independence from China by the thirteenth Dalai Lama remained hesitant and inconclusive. And as Robert Barnett emphasizes in Chapter 12, Tibet could have satisfied itself to remain loosely ruled by a distant and non-intrusive Chinese central government. Although the KMT, because of its own weaknesses as well as domestic and international challenges, performed this role well until 1949, the Chinese Communist Party (CCP)'s totalitarian project could only clash with Tibet's de facto self-rule and traditional way of life. Although the Tibetans' religious freedom and standard of living have improved since the beginning of the reforms in 1978, the CCP has been unable to address their more fundamental religious and political demands—the return of the Dalai Lama and a meaningful political autonomy. As Barnett shows, a political deal between both sides cannot be excluded because, for more than 20 years, the Dalai Lama and his government-in-exile have officially abandoned their quest for independence and agreed that Tibet remains part of China. Nevertheless, short of democratization of the Chinese regime, it is hard to foresee Beijing granting Tibet genuine political autonomy, let alone a solution that would be close to Hong Kong's "one country, two system" formula. In the foreseeable future, as the CCP continues to ostracize both the Dalai Lama and the new Prime Minister of the Tibetan government-in-exile based in northern India, China's Tibetan areas (including also Qinghai and western Sichuan) are likely to witness more tensions and conflicts and, as a result, more separatist trends.

If we apply the concept of "separatism" as defined above to China, many parts of this country may be suspected by the central government of harboring separatist intentions. One can argue, for example, that Guangdong or Shanghai have successfully fought (and will keep fighting) for more economic, financial, and even cultural autonomy while at the same time, of course, claiming to remain the most faithful Chinese patriots of the nation! It is clear that, applied to ethnic minorities, separatism takes another, deeper, and more sensitive dimension, but the majority of China's non-Han groups have not tried or even dreamed of seceding: at most, they want to acquire a degree of political autonomy that the one-party system is unable to deliver because most key positions in the CCP apparatus in minority areas are controlled by Han cadres (the well-integrated Zhuang group of Guangxi being the main exception) and the CCP has a decisive centralizing role. The absence of secessionist intent is arguably shared by Inner Mongolia's Mongols: representing around 17 percent of the population of this "autonomous region," they cultivate close personal and business links with the people of the independent and now democratic Republic of Mongolia. But the only Mongol movements of which we know aim at some kind of cultural and political autonomy, not at integration with their northern neighbors. More generally, most ethnic minorities have difficulties articulating separatist claims for two main reasons: there is a great variety of ethnic groups in the majority of China's autonomous areas (regions, prefectures, counties) and the political, economic, and demographic domination of the Han people.

Actually, if we assume that most Tibetans are now separatist (and not secessionist), China's only secessionist forces are concentrated in Xinjiang, as Dru Gladney demonstrates in Chapter 13. But here also, we need to be careful: although some violent and arguably small Islamic or pan-Turkish groupings still fight for the (re-)establishment of an independent state of East Turkestan, Rebiya Kadeer's World Uighur Congress, an opposition organization headquartered in Munich, Germany, is gradually becoming more moderate. Committed to non-violence, its mainstream component now aims only to introduce a democratic and representative system in a genuinely autonomous Xinjiang, which would still be part of China.

Two basic constraints should be emphasized: first, there is very little chance that Tibet or Xinjiang "separatists" will achieve their objectives in the foreseeable future, while the CCP is imposing on these two regions a highly unequal balance of power; second, granting these regions meaningful autonomy raises many well-known and hard to resolve issues, the control of Han migrations to these regions being one of the most pressing and complex ones. In any event, as Gladney underscores, like Tibet, Xinjiang is likely to witness increasing ethnic tensions as long as Beijing does not address the fundamental political, economic, and cultural demands and frustrations of the Uighur (and Muslim) community.

The complex issues we have just mentioned are not restricted to China, but have an impact on many secessionist and separatist movements around the world, highlighting the multiplicity of problems that any secession or even separatist/autonomization processes can trigger. For example, although accepted by Khartoum, South Sudan's declaration of independence in 2011 illustrates some of these complexities such as border delineation, oil revenue sharing, pipeline transit, and transfer of populations.

The final case examined in this volume in Chapter 14, that of Taiwan, is rather different from any of the previous ones; as Jean-Pierre Cabestan shows, it appears to a large extent to be a case *sui generis*. It is simpler in a sense that, since the end of the Chinese civil war in 1949, Taiwan, under the old

Chinese regime's official name of "Republic of China" (ROC), is de facto and even de jure independent. The question is not separation or secession but whether the Taiwanese wish or not to (re-)unify with the Chinese mainland and integrate in the People's Republic of China (PRC), as Hong Kong did in 1997. The question is also what kind of international status can be granted to Taiwan before any solution is found. But this issue is also more complex because the PRC does not recognize the ROC, which in the CCP's view disappeared in 1949, because Taipei's KMT government claims that the ROC has sovereignty over the whole of China (and as a result does not recognize the PRC) and also because, representing around 45 percent of the electorate, Taiwan's main opposition grouping, the Democratic Progressive Party (DPP), originally in favor of the island's formal independence from China, now equates the ROC with Taiwan. In these circumstances, we can understand why it is so hard for Beijing and Taipei to negotiate a deal acceptable to all the parties involved, including the USA, which continues to offer to the island a vague but critical security guarantee. Unable to fully normalize in spite of intense economic and human interactions, the two Chinese regimes probably do not have any other choice but to accept the status quo and coexist peacefully side by side for a long time to come. In this respect, a long-term separation—on purpose we avoid the taboo word "secession"—is preferable to any precipitous and unaccepted unification, provided of course that Beijing is inclined to remain as patient as it has been in the last decade and in some ways since 1949.

As we can see, Asia has not found better political recipes to address secession and separatism. If one principle continues to prevail, it is the idea that any secession should be endorsed not only by the minority that wants to secede but also by the majority of the country from which they wish to secede. In Beijing, Delhi, Colombo, or Rangoon's eyes, this principle cannot be compromised. Here, we can identify some convergences with Europe's Spanish "model" as discussed above. The Common Law countries in Europe and elsewhere (except the USA) seem to be more flexible, if we include in this category the cases of Scotland and Quebec. At the same time, we should not discount the capability of Asian countries to correct their past mistakes: supervised by the UN, the former Portuguese colony of East Timor's self-determination was eventually accepted by Indonesia in 1999, after more than 20 years of illegal and violent occupation, a political change that allowed the establishment of the new independent state of Timor-Leste in 2002. A few years later, in 2005, thanks to the EU monitoring and negotiating mission, the Free Aceh Movement and Jakarta were able to reach a peace agreement and Aceh to remain part of Indonesia. In Asia, as in Europe, therefore, democracy—and in these two cases, Indonesia's democratization—makes a difference. But in these two Asian examples, international organizations, especially the UN, have also played a crucial role. As both European and Asian states tend to accept UN intervention better than other types of intervention, the role of the UN and regional international organizations (such as the African Union) is likely to intensify in future attempts to solve secessionist or separatist tensions around the world.

This collection is far from offering a comprehensive overview of secessionism and separatism in Europe and Asia. In fact, it offers discussions on only selected aspects of a small number of secessionist and separatist cases in Europe and Asia, neglecting other continents, especially Africa. In spite of that, on the basis of these discussions, we can attempt to draw some rather general and still highly tentative conclusions. These are as follows:

First, the emergence of secessionist or separatist movements is never a result of a plot engineered by dark forces. This is the manifestation of a *malaise* between a state's specific community (or communities) and central authorities rooted in history and driven by ethnic, linguistic, and cultural differences, nationalist passions, and conflicting narratives and aspirations.

Second, many (but not all) of the issues discussed in this volume are related, as indicated above, not only to the emergence of the nation-state but also to the late survival of various kinds of empires in both Europe and Asia. For instance, at the end of World War One, while the victors were dismantling the Ottoman and Habsburg empires, parts of the latter were joined to one of the victors, Serbia, in the hope that the new creation would become a nation-state on its own. The dissolution of Yugoslavia in 1991 (Chapter 4) proved how unfounded that hope had been. Many of the problems that appeared at the end of the USSR were inherited from the expansion of the Russian empire in the nineteenth century. The separatist forces that emerged in the various heirs of the British Raj (India, Burma) or, more widely, the British colonial empire (Sri Lanka) predated the introduction of the nation-state principles in this part of the world. Although post-imperial China remained united, the newly created nation-state has encountered similar separatist tendencies: Tibet and Xinjiang were clearly part of the Manchu empires, but are they part of the Chinese nation? Can we expect the Tibetans and the Chinese to reconcile their respective approaches to Tibetan history? How can the Uighurs endorse Chinese nationalism as part of their history and identity?

Third, liberal democracies are better able to address separatist aspirations than autocracies, for the following two principal reasons: the very principles of devolution of powers and especially federation are institutional constructions that can be effective only if based on democratic foundations; and democracies are more ready to acknowledge the existence of separatist or secessionist groups and negotiate with them, especially if these groups are committed to peaceful models of political action. Conversely, violence is usually an obstacle to the recognition and the legitimization of such groups.

Fourth, secession is often the result of a failure of both (or more) sides in reaching an acceptable agreement, a solution *faute de mieux*. Secession is of course better than any kind of prolonged armed conflict or civil war. However, the cost of secession is high and usually higher than any negotiated agreement to stay together. Addressing separatist demands while negotiating meaningful devolution of power to the separatist regions appears to remain the least costly solution to many separatist conflicts.

Fifth, strong states, especially great powers, can resist secessionist and separatist forces and the pressures coming from their outside supporters more effectively than weak states. This reality, which of course goes against any idea of justice, cannot be ignored. As we know, whereas Belgrade had to abandon, after prolonged NATO bombing, its province of Kosovo, it was easier for Russia, a nuclear power, to keep Chechnya within its federation. And in Asia, as China is becoming more influential, attempts to put pressure on the Chinese government regarding Tibet or Xinjiang are becoming weaker too.

Sixth, although economic development and integration have been widely and often used and presented by central authorities as the best way to counter secessionist/separatist aspirations and to address the issue of the economic inequalities that motivate them, it is far from certain that these methods have borne the expected fruits: new prosperity, or more basically the end of poverty, can have the opposite effect and give a novel impetus to secessionist/separatist forces, in both Europe (Scotland, Slovakia) and Asia (Xinjiang, Tibet, Tamils).

Finally—following the preceding point—there is an obvious irony in witnessing a surge of secessionist and separatist movements in a world that is becoming more globalized everyday. Actually, the two forces are directly related to each other. As distances shorten and the world is arguably becoming smaller, communities, and especially minorities, feel the need to assert not only their neglected interests, but also their too easily marginalized language, culture, and identity. In this respect, the present volume offers only a small contribution to a field of political and social sciences inquiry that is not likely to fade away in the coming years.

Note

1 The part on Europe was written by Aleksandar Pavković and the part on Asia by Jean-Pierre Cabestan. The same division of labor was followed in the editing of this volume.

References

Crawford, James (2006), *The Creation of States in International Law*, Second edition, Oxford, Clarendon Press.

Geldenhuys, Deon (2011), 'Secession and Contested States' in A. Pavković and P. Radan (eds), *The Ashgate Research Companion to Secession*, Farnham, UK, Ashgate Publishing Ltd, Chapter 25, pp. 285–300.

Radan, Peter (2008), 'Secession: A Word in Search of a Meaning' in A. Pavković and P. Radan (eds), *On the Way to Statehood, Secession and Globalisation*, Aldershot, Ashgate Publishing Ltd, pp. 17–32.

——(2011), 'International Law and the Right to Unilateral Secession' in A. Pavković and P. Radan (eds), *The Ashgate Research Companion to Secession*, Farnham, UK, Ashgate Publishing Ltd, Chapter 27, pp. 345–364.

Siroky, David S. (2011) 'Explaining Secession' in A. Pavković and P. Radan (eds), *The Ashgate Research Companion to Secession*, Farnham, UK, Ashgate Publishing Ltd, Chapter 3, pp. 45–80.

Wood, John R. (1981), 'Secession: A Comparative Analytical Framework' *Canadian Journal of Political Science*, 14: 109–135.

1 Sovereignty, national self-determination and secession

Reflections on state-making and breaking in Asia and Europe

James Mayall

A glance at any historical atlas will reveal that the political map of the world has been transformed many times over the centuries. Even the most ancient states such as China or Morocco, whose core identity has been preserved for millennia, seldom if ever occupy exactly the same territory as when they were first established. In most parts of the world, and at most times, the main driver of territorial fusion has been conquest, often reinforced by dynastic marriage and/or commercial exchange. Conversely, the main driver of territorial fission has been imperial decline, often accelerated by geo-political opportunism. By this, I simply mean that insurgencies have sometimes succeeded when the rebels against established authority were either supported by a powerful neighbour as a neutral buffer between themselves and a rival empire, or were able to play off two powerful neighbours against one another, or exploit their control over high mountain passes or strategic choke points, in order to preserve their independence. There was a time, for example, before it became a Japanese prefecture, when the island kingdom of Okinawa maintained at least quasi independence under the simultaneous protection of China and Japan.[1]

This prehistory has some relevance to the modern discussion of secession, but not much. A successful secession is a very rare event but, in the contemporary world, it results in a change in the political and territorial map just as it did in the past following an imperial conquest or the disintegration of an established empire. But the similarity ceases at this point. The key distinction between the pre-modern world of imperial rivalry and the nationalist era that began with the American and French revolutions is that whereas, in the former, territory was ceded, sometimes voluntarily, more often under duress, in the latter, it is theoretically meant to reflect an act of self-(se)cession, in other words of self-determination. It was only after the universal claims of the American Declaration of Independence and the French Declaration of the Rights of Man and the Citizen had spread throughout international society that the idea of a legally grounded international order based on self-determining nation-states gradually emerged. There are those who claim that, in an age of globalization, this idea is now an anachronism, but if so, all that one can say is that it has proved an exceptionally tenacious idea,

Sovereignty, self-determination, secession 21

which shows few signs of loosening its hold on the popular imagination anywhere.

This tenacity is a mixed blessing. Once the national idea had taken hold, the tension – and sometimes open conflict – between different conceptions of justice and order, and power and law, became unavoidable. How were the national idea – and the invitation to secession that the principle of self-determination seemed to invoke – to be accommodated within international society?

I will attempt to answer this question by first looking briefly at how the principle of national self-determination has been accommodated within traditional international society, in theory and practice, before examining whether there have been any significant changes since the end of the Cold War. As we are currently witnessing, however tentatively, the beginnings of a shift in world power from west to east, I will conclude by considering whether there are major regional, cultural and ideational variations in how separatism and secession are understood, which may lead to further changes in theory and practice in the years ahead.

National self-determination and international society

Traditional international society was largely composed of dynastic sovereign states. The patrimony of the rulers – and with it the borders of their states – could be changed as the result of the fortunes of war or the construction of dynastic alliances through marriage, and consequently, by the acquisition of territory through inheritance. Think, for example, of the way in which the Normans swallowed England in the eleventh century and so laid the basis for the subsequent claims of the English crown to large parts of what is modern-day France. Or of the transfer of Quebec to the British crown under Article IV of the Treaty of Paris in 1763, transforming what these days we would be likely to think of as a wrong into a right, in other words a legal entitlement.

During the transition from the *ancien regime* to the nationalist era, territory was sometimes also bought and sold, as in the American purchases of Louisiana from France in 1803, Florida from Spain in 1819 and Alaska from Russia in 1867. In November 2008, the President of the Maldives, Mohammed Nasheed, revived this idea by suggesting that he intended to build up a sovereign wealth fund to purchase land, elsewhere in the region, to resettle the population in the event of his country being submerged by rising sea levels. It is not impossible but seems unlikely that he will find a willing seller. Neither India nor Sri Lanka, the two countries to which he referred, has a tradition of ceding territory. A transaction of this kind would breach the modern norm, which emerged as a result of the elevation of the principle of national self-determination after 1919, namely the sacralization of national territory.

Some authors have argued that the quest for self-determination need not involve territory and therefore does not automatically have to lead to an attempt to secede (Guibernau 1999; Bishai 2007). On this view, their aspirations can be achieved either by affording them full citizenship rights or by granting them a special status under the host state's constitution. It is also true that, in an era of globalization, people have been widely dispersed around the world, so that large minority communities have grown up, which may identify as much if not more with their country of origin than with their host country.

The issue of divided loyalties and the fears on the part of the majority population that they are harbouring a dangerous fifth column in their midst can have potentially serious international implications – think, for example, of the American and Canadian internment camps for Japanese during World War Two or, more recently, the fears that western countries may have provided a safe haven for jihadist terrorists from where they can plot their destruction. That the decentralized order of territorially defined sovereign states is coming under strain as a result of such developments is undeniable. But in a sense both the attempt to find non-territorial definitions of self-determination and the ability of opponents of the international order to operate away from their own homelands provides evidence of the tenacity of the traditional system rather than its eclipse. In a world where national territory has been sacralized, practical accommodations can be achieved, if the circumstances are propitious, but it remains virtually impossible to deal with these problems at the level of diplomatic theory or international law.

Why this should be so may become clearer if we briefly review the history of international society since the rise of nationalism in the nineteenth century. The traditional conception of international society as a society of sovereigns not peoples survived, dented but more or less intact, until World War One. Since 1919, international society has ostensibly been based on the principle of popular sovereignty. The collapse of the European dynastic empires and of the Ottoman empire dealt a mortal blow to the dynastic principle. It was no longer possible to defend the state as a private possession of particular individuals or families. But if prescription was out, consent had to be in: ownership of the state, in other words, had to be transferred to the people. The difficulty in effecting this transfer arose because, in the last analysis, only individuals can give or withhold consent. Yet men and women are social creatures. Which, therefore, are the appropriate collective selves, whose right to self-determination must be recognized as the basis of the new political order?

The answer to this question would be straightforward if – as most nationalists believe – the identity of the nation was self-evident. They almost invariably invoke particular historical myths and theories to justify their own claims and denigrate those of their secessionist opponents. Once in power, they generally use the school curriculum – and their monopoly over the symbols of nationhood – to construct a national culture that will both justify and run congruently with state boundaries. Sometimes they succeed; sometimes they fail, and for reasons that ultimately remain mysterious. But either way, the reality is that, although the doctrine of nationalism is clear – that is that the world is divided into nations and that consequently international society should be composed of nation-states – national identity itself is a deeply contested concept.

Sovereignty, self-determination, secession 23

Two broad accounts of national identity are on offer. Primordialists maintain that the national map of the world was laid down a very long time ago, even if very few these days cling to the belief that it accurately reflects the natural world and remains essentially unchanged since the beginning of time (Smith 1983, 1987). In contrast, except in a few anomalous or at least unexplained cases, modernists see the nation as only recently invented, imagined or constructed, dating only from the American and French Revolutions (Anderson 1983; Gellner 1983, 1997). Neither primordialists nor modernists generally pay much attention to the international implications of their theoretical accounts of the rise and spread of nationalism. To the extent that they consider the issue at all, they mostly adopt a realist approach to international relations. But although they pay little attention to legal or normative questions, implicit in their arguments is the recognition that political identity is a contingent matter. This is the crucial point. What is contingent cannot be settled by rational argument or a democratic vote. For political argument to take place, boundaries must be in place, but they lie behind or beyond such argument all the same.

Democrats, who generally still insist, as they did after 1919, that the recognition of any new state should be preceded by a plebiscite or popular vote, have difficulty in accepting this unpalatable truth. In the contemporary context, it is not difficult to understand why. After 1945, strenuous efforts were made to outlaw the use of force as an instrument of foreign policy, let alone the right of conquest. So how were new states to come into existence? A plebiscite or referendum seemed an obvious prerequisite. But, as Ivor Jennings famously put it in 1956, 'on the surface it seemed reasonable: let the people decide. It was in practice ridiculous because the people cannot decide until someone decides who are the people' (Jennings 1956, 56).

In the intervening 55 years, very little progress has been made in finding a way out of this logical impasse. Nor do I believe that one is likely to be found in the near future. Indeed, it seems likely that no general or theoretical solution to the problem is available at all, although the Australian political theorist, Harry Beran, would not agree with me. A major practical difficulty that arises in most secessionist conflicts concerns the presence of trapped minorities that prefer the status quo ante to the proposed new state. There are numerous examples of this phenomenon, but the refusal of Abkhazia and South Ossetia to accept that they should be incorporated in Georgia is a vivid and topical example. Beran maintains that a right of secessionist self-determination should be conceded if, and only if, the authorities of the new would-be state are prepared to grant a similar right to any subordinate group within their territory, and so on *ad infinitum*. Practical considerations would, he believes, call a halt to the process of fragmentation at a reasonably early stage (Beran 1984). It is an elegant solution but not one, I suspect, that is likely to appeal to any but the most enthusiastic advocates of permanent revolution.

So what to do? The answers to this question have been largely practical rather than theoretical. The extent to which the Wilsonian vision of a world

24 *J. Mayall*

made safe for democracy and self-determination would challenge, rather than support, the traditional Westphalian international order became evident immediately after World War One. The gruesome consequences of the demands for ethnic and organic democracy in much of Europe, however, were eventually submerged by World War Two and the territorial stabilization imposed on Europe by the Cold War division. As a result, in the part of the world where both nationalism and the doctrine of national self-determination had their origins, the question was effectively ignored for a generation.

Beyond Europe, this strategy was not available, partly because of the damage that the war had inflicted on both the reputation and the material power of the European imperial states; partly because of the strength of anti-colonial nationalism that increasingly challenged the attempt to restore the pre-war order; and partly because of the unholy alliance between the United States and the Soviet Union in support of the dismemberment of the European empires. The official position, to which all the major powers had signed up at San Francisco, was contained in Articles 1 and 55 of the UN Charter, which affirmed the right of all peoples to self-determination. But as we have already seen, this formula was notoriously question begging. The practical answer that gradually emerged, therefore, was to equate the right of self-determination with decolonization, a once and for all event, tied in time and space to the withdrawal of European power.

Around the edges of their inheritance, some colonial successor states consolidated their territory without suffering serious international consequences: thus India swallowed Hyderabad and Goa, Indonesia, West Irian, and then, in 1974, East Timor, and China, Tibet.[2] The Chinese absorption of Tibet was a decidedly pre-modern form of conquest, which the outside world was nonetheless able to digest, partly because no power was prepared to contemplate going to war over Tibet, but also because it had never been formally part of the British or any other empire (see also Chapter 12). The British had exercised influence over Tibet but had not challenged Chinese claims of suzerainty, a position inherited in 1947 by the government of India and endorsed, however reluctantly, by the United States. Nonetheless, throughout the Cold War, there was widespread antipathy to opening up the domestic political arrangements of sovereign states to outside scrutiny, and even more to any suggestion that the right of self-determination could be claimed by dissatisfied groups in existing states or colonies still awaiting independence.

Paradoxically, it was the expansion of international society to include most of sub-Saharan Africa in the 1960s that sealed the fate of all but the most persistent secessionists. Prior to independence, African nationalists had frequently denounced the 'Balkanization' of Africa by the European powers. At the Berlin Conference in 1884, the Europeans had partitioned the continent among themselves without paying much attention to geographical, historical or ethnic considerations. The map of Africa, nationalists argued, needed to be redrawn to reflect these realities and African interests. But how? They were no more able to answer this regional question than international society as a whole was able to distinguish between legitimate and illegitimate national selves. With hindsight, it is completely unsurprising that African governments, once independent, quickly became the most ardent defenders of the territorial status quo. When Tom Mboya, Kenya's first Foreign Minister, was asked about the rights of the Somali, the majority population in Kenya's northeast province, he replied that they could exercise their right of self-determination any time they wanted – all they had to do was to walk across the border into Somalia (Castagno 1964).

The decision to restrict the right of self-determination to European colonies could not finally dispose of the secessionist challenge to international order, even from the point of view of a legal positivist. This was because, in many parts of the world, not only had populations been divided between different colonial jurisdictions but the borders themselves had often not been demarcated. In traditional societies, where power was largely a personal attribute, this had not mattered so much but, in ostensibly national societies of citizens, it was fraught with danger. As most African states were socially heterogeneous, their governments viewed the potential threat from secessionist and irredentist movements with particular alarm. Their solution, arrived at with the assistance of Latin American lawyers, was to underpin the *Pax Africana* with the legal principle of *uti possidetis juris*, which can be loosely translated by the maxim that you hang on to what you have got at the time of independence.

Some lawyers have followed Steven Ratner in arguing that this was essentially an external imposition designed to keep the process of decolonization orderly and therefore consistent with the dominant Cold War conception of western international order (Ratner 1996, 610). It is certainly true that the major powers, like the authorities in most other states, welcomed it as a way of limiting international anarchy. But it was neither a western nor a Cold War imposition. Indeed, in agreeing to pocket their differences over territory, most African leaders were reacting to what they often perceived as continued western attempts to divide and rule. Katanga's secession in 1960 had been vigorously supported by western mining interests, and President de Gaulle of France would almost certainly have followed the four African governments that had recognized Biafra had the Federal Nigerian government not won the diplomatic battle within the OAU.[3]

Secession after the Cold War

Once the principle of *uti possidetis* had been generalized throughout international society, it successfully bottled up the aspirations for self-determination of many secessionist movements. The one Cold War exception to this statement – Bangladesh's successful bid for independence in 1972 – effectively proved the rule. Bangladesh succeeded not because of its own nationalist rebellion against the government in Islamabad, although no doubt this was an essential prerequisite for success; it succeeded because India intervened on its behalf and defeated Pakistan's army. It was able to do this because the Indian Prime

26   *J. Mayall*

Minister, Mrs Gandhi, had first neutralized the two superpowers – she signed a long-term treaty of cooperation with Moscow, which included a defence clause and ensured that the American Sixth Fleet could do nothing but sail into the Bay of Bengal and then sail out again.

In these circumstances, it was perhaps not surprising that many nationalists and their mostly liberal supporters identified the injustices of the territorial map with the ideological divisions of the Cold War. In the early 1990s, the then UN Secretary General, Boutros Boutros-Ghali, attempted to head off any optimism on this score at the pass. In *The Agenda for Peace*, he argued that, although the United Nations had not closed its doors to new members, 'if every ethnic, religious or linguistic group claimed statehood there would be no limit to fragmentation, and peace, security and economic wellbeing would become ever more difficult to achieve' (Boutros-Ghali 1993, 17 and 18). Instead, he recommended that the way to resolve the rival claims of sovereignty and self-determination was through respect for human rights, particularly the rights of minorities, on the one hand, and democratization, on the other. 'Respect for democratic rights at all levels of social existence is crucial: in communities, within states and within the community of states' (Boutros-Ghali 1993, 17 and 18).

This intimation that the old taboo against territorial change was weakening was sufficiently strong to urge the Canadian government to action. The two international experts they consulted on whether Quebec might have a unilateral right of secession provided some indication on how legal opinion on the subject was evolving. They were clear that Quebec did not have such a right, but nonetheless concluded that 'there may be developments in the principle of self-determination according to which not only colonialism but flagrant violations of human rights or undemocratic regimes could lead to a right of unilateral secession' (Department of Justice 1997).[4]

There are, so far as I know, no cases where such a right of unilateralist secessionist self-determination has been unambiguously identified, although one might argue that the peace agreements between north and south Sudan and between Papua New Guinea and Bougainville, both of which provided for referendums on independence after a transitional period of joint government, and the unilateral declaration of independence by the Kosovar majority Albanian government in February 2008, represent moves in this direction.[5] However, the circumstances are so different in each case that it is doubtful whether any attempt to generalize from them will withstand close scrutiny.

In the first two cases – the Sudan and Papua New Guinea – where self-determination disputes were the subject of international mediation, there was a deliberate attempt to resolve the conflict by constitutional means. The Peace Agreement between the government of Papua New Guinea and the Bougainville secessionist movement in 2001 established a high level of autonomy for the province and envisaged a non-binding referendum on independence sometime between 10 and 15 years after the autonomy arrangements began in 2005. Whether the referendum will take place and, if

Sovereignty, self-determination, secession   27

so, whether the result will be respected are still unknowns. The relative weight of legal theory and international norms as against power political considerations has recently been tested in the Southern Sudan, which voted in January 2011 by over 98 per cent to secede from the Republic of Sudan, although several intractable issues remain unresolved, including the division of oil revenues and the status of the border. The Abyei region, which divides the grazing lands of both the northern Arab pastoralists and the southern Dinka, is particularly troublesome. The rational solution would be to have a 'soft' border, with seasonal migration rights in both directions and cooperative arrangements to cover the shared management of water resources and the oil industry. There is little appetite for a return to civil war in either north or south, but with high levels of distrust between the two sides, negotiating a 'rational' solution will be difficult.

Kosovo's unilateral declaration of independence in February 2008 followed a period of international administration rather than mediation. The seventy-four states that had recognized Kosovo by March 2011 would also no doubt argue that the Kosovar government's independence was constitutional, although in this case, the final outcome is similarly still unclear. In October 2008, a large majority of UN member states supported a Serbian resolution in the General Assembly, against the opposition of the United States and some of its allies, requesting an advisory opinion on the legality of Kosovo's unilateral declaration of independence. Such opinions are not binding, but a ruling that the declaration was illegal would nonetheless have been a major political setback for the Kosovo government and its international supporters.

In the event, the International Court of Justice (ICJ) delivered an ambiguous verdict but one that was more favourable to Kosovo than many had anticipated. It did not rule on the substantive issue of whether Kosovo independence was legal, but on 22 July 2010, by ten votes to four, the Court found 'that the declaration of independence of Kosovo adopted on 17 February 2008 did not violate international law' (ICJ 2010). Whether this opinion is strong enough to persuade a majority of UN member states to recognize Kosovo remains to be seen; even if it does, Russia may use its veto to block admission.

So has anything really changed with the end of the Cold War? I am inclined to conclude that the answer is not much, particularly as the two successful cases of enforced secession – Eritrea's separation from Ethiopia in 1993 and East Timor's from Indonesia in 1999 – are better explained by reference to the conventional interpretation of self-determination as decolonization in accordance with *uti possidetis* than in terms of the evolution of the new democratic criteria.[6] If we discount the peaceful divorce between the Czech and Slovak Republics in 1992 and that between Serbia and Montenegro in 2006, we are still left with the question as to how state-less communities are to register their claims and grievances at the international level?

By treating the disintegration of the Soviet Union and the collapse of Yugoslavia as analogous to decolonization, international society was able to maintain the fiction that the territorial map was still based on *uti possidetis*:

28   *J. Mayall*

the internal borders of the socialist republics in the first case and the national republics in the second were accepted in the same way as colonial borders had been as the new international frontiers. But quite apart from the fact that, in Yugoslavia, the new dispensation was not accepted and therefore led to the anarchic blood-letting that *uti possidetis* was designed to prevent, there were some glaring anomalies. It is not obvious, for example, that in substantive terms the case for Chechnyan independence was any weaker than that of, say, Azerbaijan or for that matter Kosovo. But Chechnya was an autonomous republic within the Russian Federation, and so lacked international legal personality, whereas Azerbaijan was a Soviet Socialist Republic and therefore a candidate for statehood under the decolonization formula. Kosovo – according to the majority in the UN General Assembly – is in the same situation as Chechnya despite having been under international administration.

Western manoeuvring over Kosovo was followed in 2008 by Russia's intervention in Georgia and recognition of South Ossetia and Abkhazia. Both the west and Russia insist that the two cases are quite distinct, non-comparable and uniquely just or unjust as the case may be. But that is to be expected. It is hard to avoid the conclusion that we have done little more than substitute confusion for a clear principle that may sometimes have been unjust in its application, but at least offered some constraining influence on the more blatant forms of power politics.

The future of secession

The values, institutions, operating conventions and laws of contemporary international society are western in origin. They were spread around the world by the powerful forces of western imperialism and the scientific and industrial revolutions. Nationalism, the doctrine that the state belongs to the people and not to a privileged class, blood-line or self-made potentate, also arose in the west and was incorporated in the already existing state system. Inevitably, therefore, international society bears the cultural imprint of the western great powers that dominated world politics from the end of the seventeenth century to the end of the twentieth.[7] Even more than the other institutions of international society – law, diplomacy, the balance of power and even war itself – nationalist ideology became the instrument through which the hegemony of the west was first successfully challenged and may, in the end, be eclipsed.

We are still most probably a fair way off this denouement. But already we are witnessing the rise of a group of Asian powers – China most obviously, but also India – that will play an increasingly important role in shaping the evolution of international society. Great powers, whatever their leaders may say to the contrary, will always try to transform the international order in their own image. There is no logical reason that I can see why this should not be as true of China and India as it was of the European great powers and later the United States. So, will their attitude to the nationalist aspirations of minority groups within their own borders and in third countries differ markedly from their European and North American great power predecessors?

Secession in Europe and Asia compared

The short answer to this question is that, whatever other cultural differences may separate Asian and European states, attitudes to secession are not among them. The spectre of state fragmentation alarms European politicians as it does their Asian counterparts. When, in 1949, Mao Tse-tung famously announced that the Chinese people had stood up, he was quick to define the Chinese people not merely as the overwhelming Han majority, but as encompassing also the minority groups including the Tibetans and Uyghurs. Any devolution such as the creation of the Tibetan Autonomous Region has never been allowed to challenge the central authority of the Chinese state. There is no surprise, therefore, in finding China among those countries that continue to oppose the recognition of Kosovo, despite the ICJ's Advisory Opinion. But Spain, whose post-Franco constitution devolved considerable powers to the Basques and the Catalans in particular, is no less hostile to a policy that might be interpreted as setting a precedent for secessionist self-determination. In other words, hostility to secession is not primarily a cultural or regional matter: it is likely to be found wherever a state feels vulnerable to secessionist pressures.

Despite such similarities, closer scrutiny reveals contrasting dynamics beneath the surface. These have something to do with the impact of democracy on secessionist demands for self-determination, but more with attitudes towards intervention and the need to deal with the consequences of the humanitarian catastrophes that sparked many of the interventions of the post–Cold War era. I will examine each of these contrasts briefly in turn.

Democracy and secessionist self-determination

There is nothing in international law – or indeed in diplomatic convention – to prevent the voluntary dissolution of a single polity into two or more successor states. It is a rare occurrence, but examples can be culled from both Asian and European history, although there have probably been more such uncontested divorces in Europe. Thus, Singapore seceded from Malaysia in 1964; East Timor from Indonesia in 1999; Norway from Sweden in 1904; the Irish Free State from the United Kingdom in 1922; the Czech and Slovak Republics from Czechoslovakia in 1992; and Montenegro from Serbia in 2006.

None of these episodes was un-acrimonious but, in the European cases, it is probably safe to conclude that, because the parties on both sides shared the same civic and political values, it made it easier for them to reach agreement. This is likely to remain the case. If, for example, a referendum on Scottish independence is held, as the SNP government intends, and results in a majority vote in favour, it will be difficult for the government in London to

30   J. Mayall

ignore the verdict, although they would no doubt put as many obstacles in the way of dissolving the Union as possible (see also Chapter 8).

There are, so far as I am aware, no recent and successful cases where two sets of Asian democrats have attempted to resolve a self-determination dispute by negotiation, so it is impossible to say categorically that west European constitutionalism is a differentiating factor, regardless of the political context. Both India and Sri Lanka are democratic countries that have faced secessionist challenges (see Chapters 9 and 10). In Sri Lanka, after 30 years of civil war, a failed Indian peace-keeping operation between 1987 and 1990 and several failed attempts to reach a negotiated settlement, the government opted for a military solution. They finally defeated the Tamil separatists in 2010 and, in the aftermath of the war, have studiously ignored international allegations of major human rights abuses committed by both the Sinhalese government and the Tamil Tigers.

Although India is a functioning democracy and has often dealt with separatist pressures with the stratagem of creating new states to accommodate the linguistic and cultural demands of regional parties, it has been as ruthless as non-democratic China in resisting bids for outright secession whether in Kashmir, the Punjab or the northeast. Indeed, its engineered incorporation of the formerly independent kingdom of Sikkim in 1975 was less brutal but possibly even more efficient than the Chinese takeover of Tibet following its invasion in 1951 (see also Chapter 9).

But even if democracy in Europe seems to be a necessary condition for a negotiated separation, in contrast to Asia, it is certainly not sufficient even there. Where national insurgencies have tried to force the issue, as in ETA's campaign against the central government in the Basque province of Spain, or the Provisional IRA's against the British government in Northern Ireland before 1997, they have made as little headway as the Kashmiri militant separatists in India or the Tamil Tigers in Sri Lanka.

Secession and humanitarian intervention

The two judges who wrote the Advisory Opinion requested by the Canadian government on whether there could be a unilateral right of secessionist self-determination happened to come from Europe. As we have already noted, they allowed for the possibility where a government had so abused the rights of a part of its population that the basis of trust on which its legitimacy ultimately rests had been damaged beyond repair. No doubt they had in mind the savagery that had accompanied the break-up of Yugoslavia, although, as we have also seen, the unilateral declaration of independence by Kosovo remains deeply contested, and the two secessions – South Sudan and East Timor – where the circumstances most nearly fit those envisaged in the Advisory Opinion occurred outside Europe and as a result of international mediation, followed by a referendum. In neither case was there a unilateral declaration of independence.

Sovereignty, self-determination, secession   31

Asian countries, particularly Bangladesh, India and Pakistan, but increasingly also China, have played an important role in many UN peace-keeping operations, so it is as impossible to draw an unambiguous distinction between Asia and Europe on the issue of intervention as it is on democracy. Nonetheless, two observations can be made.

The first is that Asian countries are generally more resistant to any relaxation of the protection provided to governments by the sovereignty principle than their European counterparts. There are many illustrations of these contrasting attitudes in the period since the end of the Cold War, up to and including their extreme reluctance to support the NATO intervention in Libya in April 2011. Territorial integrity matters as much to the democratic Asian states such as India and Sri Lanka as it does to China. They remain deeply suspicious of what they regard as a western propensity to use humanitarian concern as a mask behind which they can justify military intervention for more traditional reasons of *Realpolitik*.

The second observation is that practical rather than theoretical considerations are almost certainly more important in shifting western countries towards the acceptance of state fragmentation in particular cases – so long of course as it is not their own. Whatever the historical verdict on western motivations for their post–Cold War interventions, they were not driven, as they had been during and immediately after World War Two, by a need to resolve an existential crisis of their own.

Western willingness, indeed initially eagerness, to police the world on behalf of the international community after the Cold War was framed from the start by the concept of limited liability. Western countries, led by the United States but with the active support of the Europeans, were not about to embark on a second age of formal empire. In order to extract themselves, either directly or as the principal paymasters of the United Nations, at some point, a political solution would have to be brokered. If this required an agreement either wholly or partially in support of secession, as in Bosnia, Kosovo and Sudan, so be it. The extreme difficulty that the Americans have had in extracting themselves from Iraq and Afghanistan, and their willingness to entertain almost any option that would allow them to exit with a minimum of honour, vividly exposes the dilemmas faced by any intervention on the basis of limited liability. There is no reason to believe that the major Asian powers will be eager to follow in their footsteps.

Convergence or regional diversity

It is possible to conclude from the evidence surveyed in this chapter that, as power shifts from west to east, there will be a retreat from such cautious relaxation of the sovereignty principle – including a willingness to entertain demands for secessionist self-determination under specific and rare circumstances – that we have witnessed since the end of the Cold War. My own conclusions are more cautious for two reasons. The first is that we still do not

32　J. Mayall

know whether the modernization of the new Asian great powers – and it this that has fuelled their rise – is dependent on their acceptance of universal values, even if these run counter to deeply held cultural beliefs that run counter to western concepts. I am genuinely agnostic on this issue, but if there is a link between modernization and universalism, it may prove more difficult for rulers everywhere to row back from the idea that the modern state relies ultimately on consent. Second, it would be unwise to underestimate the continuing power of nationalism. That power is crucially bound up with the plasticity of the concept – the fact that it can mean all things to all men – and therefore that so long as political identity remains contested, it will remain the most convenient vehicle for challenging the legitimacy of the state.

John Stuart Mill argued that when nationalism and the desire for free institutions arose simultaneously, partition might be necessary to preserve democracy.[8] Although this argument seemed peculiarly percipient in Europe after the collapse of Communism and the end of the Cold War, and although it was framed in universalist language, it seems doubtful whether it will prove sufficiently compelling to overcome the perceived strategic imperatives of the major Asian powers.

On the other hand, Thomas Hobbes's interpretation of sovereignty has proved an enormously successful western export in all parts of the world. One of the most frequent criticisms of his *Leviathan* is that he provided a blueprint for tyranny. Critics sometimes overlook the fact that Hobbes allowed all human beings to retain one natural right – the right to life – and that he believed that sovereigns, who after all remain in a state of nature in relation to one another, would have an incentive to rule well because they might have to rely on the loyalty of their subjects in war against another sovereign.

We know from experience that many rulers have preyed on their own people, but no ruler can sustain himself over the long run on the basis of terror. I do not think it very likely that territorial secession will be any easier in the future than it has been in the past. But the new elements – globalization and modern communications in particular – mean that it is now less likely that the problem will disappear over time as a result of assimilation. Whether one concludes that the prospects have improved at all in cases where a population is genuinely oppressed depends, I suspect, on whether one is temperamentally inclined to see the glass as half full or half empty. I fear I side with the pessimists more often than with the optimists, but it is at least possible to hope that self-interest will persuade governments in all parts of the world that they need to explore creative ways of meeting the desires of those who might otherwise be tempted to take up arms against the state.

Notes

1　From the fourteenth century, the Ryukyu kingdom in Okinawa and the neighbouring islands developed a tributary relationship with China. It was maintained even after the Satsuma clan from Kyoshu in Japan had invaded in 1609 and established Japanese

Sovereignty, self-determination, secession   33

hegemony over the kingdom. This did not prevent each of the three parties from maintaining the ostensible independence of the kingdom (Yokota 2010).

2 I have discussed these cases of post-colonial consolidation, prior to the re-emergence of the principle of *uti possidetis juris*, in Mayall (2000).

3 Biafra was recognized by Cote d'Ivoire, Gabon, Tanzania and Zambia. The argument for recognition was eloquently argued in a Memorandum submitted by President Julius Nyerere of Tanzania to his fellow African Heads of State in 1969. It failed, however, to win over any further states. For the text see, Kirk-Greene (1971, 429–439).

4 The two experts were Professor James Crawford, Whewell Professor of International Law, University of Cambridge, and Professor Luzius Wildhaber of the University of Basel, Switzerland, who is also a judge at the European Court of Human Rights.

5 The 2005 Comprehensive Peace Agreement in the Sudan was brokered by the United States. It provided for a referendum to be held in 2011 to ascertain whether the south wished to secede. A Southern Sudan Referendum Commission was approved by the National Assembly in July 2010. The Peace Agreement between the government of Papua New Guinea and the Bougainville secessionist movement in 2001 established a high level of autonomy for the province and envisaged a non-binding referendum on independence sometime between 10 and 15 years after the autonomy arrangements began in 2005.

6 Eritrea had been unilaterally incorporated into Ethiopia by the government in Addis Ababa in 1952 without further reference to the UN, which had been agreed as part of the solution for the problem of arranging for the administration of former Italian colonies after 1945 (see Mayall and Simpson 1992; Jacquin-Berdal 2002). Until the Indonesian army invaded East Timor in 1975, Indonesia had used civic and political rather than ethnic arguments to underpin Indonesia's national identity. State practice had by this time confirmed the principle of *uti possidetis juris* as the justification for post-colonial self-determination. As a former Portuguese colony, in theory, therefore, the principle should have applied to East Timor after the withdrawal of the Portuguese authorities (see Mayall 2000).

7 The most influential study of international society and its institutions is Bull (1977).

8 *Representative Government*, Chapter 16, numerous editions.

References

Anderson, B. (1983), *Imagined Communities, Reflections on the Rise and Spread of Nationalism*, London, Verso.

Beran, H. (1984), 'A Liberal Theory of Secession' *Political Studies*, 32: 21–31.

Bishai, L.S. (2007), *Forgetting Ourselves: Secession and the (Im)possibility of Territorial Identity*, Plymouth, UK, Lexington Books.

Boutros-Ghali, B. (1993), 'Agenda for Peace' in A. Roberts and B. Kingsbury (eds), *United Nations, Divided World*, Oxford, Oxford University Press.

Bull, H. (1977), *The Anarchical Society: A Study of Order in World Politics*, London, Macmillan.

Castagno, A.A. (1964), 'The Somali–Kenyan Controversy: Implications for the Future' *Journal of Modern African Studies*, 2(2): 165–188.

Department of Justice (1997), Ottawa, Canada.

Gellner, E. (1983), *Nations and Nationalism*, Oxford, Blackwell.

——(1997), *Nationalism*, London, Weidenfeld and Nicolson.

Guibernau, M. (1999), *Nations without States: Political Community in a Global Age*, London, Polity.

ICJ (2010), *Press Release*, International Court of Justice, No. 2010/25.

Jacquin-Berdal, D. (2002), *Nationalism and Ethnicity in the Horn of Africa: A Critique of the Ethnic Interpretation*, London, Edwin R. Mellen.

Jennings, I. (1956), *The Approach to Self Government*, Cambridge, Cambridge University Press.

Kirk-Greene, A.H.M. (1971), *Crisis and Conflict in Nigeria: A Documentary Sourcebook*, Oxford, Oxford University Press.

Leifer, M. (ed.) (2000), *Asian Nationalism*, London, Routledge.

Mayall, J. (2000), 'Nationalism and International Order' in M. Leifer (ed.), *Asian Nationalism*, London, Routledge.

Mayall, J. and Simpson, M. (1992), 'Ethnicity is not Enough' *International Journal of Comparative Sociology*, 33: 5–25.

Mayall, J. and Srinivasan, K. (2009), *Towards the New Horizon: World Order in the 21st Century*, New Delhi, Standard Publishers.

Ratner, S. (1996), 'Drawing a Better Line: Uti Possidetis and the Borders of New States' *American Journal of International Law*, 90.

Roberts, A. and Kingsbury, B. (eds) (1993), *United Nations, Divided World*, Oxford, Oxford University Press.

Smith, A.D. (1983), *Theories of Nationalism*, 2nd edition, New York, Holmes and Meir Publishers.

——(1987), *The Ethnic Origins of Nations*, Oxford, Blackwell.

Yokota, R.M. (2010), *Okinawa is a State of Mind*, at www.uchinachu.org/uchinachu/history_early.htm (accessed 13 July 2010).

Part I
Europe

2 Paradise lost

Autonomy and separatism in the South Caucasus and beyond[1]

John Cuffe and David S. Siroky

Does local ethnic autonomy satisfy the demand for self-determination or rather foster the capacity and whet the appetite for more independence? At least since the *Federalist Papers*, this has been an important question in political science, and remains a pressing concern in current world affairs for decision-makers in states that face demands for ethnic autonomy. As ethno-political movements appear to be on the rise across the globe, in democracies as well as in autocracies and hybrid regimes, the problem of self-determination concerns more and more countries. Although a large body of literature addresses the causes of ethnic mobilization, and the circumstances under which it might become violent, scholarship is considerably more scattered when it comes to evaluating possible solutions, and remains far from having reached a consensus.

Proponents of political decentralization tend to see it as the primary mechanism that policy-makers can legitimately utilize to hold together ethnically divided societies and to relieve pressure from peripheral groups on the central government (Riker 1975; Lijphart 1977; Tsebelis 1990; McGarry and O'Leary 1993; Kaufman 1996; Bunce 1999; Stepan 1999; Gurr 2000; Bermeo 2002; Hartzell and Hodie 2003; Wibbels and Bakke 2006; Brancati 2009; Miodownik and Cartrite 2010). It has been applied, with varying degrees of success, in countries as diverse as Belgium and Bosnia Herzegovina, Czechoslovakia and China, Spain and the Soviet Union. Recently, it has been proposed as a possible solution to current governance problems in Iraq and Afghanistan.

Politicians and scholars alike have extolled the virtues of decentralized governance. Politicians who cater to ethnic minority groups naturally see autonomy as an attractive campaign strategy that would enable them to dole out group-specific benefits to supporters. Majority politicians have also touted its efficacy in reducing inter-group conflict by providing a forum for expressing grievances, increasing loyalty, and reducing the incentive to exit (Brancati 2009). Advocates of autonomy of course differ in the degree of devolution they recommend—from full-blown federalism to milder forms of decentralization— but most see representation, participation, and some transfer of powers from the center to the regions as critical to addressing the self-determination demands of spatially concentrated, culturally distinct minority groups, and thus reducing the impetus to secession.

However, other scholars have argued that decentralization and the associated institutional arrangements are frequently ineffective in satisfying the demand for self-determination and often exacerbate ethnic mobilization, creating a slippery slope of increasing concessions, while at the same time reducing the government's legitimacy among its core constituency (Horowitz 1991; Roeder 1991, 2009; Slezkine 1994; Brubaker 1996; Bunce 1999; Hale 2008b). The reasons these authors provide for the belief in the adverse effects of autonomy are sundry, but the outcome is similar: the institutional architecture does not satisfy group demands for self-determination, and tends to reinforce ethnic particularism, sharpen group boundaries, providing regional leaders with access to political and economic resources that can be exploited to mobilize support for separatism. In short, autonomy provides local political actors with experience, resources, and networks that make their claims to secession more credible when the opportunity arises, and it institutionalizes ethnic differences that may have otherwise remained more fluid, thus creating the basis for secessionism and "hindering attempts to create interethnic harmony and peace" (Cornell 2002, 252–256; Rogowski 1985; Treisman 1997; Hale 2000; Kymlicka 2008).

Some attempts to resolve this apparent "paradox" have made significant progress by highlighting conditional relationships and by making nuanced threshold arguments about the point after which increasing autonomy yields decreasing returns to the state (Jolly 2006; Brancati 2009; Erk and Anderson 2009; Miodownik and Cartrite 2010). As Hechter and Okomoto (2001) put it: the empirical record is "murky": autonomy is associated with conflict in some countries and regions, and peace in others. Some scholars have therefore suggested that there is no direct link between autonomy and collective action (Horowitz 1985; Gurr and Davies 1998; Saideman et al. 2002; Sorens 2005).

Our approach

We build on this literature and seek to contribute to it theoretically and empirically by unpacking and disaggregating the heterogeneous category of "non-autonomous" groups, which typically represents the baseline for comparison. "Non-autonomous" status, we submit, includes two distinct scenarios that have very different consequences for collective action: it covers groups that have never had autonomy—the true "non-autonomous" groups— and it includes groups that had autonomy, but lost it. As the effect of autonomy on secession will depend on the composition of the reference group—non-autonomous, in this case—it stands to reason that the results will be muddled if that category includes disparate types and treats them the same. We argue that the loss of autonomy is likely to have a powerful and positive effect on separatist activity, whereas groups that were never autonomous should be highly unlikely to engage in separatism. On average, currently autonomous groups should also be unlikely to pursue secession, although they are likely to be more capable in this regard than groups that have never been autonomous.

Autonomy/separatism in the South Caucasus 39

Lumping historically autonomous and newer autonomous groups together is therefore apt to lead to confused findings. A trichotomous conceptualization enables us to observe the important behavioral differences.

Although autonomous groups may have the elite capacity to facilitate mobilization, we theorize that the masses will frequently lack the incentive to mobilize for secession on account of the considerable benefits to be gained from the status quo and the possibility of using voice to redress any outstanding grievances (Hirschman 1970). In contrast, having autonomy retracted significantly increases the motive for mobilization by increasing the cost of choosing voice over exit, while not appreciably decreasing the ability to engage in collective action.[2] It also considerably weakens the government's ability to make credible commitments that might prevent tensions from escalating (North and Weingast 1989). Groups that are not and have never been autonomous may possess grievances and motives for mobilization, but almost always lack the material and leadership resources to follow through. For these reasons, we expect groups that have recently lost autonomy to be the *most* prone to pursue secession, groups that were never autonomous to be the *least* prone, and groups that are currently autonomous to engage in *moderate* amounts of ethnic mobilization. These theoretical expectations are summarized in Table 2.1.

Although the details differ in individual cases, introducing *historic autonomy* as a theoretical category within the umbrella of non-autonomous groups contributes to our understanding of the center—periphery dynamics by disaggregating the category into more meaningful components with distinct empirical consequences. We develop this approach and test its empirical implications on a broad sample of currently, formerly, and never autonomous groups across Europe and Asia, including both democracies and autocracies, before briefly examining particular cases. We are cognizant that the meaning of autonomy may be contextual and may vary not only from place to place but also over time. In particular, we are aware of the possible measurement error that could be introduced by including autonomies in autocracies where the degree of self-rule is merely *pro forma*. In China, for instance, formal autonomy is mainly a fiction—Xinjiang and Tibet are arguably less autonomous than Shanghai or Guangdong—and we do our best to account for this crucial nuance in our coding of autonomy status across countries.

The empirical analysis reveals that historically autonomous groups do indeed exhibit the highest levels of separatism, whereas groups that are currently autonomous were significantly less likely to engage in ethnic mobilization,

Table 2.1 Theoretical expectations of ethnic mobilization

	Low capacity	*High capacity*
Weak motives	Never autonomous, included groups	Currently autonomous groups
Strong motives	Never autonomous, excluded groups	Historically autonomous groups

40 J. Cuffe and D.S. Siroky

and groups that were never autonomous are conspicuously unlikely to pursue separatism. We explain this empirical regularity by emphasizing the disparate group motives and collective action opportunities associated with these institutional arrangements. Finally, we explore these findings further through a discussion of intra-regional variation in the former Soviet space and sub-national variation in the South Caucasus, before concluding with implications for future research on separatism.

A bird's eye view of autonomy and separatism

To examine patterns in separatism across a broad sample of cases that covers different regions, we created a dataset consisting of 115 ethnic groups from Europe, Asia, and North America. Autonomy was defined using the same criteria as the Minorities at Risk (MAR) project, and each group was coded as autonomous, never autonomous, or lost autonomy (MAR 2009). The classification of the cases originates in the MAR variable, *PRSTAT*, which describes the prior status of each individual group from never autonomous to autonomous and cephalous all the way to former states and republics. We also created an index of separatism, which follows MAR's separatism index (SEPX), and codes the presence of sustained political or violent separatism over the past half century.

Table 2.2 and Figure 2.1 display the bivariate relationship between separatism and autonomous status, defined first as either autonomous or not. Table 2.3 and Figure 2.2 display this relationship once we include our trichotomous conceptualization of autonomy that disaggregates non-autonomous into "never autonomous" and "historically autonomous." These data indicate that autonomous groups engaged in far *less* separatism (19 percent) than non-autonomous groups (45 percent). We suggest that one important reason for the relatively high incidence of separatism among non-autonomous groups is that the category of "non-autonomous" includes both groups that have lost autonomy, and thus possess a high collective action capacity and an intensified sense of injustice and resentment (Petersen 2002), as well as groups that have never been autonomous. The theory suggests that the former, but not the latter, should be prone to separatist activity. When we disaggregate the data according to this logic, the results look quite different.

Table 2.2 Bivariate relationship between separatism and current autonomy status

	Non-separatist	Separatist	Total
Autonomous	17	4	21
Non-autonomous	51	42	93
Total	68	46	114

Notes: Cells represent the number of groups in the corresponding categories. Bivariate chi-square test significant at 0.05 level (4.68).

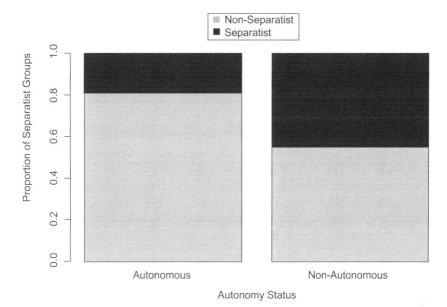

Figure 2.1 Separatism and current autonomy status

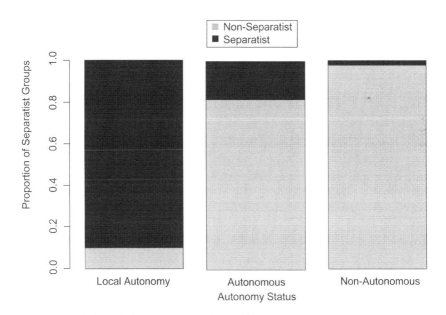

Figure 2.2 Relationship between separatism and autonomy status

42 J. Cuffe and D.S. Siroky

Table 2.3 Relationship between separatism and autonomy status

	Non-separatist	Separatist	Total
Historically autonomous	5	41	46
Autonomous	17	4	21
Never autonomous	46	1	47
Total	68	46	114

Notes: Cells represent the number of groups in the corresponding categories. Bivariate chi-square test significant at 0.05 level (4.68).

When the data are rearranged to differentiate groups that have lost autonomy from those groups that never possessed it, we find that the vast majority of groups that lost autonomy have in fact launched separatist campaigns (89 percent), compared with only a small fraction of groups that were never autonomous (2 percent) and currently autonomous groups (21 percent, see Figure 2.2). Although only associational and hardly dispositive, these findings lend support to our argument that retracted autonomy, and not the presence or absence of autonomy in general, is most liable to be associated with separatism. In fact, the incidence of separatism among non-autonomous groups that were never autonomous before is the *lowest* of the three categories examined. Although currently autonomous groups are more likely than never-autonomous groups to engage in separatism, the difference in the incidence of separatism is far less striking than the difference between either of those categories and historically autonomous groups.

Back in the USSR: paradise lost and found in the former Soviet space

Part of the existing confusion over the relationship between autonomy and separatism in the empirical record can be attributed to the selection of cases. To paraphrase one author's memorable phrase: the answers you get depend on the cases you select (Geddes 1990). Although some studies have taken a broad, cross-national view of the issue, much of the scholarly literature has focused on the post-Communist world, for this is a region where various forms of ethno-federalism have historically been and still are abundant (Gorenburg 1999, 2003; Hale 2004, 2008a; Roeder 2009). Whereas lower levels of autonomy in the Soviet context were relatively meaningless and *pro forma*, "autonomous republics look considerably more like states," writes one scholar, "than the lower-ranked autonomous oblasts and autonomous okrugs, insofar as they had their own legislatures, executives, and judiciaries. ... ASSRs were also allowed greater ... representation in the federal government ... " (Giuliano 2006, 277). Although autonomy in the Soviet context may have been more symbolic at lower levels, these higher levels of autonomy were quite meaningful, especially in cultural matters, and to a lesser degree in economic and political affairs.

Autonomy/separatism in the South Caucasus 43

In two of the seminal studies on this region, Bunce (1999, 49) and Roeder (1991) argued that autonomy in the former Soviet Union served as the critical building block "necessary for the rise of nationalist movements." The fact that all of the union republics (e.g., Estonia, Georgia, Ukraine, etc.) seceded and became independent states would seem to be *prima facie* proof of this proposition (cf. Carter and Goemans 2011). Other scholars have of course shown that the degree of separatism varied considerably *within* the Soviet Union federal republics (Hale 2008b; Giuliano 2010) from places that were exceptionally independence minded (Estonia, Georgia, Ukraine) to those that wished to preserve the Soviet Union as the most preferred outcome (Uzbekistan, Transnistria, Abkhazia) (for further discussion, see next chapter). What we observe across the former Soviet Union republics, we also see sub-nationally within those republics: for example, Georgia had two autonomous republic regions—Abkhazia and Adjaria (and one autonomous okrug, South Ossetia)— but Abkhazia pursued secession far more vigorously from Georgia than did Adjara (Derluguian 1998).

The same story has played out in many other places across the world. In both the developed and the developing worlds, we can cite cases where autonomy is associated with peace (e.g., Spain, Germany, United States, Switzerland, Australia or Nigeria, India, Mexico, Ethiopia). "Autonomy," writes Larry Diamond (1999, 156), "has done more to relieve or contain secessionist pressures than to stimulate them." Indeed, "every single longstanding democracy in a multilingual and multinational polity is a federal state" (Stepan 1999, 19). To evaluate the autonomy argument in any setting, we should first agree on a clear baseline. In the Eurasian context, the risk set might be the universe of Autonomous Soviet Socialist Republics (ASSRs). This yields a list of twenty-three ASSR cases. Most of these republics are located within Russia itself, although several exist in the other republics, particularly Crimea in Ukraine, Karakalpak in Uzbekistan, Nakhchivan in Armenia, and Abkhazia and Ajaria in Georgia (Gorenburg 1999; Treisman 1999, 237ff; Hale 2000; Giuliano 2006). Only two of the twenty-three ASSRs engaged in secessionist conflict—Abkhazia and Chechnya—whereas twenty-one (91 percent) did not. Moreover, most of the secessionist conflicts in the former USSR were not ASSRs, including the most prominent ones: Transnistria, Nagorny-Karabakh, and South Ossetia.

We could of course also take a more lenient baseline and consider Autonomous Oblasts (AOs) and not only ASSRs. Although it is true that both Karabakh and South Ossetia were AOs, the baseline should then include the other forty-seven AOs (96 percent) that did not lead to secessionist conflict. At the level of the autonomous district (okrug), the evidence is even less supportive: Chukotka, Khantia-Mansia, Nenetsia, and Yamalia *all* failed to escalate into secessionist conflict. Additionally, not a single one of the cases that the Supreme Soviet granted autonomy on July 3, 1991 (Adygeya, Gorno-Altai, Karachai-Cherkessia, and Khakassia) pursued secession (Sakwa 1996, 179; Giuliano 2010, 277). In short, many of the critical cases of secessionist conflict were *not* ASSRs, the majority of ASSRs were *not* secessionist, and most of the secessionist cases were those in which the group's status was threatened by the end of the Soviet Union with a functional downgrade in autonomy.

The Soviet Union had many autonomous administrative units, being divided into eighty-seven entities at one point: fifteen autonomous Soviet socialist republics, six kraya, forty-nine oblasti, two federal cities, five autonomous oblasti, and ten autonomous okrugi. The vast majority of autonomous entities were non-secessionist, including Adygea, Chuvashia, Dagestan, Ingushetia, Kabardino-Balkaria, Kalmykia, Karachai-Cherkessia, Karelia, Komi Republic, Mari El, Mordovia, Nenets Autonomous Okrug, North Ossetia-Alania, and Udmurtia. In the Caucasus alone, there were nine ASSRs and AOs: only three sought greater independence of any kind. Outside the Russian Federation, we observe a similar phenomenon among autonomous political entities such as Gaugazia in Moldova, Sardinia in Italy, and Vojvodina in Serbia, which did not pursue separatism. Of course, we could also mention Krajina and Republika Srpska as counterexamples of autonomous regions that became separatist, but we would argue that these regions became separatist largely once the group's status was under threat of being reversed from a privileged to a marginal one dependent upon the protection of the newly independent state's dominant ethnicity (see also Chapter 4). Italy hosts five autonomous regions—Sicily, Sardinia, Aosta Valley, Trentino-Alto Adige Sudtirol, and Friuli-Venezia Giulia—and none are associated with secessionist conflict. Portugal's autonomous regions, Azores and Madeira, are also not secessionist.

Our claim is not that autonomy is unimportant—quite the opposite, we agree it creates the capacity for collective action—our point is rather that it also frequently generates immanent and important benefits that favor the status quo. For this reason, it is less likely to lead to separatism than autonomy retraction. Autonomy is important because it can both construct and reinforce strong ethnic identities, group solidarity, and collective action (Olson 1965; Hechter 1987). Evidence from the post-Communist world, however, suggests that it is neither necessary nor sufficient to produce strong secessionist insurgencies. Three of the five main cases of violent secessionist conflict—Karabakh, South Ossetia, and Transnistria—did not have the status of autonomous republics. Even Chechnya is not a clear case, as it was only one part of the Chechen-Ingush ASSR. The only case that seems to fit the theory well in this part of the world is Abkhazia; and here, an explanation based on autonomy retraction can also account for this case (and others) quite well. Although autonomous status *per se* plays some role in understanding separatism, its effects are mixed and contingent.

Given that secessionist conflict is a rare event, even in the former Soviet context, the fact that so many of the critical cases were not ASSRs, and the fact that the overwhelming majority of ASSRs were not secessionist, casts doubt on the primacy of the theoretical framework linking autonomy directly to secession. Autonomy fosters conditions that favor secessionist conflict. It strengthens regional identity and creates the conditions for collective action, but it also engenders benefits from non-action, which remove many of the strongest motives for mobilization. Autonomy retraction is much more strongly associated with separatism, as we see in the former Communist bloc, and as we saw in the large-N analysis. In the final section, we examine this claim more closely using sub-national variation in separatism and autonomy within the South Caucasus.

Separatism in the South Caucasus: sub-national evidence from Georgia

We now examine five regions in Georgia with serious separatist potential—Abkhazia, South Ossetia, Adjara, Javakheti, and Kvemo-Kartli—and explain why the first two became virtually synonymous with secessionist conflict, whereas the last three avoided large-scale violence. Georgia is an excellent case for at least two reasons. The first is that it has experienced several secessions, and the second is that it possesses groups exhibiting all three kinds of autonomy. Our core argument is that robust secessionist movements are most likely in regions with lost autonomy—Abkhazia and South Ossetia—and least likely in the absence of autonomy—Javakheti and Kvemo-Kartli. Finally, when autonomy is upheld, as it was in Adjara, secession is also unlikely (although more probable than in cases that were never autonomous). Cornell (2002) argues that Abkhazia and South Ossetia pursued secession *because* of autonomy, which provided these groups with the necessary organizational capacity to secede. We do not disagree that autonomy fostered the capacity to engage in collective action, but we dispute the assumption that autonomy automatically generated the demand for secession. Instead, we suggest that autonomy may sometime sate the demand for self-rule. Retracting autonomy, however, more uniformly engenders resentment and provides a more compelling causal explanation for secession, for it creates the motive for independence while not significantly undermining the capacity to pursue it.

Let us consider the evidence, starting with Abkhazia. Although the Abkhaz have long been accustomed to life as a minority in their own land, their status under the Soviet Union was guaranteed through a formal autonomy arrangement that kept inter-group relations tame for many decades (1925 Constitution; 1931 revisions; Hewitt 1993, 271). Despite some tensions in the 1970s and 1980s, it was not until 1992 that conflict fully erupted (Cornell 2002, 263). Sukhumi used Tbilisi's distraction with ousting Gamsakhurdia to craft new laws that would allow the Abkhaz to override Georgian bloc voting in the regional parliament (Slider 1991, 170; Zürcher 2007, 120). While the Abkhaz sought to enshrine their status in the shadow of a rapidly changing political landscape, Georgians sought a new state that could govern a multi-ethnic periphery and embarked on a set of reforms that would strengthen the center but at the expense of the regions (Siroky and Aprasdize 2011). Although known for his nationalism, Gamsakhurdia actually secured a peaceful arrangement with the Abkhaz that granted them a high degree of disproportionality (Coppieters 2005, 383ff). It was under Shevardnadze's watch that matters

46   *J. Cuffe and D.S. Siroky*

spiraled out of control. In 1992, Georgia's Military Council declared that it would restore the 1921 Constitution of the Democratic Republic of Georgia. Many Abkhaz interpreted this to mean that its autonomous status would be revoked. Even though the 1921 constitution contained a clause for Abkhaz autonomy (1921 Constitution, XI, A. 107–108), the damage had been done and, only a few months later, the Abkhaz unilaterally declared independence (Cornell 2001, 345ff).

Like Abkhazia, South Ossetia had its autonomy revoked. It first gained its autonomy in the early 1920s and maintained it throughout the Soviet period (Saparov 2010). In 1989, South Ossetia requested an elevation of the region's status from autonomous oblast to autonomous republic. Instead of granting the request, Tbilisi increased its control over Tskhinvali. It also adopted Georgian as the official language throughout the regions, which disadvantaged many minorities that only spoke Russian and sometimes their native tongue, and then barred regional parties from competing in national elections (Fuller 1988). South Ossetians did not take these developments lying down, and proclaimed allegiance to the Soviet Union. In response, Gamsakhurdia abolished South Ossetia's autonomy altogether in December 1990 (Fuller 1990; ICG 2004). It was this move that led to the war, which commenced on January 5, 1991 (Denber 1992). The parties eventually reached a ceasefire with Moscow's backing, yet the issue of South Ossetia's status, which was the trigger that initiated the conflict, remained unresolved. Saakashvili sought to impose control over South Ossetia by establishing a parallel pro-Georgian government in South Ossetia. Tbilisi also used the police to clamp down on corruption and arrest individuals in the black market that provided the region with its principal source of revenue. The conflict was settled provisionally with another ceasefire, but exploded again in 2008, when Georgia sought to reassert control. Although a handful of states have recognized South Ossetia's independence, most states have withheld recognition, leaving its official status subject to (possibly) violent revision again in the future.

The next region is Adjara, which is a critical case, as it possessed autonomy—like Abkhazia and to a lesser degree South Ossetia—but it never lost autonomy. Consistent with the theory, Adjara also did not seek secession. We would submit that this was largely because it lacked the motive—not having lost autonomy—and not because it lacked the capacity, which it possessed because it was autonomous. Formerly part of the Ottoman Empire, Adjara became part of Georgia in 1920, and the Treaty of Kars in 1921 guaranteed its status as an ASSR. Adjara maintained this status after the dissolution of the Soviet Union and preserved a significant degree of self-rule, but this arrangement came under increasing scrutiny after the Rose Revolution in 2003. Tbilisi pursued greater control, but did so by focusing on removing Adjara's increasingly unpopular leader, Aslan Abashidze, rather than on altering the region's autonomous status. Unlike Abkhazia and South Ossetia, Adjaran autonomy was never revoked. "Abashidze never raised any question of secession from Georgia" (Fairbanks 2001, 252), arguably as a result of being

Autonomy/separatism in the South Caucasus 47

left to his own devices. Tbilisi was able to remove Abashidze without revoking the region's autonomy, and thus avoided another secession. Unfortunately, this approach proved to be the exception in Georgia rather than the rule.

Finally, the regions of Javakheti and Kvemo-Kartli were never autonomous and were also largely tranquil. Javakheti is a remote region, bordering Armenia and Turkey, composed almost entirely of ethnic Armenians (Melikishvili 1999, 21; Wheatley 2009). The conditions that many theories associate with heightened likelihood of conflict escalation are all present in Javakheti— especially grievances grounded in discrimination, isolation, and inequality, but also high group solidarity and a neighboring kin state—yet armed secessionist conflict has been largely lacking (Guretski 1998). Sometimes dubbed "Georgia's Siberia," Javakheti did not receive a single tonne of fuel for over a year, as gas supplies were cut and roads were permanently blocked with snow. Secession from Tbilisi would have been relatively easy as Javakheti was in effect already separated (Rotar 1998). Although some groups in Javakheti, especially an organization called Javakh and its paramilitary wing Vikh, called for the region to be officially recognized as an autonomous republic, the popular demand for secession was not sufficient and the support from neighboring Armenia was largely lacking (Kavkasia 1998; Dghe'has 1999). Unlike Abkhazia and South Ossetia, which were ethnically mixed, 97 percent of Javakheti is ethnically Armenian. Despite these favorable conditions for secession, Javakheti has remained firmly within Tbilisi's orbit. This has nothing to do with the pacific qualities of Armenians, who fought heartily on the other side of the border in Karabakh. The absence of sustained separatism in Javakheti results from the lack of capacity rather than desire, but lately even the demand for secession may have disappeared as well.

The final region is the Azeri-dominated breadbasket, Kvemo-Kartli, located on the border with Azerbaijan, and composed of over 90 percent Azeris who live compactly in the Rustavi, Marneuli, Bolnisi, Gabardini, Tsalka, and Dmanisi areas. As one observer noted: "they live so homogeneously that many local people don't even realize which state they live in ... " (Zerkalo 2003). Like Javakheti (and several of the other regions), Kvemo-Kartli residents possessed abundant grievances against the new state. Although these sentiments may be widespread among Azeris, they have not found a political outlet. Azeri leaders, in both Georgia and Azerbaijan, have been quick to dismiss rumors that Azeris might pursue secession (Cornell 2001, 211; CIPDD 2003). According to Alibala Akaserov, "the Azerbaijanis have never had and will not have any separatist views" (Zerkalo 2003). It may be that there is little desire for secession, even though one paper called Azeris "fourth class citizens," but a full explanation must also account for the lack of capacity. Partly this results from the absence of any autonomous institutions, but it is also partly due to Azerbaijan's stance toward its kin region, which has served to quiet any discontent and ensure stability.

The sub-national analysis of five Georgian regions primed for secession with varying autonomy arrangements affords an excellent test of the theory advanced here. The evidence is certainly not dispositive, but it provides strong support for the theory and illustrates that it provides some empirical purchase. Although the analysis of sub-national variation in secession in one country implies some important limits on what we can extrapolate to other cases, the theory is general and the empirical analysis is amenable to being tested in other countries and regions of the world. A clear advantage of examining a cluster of inter-connected cases in one country is that it allows us to hold constant many factors that vary drastically *across* states and can make drawing valid cross-national inference a thorny issue for researchers (Snyder 2001). In limiting ourselves to one country, we are able to obviate many of these challenges, although we recognize that it comes at the cost of generalizability, which we attempted to address in the first part with a large-N sample of cases.

Conclusion

This study explores the relationship between political autonomy and separatism. Rather than aggregating groups that have never possessed autonomy and those that have lost it into one category, and then comparing them together with groups that currently possess autonomy, the chapter distinguishes these three classes of ethnic groups: the currently autonomous, the historically autonomous, and the never autonomous. Our theory suggests that historically autonomous groups are most likely to engage in separatism because the retraction of autonomy stimulates the desire for self-determination, while not significantly diminishing the group's ability to pursue it through collective action. At the same time, it considerably weakens the government's ability to make credible commitments that might resolve the conflict prior to escalation.

The data that we have examined are generally supportive and show that the highest incidence of separatism is found among historically autonomous groups, and the lowest is found among groups that were never autonomous. Examining intra-regional variation in Eastern Europe and Eurasia, as well as sub-national variation in the South Caucasus, we find further empirical supports for the theory of lost autonomy. A caricature of our argument might seek to reduce our explanation for the incidence of separatism to a mono-causal institutional logic. Instead, we see autonomy retraction as an exacerbating factor that, theoretically and empirically, is strongly associated with separatism in many countries. We are of course cognizant of omitted variables in the analysis, such as the regime type, level of economic development, the availability of external support, and the manner in which the political unit was initially incorporated, and therefore the results must be treated with caution and further examined with these issues in mind. Although this result does not indicate whether, and if so when, autonomy might be a solution to ethnic conflicts, it should caution decision-makers and politicians thinking about retracting autonomy arrangements. Although centralization of this kind may build legitimacy among one constituency, it is likely to alienate another, and could engender inter-group conflict that leaves all parties worse off than before.

Notes

1 We are grateful to Aleksandar Pavković, along with the reviewers, for encouragement and comments, which have considerably improved the quality of the chapter, and of course we thank John Milton for the title. All errors are ours.
2 We recognize that organization capacity may decline over time and tested whether the results were robust by excluding cases of lost autonomy before World War Two. The results hold.

References

1921 Constitution of the Democratic Republic of Georgia: Chapter XI, Articles 107–108, at www.rrc.ge/law/konstG_1921_02_21_e.htm?lawid=108&lng_3=en (accessed 5 August 2012).

1925 Constitution of Soviet Socialist Republic of Abkhazia, Article 3, at http://abkhazia.narod.ru/constitution1.htm (accessed 5 August 2012).

Bakke, K. (2009), 'State, Society and Separatism in Punjab' *Regional & Federal Studies*, 19: 291–308.

Bermeo, N. (2002), 'The Import of Institutions' *Journal of Democracy*, 13: 96–110.

Bermeo, N. and Amoretti, U. (eds) (2003), *Federalism and Territorial Cleavages*, Baltimore, MD, Johns Hopkins University Press.

Brancati, D. (2009), *Peace by Design*, New York, Oxford University Press.

Brubaker, R. (1996), *Nationalism Reframed: Nationhood and the National Question in the New Europe.* New York: Cambridge University Press

Bunce, V. (1999). *Subversive Institutions: The Design and the Collapse of Socialism and the State*, New York, Cambridge University Press.

Carter, D. and Goemans, H.E. (2011), 'The Making of Territorial Order: New Borders and the Emergence of Interstate Conflict' *International Organization*, 65: 275–309.

CIPDD (2003), *Analysis of Conflict Factors in the Region of Marneuli Gardabani (Georgia)*, Results of sociological research.

Coppieters, B. et al. (2005), *Statehood and Security: Georgia after the Rose Revolution*, Cambridge, MA, American Academy of Arts and Sciences.

Cornell, S. (2001), *Small Nations and Great Powers: A Study of Ethnopolitical Conflict in the Caucasus*, New York, Routledge.

——(2002), 'Autonomy as a Source of Conflict: Caucasian Conflicts in Theoretical Perspective' *World Politics*, 54: 245–276.

Cunningham, K. and Beaulieu, E. (2010), 'Dissent, Repressions, and Inconsistency' in E. Cernoweth and A. Lawrence (eds), *Rethinking Violence*, Cambridge, MA, MIT Press, pp. 173–196.

Denber, R. (1992), *Bloodshed in the Caucasus: Violations of Humanitarian Law and Human Rights in the Georgia–South Ossetia Conflict*, New York, Helsinki Watch.

Derluguian, G. (1998), 'The Tale of Two Resorts: Abkhazia and Ajaria before and since the Soviet Collapse' in B. Crawford and R. Lipschutz (eds), *The Myth of Ethnic Conflict: Politics, Economics, and "Cultural" Violence*, Berkeley, CA, University of California Press, pp. 261–292.

Dghe'has (1999), 'Paper Accuses Armenian Nationalists of Stirring up Ethnic Trouble in Georgia,' 7, Tbilisi, 2 July.

Diamond, L. (1999), *Developing Democracy: Toward Consolidation*, Baltimore, MD, Johns Hopkins University Press.

50 *J. Cuffe and D.S. Siroky*

Erk, J. and Anderson, L. (2009), 'The Paradox of Federalism: Does Self-Rule Accommodate or Exacerbate Ethnic Divisions?' *Regional and Federal Studies*, 19: 191–202.

Fairbanks, C.H. Jr. (2001), 'Party, Ideology and the Public World in the Former Soviet Space' in A.M. Meltzer, J. Einberger and Richard Zinman (eds), *Politics at the Turn of the Century*, Lanham, MD, Rowman and Littlefield, pp. 236–279.

Fuller, E. (1988), 'Draft State Program on Georgian Language' *Radio Liberty Report*, 559.

——(1990), 'Parliament Votes to Abolish Ossetian Autonomy' *Radio Liberty Report*, 512/90.

Geddes, B. (1990), 'How the Cases You Choose Affect the Answers You Get: Selection Bias in Comparative Politics' *Political Analysis*, 2: 131–150.

Giuliano, E. (2006), 'Secessionism from the Bottom-Up: Democratization, Nationalism, and Local Accountability in the Russian Transition' *World Politics*, 58: 276–310.

——(2010), *Constructing Ethnic Grievance: The Rise and Decline of Ethnic Nationalism in Russia*, Ithaca, NJ, Cornell University Press.

Gorenburg, D. (1999), 'Regional Separatism in Russia: Ethnic Mobilization or Power Grab?' *Europe–Asia Studies* 51: 245–275.

——(2003), *Minority Ethnic Mobilization in the Russian Federation*, New York, Cambridge University Press.

Guretski, V. (1998), 'The Question of Javakheti' *Caucasian Regional Studies*, 3(1), at http://poli.vub.ac.be/publi/crs/eng/0301-05.htm (accessed 5 August 2012).

Gurr, T. (2000), *Peoples versus States: Minorities at Risk in the New Century*, Washington, DC, United States Institute of Peace.

Gurr, T. and Davies, J. (1998), *Preventative Measures*, New York, Rowman and Littlefield.

Hale, H.E. (2000), 'The Parade of Sovereignties: Testing Theories of Secession in the Soviet Setting' *British Journal of Political Science*, 30: 31–56.

——(2004), 'Divided We Stand: Institutional Sources of Ethnofederal State Survival and Collapse' *World Politics*, 56: 165–193.

——(2008a), *The Foundations of Ethnic Politics: Separatism of States and Nations in Eurasia and the World*, New York, Cambridge University Press.

——(2008b), 'The Double-Edged Sword of Ethnofederalism: Ukraine and the USSR in Comparative Perspective' *Comparative Politics*, 40: 293–312.

Hartzell, C. and Hodie, M. (2003), 'Institutionalizing Peace: Power Sharing and Post-Civil War Conflict Management' *American Journal of Political Science*, 47: 318–332.

Hechter, M. (1987), *Principles of Group Solidarity*, Berkeley, CA, University of California Press.

Hechter, M. and Okamoto, D. (2001), 'Political Consequences of Minority Group Formation' *Annual Review of Political Science*, 4: 189–215.

Hewitt, G. (1993), 'Abkhazia: A Problem of Identity and Ownership' *Central Asian Survey*, 12: 267–323.

Hirschman, A. (1970), *Exit, Voice, and Loyalty: Responses to Declines in Firms*, Cambridge, MA, Harvard University Press.

Horowitz, D. (1985), *Ethnic Groups in Conflict*, Berkeley, CA, University of California Press.

——(1991), *A Democratic South Africa? Constitutional Engineering in a Divided Society*, Berkeley, CA, University of California Press.

International Crisis Group (2004), *Georgia: Avoiding War in South Ossetia*, ICG Europe Report 159.

Jolly, S. (2006), *A Europe of Regions? Regional Integration, Sub-National Mobilization and the Optimal Size of States*, PhD Dissertation, Department of Political Science, Duke University, Durham, NC.

Kars Treaty of 1921 (in Russian), at www.amsi.ge/istoria/sab/yarsi.html (accessed 5 August 2012).

Kaufman, C. (1996), 'Possible and Impossible Solutions to Ethnic Civil Wars' *International Security*, 20: 136–175.

Kavkasia-Press News Agency (1998), '*Ethnic Armenians in Southern Georgia Demand Autonomy*' Tbilisi, 22 August.

Kymlicka, W. (2008), *Finding Our Way: Rethinking Ethnocultural Relations in Canada*, New York, Oxford University Press.

Lijphart, A. (1977), *Democracy in Plural Societies: A Comparative Exploration*, New Haven, CT, Yale University Press.

McGarry, J. and O'Leary, B. (1993), 'Introduction: The Macro-political Regulation of Ethnic Conflict' in J. McGarry and B. O'Leary (eds), *The Politics of Ethnic Conflict Regulation: Case Studies of Protracted Ethnic Conflicts*, London, Routledge, pp. 1–40.

Melikishvili, L. (1999), *Latent Conflict in Polyethnic Society*, Tbilisi, Tbilisi University Press.

Minorities at Risk Project (2009), 'Minorities at Risk Dataset', College Park, MD, Center for International Development and Conflict Management, at www.cidcm.umd.edu/mar/ (accessed 6 June 2011).

Miodownik, D. and Cartrite, B. (2010), 'Does Political Decentralization Exacerbate or Ameliorate Ethnopolitical Mobilization? A Test of Contesting Propositions' *Political Research Quarterly*, 63: 731–746.

North, D. and Weingast, B. (1989), 'Constitutions and Commitment: The Evolution of Institutions Governing Public Choice in 17th Century England' *Journal of Economic History*, 49: 803–832.

Olson, M. (1965), *The Logic of Collective Action: Public Goods and the Theory of Groups*, Cambridge, MA, Harvard University Press.

Pavkovic, S. (2007), *Creating New States*, Burlington, VT, Ashgate Publishing Company.

Pavkovic, S. and Radan, P. (eds) (2011), *Research Companion on Secession*, Burlington, VT, Ashgate Publishing Company.

Petersen, R. (2002). *Understanding Ethnic Violence: Fear, Hatred, and Resentment in Twentieth Century Eastern Europe.* New York: Cambridge University Press.

R Development Core Team (2011), *R: A Language and Environment for Statistical Computing*, R Foundation for Statistical Computing, Vienna, Austria, at www.R-project.org (accessed 5 August 2012).

Riker, W. (1975), 'Federalism' in F. Greenstein and N. Polsby (eds), *Handbook of Political Science*, 5: 93–172.

Roeder, P. (1991), 'Soviet Federalism and Ethnic Mobilization' *World Politics*, 43: 196–232.

——(2009), 'Ethnofederalism and the Mismanagement of Conflicting Nationalisms' *Regional & Federal Studies*, 19: 203–219.

Rogowski, R. (1985), 'Causes and Varieties of Nationalism: A Rationalist Account' in E. A. Tiryakian and R. Rogowski (eds), *New Nationalisms of the Developed West*, New York, Allen and Unwin, pp. 87–108.

Rotar, I. (1998), 'Tbilisi Has Only Partial Control over Georgia's Armenian Regions' *Prism*, 4: 10.

Saideman, S., Lanoue, D., Campenni, M. and Stanton, S. (2002), 'Democratization, Political Institutions, and Ethnic Conflict: A Pooled, Cross-Sectional Time Series Analysis from 1985–1998' *Comparative Political Studies*, 35: 103–129.

Sakwa, R (1996), *Russian Politics and Society*, New York, Routledge.

Saparov, A. (2010), 'From Conflict to Autonomy: The Making of the South Ossetian Autonomous Region, 1918–1922' *Europe and Asia Studies*, 62: 99–123.

Siroky, D. and Aprasidze, D. (2011), 'Guns, Roses and Democratization: Huntington's Secret Admirer in the Caucasus' *Democratization*, 18(5): 1227–1245.

Slezkine, Y. (1994), 'The USSR as a Communal Apartment, or How a Socialist State Promoted Ethnic Particularism' *Slavic Review*, 53: 414–452.

Slider, D. (1991), 'Democratization in Georgia' in K. Dawisha and B. Parrott (eds), *Conflict and Cleavage in Central Asia and the Caucasus*, New York, Cambridge University Press, pp. 156–201.

Snyder, R. (2001), 'Scaling Down: The Subnational Comparative Method' *Studies in Comparative International Development*, 36: 93–110.

Sorens, J. (2005), 'The Cross-sectional Determinants of Secessionism in Advanced Democracies' *Comparative Political Studies*, 38: 304–326.

Stepan, A. (1999), 'Federalism and Democracy: Beyond the U.S. Model' *Journal of Democracy*, 10: 19–34.

Treisman, D. (1997), 'Russia's "Ethnic Revival": The Separatist Activism of Regional Leaders in a Postcommunist Order' *World Politics*, 49: 212–249.

——(1999), 'Political Decentralization and Economic Reform: A Game Theoretic Analysis' *American Journal of Political Science*, 43: 488–517.

Tsebelis, G. (1990), 'Elite Interaction and Constitution Building in Consociational Societies' *Journal of Theoretical Politics*, 2: 5–29.

Wheatley, J. (2009), 'The Integration of National Minorities in the Samtskhe-Javakheti and Kvemo Kartli Provinces of Georgia Five Years into the Presidency of Mikheil Saakashvili', ECMI Working Paper, No. 44, September.

Wibbels, E. and Bakke, K. (2006), 'Diversity, Disparity, and Civil Conflict in Federal States' *World Politics*, 59: 1–50.

Zerkalo, Baku (23 Dec 2003), 'Paper warns against use of Georgia's Azeri for "inter-political feuding"', Interview with Zurab Melikishvili, Governor of the region.

Zürcher, C. (2007), *The Post-Soviet Wars: Rebellion, Ethnic Conflict and Nationhood in the Caucasus*, New York, New York University Press.

3 Patterns of secession and disintegration in the USSR

Richard Sakwa

All three Communist federations disintegrated, but each did so in its own way. Czechoslovakia was peacefully divided in 1992 into its two constituent units, whereas Yugoslavia's dissolution was accompanied by war and bitter inter-ethnic conflict (see Chapter 4).[1] The case of the disintegration of the Union of Soviet Socialist Republics (USSR) in 1991 falls somewhere in between, with some violence, notably in the Baltic republics and the South Caucasus, but overall the process was remarkably devoid of large-scale conflict. The secession process in the first instance took place cleanly along the lines of the already constituted sub-national sovereign legal entities, a process in which all the union republics participated with greater or lesser enthusiasm. In the long term, however, the formal dissolution of the USSR in December 1991 was the easy part. In the Caucasus and Moldova, the disappearance of the USSR provoked a number of secessions within secessions in which the next layer of sub-national territories (notably Abkhazia, South Ossetia, Nagorno-Karabakh, and Transnistria) sought to break away from the newly established independent states. Although the legal framework for the independence of union republics was relatively clear, the emergence of secessionist movements provoked entrenched conflicts that assumed a 'frozen' character until the recognition of the independence of Kosovo in February 2008 and, following the Russo-Georgian war of August 2008, that of Abkhazia and South Ossetia. As with the peculiar status of the Turkish Republic of Northern Cyprus, whose declaration of independence on 15 November 1983 was recognized only by Turkey, this second wave of post-Soviet secessions entered uncharted legal and constitutional waters.

The Soviet Union and its progeny

The experience of secession in the Soviet case is distinctive in a number of respects. First, the nature of the host state from which secession was achieved remains a matter of considerable debate. The USSR was created in December 1922 as the apparently voluntary union of four original union republics: the Russian Soviet Federative Socialist Republic (RSFSR), Belorussia, Ukraine and the Transcaucasian Federation of Armenia, Azerbaijan and Georgia, which later became union republics in their own right. Union republics retained the constitutional right to secede, something once again recognized in the USSR's last constitution adopted in 1977 and formalized starkly in Article 69 of the Russian constitution: 'The RSFSR has the right freely to leave the USSR' (*Konstitutsiya* 1989, 21). By the time the USSR disintegrated in 1991, there were fifteen union republics, four of which represented territorial conquest during World War Two: the Baltic republics of Estonia, Latvia and Lithuania, and Moldavia (carved out of Bessarabia and North Bukovina). These four can be considered 'colonies' in some sense but, for the other eleven, such a designation would be misleading. The characterization of the USSR as an empire, although appropriate in some abstract conceptual sense while recalling the overlapping sovereignties of medieval empires, would be at best partial if applied in the stronger colonial meaning of the term (Beissinger 1995). Even for the four republics seized by Soviet arms, their incorporation into the USSR did not entail the establishment of a simple exploitative model, and instead membership in the USSR extended to them the Communist developmental model, with all its achievements and drawbacks.

Second, the political character of the host state is no less complex. The first Soviet constitution of January 1924 entrenched a type of ethno-federalism that guaranteed certain legal rights to a hierarchy of constituent entities, with union republics at the top formally retaining a degree of sovereignty, followed by autonomous republics, autonomous oblasts and then ordinary units (oblasts and krais). As we shall see, the Soviet theory of sovereignty differed from typical western appreciations and allowed a hierarchy of sovereign powers. Overlapping sovereignty, however, did not matter very much as the governing and only party, the Communist Party of the Soviet Union (CPSU), was a firmly unitary entity superimposed over the federal system as some sort of 'virtual' sixteenth republic. It represented a whole apparatus of governance without a territorial base. This was a distinctive type of governmentality that generated a whole pathology of double identities and deceptions, with power both alienated and distant while reaching into the very souls of its citizens. The supra-territorial aspect was pointedly emphasized by depriving the RSFSR, the largest republic by far, of its own Communist party and certain other attributes of statehood, such as an academy of sciences, its own security services and even a national anthem, established in the other fourteen union republics.

The tension between the virtual 'Communist' republic and the real physical entities became increasingly intolerable for all as Mikhail Gorbachev's *perestroika* (restructuring) of the Soviet system, launched in 1985, became increasingly radical, accompanied by the delegitimation of the Communist system in its entirety. Thus, the original dynamic of secession had more of a political than a national character, designed to achieve the dissolution of the Communist order and not in the first instance the disintegration of the country. It was the mismanagement of this process by the Gorbachev leadership from 1989 that transformed a dissolution agenda, designed to destroy the powers of the Communist virtual sixteenth republic, into a genuine territorial secessionist process. In the absence of the unitary glue of the CPSU, Gorbachev hoped to

Secession and disintegration in the USSR 55

transform the USSR into a genuinely voluntary confederation of sovereign states through the negotiation of a new union treaty but, in the end, these attempts failed, and dissolution of the Communist system was soon followed by the disintegration of the USSR.

The third feature focuses on the nature of the secessionist movements. Here, we need to recognize that, in each of the union republics, the situation was different. In the Baltic republics, the reformist Communist leaderships elected from 1988 sought at first to participate in the renewal of the Soviet political system, but very soon their aspirations were radicalized as a result of the various blockages on reform at the federal level. With remarkable speed, secessionist movements, encompassing the new Communist leaderships all the way to extremist nationalist groups, advanced radical plans for separation from the USSR. Only Sweden and a few other states had formally recognized the annexation of the Baltic republics after World War Two, and thus their independence can be seen as the restoration of a prior legal order. In Moldova, the issue was complicated by the aspirations of some of the secessionists to unite with Romania, an idea that provoked the secession of Transnistria, a territory strung along the left bank of the Dniester, from Moldova.

In the South Caucasus, the republics of Armenia, Azerbaijan and Georgia had enjoyed independence between 1918 and their reincorporation in 1920–1921 into Soviet Russia, but now their renewed independence was accompanied by internal disintegration (with Abkhazia and South Ossetia effectively splitting away from the radical nationalist Georgian state) and inter-state conflict between Armenia and Azerbaijan over the Armenian-populated enclave of Nagorno-Karabakh. Abkhazia had enjoyed union republic status when it participated in the formation of the USSR in December 1922, within the framework of the Transcaucasian Federation and later joined with Georgia in a confederal 'Treaty of Union' until, on 19 February 1931, Stalin subordinated the republic to Georgia (Harzl 2011) (see also Chapter 2). In the five Central Asian republics (Kazakhstan, Kyrgyzstan, Tajikistan, Turkmenistan and Uzbekistan), secessionist movements were lacking, in large part because of the subsidies and other sources of support from Moscow. This is not to deny the profound nation-building process that had taken place within the framework of Soviet nationality policy (Suny 2002). Out of a largely clan-based entity, for example, Turkmen leaders had exploited opportunities within the Soviet framework to forge a new nation that welcomed the chance to become a sovereign state in 1991 (Edgar 2004). Independence had not been sought, however, and in those chaotic months, the Soviet Union effectively left them: secession was achieved without the instrumentality of a secessionist movement. Thus, these republics fell into the lap of the former Communist ruling elites, where they remain to this day (with the partial exception of Kyrgyzstan). This also applies in large part to Belarus, where secessionist sentiments were minimal. In 1994, however, the rule of the old elites gave way to a populist outsider, Alexander Lukashenko, who proceeded to create a sultanist regime. In Ukraine, secessionism up to 1988 was largely limited to émigré intellectuals

56 R. Sakwa

and Galicia (incorporated from Poland in 1945), but it swiftly gained traction following the attempted conservative coup in Moscow in August 1991. Ukrainian secession in 1991 reflected less a national narrative of statehood but in large part was a response to the immediate political needs of the political elite. The myth of the ineluctable necessity of Ukrainian statehood only came later (Beissinger 2002). The relative weakness of secessionist sentiments, until stimulated by the crises in the regime and the state from August 1991, is reflected in the outcome of Gorbachev's appeal to the people over the heads of the fractious elites. The referendum of 17 March 1991 confirmed that the majority of the electorate favoured the preservation of the Soviet Union 'as a renewed federation of equal sovereign republics', with an 80 per cent turnout of the 184 million registered electors in which 76.4 per cent voted in favour. Although the question was multifaceted, and modified in some republics, accompanied by another question in others, and blocked altogether in Armenia, Estonia, Georgia, Latvia, Lithuania and Moldova, the vote seemed to endorse Gorbachev's view that the USSR was a viable political community. In Russia, 71 per cent voted to preserve the union on a 75 per cent turnout, although the vote in support was higher in the autonomous republics, revealing greater fear of Russia than the union authorities, and even in Ukraine 70 per cent voted in favour, but this was as nothing compared with the 98 per cent in favour of the union in Turkmenistan (Walker 2003, 117–118). In Russia, the vote was accompanied by a referendum on the creation of an executive presidency, which inherently undermined support for the union. After all, simple logic dictates that two presidents in a single country is one too many.

The fourth and final feature concerns the response of the Soviet authorities. Gorbachev's initial reaction was bewilderment that the 'nationalities question' re-emerged because, as late as 1986, the twenty-sixth party congress had asserted that the problem had, 'in the main', been resolved. This gave way to attempts to incorporate separatist aspirations, which initially, as we have seen, fell short of secession, into a revised union. However, once a new constituent treaty was mooted, the Baltic republics wanted out, and even the remaining twelve could find no adequate basis for agreement. By the end, five drafts of a new union treaty were proposed, each granting more rights to the republics in what was planned to be a post-Communist Union of Sovereign States (USS).[2] The August 1991 putsch was provoked by plans to sign the fourth version of the union treaty on 19 August, which would have granted the republics extensive powers. With central authority disintegration, the final version on 14 November 1991 conceded yet more powers to the union republics while retaining some central institutions such as a directly elected president and a bicameral legislature, but even this was too much for Ukraine.

Without Ukraine, the renewed union was considered pointless and, by this stage, Russia had also lost faith in the renewal process. On 7–8 December 1991, the leaders of Russia, Ukraine and Belarus met to discuss the future of the union in a hunting lodge in the Belovezhskaya Pushcha nature reserve in western Belarus. As the three countries were original signatories in December

1922, they claimed the right to dissolve what they had previously formed and, in place of the USSR, they created the Commonwealth of Independent States (CIS), joined two weeks later by all the other republics except Georgia and the Baltic republics. According to the Soviet constitution, the only way that a republic could secede was by referendum, but this was ignored. Russia was impatient to free itself of Soviet tutelage in general and Gorbachev's leadership in particular, but this act of legal nihilism instituted a tradition that remains to this day. It also provoked a crisis of identity in Russia that persists to the present, as it was not clear who was seceding from what. After all, the Soviet system enshrined a form of Russian greatness and, in withdrawing from that shell, Russia emerged with a reduced status to which it has not yet fully reconciled itself. Russia makes no territorial claims on its neighbours, yet it is not quite comfortable in its reduced skin.

While trying to renew the union, Gorbachev also pursued three other strategies. The first was to create a legal framework for secession. Although the right had been granted by the constitution, no practical mechanism existed to manage the process. A new law of 3 April 1990 provided a detailed and extremely onerous procedure, including the need for a referendum and some other detailed stipulations including a 5-year transition period, that in effect rendered the legislation a 'law on non-secession'. The second was the attempt to delineate the precise powers of the federal centre and the republics, and thus to obviate the need for independence. The landmark law of 26 April 1990 sought in laborious detail to delineate the powers of the federal government and the union republics, but its effect was only to exacerbate tensions between the union republics and the autonomous republics within them, while reinforcing the perception that secession would be prevented at almost any cost (Walker 2003, 74–75). To pre-empt the gate coming down on their aspirations, on 11 March 1990, Lithuania declared independence.

The third element was to raise the penalty threshold for major putative secessionist states. This Gorbachev did by diluting what had hitherto been the jealously guarded prerogative of union republics, and encouraged sub-subnational separatism by suggesting that the autonomous republics could be granted the right to join the new union treaty as signatories in their own right. This stimulated a wave of separatism within Russia, against whom the measure was designed, and in particular in Tatarstan and Chechnya, in the vanguard of movements seeking greater sovereignty. Chechen separatists under Johar Dudaev continued to insist right up to his death in 1995 that Chechnya would be happy to remain a member of the redesigned Soviet Union but not of Russia, a possibility opened up by Gorbachev's constitutional innovations but nonsense in political terms. Gorbachev's attempt to outflank the Russian leadership would leave a terrible legacy as Russia tried to avoid going the way of the USSR. The struggle for Russian territorial integrity would be the dominant motif of its early years of independence, as it remains for Azerbaijan, Georgia and Moldova and, even in Uzbekistan, the autonomous Karakalpak republic jealously defends its historical prerogatives.

58   R. Sakwa

Secessionist dynamics

Most Third World federations remain intact because of the authoritarian practices of their central leaderships, but this is a highly inefficient mode of governance. Of the forty-four federations created in the Third World, twenty-seven have broken apart or become fully centralized unitary states. Even in countries where federalism has sunk deep roots, as in Malaysia and Nigeria, it has assumed centralized forms (Mawhood 1984, 521). Democratizing federations find themselves in a particularly parlous situation and, in the Soviet case, provoked the disintegration of the state (Horowitz 1993; Hale 2004). The latent powers of the republics now came to life, and were exploited by entrepreneurial elites to advance their own agendas (Bunce 1999).

Randall Collins's geo-political theory offered a theoretical approach to the Soviet system that allowed him to predict the disintegration of the state. It focuses on three inter-related factors: size and resource advantage (size of the economy and the population); positional advantage (number and attitude of neighbours); and internal state fragmentation. Associated factors included stalemate between the great powers and imperial overextension. Collins argued that the 'Russian empire' (his term for the Soviet Union) suffered from critical structural weaknesses and predicted that 'in the long-term future Russia will fragment into successively smaller states' (Collins 1986, 196). By the 1980s, the USSR was suffering declining economic growth rates, a growing burden of defence spending and a general cultural and demographic malaise accompanied by the subjective appreciation, admitted by Gorbachev, that the political system was becoming increasingly dysfunctional.

What the country was not suffering from, however, was nationalist mobilization or any but very marginal separatist sentiments. Inter-ethnic tensions certainly existed but, on the whole, in cultural terms a 'Soviet people' had been created; but the crucial point is that, in political terms, this was given weak representation and was fragmented. A 'Soviet' nation had not come into being, and the option of identifying oneself as 'Soviet', unlike the availability of a 'Yugoslav' identifier in that Balkan multinational federation, was not even offered in Soviet census returns. The notorious 'point 5' in the Soviet passport stated the holder's nationality but precluded the category 'Soviet', unlike in the Balkans where self-identification as 'Yugoslav' was allowed. The failure to give institutional form to a supra-national Soviet identity perpetuated, and indeed intensified, sub-national identification. Nationalism as such, however, was a product rather than the cause of the Soviet disintegration.

The Soviet disintegration was the product of a triple process. The first could be labelled the 'decolonization' model, and this applies primarily to the Baltic republics, Moldova and to a degree to the South Caucasus (and the Galician part of Ukraine should certainly be included in this list). Here, we have territories that were effectively forcibly reincorporated into the Soviet Union, as most have a long relationship with the Russian empire. Georgia, for example, joined the Russian empire in 1801 as a way of protecting itself from Ottoman

Secession and disintegration in the USSR 59

and Persian threats, whereas the Baltic republics had been within the Russian sphere for several centuries. As part of the Russian and Soviet system, these territories had maintained their own cultural identities, including their languages and festivals. Inevitably, there had been a natural process of Russianization, although forced Russification was the exception rather than the rule.

The titular nations in Estonia and Latvia, however, felt increasingly threatened by the influx of Slavic workers employed in their burgeoning manufacturing industries and military establishments. The demographic balance had changed to the point that non-Latvians comprised nearly half the population by 1991. In political terms, however, the Communist parties in these republics, although part of a unitary system, were able to voice republic concerns. The memory of the Soviet occupation in 1940 and the Stalinist deportations following 1945, however, continued to rankle but, during the long period of Brezhnevite stability from 1964, political repression was no more intense here than in any other Soviet republic. Neither was economic exploitation any different than throughout the Soviet union; and indeed standards of living in the Baltic republics were much higher than in Russia. This was a very peculiar 'empire', in which the peripheries (except in Central Asia) were more economically developed and prosperous than the alleged 'core' (Suny 1993). On 16 November 1988, the Estonian Supreme Soviet adopted a Declaration affirming the sovereignty of the republic, and thus launched what in due course would become a 'parade of sovereignties' that in the end turned into a 'war of the laws' and the disintegration of the union.

The second process can be called the 'affirmation' model, which primarily concerns Russia. In effect, Russia seceded from the state that nationalists in non-Russian republics accused Russia of dominating. Since the 1960s, there had been a growing Russian national awareness that the Soviet Union was not the best framework to advance Russia's specific national interests. Not only did it lack some of the political and social institutions present in the other republics, but there was also a perception that Russia was shouldering a disproportionate share of the burden of the Soviet enterprise, and was getting an unfair share in return (Brudny 1999). Russia felt that it was subsidising the other republics, and only gained opprobrium in return. Alexander Solzhenitsyn led the calls for Russia to shed the imperial burden and to focus on its own cultural and national development. On his election to the chair the Russian Congress of People's Deputies (the new-style parliament) in May 1989, Boris Yeltsin gave expression to these sentiments, exacerbated by his personal conflict with Gorbachev. Russia issued its own declaration of state sovereignty on 12 June 1990, followed in rapid succession by Ukraine and other republics; and as we have seen, it was Russia that declared the Soviet Union defunct in December 1991.

Ukraine is the second main case of the affirmation model. Here, a number of specific grievances came together to fuel a powerful secessionist movement, which the former Communist leadership (embarrassed by its failure to condemn the 1991 August coup in time) came to head. The Ukrainian language

60   R. Sakwa

had indeed been squeezed out by Russian, with few schools teaching the language and higher education entirely Russianized. The famine of 1932–1933 (*golodomor*, in Ukrainian *holodomor*) was interpreted by nationalists as a deliberate Stalinist policy of anti-Ukrainian genocide, although Russian regions in the Kuban and lower Volga suffered equally. In economic terms, there had long been a struggle between investment in Siberia and Ukraine, and in broad terms Ukraine had won out (the lack of a Russian Communist party was a factor here), provoking Siberian regional separatism after 1991. Above all, the Cossack tradition and memories of Ukrainian statehood before unification with Russia in 1654 and during the Russian civil war fostered a powerful sense of nationhood. Whether this required independent statehood is another issue: western Ukraine, with its distinctive religious tradition (the Uniates), certainly thought it did; whereas the Donbas to this day retains close cultural ties and economic affiliations with Russia.

The third model is 'secession by default'. This encompasses those countries that effectively had secession thrust upon them in the course of the Soviet disintegration. This includes Belarus, which shares a close cultural connection with Russia. The election of the anti-nationalist Lukashenko in 1994 reflected the ambivalence of Belarusian statehood; but once in power, the entrenched national elites, despite much talk of creating a common state with Russia, were not willing to sacrifice their unexpected statehood. The Central Asian states had been latecomers to the Russian empire and resisted Bolshevik modernization plans, and had suffered terribly from Stalinist collectivization but, by the 1990s, the Soviet Union offered them a comfortable framework for modernization and membership of a world civilization. Corruption in the republics was tolerated in exchange for loyalty in the Brezhnev years, and Gorbachev's anti-corruption campaigns were an affront to national pride. There were no secessionist movements here, and instead Communist leaders simply re-branded themselves as national elites and continued to rule as before, sans supervision from Moscow. Only in Kyrgyzstan was there some circulation of elites, but even here the newcomers soon succumbed to the clan politics and crony capitalism prevalent in the region.

Post-Communist secessionism

There is a large literature devoted to the question of whether Russia will disintegrate in a manner reminiscent of the Soviet collapse. One major difference is the demographic balance. Whereas ethnic Russians comprised just over half the population of the USSR, they now make up 80 per cent of the Russian Federation. The nature of the state also differs. Whereas the USSR was a *treaty* federation, in which the contracting parties retained the right to secede, Russia is a *constitutional* federation, where its members are considered to be part of a pre-existing political entity and have no constitutional right to secede.

There are some similarities, however. Above all, the peculiar type of 'matrëshka federalism', formalized by the 1924 constitution, remains, based on a hierarchy of ethno-federal units. The American model of federalism, where ethnicity does not define any of the federal components, is an attractive model for many in Russia, where the ethnic republics act as a standing reproach to the view that ethnicity should be an individual attribute and not given political form in sub-national state construction. However, the logic of path dependency means that it would take a revolution to repudiate the federal representation of ethnicity and, despite attempts to foster a civic Russian nationalism, notably in the advocacy of the neutral term *Rossiyanin* (as opposed to the ethnic signifier *Russkii*) in the Yeltsin years, the political identity of titular ethnic groups remains as strong as ever.

This is particularly in evidence in the Caucasus. The attempt to push the boundaries of the 'Grotian moment', when state sovereignty is up for grabs, to encompass former autonomous (rather than union) entities such as Chechnya, South Ossetia and Abkhazia engendered prolonged confrontation that at times turned into outright war. The logical problem of differentiating between peoples that the Soviet system decided had matured enough for statehood and those that had not (notably Tatarstan and Abkhazia) in the early 1990s provoked a 'parade of sovereignties' that, in the Chechen and Abkhaz cases, turned into outright declarations of independence. It was clear that the Soviet Union had been far from a 'melting pot' of nations or even a sustainable union of peoples, but the post-Soviet states were no less challenged to define their national character and state identity (Sukhov 2007). In the Russian case, a Federative Treaty in March 1992 stabilized the situation by granting extensive powers to what had become twenty-one sub-national republics and the other 'subject of the federation', in exchange for unity and loyalty (a deal refused at the time by Chechnya and Tatarstan).

This principle was entrenched in the December 1993 constitution, although the sub-national units were deprived of even the formal entitlement to sovereignty. Different interpretations of sovereignty remained, however, with a type of relative sovereignty still prevalent in Russian debates, whereas most other post-Soviet republics adopted the stronger western definition focused on the pre-eminence of a single authoritative state (Deyermond 2007). In the 1990s, Russian regionalism took a segmented form, where both the centre and the federal subjects engaged in mutually exclusive power accumulation strategies that rendered the system highly asymmetrical (Stepan 2000). The 'new federalism' under Vladimir Putin from 2000 sought to equalize federal imbalances and to overcome segmentation, but the centralization drive threatened federalism in its entirety. The abolition of gubernatorial elections in 2004 signified the consolidation of the 'power vertical', but the principle of federalism was not repudiated, although unitary practices increasingly jeopardized its operation.

The cases of post-Soviet separatism challenge existing practices of regulating sub-national conflicts but, above all, raise the question whether secession really is the best option when peoples cannot or will not coexist within a single state. There is, moreover, no internationally recognized mechanism to decide what would be the optimal option in any given case, and thus brute

62   *R. Sakwa*

force and geo-political expediency tend to govern the process of state formation. This certainly applies to Kosovo's independence, as it does to Abkhazia and South Ossetia. The tension between the opposed UN principles of territorial integrity and national self-determination is endemic, and there is no universal mechanism to reconcile the two. Thus, in 1991, the international community recognized republics not on the basis of the principle of national self-determination but on whether the Soviet (and Yugoslav) systems had accorded a particular people union republic status. The vast majority of the 6,000-odd cultural–linguistic groups on the planet have no territorial recognition as states and thus no voice in international affairs, and yet decolonization and the disintegration of the Soviet Union and the Soviet bloc accelerated state formation in a process that is not yet over. Hence, secession today in post-Soviet Eurasia has become a *force majeure* form of state formation in the absence of a mechanism to adjudicate between competing claims to statehood.

The differences between republics are significant, as Chechnya was formally part of a federal system and thus its claim to self-determination stopping short of independence could be encompassed by Russia's ethno-federal system. Following two terrible wars (1994–1996 and 1999–2009), Chechnya, under the leadership of Ramzan Kadyrov (he formally assumed the presidency in March 2007), was granted extensive autonomy to manage its own affairs. However, this was less an example of the asymmetrical federalism that has characterized Russian politics since independence in 1991 than a case of the extreme segmentation that, in certain respects, repudiates the fundamental federal principle of power sharing. Nevertheless, by the time the 'counter-terrorist operation', as the second war was called, was formally ended on 16 April 2009, Chechnya had been brought back into the Russian political sphere, although its subordination to constitutionalism was rather more in doubt. Although the secessionist *movement* had been defeated, this was at the cost of consolidating a potentially separatist *leadership* (Sakwa 2010).

In Georgia, matters had an opposed dynamic (see also Chapter 2). The republic was proclaimed a unitary state in 1990, which immediately provoked the counter-mobilization of threatened minorities (Coppieters and Levgold 2005). Both Abkhazia and South Ossetia declared their independence and, following various wars, emerged as de facto independent states. They were recognized as such by Russia on 26 August 2008, although few other countries followed suit. The two republics appealed to a long history of separate political identity from Georgia as well as discrimination ('just cause' in the just war tradition) to bolster their claims to independence (Coppieters and Sakwa 2003).

At the heart of the post-Soviet secession struggles lies the question of just cause; that is, the prevention or remedying of injustices. Whereas the normative framework of the Soviet disintegration lay in the sphere of constitutionalism, after 1991, sub-national separatist claims could only be justified by devising arguments based on political practices and mythologized national narratives. Even where elements of just cause could be demonstrated, separatist or secessionist movements are constrained by a set of other considerations, notably 'right intentions' (i.e. motives consistent with just cause), proportionality in methods and the recourse to violence only as a last resort (Coppieters 2003). No less important are the dynamics of ethnic secession, with Horowitz's model of interest-based interactions inadequate in most dimensions when applied to post-Soviet cases (Laitin 2007).

The well-known claim about the 'artificiality' of the Soviet borders applies equally to the attempt by Nagorno-Karabakh to secede from Azerbaijan, to which it was given by Stalin's personal decision, to join Armenia. It also applies to Transnistria, a thin sliver of land on the west bank of the Dniester that was an autonomous republic of interwar Ukraine but which was attached to the new republic of Moldavia (carved out of Romanian territory) after World War Two. It could equally apply to the Crimea, which was transferred from Russian to Ukrainian jurisdiction in 1954, in large part based on economic considerations, although the date was chosen to celebrate the 300th anniversary of the union of the two countries. Every post-Soviet republic (like most African states) could be accused of artificiality, and populations remain mixed throughout the region. The 1989 census, for example, revealed that, of the 44.2 million Ukrainians in the USSR, only 37.4 million lived in Ukraine and Russia was host to 3.7 million. The figure would undoubtedly be higher if Stalin had not ordered that Ukrainian be replaced by Russian in the Kuban's schools in 1934, and the Ukrainian accent remains prevalent in south Russia.

As in the case of Kosovo, the language of the right of a nation to 'self-determination' is avoided in post-Soviet conflicts (Muharremi 2008). When discourse over the protection of national minorities is exhausted, historical and remedial arguments take precedence.[3] The problem in the post-Soviet area as elsewhere is that there are endless problems of minorities within minorities, provoking a possible cascade of secessionist conflicts whose peaceful resolution is almost impossible. The former administrative borders of federal states were the primary line of division, representing three-quarters of all the borders in the region. For the minorities within the new republics, secession is only one possible form of self-determination. Federal solutions are usually posited as a way of combining minority rights with political representation; and in extreme cases, as in Georgia before 2008, the confederal option was probably the only way in which the integrity of the country could have been maintained. In Estonia, however, talk in the early 1990s of the secession of the predominantly ethnic Russian Narva area has largely disappeared. The idea of the pre-emptive revision of borders holds little attraction; but delay sometimes leads to their forcible change, typically accompanied by ethnic cleansing. Cosmopolitan solutions that call for transparent borders as part of larger transnational communities are something yet to be achieved in the region.

Notes

1 The chapter draws on my earlier 'Secession as a Way of Dissolving Federations: The USSR', Chapter 8 in Pavković and Radan (2011).

64   R. Sakwa

2 The five Union Treaties were published in *Izvestiya*: 24 November 1990, 9 March, 27 June, 15 August and 25 November 1991.
3 For a discussion of theory and practice, see Osipov (1997).

References

Beissinger, M. (1995), 'The Persisting Ambiguity of Empire' *Post-Soviet Affairs*, 11(2): 149–184.

——(2002), *Nationalist Mobilization and the Collapse of the Soviet State*, Cambridge, Cambridge University Press.

Brudny, Y.M. (1999), *Reinventing Russia: Russian Nationalism and the Soviet State, 1953–1991*, Cambridge, MA, Harvard University Press.

Bunce, V. (1999), *Subversive Institutions: The Design and the Destruction of Socialism and the State*, Cambridge, Cambridge University Press.

Collins, R. (1986), *Weberian Sociological Theory*, Cambridge, Cambridge University Press.

Coppieters, B. (2003), 'Secession and War: A Moral Analysis of the Russian–Chechen Conflict' *Central Asian Survey*, 22(4): 377–404.

Coppieters, B. and Levgold, R. (eds) (2005), *Revolution, Statehood and Security: Georgia after the Rose*, Cambridge, MA, The MIT Press.

Coppieters, B. and Sakwa, R. (eds) (2003), *Contextualizing Secession: Normative Studies in Comparative Perspective*, Oxford, Oxford University Press.

Deyermond, R. (2007), *Security and Sovereignty in the Former Soviet Union*, Boulder, CO, Lynne Rienner.

Edgar, A.L. (2004), *Tribal Nation: The Making of Soviet Turkmenistan*, Princeton, NJ, Princeton University Press.

Hale, H. (2004), 'Divided We Stand: Institutional Sources of Ethnofederal State Survival and Collapse' *World Politics*, 56(2): 165–193.

Harzl, B.C. (2011), 'Nationalism and Politics of the Past: The Cases of Kosovo and Abkhazia' *Review of Central and East European Law*, 36: 53–77.

Horowitz, D. (1993), 'Democracy in Divided Societies' *Journal of Democracy*, 4(4): 18–38.

Konstitutsiya (1989), *Konstitutsiya (osnovnoi zakon) Rossiiskoi Sovetskoi Federativnoi Sotsialisticheskoi Respubliki* (first adopted in 1978, with changes of 27 October 1989), Moscow, Sovetskaya Rossiya.

Laitin, D.D. (2007), *Nations, States and Violence*, Oxford, Oxford University Press.

Mawhood, P. (1984), 'The Politics of Survival: Federal States in the Third World' *International Political Science Review*, 5(4).

Muharremi, R. (2008), 'Kosovo's Declaration of Independence: Self-Determination and Sovereignty Revisited' *Review of Central and East European Law*, 33: 401–435.

Osipov, A.G. (ed.) (1997), *Pravo narodov na samoopredelenie: ideya i voploshchenie*, Moscow, Zven'ya.

Pavković, A. and Radan, P. (eds) (2011), *Ashgate Research Companion to Secession*, Farnham, UK, Ashgate.

Sakwa, R. (2010), 'The Revenge of the Caucasus: Chechenization and the Dual State in Russia' *Nationalities Papers*, 38(5): 601–622.

Stepan, A. (2000) 'Russian Federalism in Comparative Perspective' *Post-Soviet Affairs*, 16(2): 133–176.

Sukhov, I. (2007), 'Russian Federalism and Evolution of Self-Determination' *Russia in Global Affairs*, 5(2), at http://eng.globalaffairs.ru/numbers/20/ (accessed 5 August 2012).

Suny, R.G. (1993), *The Revenge of the Past: Nationalism, Revolution and the Collapse of the Soviet Union*, Stanford, CA, Stanford University Press.

——(2002), *A State of Nations: Empire and Nation-Making in the Age of Lenin and Stalin*, Oxford, Oxford University Press.

Walker, E.W. (2003), *Dissolution: Sovereignty and the Breakup of the Soviet Union*, Lanham, MD, Rowman and Littlefield.

4 From Yugoslavia to the western Balkans

Radmila Nakarada

Introduction

Twenty years after the disappearance of the Socialist Federative Republic of Yugoslavia (SFRY) the existing plenitude of books and articles are still attempting to decipher the causes of its ill fate, Yugoslavia still remains a subject of scholarly interest and research. This may suggest either that the full tale has yet to be recounted or that the tale has still not reached its end. Whether one or the other, the tale is interesting because the disintegration of Yugoslavia descended into unexpected flames of violence caused by secessions and has had global implications that may still be unfolding.

The violent disintegration of Yugoslavia represented the first war(s) to be fought on European soil after the end of World War Two. The result of these wars was a violent change to the borders of the SFRY, which appeared to be justified, by the Arbitration Commission on the Conference of Yugoslavia (convened by the European Community (the EC)), by reference to the peoples' right to self-determination and the principle of *uti possedetis* (Nakarada 2008). The use of force to change the borders of sovereign states was at the time a novelty in post-1945 Europe; but similar attempts at violent border changes were made later in the former USSR and the Middle East.

Prior to the end of the Cold War, in spite of all the economic difficulties and political strains, Yugoslavia was still considered a relative success story, having established an apparently organic community within a multicultural milieu (in mid-1980, 12 percent of all marriages in the SFRY were mixed), developed extensive economic ties and interdependencies between its federal units, and attained a higher standard of living than any other Communist-ruled state. It also enjoyed a respectable international status based on its contribution to the victory of the allies in World War Two, its break with Stalin's international Communist organization, its participation in the creation of the non-aligned movement, and the fact that it was the first Communist-ruled state that had signed bilateral agreements with the EC (Skopjak 2004, 99–100).[1] Having recognized Yugoslavia as a creator of the so called Third Way, self-managing socialism, "socialism with a human face," some observers had expected that, at the end of the Cold War, Yugoslavia would easily find its place in the new global environment and the reintegration of the Communist-ruled countries

Yugoslavia to the western Balkans 67

into western Europe. Instead, the country disintegrated, undergoing a chain of secessions and a series of tragic wars. When the wars ended in 1995, only its former Republic of Slovenia became a member of the European Union (EU) in 2004, whereas the rest of the newly created states become part of the new region—western Balkans.[2] The magnitude of the violence and the protracted process of the break-up inspired a number of attempted explanations of why Yugoslavia disintegrated (see Soso 2002; Jovic 2008).[3] These explanations included, among others, the view that Yugoslavia was, in fact, an "artificial state" predetermined to vanish, because it was the result of Serbian imperial expansionism (analogous to the role of Russia in creating the USSR); and the view that the SFRY was an authoritarian interlude of peace in a frozen ethnic conflict between eternal enemies that exploded when external circumstances changed dramatically. If we discard these deterministic interpretations often based on false analogies, we face an intricate "ensemble" of factors that have played themselves out, albeit unevenly, in the process of disintegration of the SFRY. They include, among others, the following ambiguities built into its very foundations—the simultaneous capacities for integration and disintegration;[4] the tension between shared traits and divergences, between common and competing interests (and memories) that strained the possibilities of creating social cohesion and a homogeneous nation state; the protracted structural crisis of a European semi-periphery (see Berend 1996, 412)[5] and limited policy options advanced by the intellectual and political elites that lost their ability to distinguish between the (political) system and the state[6] as well as various local and global interactions, which appeared to simultaneously annul both the capacities of state reorganization and the mechanisms of non-violent break-up. This brief inventory is just an indication that the Yugoslav disintegration involved historical legacies, the failure of the Yugoslav self-managing socialism to devise a formula accommodating multiethnic and regional differences as well as the changing international environment following the end of the Cold War. The process was also influenced by the limited capacities of the political and intellectual elites in Yugoslav republics to envisage peaceful and mutually agreed political change. Secession came at the end of the process of non-violent disintegration and at the beginning of its violent chapter—resulting in four wars. The following is a brief outline of several dimensions of the disintegration process that reinforced each other.

Sequences of disintegration

The major disintegrative factors in the political realm can be listed in the following sequence:

- The 1974 Yugoslav Constitution, promulgated under the rule of the Communist leader Tito, transformed the country into a loose federation, weakening the central authority and turning the republics (federal units) and autonomous provinces into proto-states with veto power.

68 R. Nakarada

- In 1989, the Republic of Slovenia unilaterally amended its own constitution overriding the Yugoslav federal constitution. It proclaimed the right to self-determination of Slovenia including the right to secession and the supremacy of its republican authorities over the federal government.
- In 1989, Serbia unilaterally amended its constitution curtailing the state and political autonomy of the Kosovo province but leaving its cultural autonomy unchanged.[7] Kosovo Albanian elites and population interpreted this as a violation of their acquired rights; this change triggered the first attempt at secession in the SFRY—the attempt to secede Kosovo from Serbia in 1990 (see the next section: Secession and wars).
- In October 1990, Slovenia and Croatia proposed a confederal model of Yugoslavia according to which any member had the right to leave the confederation at any time unilaterally. Serbia and Montenegro proposed a model of democratic federalism (which would not allow unilateral secession), and Macedonia and Bosnia and Herzegovina a somewhat modified confederal model. All of them were, by and large, presented in "take it or leave it" form. As Jan Oberg says, "each actor acted as if the others did not exist, or could be forced to disappear ... Each actor usually took the worst possible step at the worst possible moment, only to confirm the other actors in their worst fears and assumptions" (Oberg 1994, 127).
- In November 1990, the Slovenian parliament concluded that the Yugoslav state was no longer functional and that Slovenia therefore had no future in Yugoslavia because "economic and national death awaits us in it" (Jovic 2008, 274). This ruled out any elections held at the Yugoslav federal level.

In the economic realm, one can note the following disintegrative factors. The SFRY economy was an export-oriented economy based on a socialist (non-private) market with rudimentary forms of regional integration with western Europe. But the oil crisis and the resulting recessions in the west in the mid-1970s and mid-1980s hit the heavily indebted Yugoslav economy hard. As international interest rates shot up, the economy, whose expansion was sustained by cheap credit from the west, suddenly contracted. The recession also limited export opportunities from Yugoslavia to the west. This decreased the economic growth rate and the general standard of living, which in turn caused political dissatisfaction among the citizens; this dissatisfaction easily took on ethno-national coloring. The economic crisis led to the conflict between, on one hand, the Keynesian segments of national elites (Woodward 1995) who wanted to strengthen the federal institutions, its redistributive capacities, and its central bank and, on the other, the local Yugoslav factions of the "transnational elite" (Robinson 2003), the internal supporters of neo-liberalism. The latter resisted recentralization believing that the economic crisis could not be resolved by strengthening the federation. Resistance emerged in those republics (Slovenia and Croatia) that did not want to erode their sovereignty attained by the constitution of 1974 and the right to freely dispose of resources on their territory (Woodward 1995). Instead of opting for reform, they chose independence, an option that was made easier by the end of the Cold War, the unification of Germany, and the emerging celebration of the principle of self-determination that served their interest in independence well. For these reasons, Susan Woodward argues,[8] it is incorrect to define the Yugoslav conflict as originally being ethnic (see also Allcock 2000, 89). It is above all the result of simultaneous transformation of the existing international order (moving from Keynesianism to neoliberalism) and internal order (moving from socialism to capitalism). From this, one can infer that the apparent advantages of the Yugoslav economic model—the socialist market and its openness to global economic trends—in fact increased its internal vulnerabilities and contributed to its disintegrative tendencies.

Secession and wars

In our discussion of the secessionist chain, we will group the cases according to their shared characteristics and not follow a strict chronology of events. The first group consists of the initiators of secession—Slovenia and Croatia. Bosnia and Herzegovina and Kosovo (or Kosovo and Metohija) are each in themselves unique cases, particularly in relation to the extreme violence involved in their establishment, whereas Macedonia and Montenegro are to a certain extent by-products of the federal break-up, "collateral states" whose secession was not accompanied by violence.

The initiators—Slovenia and Croatia

Slovenia's secession had its roots in the so called "cestna afera" (the road affair) in 1969, sparked by the distribution of loans from western banks that failed to finance building a highway in Slovenia. This was the first open conflict between one federal republic and the central federal government. In the background of this conflict was the demand for greater independence for Slovenia, a reform of the federation, as well as the revision of Slovenia's financial obligations toward the federation, in particular to the federal Fund for the Undeveloped Regions (Bilandžić 1979). A decade later, voices among the intellectual elite gathered round the journal *Nova revija* re-emerged advocating the need for Slovenia to break away from the Balkans and rejoin its natural habitat—western Europe. This advocacy led to the formulation of the Slovenian national program in 1986 under the title "Contributions for a Slovenian national program" (Soso 2002, 171–176), which later provided the basis/inspiration for the actions of Slovenian politicians, including the amendments to the republic's constitution aiming at the subordination of the Yugoslav federal authorities to that of the Republic of Slovenia. The essays constituting the Slovenian national program were, in part, a response to the leaked draft of the "Memorandum of the Serbian Academy of Arts and Sciences," which listed a series of Serb nationalist grievances and at the end raised the possibility of Serbia leaving Yugoslavia. At the time (1986), Slobodan

Milošević (the Serb leader who later emerged as the advocate of Serb nationalism) was a mainstream Communist apparatchik, who denounced Serbian nationalism and the "Memorandum." The Slovenian program of secession, contained in the *Nova Revija* contributions, was not simply a reaction to his aggressive policies in the 1990s (he was only an additional good excuse), but an autochthonous project that later gained external (primarily German) support. As this was primarily a project of the political and intellectual elite, a lot of energy had to be invested in order to win over the majority of the Slovene population to the idea of an independent Slovenia. A poll conducted by the newspaper *Delo* in Ljubljana in the early 1990s showed that 52 percent of the population was in favor of confederative association with Yugoslavia, and 28 percent was for complete secession, whereas 8 percent was for the status quo. It took a half a year of intensive media campaigning to win over the majority of the population for secession (Bookman 1992).

The formal procedure of separation included the removal of the adjective "socialist" from the republic's name by a Slovenian parliament in 1990, which issued a *Declaration on the Sovereignty of the State* in the same year, giving the republican laws priority over the federal ones, and submitting (together with Croatia) to the SFRY presidency the proposal for a confederal model of Yugoslavia. The proposal was submitted in October; only 2 months later, in December 1990, a referendum was carried out in Slovenia in which 86 percent of those voting voted for an independent state. Following the referendum, Slovenian soldiers were withdrawn from the Yugoslav People's Army (YPA), but its political representatives continued to take part in the negotiations among the leaders of the six federal units (republics) on the constitutional reorganization of the federation. Six months later, following its May *Declaration on Disassociation*, on June 25, 1991, the Slovenian parliament passed acts of separation from the SFRY and a declaration of independence, followed by its Territorial Defense (TD) taking over the customs and border crossings of Slovenia. The TD, previously secretly armed (primarily by the Austrian agencies) and de facto transformed into an army, demanded the pull-out of the federal YPA. The next day, a 10-day war broke out between the YPA units and the Slovenian TD. There were few casualties on the Slovenian side (around ten members of the TD), whereas the young, badly trained recruits of the Yugoslav army suffered greater losses (around sixty). The SFRY Presidency decided to withdraw the YPA units from Slovenia soon afterwards. The European Community (EC) attempted to mediate, negotiating the Brioni Declaration, which called for a 3-month moratorium on the declaration of independence of both Slovenia and Croatia and the reinstatement of the previous border arrangements. However, it failed to implement its own policy consistently, a weakness that reoccurred in the succeeding EC (later European Union) efforts to play a role in resolving the Yugoslav crisis (see Nakarada and Račić 1998). At the end of the year, on December 23, 1991, the German government, violating the decision of the EC Ministerial Council, recognized Slovenia on its own. The other EC member states followed suit in January 1992.

As in the case of Slovenia, Croat secessionism cannot be explained away as a reaction to the awakened and threatening Serbian nationalism of the 1990s. Already in the early 1970s, during the rule of the Yugoslav Communist leader (of Croatian origin), Marshal Tito, a nationalist movement emerged in Croatia, the so-called *Maspok* (mass movement), for the first time leading to national homogenization in one republic, uniting the Croatian Communist party leadership, intellectuals, and citizens around a common goal—creating an independent national state. The leaders of the movement demanded that Croatia had its own army and seat in the UN. The similarities of the aims articulated in the 1970s and 1990s and the fact that some of the leaders of *Maspok*, such as Dr. Franjo Tudjman, became key political actors in the early 1990s points out the autochthonous aspect of the secession of Croatia.

The Slovenian example encouraged radical secessionists in Croatia, dramatically dividing the Serb and Croat population. Thus, two parallel processes ensued, one successful, the other not: the secession of Croatia from the SFRY, and the attempt of the Serb-inhabited parts of Croatia to secede from independent Croatia by remaining in the SFRY. Ironically, during the process of democratization in the early 1990s, in the multiethnic environment in Croatia, political parties were formed along the ethnic axis. The first post-Communist multi-party elections to be held in Croatia in April 1990 were won by Dr. Tudjman and his nationalist Croatian Democratic Union (CDU). Thanks to the electoral system based on the majority principle, his coalition won a two-thirds majority on the basis of 41 percent of the votes. Before and after the elections, armed conformation and skirmishes with the Serbs began in Croatia. They grew in intensity as the CDU proceeded to introduce constitutional changes in the parliament. First, the designation "socialist" was removed as in Slovenia, and state symbols changed. With the appearance of the flag with an Ustasha emblem (chessboard), the Serb political parties decided to establish a regional union of the Serb-populated areas of Croatia and issue a *Declaration on the sovereignty and independence of Serbs in Croatia*. The Serbian National Council was established as their representative body and, on August 16, it decided to hold a referendum on the autonomy of Serbs in Croatia. The "unarmed uprising" of the Serbs turned into an armed one the next day, when the Croatian special police attacked a police station in the town of Benkovac. Serbs armed themselves and set up barricades, while the Croatian state proceeded to import weaponry. By the end of the year, a new constitution of the Republic of Croatia was adopted, defining Croatia as the national state of the Croatian nation. It also changed the status of Serbs from a constituent nation in Croatia into a minority. Exclusionary practices, including the marginalization of the Serbian dialect and Cyrillic alphabet, firing of Serbs working in state administration and police and obliging them to sign loyalty oaths, revived among the Serbs in Croatia the fears and insecurities of the past, in particular the period of the pro-fascist Ustasha state during World War Two.

Shortly after, Croatia, like Slovenia, also suspended the constitution of the SFRY; only Croatian laws were to be valid on its territory. In February 1991,

Serbs responded by deciding that its regional union, by the name of "Krajina" (the Frontier), would separate from the Republic of Croatia and remain in the SFRY. Amid the growing tension and small-scale armed conflicts, on the same date as Slovenia, June 25, 1991, the Croatian Parliament proclaimed Croatia an independent and sovereign republic, later gaining the recognition[9] of Germany, followed by other European countries and the USA. As the conflicts between the Serb and Croatian police forces intensified, the Croatian government, like the Slovenian one before it, demanded the withdrawal of the YPA units from Croatia and, failing to achieve this, blockaded the YPA barracks in Croatia. The YPA responded by a full-scale invasion of Croatia, relieving most of its units blockaded in the barracks and extending the territory controlled by the Serb militias. In the ensuing period, the EC negotiated around fifteen ceasefires but with no lasting success.[10] In December 1991, the Serbian National Council declared the Republic of Srpska Krajina (uniting two territorially disjointed areas in Croatia: Krajina and Eastern Slavonia) independent from Croatia. In an attempt to end the violence, in 1992, the UN initiated the so called Vance plan establishing UN protected areas (UNPA) with UN peace-keeping forces. However, the engagement of the UN did not result in the end of this conflict. As Robert Hayden (2000) points out, a "final solution" is inevitable when a national state is created in a multinational region. The "final solution" in Croatia came in the form of two military operations in 1995—operation "Flash" in eastern Slavonija and operation "Storm" in the Republic of Krajina. The aim was to reintegrate these two seceding territories, and this resulted in the forced eviction of the Serb population, around 300,000 people from the UN protected areas (which the UN forces did nothing to stop).

Secession and NATO military intervention—Bosnia and Herzegovina and Kosovo

Following the secessions of Slovenia and Croatia in June 1991, a profound crisis opened in Bosnia and Herzegovina. It had a unique demographic structure; three nations shared a territory, without any one nation having an overwhelming majority.[11] The three nations had two different goals in relation to the ongoing disintegration. Most of the Serbs wanted to remain in the SFRY, whereas most of the Muslims/Bosniaks and Croats wanted an independent Bosnian state. The Muslim leader made it clear that he was prepared to sacrifice peace for a sovereign state, and not the sovereign state for peace (Kovacevic and Dajic 1994). The first multi-party elections held in 1990 divided the electorate along ethnic lines, as in the case of Croatia. The Muslim Party of Democratic Action (PDA) won the greatest number of seats (82), followed by the Serbian Democratic Party (SDP, 72), and the Croatian Democratic Union (CDU, 44). Outnumbering the Serbs, the PDA and CDU adopted a Memorandum on the sovereignty of Bosnia on October 15, 1991, while the Serbian deputies left the session in protest. This indicated that

Yugoslavia to the western Balkans 73

outvoting would be the model applied in resolving the future fate of Bosnia. As a result, the Bosnian Serbs organized a plebiscite outside the institutional framework of the republic in support of remaining in Yugoslavia. Thus, again, two parallel processes of secession were being initiated, the secession of Bosnia from Yugoslavia and the secession of the Serbs from Bosnia. As in the case of Slovenia and Croatia, the EC became involved in the Bosnian crisis and, as a result of the recommendation of its Arbitration Commission of the Conference on Yugoslavia, a referendum on the independence of Bosnia was held at the end of February 1992, boycotted, however, by most Serb voters. As expected, the majority of those voting (Bosnian Muslims and Croats) voted for independence. Many observers interpret this referendum as the ultimate step in the dissolution of the possible political consensus that could have resulted in the non-violent creation of the Bosnian state. On April 7, 1992, the EC and US recognized the independence of the Republic of Bosnia and Herzegovina, while the Parliament of the Serbian people declared the independence of the Serbian Republic of Bosnia and Herzegovina (*Republika Srpska*). Prior to the referendum, the first peace plan proposing con-federalization on ethnic principles—the so called Cutillero plan—was rejected by the Muslim leaders and, by early 1993, a full-scale war broke out, initially between the Serb military (which inherited the heavy weaponry and officers of the YPA) and the Muslim/Croat forces. The war resulted in shifting alliances: Serbs fought against Muslims and Croats, Muslims and Croats fought each other, and there were episodes of intra-Muslim violence. The violence of the Yugoslav disintegration processes reached its peak in the case of Bosnia and Herzegovina: according to the International Criminal Tribunal on Yugoslavia (ICTY), in the period 1992–1995, a total of 104,731 people were killed; of these, 62,625 victims were soldiers. The ethnic structure of the victims is the following: 68,000 Muslim, 22,000 Serbs, 8,580 Croatian, and 4,495 others (ICTY 2011). The war in Bosnia included massacres of civilians (the town of Srebrenica being one of the biggest), ethnic cleansing, detention camps, torture and rape, the siege of the capital Sarajevo, urbanicide, and the demolition of cultural and religious monuments. In 1995, NATO started to bomb Serb military positions in order to force the Bosnian Serb leadership to negotiate the end of the conflict; in this way, NATO became engaged for the first time in an Out of Area Mission and, after almost half a century, Germany parti-cipated for the first time in military operations (in securing the no-fly zone over Bosnia and Herzegovina).

Following Cutillero's plan, several other unsuccessful peace proposals ensued (in 1992, the Vance–Owen plan, rejected by the Serbs; in 1993, the Owen–Stoltenberg plan, rejected by the Muslims), but the war finally ended in 1995 as a result of the US-brokered Dayton Agreements. Bosnia and Herzegovina became an independent state with two entities, *Republika Srpska* and the Bosnian–Croat federation, consisting of ten cantons.

Kosovo (in its Serbian appellation, Kosovo and Metohija) is a seceding province of Serbia with a history of attempted secessions from Serbia. In June

1990, having been locked out of the Kosovo assembly's building by the Serbian authorities, the Kosovo Albanian deputies in the Communist-controlled provincial assembly proclaimed secession from the Socialist Republic of Serbia, a federal unit of the SFRY. This was the first in the series of secessions in or from the SFRY. Following the repeated proclamations of independence of Croatia and Slovenia in October 1991, the same deputies declared the independence of Kosovo from the SFRY. No state apart from Albania recognized Kosovo's independence at that time.

In the Kosovo province, one can observe a continuous conflict of the claims of the historical rights of the Serbs (Kosovo is the cradle of Serbian statehood) and the ethnic rights of the Albanians who make up an overwhelming majority of the population. Under Communist rule, the conflict started with Kosovo Albanian protests against discrimination and their repeated large-scale public demonstrations demanding a separate federal unit, the Republic of Kosovo (1968, 1981, 1988), declarations of a state emergency by the Yugoslav state authorities (1981), the forced emigration of Serbs from Kosovo and their protests in Belgrade (1986, 1988), the dissolution of the Kosovo provincial assembly and other institutions countered by setting up parallel Kosovo Albanian institutions (1990), the boycott of Serbian elections by the Kosovo Albanians and holding of their own elections and referenda (1992) and, in 1996, the emergence of Kosovo Albanian paramilitary forces trained and equipped outside the country. The conflict was rather intense until the 1990s, reaching the edge of civil war, but subsided during the wars in Croatia and in particular Bosnia (1991–1995). The Kosovo Albanian leadership expected that, when the final peace treaty was negotiated in Dayton, Ohio, in 1995, the question of Kosovo's independence would be part of the agreement. When these expectations were unfulfilled, a new Kosovo Albanian organization, the Kosovo Liberation Army (KLA), emerged: in 1996, the KLA began attacking Serbian police, provoking large-scale operations of the Serbian military and police that led to civilian casualties. The KLA's strategy appears to have been to provoke violent reactions that would lead to outside intervention similar to that in Bosnia and Herzegovina. By 1998, the conflict became internationalized, involving foreign mediators, diplomatic actions of the Contact group, sanctions against Serbia, and NATO plans for military intervention. At the beginning of 1999, the Contact group initiated a series of negotiations (similar to those that had taken place in Dayton, Ohio) in Rambouillet, France. And when it seemed that a political solution was reached, the so called Annex B to the proposed agreement suddenly appeared on the table in the form of an ultimatum, demanding that Serbia allowed the deployment of NATO forces on all its territory. This Annex was not acceptable to the Serb leaders and NATO bombing ensued (March 24, 1999), causing a major humanitarian crisis in Kosovo with hundreds of thousands of Kosovo Albanians leaving Kosovo. The bombing by NATO ended by June 9 when an agreement was negotiated between the EU and Russian negotiators and the Serb leader Milošević, and the Serbian forces withdrew from Kosovo. UNSC Resolution

Yugoslavia to the western Balkans 75

1244 was passed, formally preserving the sovereignty of Serbia on the territory of Kosovo, but in fact establishing a protectorate under the combined auspices of NATO, the UN, the EU, and the Organization for Security and Cooperation in Europe (OSCE). The final status of Kosovo was to be the subject of negotiations that were started in 2006 by the former Finnish president M. Ahtisari, representing the Contact group. They were cut short after a year with the conclusion that all diplomatic possibilities were exhausted and that the two sides could not agree on a solution. This was followed on February 17, 2008 by the Kosovo Albanian proclamation of independence, which was immediately recognized by the US and twenty-two out of twenty-seven members of the EU.

In the unraveling of Yugoslavia, this is the *only case* in which (a) the boundaries of a federal unit (Serbia) were redrawn without the consent of the government of the federal unit; (b) the right to self-determination including the right to secession was granted to a minority, Kosovo Albanians, but denied to all other minorities in former Yugoslav republics; and (c) the secession was a consequence of a combined military intervention by NATO (not authorized by the UN Security Council) and the actions of the local paramilitary forces (Kosovo Liberation Army, KLA) against the Yugoslav/Serbian forces. Although not sanctioned by international law, some observers believe that the NATO bombing and Kosovo's secession were legitimate because of the gross violation of human and minority rights carried out by the repressive regime of Slobodan Milošević in Serbia.

"Collateral states"—Macedonia and Montenegro

Macedonia's departure from Yugoslavia was in fact unwilling, more an unintended consequence of the disintegration of the federation and the devastating wars that ensued than an articulated intention or developed strategy. For Macedonia, secession became inevitable when Slovenia and Croatia departed. Secession was also a defensive mechanism, preventing the spillover effect of the ongoing wars to Macedonian territory. The first step in constituting an independent state was taken by the Macedonian Parliament, which adopted a *Declaration of Sovereignty of Socialist Republic of Macedonia* at the end of January 1991. The next step was the organization of a referendum. On September 8, a referendum was held, and the citizens voted for independence by an overwhelming majority. However, the referendum that "set up the Republic of Macedonia as a sovereign and independent state" was boycotted by most Albanians living in Macedonia. The Albanian political leaders then organized a parallel referendum on the establishment of their own state, the Republic of Ilirida. As S. Slavevski (2003) points out, this was a signal for Macedonians that Macedonian Albanians did not want to live together with them in the same state. Thus, in the case of Macedonia, we see that attempts by multinational federal units in the SFRY to establish themselves as independent states simultaneously produced deep internal divisions along ethno-national lines. The Macedonians, however, proceeded with their constitutional construction of the state. On November 17, 1991, the first constitution of the Republic of Macedonia was enacted by majority vote in the parliament. However, the Macedonian Albanians were dissatisfied because their political and constitutional role was left unrecognized in the constitution. The final end to Macedonia's ties with Yugoslavia, completing its secession, came in January 1992, when a constitutional law was passed declaring that Macedonia was formally withdrawing from all federal institutions and terminating the mandates of all federal officials. Following the formal secession of Macedonia, the YPA departed peacefully from Macedonia. At the same time, the Arbitration Commission of the Conference on Yugoslavia stated that, besides Slovenia, only Macedonia fulfilled the conditions for international recognition. However, the recognition of Macedonia by the EC member states was postponed because Greece disagreed, above all because of its name—the Republic of Macedonia—asserting that the name implied pretensions on Greek territory which has an adjacent province of the same name. Thus, together with the process of establishing itself as an independent country, a battle began with Greece for its proper name; Macedonia is still designated as the Former Republic of Yugoslavia Macedonia.

Until 1997, the political leaders of Montenegro cooperated with the Milošević regime in Serbia, participated in YPA military campaigns, and executed his strategic plans, in 1992 creating, together with Serbia, the Federal Republic of Yugoslavia. This was the period when the strongman of Montenegro, the Prime Minister, Milan Djukanović, was declaring that he was a proud supporter of Milošević, of the Serbian heritage, and of Montenegrin statehood. Following the wars, sanctions, isolation, and divisions within his own party, in 1997, Djukanović embarked on an increasingly independent policy path, promoting democracy, introducing the German mark as local currency, criticizing Milošević for his old-fashioned politics, and forging ties with the Serbian opposition parties. He was actually promoting a form of creeping secession, supported by the US and its allies. In the EU and US media and policy statements, the split between yesterday's allies, Milošević and Djukanović, was presented as a split between authoritarian and democratic forces. Djukanović's Communist past, suspected connections with the mafia, and his treatment of opposition were systematically ignored. Near the end of Milošević's reign in 1999, when the state crisis become particularly acute, Djukanović proposed a *Platform for the redefinition of the relationship between Serbia and Montenegro* calling for major changes in the division of governing responsibilities within the FR Yugoslavia. After the fall of Milošević in 2000, Djukanović abandoned his earlier project of reforming the federation and opted for the independence of Montenegro, arguing that remaining in the union meant preserving the Great Serbia project. Before independence was achieved, the EU sponsored an attempt at reconstituting the relationship between the two federal units. As a result, in 2003, the State Union of Serbia and Montenegro replaced the FR Yugoslavia as a loose confederation, with one unit (Serbia) being twenty times larger than the other. Finally, on May 21,

2006, a referendum was organized with the support and under the supervision of the EU, and 55.5 percent of those voting voted in favor of the independence of Montenegro. The Montenegrin citizens residing in Serbia—but not in other countries—were not allowed to vote.

Disintegration and violence

Unlike the disintegration of the other two Communist federations—the USSR and Czechoslovakia—the disintegration of Yugoslavia was accompanied by large-scale violence including conventional warfare, which was stopped only by outside military intervention. The degree and the repertoire of the perpetrated violence among members of the local communities are indeed shocking and difficult to explain, but it is in no way a specificity of the region, nor is it comparable to the Holocaust.[12] Why did this violence occur? While not aspiring to a comprehensive explanation, one could point out the following factors that may contribute to an explanation.

1. The Balkans and especially the space of former Yugoslavia have been the object of extreme violence in the course of history. This included forced deportations, purges, imposed change of religion, violent drawing of the border lines, the use of force to prevent the development of national states, large-scale military conflicts and communal violence during both World Wars. The violence experienced in the 1990s appears to be a continuation or replication of the violence experienced in the past two centuries. Maria Todorova argues convincingly that the peoples of the Balkans had little influence in shaping the fate of their nations and states because "their size, form, stage of development and even the very existence of Balkan states were almost entirely regulated by the interests of great powers, in accordance with the rules of the power balance game" (Todorova 2009, 169).
2. Some scholars argue that members of the same or similar cultures, whose identity is based on common features, have a better chance of de-escalating a conflict and reconciling more easily.[13] The case of the former Yugoslavia, however, points to a different conclusion. Instead of commonalities de-escalating the conflict, the "narcissism of minor differences" became part of the configuration that fueled the conflicts, justifying separation from the different Other (Ignatieff 1999, 57)[14] In communities where the narcissism of minor differences reigns, violence may be viewed as an attempt to translate them into insurmountable, irreconcilable differences.
3. With the end of the Cold War, Yugoslavia was, to paraphrase Claus Offe, exposed to an overload of simultaneous challenges. The crisis in Yugoslavia involved the following variety of factors: personal existential uncertainty due to the deepening economic crisis (without any parallel since 1948), the loss of privileged international status resulting from the end of the Cold War, dismantling not only of the political system but of the state and thus

the dissolution of a community with whose values ("brotherhood and unity of the peoples of Yugoslavia") many of the citizens identified for half a century. The local world of many Yugoslav citizens disintegrated in its totality with the end of the Cold War order, so one can say that the measure of violence corresponded directly with the depth of the crisis, with the historical overload of challenges that "denaturalized" (K. Polanyi) the Yugoslav citizens and turned them into beings capable of hatred, massive violence, and crimes.

Notes

1 In October 1968, formal relations were established between the SFRY and the EEC, with an accredited Yugoslav representative in the EC. In March 1970, a trade agreement was signed. Three years later, a new 5-year agreement was signed between the SFRY and the EEC, mutually granting the status of most favored nation. In April 1980, an agreement on cooperation between the two sides was signed with no time limitation. As late as December 1987, a new protocol was signed on cooperation between the SFRY and the EEC.

2 Over the years, the region underwent different designations, from southeast Europe to western Balkans. Western Balkans at present includes all of the ex-Yugoslav Republics, minus Slovenia but including Albania.

3 Dragovic Soso identifies five categories of explanations to be found in academic writings. They include explanations focusing on ancient hatreds/clash of civilizations, on the historical legacy of nineteenth-century South Slav national ideology, on the legacy of the Yugoslav socialist system, the role of political and intellectual agency, as well as on the impact of external factors. D. Jovic insists that the disintegration of Yugoslavia was multicausal but firmly rejects the ancient hatred explanation and gives primacy to the ideological factor, i.e., the concept of withering away of the state that the Communist party of Yugoslavia systematically implemented from 1974 onward.

4 Established in 1918, the state unified South Slav peoples with similar languages and cultures. But the state was also characterized by powerful disintegrative forces, above all different religions and different historical backgrounds—these peoples, before their unification, were part of rival multinational and multiconfessional empires. However, these deeply rooted disintegrative tendencies were played out only under the conditions of radical change in the European space—World War Two brought the end of the first Yugoslavia (Kingdom of Yugoslavia), and the end of the Cold War brought the end of the second (the SFRY).

5 Writing in the early stages of the transition process in former socialist countries, I. Berend was of the opinion that Europe was continuing to be polarized into a dynamic center and an unsuccessful periphery that once again is not capable of responding to the challenges of the world market, and thus is lagging behind.

6 Paraphrasing A. Toynbee, this would mean that the elite lost its "gift for creation," i.e., creative response to challenges, as well as the "faculty for attracting the allegiance of the majority without having to resort to force." Toynbee's description of the breakdown of the society is also relevant, for it means that it has entered a "critical period" marked "by the collapse of the consensus and by the disintegration of society into dissenting and mutually hostile fragments; status is questioned, relationships become fluid, and in the ensuing struggle for power the relative capabilities of the contending classes and individuals are forgotten" (Toynbee 1977, 224–225).

7 Until 1989, Serbia was constitutionally divided into three parts—central or "narrow" Serbia plus two provinces (Kosovo and Vojvodina)—and each province had a position equal to the central Serbian government. No other republic in Yugoslavia had sub-federal units—provinces.

8 "In the wake of the disintegration of the Yugoslav federation, and perhaps understandably so in view of the seriousness of the accompanying armed conflict, the attempt to provide an explanation has dwelt quite disproportionately upon the factor of ethnic diversity. Nevertheless, I contend that no explanation which does not place at its heart economic factors deserves to be taken seriously" (Woodward 1995).

9 The premature recognition, against the advice of Lord Carrington, the Chairman of the Peace Conference on Yugoslavia, was supposedly based on the calculation that "turning yesterday Republics into new states within the given administrative borders" would deter future conflicts (Hayden 2000). Instead, it led to the bloodiest chapter of the war in Bosnia and Herzegovina.

10 The ICTY concluded that, although it researched for more than a decade, it does not have reliable numbers as far as the number of victims of the war in Croatia is concerned. Croatian officials speak of 12,000 dead Croatians, and the NGO Veritas (2011) estimates 8,000 dead Croatian Serbs.

11 According to the last census (1991), there were 43.5 percent Bosniaks, 31 percent Serbs, 17.4 percent Croats, and 5.5 per cent Yugoslavs.

12 The activities of the US PR Agency Ruder Finn hired by the Bosnian government set the stage for this analogy. The famous interview with James Harff, director of Ruder Finn's Global Public Affairs section, has often been cited, among others recently by Richard Palmer (2011). "Nobody understood what was going on in (former) Yugoslavia," he said in an October 1993 interview with French journalist Jacques Merlino. "The great majority of Americans were probably asking themselves in which African country Bosnia was situated." Ruder Finn took advantage of this ignorance. Its first goal was to persuade the Jews to oppose the Serbs—not an easy task. "The Croatian and Bosnian past was marked by a real and cruel anti-Semitism," said Harff. "Tens of thousands of Jews perished in Croatian camps. So there was every reason for intellectuals and Jewish organizations to be hostile towards the Croats and Bosnians." Harff used a couple of reports in the *New York Newsday* about Serbian concentration camps to persuade Jewish groups to demonstrate against the Serbs. "This was a tremendous coup," said Harff. "When the Jewish organizations entered the game on the side of the Bosnians, we could promptly equate the Serbs with the Nazis in the public mind. … By a single move, we were able to present a simple story of good guys and bad guys which would hereafter play itself. We won by targeting a Jewish audience, the right target. Almost immediately there was a clear change of language in the press, with the use of words with high emotional content, such as 'ethnic cleansing,' 'concentration camps,' etc., which evoked inmates of Nazi Germany and the gas chambers of Auschwitz. The emotional change was so powerful that nobody could go against it."

13 "Peoples who believe they share the same culture tend to have a decent regard for each other and resist dehumanizing each other. This also helps inhibit the destructive escalation of a conflict. Peoples in different countries may also have some degree of a shared culture and insofar as they do, conflict escalation is limited" (Kriesberg 2004, 94).

14 Michael Ignatieff develops Freud's idea of "narcissism of minor differences," according to which the very minor differences between similar peoples become the basis for hostility. The live tissue of connectedness has to be destroyed in order for the next door neighbor to be transformed into an enemy. "As less and less distinguishes you from anybody else," notes Ignatieff, "the more important it becomes to wear the differentiating mask" (Ignatieff 1999, 57).

80 R. Nakarada

References

Allcock, J.B. (2000), *Explaining Yugoslavia*, New York, Columbia University Press.

Berend, I. (1996), *Central and Eastern Europe, 1944–1993*, Cambridge, Cambridge University Press; trans. Vera Nenadov Palcic (2001) Centralna i Istočna Evropa, 1944–1993, Podgorica, CID.

Bilandžić, D. (1979), *Historija Socijalističke Federativne Republike Jugoslavije. Glavni procesi (History of the Socialist Federative Republic of Yugoslavia. Main Processes)*, Zagreb, Skolska knjiga.

Bookman, Z.M. (1992), *The Economics of Secession*, New York, St. Martin's Press.

Briscoe, I. and Price, M. (2011), *Kosovo's New Map of Power: Governance and Crime in the Wake of Independence*, The Hague, Netherlands Institute of International Relations 'Clingendael'.

Chandler, D. (2006), *Empire in Denial: The Politics of State-building*, London, Pluto Press.

Cohen, J.L. and Soso, D.J. (eds) (2008), *State Collapse in South-Eastern Europe. New Perspectives on Yugoslavia's Disintegration*, West Lafayette, IN, Purdue University Press.

European Commission (2011), *Key Findings of the 2011 Progress Report for Bosnia and Herzegovina, Brussels: European Commission*, at http://europa.eu/rapid/press-ReleasesAction.do?reference=MEMO/11/687 (accessed 15 October 2011).

Hayden, R.M. (2000), *Blueprints for a House Divided. The Constitutional Logic of the Yugoslav Conflicts*, Ann Arbor, MI, The University of Michigan Press.

Hobsbawm, E. (2007), *Globalisation, Democracy and Terrorism*, London, Little Brown & Co.

ICTY (2011), *War Demographics* (online), The Hague, International Court Tribunal for the former Yugoslavia, at www.icty.org/sid/10622 (accessed 15 October 2011).

Ignatieff, M. (1999), *The Warrior's Honor*, London, Vintage.

Jovic, D. (2008), *Yugoslavia: The State that Withered Away*, West Lafayette, IN, Purdue University Press.

Judah, T. (2009), *Yugoslavia is Dead, Long Live the Yugosphere*, London, LSEE Papers on South Eastern Europe, European Institute LSE.

Kovacevic, S. and Dajic, P. (1994), *Chronology of Yugoslav Crisis: 1942–1993*, Belgrade, IES.

Kriesberg, L. (2004), 'Comparing Reconciliation Actions within and between Countries' in B.S.T. Yaacov (ed.), *From Conflict Resolution to Reconciliation*, Oxford, Oxford University Press.

Kuzmanovic, J. (2011), *Croatia Government must cut spending more, Rohatinski says* (online). Bloomberg Businessweek, at www.businessweek.com/news/2011-10-21/croatia-government-must-cut-spending-more-rohatinski-says.html (accessed 21 October 2011).

Levick, R. (2011), *Croatia in EU: A Disaster Waiting to Happen* (online). Forbes, at www.forbes.com/sites/richardlevick/2011/10/27/croatia-in-the-eu-a-disaster-waiting-to-happen/ (accessed 29 October 2011).

Nakarada, R. (2008), *Raspad Jugoslavije*, Beograd, Sluzbeni glasnik.

Nakarada, R. and Račić, O. (1998), *Raspad Jugoslavije izazov evropskoj bezbednosti (Disintegration of Yugoslavia a Challenge to European Security)*, Beograd, IES, FEE.

Oberg, J. (1994), 'Conflict-mitigation in Former Yugoslavia – it could still be possible' in R. Nakarada (ed.), *Europe and the Disintegration of Yugoslavia*, Belgrade, IES.

Palmer, R. (2011), 'What really happened in Bosnia' *The Philadelphia Trumpet*, 7(22): 22–25.

Pavković, A. (2000), 'Recursive Secessions in Former Yugoslavia: Too Hard a Case for Theories of Secession?' *Political Studies*, 48: 485–502.

Pavković, A. and Radan, P. (2007), *Creating New States: Theory and Practice of Secession*, Aldershot, Ashgate.

Robinson, W. (2003), *Transnational Conflicts. Central America, Social Change and Globalization*, London, Verso.

Ross, H.M. (2004), 'Ritual and the Politics of Reconciliation' in B.S.T. Yaacov (ed.), *From Conflict Resolution to Reconciliation*, Oxford, Oxford University Press, pp. 197–223.

Santos, B.S. (2007), *Beyond Abyssal Thinking* (online). Eurozine, at www.eurozine.com/articles/2007-06-29-santos-en.html (accessed 30 October 2011).

Skopjak, Z. (2004), 'Chronologies' in J. Teokarevic (ed.), *Kako ubrzati pridruživanje Republike Srbije Evropskoj uniji (How to speed up the accession of the Republic of Serbia to the EU)*, Belgrade, IES.

Slavevski, S. (2003), 'The Macedonian Societal Security Dilemma' in B. Vankovska (ed.), *Challenges of the Post-Conflict Reconciliation and Peace-building in Macedonia*, Skopje, Faculty of Philosophy and Geneva Centre for the Democratic Control of Armed Forces.

Soso, J.D. (2002), *Saviours of the Nation: Serbia's Intellectual Opposition and the Revival of Nationalism*, London, Hurst & Co.

Srdoc, N. (2009), *Europe's Authoritarian States* (online). Reflections, at www.ebireflections.com/1/4/4 (accessed 30 October 2011).

Thomas, R.G.C. (ed.) (2003), *Yugoslavia Unraveled*, Lanham, MD, Lexington Books.

Todorova, M. (2009), *Imaginary Balkan*, Oxford, Oxford University Press.

Toynbee, A. (1977), *A Study of History*. Oxford, Oxford University Press.

Veritas (2011), *Poginuli i nestali Srbi u Hrvatskoj i RSK: 1990–1998 (Dead and missing Serbs in Croatia and RSK: 1990–1998)* (online), at www.veritas.org.rs/srpski/spiskovila.htm (accessed 28 October 2011).

Woodward, S.L. (1995), *Balkan Tragedy. Chaos and Dissolution after the Cold War*, Washington, DC, The Brookings Institution.

5 Host state responses to ethnic rebellion

Serbia and Macedonia in comparison

Keiichi Kubo

Introduction

In the literature of ethnic conflict, various scholars have asked why ethnic groups rebel. Compared with the extensive scholarly attention to the rebels, however, state responses to rebellion have attracted much less attention or systematic enquiry. This lack of sufficient attention is regrettable, and one should focus more on the actions taken by the state authorities in a systematic manner, as advised by Eckstein (1965) and Premdas (1990).

This chapter conducts a comparative analysis of the state responses to the ethnic rebellion in Serbia and Macedonia, as these two cases present an interesting contrast. Whereas both countries experienced the onset of a low-intensity rebellion, the state authorities responded with severe military repression in Serbia, but in a more conciliatory manner in Macedonia. The outcome is starkly different: Serbia experienced an escalation of rebellion, causing a large number of casualties, whereas Macedonia experienced a de-escalation of rebellion with a fairly small number of casualties.

This chapter consists of three sections. The first section briefly presents a theoretical overview. The second section analyzes how the state authorities responded to the initial onset of low-intensity rebellion in Serbia and Macedonia, and how the different state responses affected the course of conflict. The third section then attempts to conduct a comparative analysis to explain why the state authorities responded differently.

Theoretical overview

State response as a crucial factor that explains escalation

Why do some ethnic groups experience an escalation of rebellion after the onset of low-intensity rebellion, while others do not? One of the answers lies in dynamics between the ethnic group and the state authorities. In many cases, the occurrence of low-intensity rebellion is perceived by the state authorities as a signal that the security and integrity of the state is being threatened. Thus, state institutions such as the government, police, and

Responses to rebellion: Macedonia/Serbia 83

military would consider taking some measures in order to eliminate the threat to the country.

The option often considered by the state authorities is repression. The state authorities try to eliminate the problem by suppressing the rebel activities by force or even by physically destroying the rebel organizations. If successful, this option will "solve" the problem without making any concession to the rebels. When repression by the state authorities becomes excessive, however, it can be counterproductive and radicalize the ethnic group. Indeed, many authors have pointed to the counterproductive effect of repression. For example, Bose (2003, 116) points out that the "regime of repression had the effects of further radicalizing public opinion and of convincing thousands of Kashmiri youths to take up arms to fight the Indian state." In the case of the Kurdish question in Turkey, the security operations and the practice of village burning was fuelling Kurdish nationalism and forcing especially young people to join the ranks of the rebels (Kirişci and Winrow 1997, 131). In Sri Lanka, the military terror and repression directed against the Tamil population played a "vital catalytic role" and contributed to the ascendancy of the LTTE (Bose 1994, 91). Hibbs (1973, 182) concluded that "the nearly instantaneous response to repression is most often more mass violence."

If the repressive measures lead to the radicalization of the ethnic group and thus lead to the escalation of conflict,[1] it is important to analyze the state response as a dependent variable, that is, to explain why some state authorities resort to repression while others do not. The following section explores some possible factors that might explain the variance in this regard.

Explaining state response: repression or conciliation?

Why do some state authorities choose repression while others choose conciliation? This section briefly examines five factors that might explain the difference, namely (a) political regime; (b) level of economic development; (c) "institutional settings"; (d) electoral incentives; and (e) role of external actor.

First, the political regime of the country may affect the level of state repression. For example, analyzing the determinants of the level of political repression (such as suspension of civil rights and liberties), King (2000) found that democracy has "pacifying effects" on the behavior of repressors toward dissidents: although the increase in political dissent tends to increase the level of political repression when democracy is weak, it does not increase the level of political repression so much when democracy is strong. A similar argument can be made for military repression. In other words, the level of state repression may be lower in a country under a democratic regime, because it would be more difficult to resort to the arbitrary use of police/ military force against its population if there are strong democratic constraints on the government.

Second, the level of economic development may affect government decisions on military repression. If a country enjoys a higher level of economic development, the government would try to avoid the risk of disturbing normal economic activities and of earning a bad reputation among the international community. If a country is poor, on the other hand, there will be much less at risk compared with rich countries and, in addition, poorer countries lack sufficient resources to share with rebelling groups to solve the conflict more peacefully. Therefore, one may expect that the government in poorer countries is more likely to take repressive military measures than richer countries.

Third, one should consider what Ron (2003) calls "institutional settings." Comparing Serbia and Israel, he argues that Serbia resorted to ethnic cleansing (i.e., an extremely high level of state violence) because Bosnia was "frontier" and *external to* Serbia's core, and thus the state authorities did not feel a bureaucratic, moral, and political sense of responsibility for its fate, whereas Israeli state violence in Palestine was more restrained because it was "ghetto" and *inside* the Israeli core, and thus the state authorities felt more responsibility (Ron 2003, 8–9, 13–24). As for Kosovo, the Serbian authorities employed the tactics of ethnic policing until 1999, but they started ethnic cleansing when NATO intervention began and Kosovo's ghetto status evaporated and became "externalized" (Ron 2003, 87–111).

Fourth, electoral incentives might explain the actions taken by the key politicians who control the state authorities, if a country is under democratic control. The radicalizing effect of elections in a multiethnic country has been pointed out by various authors. For example, Rabushka and Shepsle (1972) argue that, when elections are conducted in a plural society, candidates outside the multiethnic coalition emerge, raise local issues, and take radical and extreme positions to win the elections, which leads to the victory of radicals and the "bankruptcy of moderation." This process of radicalization is often called "ethnic outbidding" or "flanking" (cf. Hislope 1996; Aklaev 1999). The politicians who control the state authorities, therefore, may follow electoral incentives to take a more radical stance against the rebels in order to win support from the ethnic majority.

The key condition for such "ethnic outbidding" is the lack of cross-ethnic voting. As Horowitz (1985, 1991, 2002) and Reilly (2001) argue, when there is no cross-ethnic voting, taking a moderate position toward other ethnic groups is not rewarded, and thus there is no electoral incentive for moderation. Horowitz and Reilly thus claim that the electoral system that fosters cross-ethnic voting will give electoral incentives for moderation. If their arguments hold, one may expect that the politicians whose electoral performance is affected by the voting behavior of the ethnic minorities are more likely to take a more conciliatory stance.

Finally, the role of external actor should not be ignored. The significance of external actors in the actions of the ethnic minority is pointed out by various scholars, such as Brubaker (1996), Fearon (1998), and Jenne (2007). If the external actors support the radical actions of the ethnic group and provide resources for the rebellion, this ethnic group is more likely to take radical action. The same point can be made for the actions of the state authorities.

One may expect that the state authorities are more likely to take repressive measures against the rebels if the external actors show their support, explicit or implicit, for such actions.

The determinants of the state response to the low-intensity rebellion in Serbia and Macedonia will be examined based on the analytical framework presented above. In order to do so, the following section will briefly examine the nature of the state response and the consequences for the course of rebellion.

State response to low-intensity ethnic rebellion

Serbia: military repression and the escalation

In Serbia, a low-intensity rebellion was started in 1996 by a small resistance group named the Kosovo Liberation Army (KLA hereafter). The KLA was founded in 1993 and grew out of the Popular Movement for Kosovo, a Marxist underground party formed in the early 1980s.[2] Those who organized the KLA were mainly the activists or students who went abroad after being punished in Serbia, and the resources at their disposal were very limited when they started their rebellion. For example, up to 1997, the KLA had only about 150 active men (Judah 2000, 118), and "until late 1997, active armed resistance groups in Kosovo were very small and without permanent bases in the province" (IICK 2000, 52). As a result, the initial intensity of rebellion was not very great. From 1996, the number of attacks increased (thirty-one in 1996, fifty-five in 1997, and sixty-six in January and February 1998 alone), but the death toll remained fairly low until the beginning of 1998.

Since the emergence of the KLA, the Serbian authorities tolerated their activities for some time, but police operations were started to repress the movement in early 1998 in the Drenica region. One of the most serious incidents occurred in Prekaz in March 1998, where the Serbian police killed almost all members of the Jashari clan, a total of fifty-nine people, including civilians, women, and children (AI 1998, 18). By the end of May, 300 people were estimated to have been killed since the start of police operations in February 1998 (IICK 2000, 72).

The effect of these police operations, however, was not to pacify but to "electrify" Kosovo (Judah 2001, 23). After the deaths of the Jasharis, many Kosovo Albanians, especially young people, started joining the KLA as volunteers and the KLA began to expand quickly. It is suggested that the KLA had about 1,200 members in May 1998, but had grown to 25,000 members by July 1998 (Mijalkovski and Damjanov 2002, 128). The rapid expansion of the KLA naturally led to an escalation of the conflict in Kosovo. For example, according to one Serbian general, there was a sharp increase in the number of attacks by the KLA from March 1998.[3] The KLA had taken control of three major routes in Kosovo by the summer of 1998. This, in turn, led to the massive military operations against the KLA by the Serbian army and police in the summer of 1998. One can safely conclude, therefore, that the

86   K. Kubo

repressive measures taken by the Serbian authorities in early 1998 turned out to be rather counterproductive, leading to escalation of the rebellion.

Macedonia: peace process and prevention of escalation

In Macedonia, a low-intensity rebellion was started in 2001 by a small guerrilla group named the National Liberation Army (NLA hereafter). The leader of the NLA, Ali Ahmeti, was one of four men who prepared to set up the KLA.[4] As the organizers of the NLA were former students, such as Ahmeti, and their friends or relatives, such as Fazli Veliu (Ahmeti's uncle, a high-school teacher), resources at their disposal were limited. In addition, the lack of systematic support from the Albanians in Kosovo further limited the resources available to the NLA. Certainly, Ahmeti and Veliu were heavily involved in KLA activities. This does not mean, however, that the KLA people systematically decided to organize another "liberation struggle" in Macedonia. On the contrary, the Popular Movement for Kosovo held a convention in Prizren in August 1999 and decided to dissolve itself now that its mission had been completed, which meant that the Albanians outside Kosovo needed to organize their movement again.[5] When Ahmeti later decided to establish the NLA, "even the best friends from the KLA, such as Thaçi and Mahmuti, were against such action."[6]

Therefore, the NLA started its rebel activities at only a low level of intensity. The first NLA actions occurred in January 2001, when a police station in the predominantly Albanian village of Tearce was attacked by grenade and one policeman was killed (Rusi 2004, 2). After that, the armed conflict between the NLA and the Macedonian forces continued until August 2001, but the level of intensity of the rebellion remained relatively low and never reached the level of a protracted civil war: it is estimated that between 150 and 250 people were killed in the conflict (Phillips 2004, 161).

The conciliatory stance taken by the state authorities was one crucial factor for this relatively quick de-escalation of the conflict. The key figure was the then President of Macedonia, Boris Trajkovski, who worked continuously to solve the conflict peacefully. For example, when the conflict started, he convened meetings of all political parties to address inter-ethnic issues, which eventually led to the formation of a national unity government in May 2001 (Daskalovski 2005, 91–92). When this coalition went into deep disarray at the end of May, Trajkovski presented parliament with a "crisis resolution plan" to continue the negotiations to solve the conflict peacefully (Daskalovski 2005, 94). As a result of the continuous efforts made by Trajkovski, the Ohrid negotiations began on July 28, and the "Framework Agreement" for constitutional changes (so-called "Ohrid Agreement") was signed at the presidential residence on August 13, 2001, which led to the end of the conflict. The NLA leader, Ali Ahmeti, said that, "If the Ohrid Agreement had not been signed, a new Bosnia would have unfolded with one or two hundred thousand victims" (Popetrevski and Latifi 2004, 36).

The role played by Trajkovski was particularly important because other leading politicians, such as Prime Minister Ljubco Georgievski and Minister of Interior Ljube Boškoski, showed much more radical attitudes toward the Albanian rebels. For example, when Trajkovski was making his efforts to form a "government of national unity," Georgievski was pressing for a declaration of war, arguing that it would lead to a more efficient fight against the guerrillas (Balalovska et al. 2002, 29). For Boškoski, the elimination of the "terrorists" was a "holy task" (Balalovska et al. 2002, 29), and he was reported to be personally present in Ljuboten during the entire operation on August 12 when the Macedonian police forces conducted a house-to-house attack.[7] If Trajkovski had not started and fostered the peace process, therefore, the cycle of violence between the state authorities and the rebels might have escalated into a large-scale conflict.

Explaining the state responses

Why did the state authorities choose repression in Serbia but not in Macedonia? Let us examine the effect of the factors examined in the first section. Some factors cannot explain the difference. First, the level of economic development does not seem to be relevant, as the level of economic development in Serbia was 50 percent higher than in Macedonia as of 1988 (Pleština 1992, 180–181). Although the lack of data in former Yugoslavia hinders the precise comparison of the two countries in the 1990s, the difference would not have been so large that it could explain the different reactions in Serbia and Macedonia.[8] Second, the "institutional settings" emphasized by Ron cannot explain the difference either. According to his criteria, both Kosovo and northwestern Macedonia were inside the "core" of the state when the state authorities made their reactions to the initial rebellion. As for the political regime, it may explain the difference to a certain extent: while Serbia had an authoritarian regime, the political regime in Macedonia was relatively democratic. This factor, however, cannot explain why Trajkovski took a moderate stance toward rebels whereas other politicians, such as Georgievski and Boškoski, took a more radical position, as all of them were democratically elected in Macedonia.

Thus, in order to explain the different policy choices made by Milošević and Trajkovski, this section examines two remaining factors, namely (a) electoral incentives and (b) the role of external actors.

Case of Serbia

Electoral incentives

Why did Milošević decide to take repressive measures against the KLA? In order to answer this question, one needs to go back to the origin of his ascent to power in the late 1980s and see what his agenda was. Indeed, it was

88 *K. Kubo*

precisely the issue of Kosovo that Milošević used to foster nationalism as his power base. For example, on June 28, 1989, at the Gazimestan shrine which memorializes the 1389 Battle of Kosovo, Milošević made a famous speech to commemorate the 600th anniversary of the battle. When Milošević walked onto the platform, he was greeted by shouts of "Slobo! Slobo!" and "Kosovo is Serbia!" (Cohen 2002, 144). When the first multi-party elections were held in Serbia in 1990, Milošević consolidated his power with a landslide victory in the elections.

Kosovo thus had a critical political importance for Milošević's electoral victory, which made it difficult, or even impossible, for him to make concessions on the issue of Kosovo. A number of western officials, such as Warren Zimmerman (1996, 57), Lord Owen (1995, 137), and General Clark (2001, 65), recalled that Milošević became difficult whenever the issue of Kosovo was raised. Louis Sell (2002, 281–282) observed that Serbian control over Kosovo was "virtually all that he had left to show for a decade of disastrous rule" by the end of the 1990s and "Milošević could not afford to give up Kosovo voluntarily, even if he had wanted to." Milošević told a US diplomat in early 1998: "Kosovo is not Bosnia. Kosovo is my head" (Sell 2002, 281).

The electoral incentives were reinforced by the context of domestic politics, namely the declining legitimacy of the regime. The decreasing support for Milošević and the declining legitimacy of his regime in 1996–1997 are well documented. According to Sekelj (2000, 72), for example, opinion polls show that Milošević's popularity had dropped from the active support of more than half the population in 1992 to only 12 percent before the 1997 elections. Slavujević (1999, 100) concluded that the Serbian political system enjoyed the support of only one-fifth of citizens and was completely de-legitimized by 1997. As a result, serious challenges were posed to the regime in 1996 and 1997. First, the reformist coalition *Zajedno* won in major cities including the capital, Belgrade, in the 1996 local elections (Thomas 1999, 285). When the authorities refused to recognize the results, the opposition organized huge demonstrations for more than 2 months, and the regime was finally forced to admit the victory of the opposition (Thomas 1999, 285–318). Second, in Montenegro, reformist Milo Djukanović ran as a presidential candidate against incumbent Momir Bulatović, Milošević's close ally, in the 1997 presidential elections, and the former won (Thomas 1999, 379–386, Goati 2001, 138–148).

Furthermore, even Serb nationalists became unsatisfied with him and started shifting their support to the Serbian Radical Party (SRS hereafter), led by ultranationalist Vojislav Šešelj. Cohen (2002, 267–271) points out that Milošević was condemned by many Serbs for having "betrayed" Serb national interests in Bosnia, and that Milošević could no longer portray himself as a heroic patriot in the second half of the 1990s. Thus, in the 1997 elections, the SRS won 82 out of a total of 250 seats in the Serbian Parliament, and Šešelj even defeated the candidate from Milošević's party, the Socialist Party of Serbia (SPS hereafter), for the Serbian President, even though the overall turnout did not reach 50 percent and thus the election was declared invalid.[9]

Responses to rebellion: Macedonia/Serbia 89

In this context of declining legitimacy, it was even more dangerous for Milošević to take a conciliatory stance on Kosovo. Instead, Milošević chose to re-establish his legitimacy by taking a firm stance. For example, in December 1997, the Yugoslav delegations walked out of the international conference when an attempt was made to place Kosovo on the agenda: in the run-up to the December presidential elections, the SPS had to appear to be taking a firm line on Kosovo (Thomas 1999, 403; Simić 2000, 179). Furthermore, Milošević decided to co-opt Šešelj into the ruling coalition exactly when he started an offensive against Albanian "terrorists": on March 24, 1998, a new government was formed by a so called "patriotic coalition" of the SPS, the JUL, and the SRS (Simić 2000, 103); the SRS received sixteen of thirty-six portfolios, with Šešelj taking the post of deputy prime minister. As Thomas (1999, 418) argued, "the entry of the Radicals into positions of power meant that there would be no moderation in the government's stance on the issue of Kosovo." Some analysts even speculated that Milošević's decision to launch an offensive in Kosovo may have been influenced by his desire to create a psychology of acute threat: although any rapprochement between the ruling parties and the SRS had appeared impossible after the December 1997 presidential elections, a new atmosphere of crisis over Kosovo brought the two camps closer and weakened criticism against the regime (Thomas 1999, 416). Mihailović (1999, 145) also argues that the Serbian elite invented a "legitimacy formula" by activating a crisis in Kosovo.

Ambiguous signals from external actors

In addition to the electoral incentives, ambiguous signals from external actors also encouraged the Serbian authorities to take repressive measures. The behavior of Robert Gelbard, then US special envoy for the Balkans, was crucial. When he made his first visit to Kosovo in January 1998, Gelbard was quoted in Serbian newspapers as saying that Washington was considering putting the KLA on its list of terrorist organizations.[10] Importantly, as early as January 1998, the US was well aware of the preparations for police operations in Kosovo (Albright 2004, 380). This awareness notwithstanding, in February 1998, immediately before the Serbian police operations in Kosovo, Gelbard condemned attacks carried out by the KLA, which he described as a "terrorist organization."[11] Furthermore, the US even made some concessions toward Yugoslavia in February 1998. For example, Gelbard told Milošević that Washington was prepared to let Yugoslavia join the Southeast European Co-operative Initiative, a US-backed body promoting economic development in the region.[12]

These acts sent a signal to the Serbian authorities that the repressive measures against the KLA were legitimate. Indeed, General Delić and Milošević quoted Gelbard's remarks to argue that the KLA was a "terrorist" organization.[13] Cohen (2002, 283) argued that "inadvertently perhaps, Gelbard had provided Milošević with a green light to launch his March 1998 offensive in Kosovo.

90 *K. Kubo*

Indeed, Serbian action in Kosovo escalated only four days after Gelbard's remarks." Simić (2000, 194) observed that Gelbard's condemnation of the KLA as a terrorist organization was interpreted as a "signal for action" in Serbian government circles. Petritsch and Pihler also pointed out that "it was not by chance that the attack followed immediately after the visit of Gelbard … For Milošević, Gelbard's signal meant a green light for military solution" (Petrič and Pihler 2002, 82).

Even after the Prekaz massacre, which the US officials condemned, they still continued calling the KLA "terrorists." In May 1998, for example, US envoys Holbrooke and Gelbard again condemned the KLA as terrorists.[14] The attitude of the US clearly changed in June in favor of the KLA, apparently as a result of the continuing atrocities in Kosovo. In mid-June, NATO started an air exercise code named "Determined Falcon" in Macedonia and Albania.[15] At the end of June, Holbrooke talked to the KLA members for the first time in the border town of Junik.[16] Only a few days later, he revealed that Gelbard had made official contact with KLA representatives in Geneva,[17] and the US even suggested that the KLA should participate in peace talks with Belgrade.[18] Albright (2004, 286) recalls as follows: "By mid June, it had become obvious that no political settlement would be possible without the rebels, so our diplomats began meeting with the KLA representatives. This infuriated Milošević and nettled the Europeans, but it was the only way to make progress."

Even after western officials stopped condemning the KLA as "terrorists," Milošević was not deterred from using force. One may argue that the diplomatic pressure from outside generally had a limited effect, as Milošević had "rarely been bothered about international criticism before."[19] In addition, however, the division in the major powers also made the external pressure ineffective. Most important in this regard was the Russian factor:[20] Russia consistently opposed military intervention against Serbia. For example, when NATO started the air exercise "Determined Falcon," Milošević visited Moscow and received an assurance that Russia would veto NATO's military intervention in the UN Security Council.[21] The western countries were also not always monolithic. For example, when the US started taking a tougher stance against Milošević, it was supported by the UK and Germany but less so by France and Italy.[22] As Wolff (2003, 87) pointed out, a "major problem that inhibited the international community's ability to devise and implement effective conflict prevention, management and resolution policies resulted from the fact that there was no unified approach to the Kosovo crisis."

Case of Macedonia

Electoral incentives

Unlike Milošević, Trajkovski won the presidential elections in 1999 with the support of the Albanians. The electoral system played a crucial role. In

Macedonia, the two-ballot majority system is used for presidential elections, in which the second round is fought only by the two leading candidates in the first round vote (assuming that no candidate won a majority on the first ballot). In the 1999 presidential elections, Petkovski was leading in the first round vote (343,606 votes or 32.7 percent) while Trajkovski ranked second (219,098 votes or 20.9 percent), but Trajkovski won in the second round by a narrow margin (591,972 votes for Trajkovski and 514,599 votes for Petkovski). Albanian voters had a decisive role: they voted en masse for Trajkovski in the second round. According to Arben Xhaferi, he suggested to Albanian voters that they should vote for Trajkovski in the second round "because he was new, atypical (Protestant rather than Orthodox), young and moderate."[23] If one compares the election results at the municipality level, it is clear that the votes received by two Albanian candidates in the first round shifted massively to Trajkovski in the second round.[24] The number of votes received by two Albanian candidates in the first round exceeded 200,000, which is more than half the additional votes received by Trajkovski in the second round. Clearly, Trajkovski could not have won the elections if there had been no support from Albanians.

Trajkovski thus delivered a moderate message regarding inter-ethnic relations in Macedonia. In his inauguration speech, for example, he said: "I will not allow ethnic hatred, jingoism and intolerance to threaten the stability of the country."[25] His religious beliefs also had a significant impact on his moderate stance toward the Albanians. Robert Milcev, a brother-in-law of Trajkovski, and Jason Miko, who worked closely with Trajkovski for the government's lobbying activities in the US, both said that it was the "Christian perspective that it is better to talk than to fight" that affected his decisions and actions during the armed conflict.[26] Thus, it was natural for him to take an initiative to foster political dialogue between the Macedonian and Albanian parties.

Electoral incentives did not motivate other politicians, such as Georgievski and Boškoski, to take a conciliatory stance, because of the nature of the party system in Macedonia: the Albanians in Macedonia vote overwhelmingly for their own ethnic parties, and there was virtually no cross-ethnic voting in the parliamentary elections (for the elections and party system in Macedonia, see e.g., Mojanoski 1996, 2000; Nikolovska and Siljanovska-Davkova 2001; Karakamiševa 2004). For the Macedonian parties, therefore, there was no incentive to take a moderate stance. Rather, the Macedonian political parties were motivated to take a more radical stance toward the Albanian rebels to win support from ethnic Macedonians, who were becoming increasingly radicalized. For example, the former Foreign Minister Ljubomir Frčkoski, Trajkovski's advisor during the conflict, pointed out as follows:

> Trajkovski played a crucial role for the peaceful solution of conflict, because he was the only politician who could take the responsibility to take care of negotiations. No other Macedonian politicians wanted to

92   *K. Kubo*

lead the peace negotiations with Albanian parties, because they thought they would lose the elections if they did so.[27]

The electoral incentives, therefore, can explain not only the difference between Serbia and Macedonia (Milošević and Trajkovski) but also the difference between the politicians in the case of Macedonia (Trajkovski and Georgievski or Boškoski).

External pressures from the international community

International factors also played a critical role. In the case of Macedonia, signals sent from the external actors were more coherent. Until the Ohrid Agreement was signed, western officials kept putting strong pressure on the Macedonian authorities to restrain the use of force against the rebels and to find a political solution to the conflict. For example, when the Macedonian forces launched an offensive against the NLA around Tetovo at the end of March 2001, NATO Secretary-General George Robertson and the EU High Representative Javier Solana arrived in Skopje to put pressure on the Macedonian authorities to halt the offensive (Phillips 2004, 97). At the end of June, when the Macedonian forces started a massive offensive against the village of Aracinovo, Robertson called this action "sheer madness," demanded its suspension, and visited Skopje to persuade the Macedonian state leaders to agree to a ceasefire.[28] Eventually, NATO and OSCE intervened to implement the pull-out of the NLA rebels, together with their arms, and to transfer them to an undisclosed location.[29]

It is argued above that labeling the KLA as "terrorists" sent the wrong signal to the Serbian authorities. In this regard, western officials were much more careful in the case of Macedonia, probably because they had learned from their earlier experiences in the Kosovo conflict. When the NLA emerged, Solana condemned the violence and urged Albanian leaders to isolate "extremists,"[30] and NATO also called them an "extremist Albanian group,"[31] but both avoided the word "terrorist." Solana used the term "terrorist" once to condemn the ambush by the NLA that killed eight Macedonian commandos, but he did not forget to emphasize the importance of a political solution to the conflict, saying "by remaining steadfastly on the course of dialogue and reform, the responsible political leaders can effectively counter the threat of extremist nationalism and help their country advance on the road to full participation in a prosperous and stable Europe."[32]

Western countries kept putting pressure on the Macedonian government to foster a political process to solve the conflict. In May 2001, Solana appointed Mark Dickinson, UK Ambassador in Skopje, as his personal representative in Macedonia to push forward the political dialogue.[33] At the beginning of June, Solana visited Macedonia twice, which led to the offer of an amnesty by Trajkovski.[34] At the end of June, when European foreign ministers met in Luxembourg, they expressed their dissatisfaction with the progress achieved so far and made the granting of aid to Macedonia conditional upon progress in political dialogue.[35] They appointed the former French Defense Minister, François Léotard, as a full-time special envoy in Macedonia;[36] he held intensive individual and joint discussions with local political leaders. When negotiations faced deadlock at the end of July, Solana and Robertson flew to Macedonia to provide additional pressure again, saying "95 percent of the agreement has been already agreed and only 5 percent remains to be agreed upon, which is not worth waging a war."[37] Western diplomats in Skopje concurred that Solana's dedication to the peace process in Macedonia turned out to be essential (Phillips 2004, 117).

It seems that the external pressure was more effective in the case of Macedonia for several reasons. First, some scholars suggest that it was effective because it was timely. For example, the former Foreign Minister of Macedonia Denko Maleski argues that "the West intervened *timely* to peacefully solve the conflict, and they did so because of their earlier experiences in the Balkans."[38] Indeed, the west responded fairly quickly, at a very early stage in the conflict, and it certainly increased the effectiveness of external pressure. Second, external actors were more unified and coherent and did not show internal disagreements. The third important factor was the dependency of Macedonia on external support. The fact that Macedonia was seeking membership of the EU and NATO gave them leverage on the Macedonian leadership. For example, in April 2001, Macedonia signed a Stabilization and Association Agreement with the EU, and at the signing ceremony, Prime Minister Georgievski promised to meet the June deadline for improved relations between Macedonians and Albanians.[39] Macedonian politicians were aware that Macedonia needed external assistance, and this awareness certainly made them more responsive to the demands of the international community.

Conclusion

This chapter has analyzed the cases of Serbia and Macedonia regarding the state response to ethnic rebellion. Whereas the Serbian authorities resorted to excessively repressive measures, the Macedonian authorities showed a much more conciliatory stance toward the rebels. This difference affected the course of the conflict in these two countries: the ethnic rebellion escalated into a large-scale one in Serbia, whereas the conflict in Macedonia de-escalated relatively quickly after the political parties signed the Ohrid Agreement. This chapter then examined which factors can explain the difference and demonstrated that electoral incentives and the role of external actors played an important role.

The findings in this chapter are confined, naturally, to the cases of Serbia and Macedonia, and it remains to be seen whether these factors can explain the state response to ethnic rebellion in other countries as well. This chapter only constitutes a starting point for further systematic analysis of the actions of state authorities in ethnic conflict, and further research is required to broaden and deepen our knowledge on this matter.

Notes

1 In the present chapter, there is no space to empirically test this argument on the radicalizing effect of state repression. I have conducted some statistical analyses using the MAR dataset elsewhere (Kubo 2007) to test the two interconnected hypotheses (if a low-intensity rebellion occurs in a country, the state authorities are more likely to take more repressive measures against rebels; and, as the level of state repression becomes higher, the level of intensity of rebellion in a country is more likely to increase) and found some empirical support for these hypotheses.

2 For the LPK and other Marxist–Enverist underground parties, see Judah (2000, 102–120); Çeku (2003, 2004). I have analyzed the origins of the KLA and the process of its expansion in detail elsewhere. See Kubo (2010).

3 He did so, of course, without admitting that the sharp increase in the number of KLA attacks was a result of the excessive use of force by the Serbian security forces. Indeed, he denied any excessive use of force by the Serbian authorities. See ICTY transcript of case IT-02-54 (Slobodan Milošević): 9327–9329 (June 22, 2005).

4 Phillips (2004, 8). As for the four-man branch of the LPK, see also Judah (2000, 115–116).

5 Interview with Ibrahim Kelmendi, Tetovo, May 30, 2006.

6 Interview with Ibrahim Kelmendi, Tetovo, May 30, 2006.

7 HRW (2001). Boškoski was prosecuted by the Hague Tribunal for "violations of the laws or customs of war" in Ljuboten. See the indictment against Ljube Boškoski and Johan Tarculovski, case no. IT-04-82, at www.un.org/icty/indictment/english/bos-ii050309e.htm.

8 In the Penn World Table 6.1 used in the present research, the data for gross domestic product (GDP) per capita in Yugoslavia is missing for the entire period from 1990 to 2000. See Penn World Tables at http://dc2.chass.utoronto.ca/pwt/alphacountries.html.

9 SRS officials protested that the authorities had manipulated the turn-out figures in order to deprive Šešelj of his victory. See Thomas (1999, 352). Eventually another candidate from the SPS, Milutinović, defeated Šešelj in the presidential election in December 1997 and the SPS managed to remain in power.

10 *Financial Times*, January 9, 1998.

11 *Financial Times*, February 24, 1998; *The Times* March 2, 1998; *Sunday Times* March 1, 1998.

12 *Financial Times*, February 24, 1998.

13 ICTY transcript of case IT-02-54 (Slobodan Milošević): 4266 (May 3, 2002), 41248 (June 21, 2005).

14 *Financial Times*, May 11, 1998; May 12, 1998; May 13, 1998.

15 *Observer*, June 14, 1998.

16 *Times*, June 25, 1998.

17 *Financial Times*, June 30, 1998.

18 *Guardian*, June 30, 1998.

19 *Independent*, March 25, 1998.

20 For a good review of the "Russian factor" in the Balkans since the end of Cold War, see Simić (2000, 137–161). For the relationship between NATO and Russia during the Kosovo crisis, see also Norris (2005).

21 Petrič and Pihler (2002, 95–96). This Milošević–Yeltsin agreement led to the establishment of the KDOM (Kosovo Diplomatic Observer Mission), which turned into the KVM (Kosovo Verification Mission) after the Milošević–Holbrooke agreement in October 1998. See Petrič and Pihler (2002, 96–97).

22 *Financial Times*, April 29, 1998. See also Albright (2004, 381–382) for the attitude of France, Italy, and Russia.

23 Interview with Arbën Xhaferi, Tetovo, May 30, 2006. Xhaferi was then the president of the DPA, the largest Albanian party, which had been in the ruling coalition with the VMRO–DPMNE since 1998. Therefore, his recommendation was highly influential with Albanian voters.
24 Pearson's correlation coefficient between these two figures is extremely high (0.976) and statistically significant at the 0.01 level (two-tailed test).
25 Inauguration speech of President Trajkovski, December 15, 1999. For the English translation of the original text, see www.boristrajkovski.org/.
26 Interview with Robert Milcev and Jason Miko, Skopje, June 1, 2006. Trajkovski was a devout Methodist and religiously very active since his youth. For example, in 1978, when he was 22 years old, he was elected president of the Evangelical Methodist Youth of Yugoslavia. See Miko (2004).
27 Interview with Ljubomir Frčkoski, Skopje, June 7, 2006.
28 *AIM Press*, July 1, 2001.
29 *AIM Press*, July 1, 2001.
30 Solana's statement on the violent incidents in the border region of the former Yugoslav Republic of Macedonia, March 5, 2001, at http://ue.eu.int/.
31 *Daily Telegraph*, March 9, 2001.
32 Solana's statement after the killing of eight soldiers near Tetovo, April 29, 2001, at http://ue.eu.int/.
33 Solana's statement on the confirmation of the appointment of Ambassador Dickinson as his personal representative in FYROM, May 18, 2001, at http://ue.eu.int/.
34 *Guardian*, June 1, 2001.
35 *AIM Press*, July 1, 2001.
36 *AIM Press*, July 1, 2001.
37 *AIM Press*, August 21, 2001.
38 Interview with Denko Maleski, Skopje, June 1, 2006.
39 *Guardian*, April 10, 2001.

References

AI (Amnesty International) (1998), *Kosovo: The Evidence*, London, Amnesty International.
Aklaev, Airat R. (1999), *Democratization and Ethnic Peace: Patterns of Ethnopolitical Crisis Management in Post-Soviet Settings*, Aldershot, Ashgate.
Albright, Madeleine (2004), *Madam Secretary: A Memoir*, London, Pan Macmillan.
Balalovska, Kristina, Alessandro Silj and Mario Zucconi (2002), *Crisis in Macedonia*, Rome, Ethnobarometer.
Bieber, Florian and Židas Daskalovski (eds) (2003), *Understanding the War in Kosovo*, London, Frank Cass.
Bose, Sumantra (1994), *States, Nations, Sovereignty: Sri Lanka, India and the Tamil Eelam Movement*, Thousand Oaks, CA, Sage Publications.
——(2003), *Kashmir: Roots of Conflict, Paths to Peace*, Cambridge, MA, Harvard University Press.
Brubaker, Rogers (1996), *Nationalism Reframed: Nationhood and the National Question in the New Europe*, Cambridge, Cambridge University Press.
Çeku, Ethem (2003), *Mendimi Politik i Lëvizjes Ilegale në Kosovë 1945–1981*, Prishtinë, Brezi'81.
——(2004). *Shekulli i Ilegales: Proceset gjuqësore kundër ilegales në Kosovë (Dokumente)*, Prishtinë, Brezi'81.
Clark, Wesley K. (2001), *Waging Modern War: Bosnia, Kosovo and the Future of Combat*, Oxford, Public Affairs.

96   *K. Kubo*

Cohen, Lenard J. (2002), *Serpent in the Bosom: The Rise and Fall of Slobodan Milošević*, Boulder, CO, Westview.

Daskalovski, Židas (2005), *Walking on the Edge: Consolidating Multiethnic Macedonia 1989–2004*, Skopje, Dominant.

Davenport, Christian (ed.) (2000), *Paths to State Repression: Human Rights Violations and Contentious Politics*, Lanham, MD, Rowman & Littlefield.

Eckstein, Harry (1965), 'On the Etiology of Internal Wars' *History and Theory*, 4(2): 133–163.

Fearon, James D. (1998), 'Commitment Problems and the Spread of Ethnic Conflict' in David D. Lake and Donald Rothchild (eds), *The International Spread of Ethnic Conflict: Fear, Diffusion and Escalation*, Princeton, NJ, Princeton University Press, pp. 107–126.

Goati, Vladimir (2001), *Izbori u SRJ od 1990. do 1998.: Volja Gradana ili Izborna Manipulacija*, II dopunjeno izdanje, Beograd, Centar za Slobodne Izbore i Demokratiju.

Hibbs, Douglas A. (1973), *Mass Political Violence: A Cross-national Causal Analysis*, New York, Wiley-Interscience.

Hislope, Robert (1996), 'Intra-Ethnic Conflict in Croatia and Serbia: Flanking and the Consequences for Democracy' *East European Quarterly*, 30(4): 471–494.

Horowitz, Donald L. (1985), *Ethnic Groups in Conflict*, Berkeley, CA, University of California Press.

——(1991), *A Democratic South Africa? Constitutional Engineering in a Divided Society*, Berkeley, CA, University of California Press.

——(2002), 'Constitutional Design: Proposals versus Processes' in Andrew Reynolds et al. (eds), *The Architecture of Democracy*, Oxford, Oxford University Press.

HRW (Human Rights Watch) (2001), *Macedonia – Crimes Against Civilians: Abuses by Macedonian Forces in Ljuboten, August 10–12, 2001*, at www.hrw.org/reports/2001/macedonia/ (accessed 5 August 2012).

IICK (Independent International Commission on Kosovo) (2000), *Kosovo Report: Conflict, International Response, Lessons Learned*, Oxford, Oxford University Press.

IWPR (Institute of War and Peace Reporting) (2004), *The 2001 Conflict in FYROM: Reflections*, London, Conflict Studies Research Centre, at www.da.mod.uk/CSRC/documents/balkans/ (accessed 5 August 2012).

Jenne, Erin K. (2007), *Ethnic Bargaining: The Paradox of Minority Empowerment*, Ithaca, NY, Cornell University Press.

Judah, Tim (2000), *Kosovo: War and Revenge*, New Haven, CT, Yale University Press.

——(2001), 'The Growing Pains of the Kosovo Liberation Army' in Michael Waller, Kyril Drezov and Bülent Gökay (eds), *Kosovo: The Politics of Delusion*, London, Frank Cass, pp. 20–24.

Karakamiševa, Tanja (2004), *Elections and Electoral Systems*, Skopje, Kultura.

King, John C. (2000), 'Exploring the Ameliorating Effects of Democracy on Political Repression: Cross-National Evidence,' in Christian Davenport (ed.), *Paths to State Repression: Human Rights Violations and Contentious Politics*, Lanham, MD, Rowman & Littlefield, pp. 217–239.

Kirişci, Kemal and Gareth M. Winrow (1997), *The Kurdish Question and Turkey: An Example of a Trans-state Ethnic Conflict*, London, Frank Cass.

Kubo, Keiichi (2007), *Why Ethnic Groups Rebel: Intra-ethnic Division, Dynamic Grievances, State Repression and Escalation*, PhD Thesis, London School of Economics and Political Science.

——(2010), 'Why Kosovar Albanians Took Up Arms against the Serbian Regime: The Genesis and Expansion of the UÇK in Kosovo' *Europe–Asia Studies*, 62(7): 1135–1152.

Responses to rebellion: Macedonia/Serbia 97

Lake, David D. and Donald Rothchild (eds) (1998), *The International Spread of Ethnic Conflict: Fear, Diffusion and Escalation*, Princeton, NJ, Princeton University Press.

Mihailović, Srećko (1999), 'Virtuelna Legitimacija Treće Jugoslavije' in Zoran Đ. Slavujević and Srećko Mihailović (eds), *Dva Ogleda o Legitimitetu: Javno Mnenje o Legitimitetu Treće Jugoslavije*, Beograd, Institut društvenih nauka, pp. 137–252.

Mijalkovski, Milan and Petar Damjanov (2002), *Terorizam Albanskih Ekstremista*, Beograd, Vojska.

Miko, Jason (2004), *Boris Trajkovski: President of the Republic of Macedonia, 1999–2004*, Skopje, The Boris Trajkovski International Foundation.

Mojanoski, Cane T. (1996), *Socijalen i Politički Profil na Političkite Partii vo Makedonija*, Skopje, Liber.

——(2000), *Letopis na Makedonskata Demokratija*, Skopje, Pakung.

Nikolovska, Natalija and Gordana Siljanovska-Davkova (2001), *Macedonian Transition in Deficiency: From Unitarian to a Bi-National State*, Skopje, Magor.

Norris, John (2005), *Collision Course: NATO, Russia, and Kosovo*, Westport, CT, Praeger.

Owen, David (1995), *Balkan Odyssey*, San Diego, CA, Harcourt Brace.

Petrič, Volfgang and Robert Pihler (2002), *Dugi Put u Rat: Kosovo i Međunarodna Zajednica, 1989–1999*, Beograd, Samizdat B92.

Phillips, John (2004), *Macedonia: Warlords and Rebels in the Balkans*, London, I.B. Tauris.

Pleština, Dijana (1992), *Regional Development in Communist Yugoslavia: Success, Failure, and Consequences*, Boulder, CO, Westview.

Popetrevski, Vasko and Veton Latifi (2004) 'The Ohrid Framework Agreement Negotiations' in IWPR (Institute of War and Peace Reporting), *The 2001 Conflict in FYROM: Reflections*, London, Conflict Studies Research Centre, at www.da.mod.uk/colleges/arag/document-listings/balkan/csrc_mpf-2004-07-22, pp. 29–36 (accessed 5 August 2012).

Premdas, Ralph R. (1990), 'Secessionist Movements in Comparative Perspective' in Ralph R. Premdas, S.W.R. de A. Samarasinghe and Alan B. Anderson (eds), *Secessionist Movements in Comparative Perspective*, London, Pinter Publishers, pp. 12–29.

Rabushka, Alvin and Kenneth A. Shepsle (1972), *Politics in Plural Societies: a Theory of Democratic Instability*, Columbus, OH, Charles E. Merrill.

Reilly, Benjamin (2001), *Democracy in Divided Societies: Electoral Engineering for Conflict Management*, Cambridge, Cambridge University Press.

Ron, James (2003), *Frontiers and Ghettos: State Violence in Serbia and Israel*, Berkeley, CA, University of California Press.

Rusi, Iso (2004), 'From Army to Party: The Politics of the NLA' in IWPR (Institute of War and Peace Reporting), *The 2001 Conflict in FYROM: Reflections*, London, Conflict Studies Research Centre, at www.da.mod.uk/colleges/arag/document-listings/balkan/csrc_mpf-2004-07-22, pp. 1–16 (accessed 5 August 2012).

Sekelj, Laslo (2000), 'Parties and Elections: The Federal Republic of Yugoslavia. Change without Transformation' *Europe–Asia Studies*, 52(1): 57–75.

Sell, Louis (2002), *Slobodan Milosevic and the Destruction of Yugoslavia*, Durham, NC, Duke University Press.

Simić, Predrag (2000), *Put u Rambuje: Kosovska Kriza 1995–2000*, Beograd, Nea.

Slavujević, Zoran Đ. (1999), 'Delegitimizacija Sistema i Njegovih Institucija' in Zoran Đ. Slavujević, and Srećko Mihailović (eds), *Dva Ogleda o Legitimitetu: Javno Mnenje o Legitimitetu Treće Jugoslavije*, Beograd, Institut društvenih nauka, pp. 9–136.

98   *K. Kubo*

Slavujević, Zoran D. and Srećko Mihailović (1999), *Dva Ogleda o Legitimitetu: Javno Mnenje o Legitimitetu Treće Jugoslavije*, Beograd, Institut društvenih nauka.

Thomas, Robert (1999), *The Politics in Serbia in the 1990s*, New York, Columbia University Press.

Waller, Michael, Kyril Drezov and Bülent Gökay (eds) (2001), *Kosovo: The Politics of Delusion*, London, Frank Cass.

Wolff, Stefan (2003), 'The Limits of Non-Military International Intervention: A Case Study of the Kosovo Conflict' in Florian Bieber and Židas Daskalovski (eds), *Understanding the War in Kosovo*, London, Frank Cass, pp. 79–100.

Zimmermann, Warren (1996), *Origins of a Catastrophe: Yugoslavia and Its Destroyers*, New York, Times Books.

6 Seceding by the force of arms
Chechnya and Kosovo

Aleksandar Pavković

Some attempts at secession involve the use of violence and some do not. More specifically, in some cases, secessionist movements or organizations use armed force in pursuit of their secessionist claims and in some they do not. This has been a general feature of all attempts at secessions in the past and present century: for example, in the 1990s, the secessionist movements in the Baltic republics, Slovakia and Kosovo eschewed the use of force or violent confrontation, whereas those in Slovenia, Eritrea and Sri Lanka did not.

To explain why some secessionist movements use armed force and some do not, one can attempt first to identify those structural components that favour armed insurgency and then argue that secessionist movements, like any other insurgent political movement, respond to favourable opportunities – of a structural kind – for armed insurgency. In those cases in which there were favourable opportunities, secessionist movements responded to them and initiated armed insurgency against the host state and in those in which there were no such opportunities, they did not. In this chapter, I shall attempt to argue that the response-to-opportunity model is not quite sufficient to explain the difference in the use of armed force between Chechnya and Kosovo. In particular, I shall argue that the same opportunities – 'structural' factors – that gave rise to the use of armed force in Chechnya did not do so in the case of Kosovo. This suggests, I hope to show, that the 'human agency' may be a significant and possibly overlooked factor in the use of armed force in secessionist conflicts.

Structural similarities

Both Chechnya and Kosovo (or, in its Serbian appellation, Kosovo and Metohija) were sub-federal units – an autonomous republic and a province respectively – *within* top-tier federal units in their respective Communist-ruled federations, the Union of Soviet Socialist Republics (USSR) and the Socialist Federative Republic of Yugoslavia (SFRY). In the late 1980s, both offered almost all of the opportunities that are considered favourable for armed insurgency in contemporary scholarly literature. First, large segments of those regions are covered by rough terrain – wooded mountains – which provided both the base and the operational terrain for insurgent groups (Fearon and Laitin 2003). Second, both regions have been the poorest and least economically developed regions in their respective host states with quite limited natural resources and a rapidly increasing population (of the potentially secessionist national group). Third, in the circumstances of rapid and continuous deterioration in the economy of the host state as a whole, economic underdevelopment resulted in higher unemployment in these two relatively poor regions (Dunlop 1998, 86–87; Giuliano 2006, 280; Kubo 2011). In both regions, there was, in particular, very high youth unemployment. Persistently high youth unemployment, one could argue, favours insurgent mobilization – unemployed youngsters can see more of a future in joining an insurgent group than in waiting for employment that never comes.

Fourth, structural weakening of the host state – due to the disintegration of its institutional structures – provided both Kosovo Albanian and Chechen political leaders with an opportunity to remove the existing state organs (including their armed forces) from the territory they claimed. Let us start with Kosovo. From 1987 on, the Communist regime in the federal unit of Serbia under its new leader Slobodan Milošević quickly lost legitimacy and support among the Kosovo Albanian population (as it rapidly restricted the autonomy of the province) and had to rely on overt coercion to maintain its control of the Kosovo province. In June 1991, two federal republics, Croatia and Slovenia, seceded from the SFRY. Even before the official proclamation of independence of these two federal units, Serbia offered substantial military, logistic and economic support to its co-nationals' uprisings in Croatia and Bosnia and Herzegovina. As the fighting in these two federal units intensified, the EU and, under US and EU member states' pressure, the UN imposed severe economic and diplomatic sanctions on Serbia in order to stop its support for the Serb secessionists in these two republics. This greatly weakened the Serbian government's capacity to use coercion in Kosovo and offered significant opportunities to the secessionist parties for armed insurgency. However, as we shall see below, their leaders rejected the option of armed insurgency against the Serbian regime.

This is in sharp contrast to the main Chechen secessionist organization which staged an armed insurgency against the Soviet Chechen authorities and then proceeded to use force against both its Chechen political opponents and the Russian armed forces. In August 1991, a group of Communist political and military leaders staged a short-lived coup in Moscow in a futile attempt to stop further disintegration of the USSR. The Soviet Communist leaders in Chechnya appeared to have supported this coup and, in September 1991, the principal secessionist organization in Chechnya, the All-National Congress of Chechen Peoples (OKChN in its Russian abbreviation), led by the former Soviet Air Force General Dokhar Dudaev, removed, by force, the Soviet (Communist) Chechen political leadership in this republic (Dunlop 1998, 104–106). The Soviet military or police, still stationed in Chechnya, did not attempt to stop this removal from power (Seely 2001, 99–108). In November

1991, the then Soviet President Gorbachev countermanded the Russian government's orders for military intervention against the OKChN secessionist authorities. By the spring of 1992, the Soviet military had departed from Chechnya leaving an estimated half of its weaponry in the hands of the secessionist regime. The retreat of the Soviet military left Dudaev's secessionist regime in control of most of Chechnya except for a few northern areas under the control of the deposed Soviet Chechen leaders. Thus, the disintegration of the host state – the USSR – provided the opportunity for the main secessionist party to use its armed militia against the existing political authorities and rival political groups and to create a well-equipped armed force that no political rival in Chechnya could match.

Fifth, both national groups – Chechens and Kosovo Albanians – have a long standing historic grievance against the host state, which the host state appeared to have no means of resolving apart from acceding to their secession. Both Serbia and Russia incorporated the territory of these two regions by military conquest: Russia achieved this by the military campaigns in the 1820s and Serbia in the First Balkan War in 1912. The conquests led to protracted armed resistance by Kosovo Albanians and, in particular, Chechens; the Chechen resistance lasted until 1859. Following the incorporation, there were frequent mass armed insurrections against the host state rule whenever the host state was militarily weak and whenever its military forces had either been defeated or were engaged elsewhere. In both regions, there were armed insurrections against the host state during and following World War One and during World War Two. In both cases, the host state, once it regained its military capacity, responded to the mass insurrection with military force, which led to large-scale civilian displacement and loss of life. During World War Two, in 1944, the Soviet regime under Stalin deported most of the Chechen and other North Caucasian populations to Kazakhstan; this mass deportation has no parallel in Kosovo.[1] In 1944–1945, Tito's Communist regime in Yugoslavia responded to the mass insurrection of Kosovo Albanians by military invasion of the region, the imposition of military rule on the Albanian population, mass arrests of those suspected of disloyalty and selective extrajudicial murders. In addition, selected Kosovo Albanian Communist cadres were given high governmental and Party offices in the sub-federal province of Kosovo, and attempts were made to recruit Kosovo Albanians for membership of the Yugoslav Communist Party (that is, its Kosovo provincial branch). In short, the response of the Yugoslav Communist regime to the 1944 mass insurrection of Kosovo Albanians (which appeared to have had much wider popular support than its counterpart insurrection in 1942 in Chechnya) was less drastic and followed the conventional Leninist formula of ruthless military suppression of the armed insurrection and parallel creation of a collaborationist Communist elite from the aggrieved national group.

Sixth, in both regions, various narratives of heroic resistance to the foreign occupier are an element of family education and popular folklore. In this narrative, the national heroes of past resistance – Shamil in the case of the

Chechens and Skenderbeg in the case of the Albanians – provide a model and ideal of manly behaviour. The narrative of historical resistance thus provides a framework within which contemporary political grievances can be easily placed and explained in terms of their historical continuity (Judah 2008, 25–27). The underlying grievance is that of having been forced, in spite of manly resistance, to live in a host state politically dominated by an alien group. The continued alien domination in an alien state thus provides an explanation for political powerlessness and marginalization as well as for poverty and relative economic underdevelopment of the insurgent national groups.

A history of resistance and a popular narrative of resistance in these two cases provided a basis for a national liberation ideology that justifies armed insurrection on the grounds of historical continuity and historical necessity: history is thus mobilized to show that only armed struggle can liberate the oppressed from the oppression and the oppressors.

Seventh, clans or extended families still play an important (some would say the principal) role in the social organization of both Kosovo Albanians and Chechens. Individuals in these societies are well aware of their clan or extended family membership, usually feel pride in belonging to their clan or family and feel solidarity with other clan or family members. Clan or family loyalties often override political or any other allegiances and are, in consequence, mobilized for political (as well as business and criminal) purposes. Upon the disintegration of the Communist judicial and coercive systems, both societies have experienced a resurgence of blood feud – vendetta – as a means of resolving disputes among families (Dunlop 1998, 20–22; Judah 2008, 28–29). Within the system of blood feud, violence against members of other groups is a socially accepted and even required behaviour. The acceptance of violence as a means of resolving disputes, one can argue, may facilitate the mobilization of members of such societies for violence against the members of 'outside' groups who are alleged to be oppressors or 'wrongdoers'.

Seventh, the religious background of most Kosovo Albanians and Chechens is Islamic, even if not all persons of this background are practising Muslims. This sharply differentiates them from the population of the host state, which is predominantly Eastern Orthodox. In the popular narrative of both Russian and Serbian history, Islam is presented primarily as the religion of the foreign invaders and oppressors: in the case of Russia with Tatars and Ottomans and in the case of Serbia with Ottomans. Partly as a consequence of this type of narrative, there is a popular mistrust or at least absence of solidarity with members of the 'opposing' religious groups.[2]

Finally, in both cases, the principal secessionist movements/parties made essentially non-negotiable claims: they demanded full sovereignty and independence of the province/republic they claimed as their homeland. In their negotiations with the host state representatives, the secessionist leaders repeatedly refused to make any concessions on this issue. These non-negotiable demands, as Toft (2005, 123–133) indicates, increase the likelihood of violent conflict over them.

Kosovo: secession without an armed insurgency

And yet, in spite of all the conditions favourable for armed insurgency, there was no armed insurgency in Kosovo preceding or following its declaration (in October 1991) of independence from the SFRY (Kosovo's first declaration of independence, in June 1990, was from the Republic of Serbia but not Yugoslavia). The mass insurgency in Kosovo started 7 years later – in February 1998 (see also Chapter 5). Following the trail of a leading Kosovo Liberation Army (KLA) militant, Adem Jashari (who was accused of murder), the Serbian special police surrounded his family compound and, after a short siege, destroyed it, killing the suspect as well as others, including women and children. In response to this, Kosovo Albanians in west Kosovo joined the insurgent organization, the KLA, en masse. The KLA, an offshoot of a Marxist revolutionary and irredentist organization, started its campaign of bombings and assassination in 1996, but lacked wider support among the Kosovo Albanian population until this incident in 1998. The principal secessionist party – the Democratic League of Kosovo (LDK) – had been, since its foundation in 1989, committed to non-violent struggle for independence. Until the end of 1996, the LDK leaders claimed that the KLA was a front organization for the Serbian government and police which, according to them, were intent on fomenting violent conflict (Pavković 2000, 190; Kubo 2010, 1145).

The LDK and KLA had one goal in common – the secession of Kosovo from Serbia (then a federal unit in the Federal Republic of Yugoslavia). The KLA, until 1999, wanted the secession to follow unification with Albania, whereas from October 1991, the LDK's goal was for an independent state of Kosovo. Their major difference was in tactics: the KLA leaders believed that Serbian rule over Kosovo could be overthrown only through armed struggle, whereas the LDK leadership renounced the use of violence on both tactical and ideological grounds. In the view of their leader, the first president of the Republic of Kosovo, Dr Ibrahim Rugova, the use of violence is wrong, in particular if the goal can be achieved in a non-violent way. Moreover, he repeatedly warned that Kosovo Albanian armed rebellion would lead to the mass killing and displacement of civilians and that it could not succeed because Serbia had a military force superior to and larger than anything that the Kosovo Albanians could deploy (Judah 2008, 69–71). His warnings proved to be right – the mass rebellion led by the KLA in 1998 led to huge displacement and indiscriminate killing of civilians in the areas of violent conflict. The KLA on its own proved unable to conquer any towns or to remove the Serbian/Yugoslav military from Kosovo. The Serbian/Yugoslav military was removed by an agreement with NATO/UN after 78 days of bombing of Serbia and its military and industrial infrastructure (Judah 2008, 90–91)

In contrast, the All-National Congress of Chechen Peoples (OKChN), under the leadership of General Dudaev, prior to the declaration of independence in December 1991, deployed its armed units – called the Chechen National Guard – first against the Soviet Chechen leadership (in September 1991) and

104 *A. Pavković*

then against its main political rival, the Provisional Council formed by the Chechen Supreme Soviet (in November 1991). The first targets of armed action were thus rival but unarmed Chechen groups, not Russian or Soviet forces. The Chechen National Guard, armed in 1991–1992 from the arsenal of the retreating Soviet armed forces, was transformed into a well-equipped army that was able to ultimately defeat, in 1996, the much larger Russian invasion force without any assistance from other states or international organizations. The party's dominance in Chechnya in the period from 1991 to 1994 was in part based on having an armed force superior to any other Chechen political organization.

The Kosovo LDK, in contrast, had no plans to create a large armed force,[3] and gained its political dominance in Kosovo through electoral means: it won the largest number of votes (76 per cent) in the first semi-clandestine[4] elections held in 1992 and, again, under the UN protectorate, in 2000 and 2004. The LDK lost its lead only in the 2007 parliamentary elections to the Democratic Party of Kosovo (DPK, not to be confused with LDK), a party that originated in the KLA and whose leader was the political leader of the KLA during the insurgency. This suggests that the KLA, at the time of the insurgency and long after, did not have the popular support to match that of the LDK.

Instead of asking why the LDK platform of non-violent struggle for independence appeared to have won wider popular support than the KLA's platform of violent struggle, we could perhaps ask, first, why did the OKChN resort to the use of force against its Chechen political rivals in 1991, before it was forced to confront, in late 1994, the non-Chechen forces, that is the Russian army? I have no access to any sources regarding the decision-making of the OKChN leadership; in consequence, I would have to rely on the available circumstantial evidence, that is the political context under which these decisions were made.

In September 1991, the following two factors favoured the use of armed force against the Soviet Chechen authorities or any other political rivals: first, the Russian government, under Boris Yeltsin, withdrew its support from the Soviet Chechen leadership under Doku Zavgayev because Zavgayev had an ambivalent attitude towards the August coup in Moscow which Yeltsin opposed; second, the Soviet central government, under Mikhail Gorbachev, appeared to exercise no effective control over the Soviet police and military forces in Chechnya. This provided a window of opportunity for a quick removal of the Soviet Chechen leadership and its administration. The quickest and most reliable way of gaining power – before the Soviet Chechen leaders were able to resume their control over the forces of coercion – was to use force: at the time, speed appeared to be essential to prevent the reassertion of the authority of the Soviet Chechen leaders and the Chechen Communists (Seely 2001, 102–109).

As already mentioned, on account of the broken lines of command and authority resulting from the attempted coup in Moscow, the Soviet coercive apparatus in Chechnya – the police, the internal paramilitary forces and the military – appeared to lack direction as to how to operate in the new political environment in which the power and authority of the local Communist party were contested. They appeared to have had no orders from the Soviet central government as to whom to support in this conflict. Moreover, as a result of the continuing contest for authority over Russia between the Russian President Yeltsin and the Soviet leader Gorbachev, it was no longer clear who, if anyone, was in authority to issue orders to use force against any of the actors in this conflict. This was a classic case of a power vacuum which the OKChN was ready to fill with its own armed units.

This power vacuum and the possibility of the reassertion of the power of the Soviet Chechen authorities favoured the use of armed force. But in order to use armed force, one has first to possess it. Why did the OKChN create its own armed force well before the August 1991 Moscow coup? Again I have no access to relevant sources regarding the Chechen leadership's decision-making. But, again, circumstantial evidence suggests that the leaders of OKChN were not certain that they could rely on the electoral or peaceful means of winning (and keeping) power in Chechnya. This is also the view of at least some observers/participants in Chechnya itself. One of them quotes Dudaev as saying, 'If you wait for elections, the Communists will take power again.'[5] Under these conditions, their own armed force would have appeared to be a more reliable instrument of gaining and keeping power.

In contrast to the OKChN's use of armed units against the Soviet Chechen authorities as well as other political rivals, the LDK leader Rugova and his circle not only avoided the use of force but did not regard any other Kosovo Albanian political party as a serious competitor for power. Rugova's model for his political movement or party was Polish Solidarnosc' from the 1980s; and, as a result, the LDK was organized as a mass movement that attempted to *include* all shades of Kosovo Albanian political opinion, including the Kosovo Albanian Communist party leaders as well as its rank and file. Its inclusive policies appeared to work, as other parties – except for the small militant groups such as KLA joined in the coalition cabinet formed by the LDK in 1992. In contrast to the LDK, the OKChN was an openly anti-Communist national liberation organization that *excluded* those Chechen political groups that did not share its national liberation ideology and regarded Chechen independence as a long-term and not an immediate goal. In particular, in line with its national liberation rhetoric, OKChN leaders considered as traitors to the national cause any political group that showed readiness to negotiate a deal which would deny the full independence of Chechnya from Russia. For them, the cause of national independence was not subject to negotiation: full and immediate independence was the only acceptable political option for them. National liberation organizations often regard the necessity of liberation from foreign rule as the highest and overriding goal that trumps any need for a democratic procedure or wider political support. In short, such a liberation needs to be achieved, even if most of the population to be liberated does not support it.[6] This, I believe, was the position that Dudaev

106 *A. Pavković*

and the OKChN leadership took even before the failed Moscow coup in August 1991.

In contrast, from its inception in 1989, the LDK was assured of widespread popular support: it had no serious political competitors among the numerous Kosovo Albanian parties. The KLA, formed in 1993, was a marginal group that the LDK leaders did not take seriously at all. The sole opponent of the LDK was the Milošević regime in Serbia, which had no popular support among Kosovo Albanians. The Milošević regime was ready to tolerate the LDK and its parallel state structures in Kosovo as long as the LDK was not attacking its state institutions in Kosovo and non-Albanians (including Serbs) living in Kosovo. The LDK was even ready to negotiate with Milošević (who, in turn, was ready to receive Rugova as a representative of the Kosovo Albanians) but was not ready to compromise on its demand for full independence (Judah 2008, 68–72). In view of its Solidarnosc' model, the wide political support, the dominant political position it had in Kosovo and the relative tolerance of the Milošević regime, the LDK had nothing to gain by using force. By using force, it would be open to suppression by the Milošević regime and would, possibly, lose its dominant political position.

One should note that, although the Milošević regime had no popular support among Kosovo Albanians, at no time did it leave a power vacuum in Kosovo similar to the one created in Chechnya in the wake of the failed August 1991 Moscow coup. In response to the Kosovo Albanian political demonstrations in Kosovo in 1988, the Milošević regime maintained a large police force with clear directives to crush any public political protest among Kosovo Albanians. As a result, from 1988 onwards, any attempt by Kosovo Albanian armed groups to remove the Serbian political authorities by force would have been effectively countered – as similar attempts by the KLA in 1998–1999 were indeed countered. In short, in spite of the weakening of the Serbian state and its capacity to deploy force, the Serbian government was still ready and able to use its coercive apparatus against any Kosovo Albanian force that attempted to remove its institutions from Kosovo. As Rugova had stated in the early 1990s, the use of force by Kosovo Albanians against the Serbian government could not have succeeded in removing its rule over Kosovo. In contrast, in 1991–1992, the successive Soviet and Russian authorities were not ready or able to use their own military force against the insurgent Chechen regime led by Dudaev, although they commanded much larger armed forces than the Serbian/Yugoslav government did.

Using force as an adaptive tactic?

In spite of the similarities in social, economic and political circumstances in pre-secession Kosovo and Chechnya, there were, as noted above, two key differences: first, the disintegration of the Soviet federal state created a power vacuum in Chechnya that had no parallel in Kosovo. Second, the principal Chechen secessionist party, the OKChN, was ready to fill this power vacuum with its own armed force which it had organized beforehand. The principal Kosovo secessionist party, the LDK, had no comparable armed forces and had not used armed force in pursuit of its secessionist aims.

The organization and the use of armed force in Chechnya can thus be interpreted as an adaptive tactic of a political group whose political ideology – that of national liberation – justified the use of force in pursuit of selected political goals. This tactic could be considered both an appropriate response to the emerging power vacuum in the region and an ideologically justifiable instrument in the struggle against political rivals or opponents. If interpreted in this way, the use of force by the Chechen secessionists was not determined by any set of structural features of Chechen social and economic circumstances. In fact, one could argue that the OKChN could also have opted for the same tactics that the LDK adopted – that is, it could have opted to become an inclusive political organization that relied exclusively on its organizational superiority and electoral support to gain and maintain a politically dominant position in Chechen society. Whether it could have been as successful in this as the LDK was in Kosovo is, of course, an open counterfactual question, which perhaps cannot be answered at all. Consequently, it is an open question whether such a political option would have been equally effective from an instrumental point of view; that is, whether it would have yielded the same results – the takeover of power in Chechnya – as the other option (the use of force) did. The main point of this chapter is that this political option was available to the OKChN leadership. Likewise, the LDK also had the option of initiating an armed rebellion before the KLA in 1996, but its leader decided not to take it (Kubo 2010, 1144).

If so, the use of force or the abstention from the use of force, at least in these two cases, does not appear to be a tactic that is or was determined by the structural features listed at the beginning of the chapter. As we have listed only some of the features that the cases appear to share, perhaps there are other structural features that cause or lead to the use of force or the abstention from the use of force.

Let us consider one feature – if one may call it so – that the two cases *do not* share: the personal background of the top leaders in Chechnya and in Kosovo. General Dokhar Dudaev was a professional air force officer and pilot, trained to use force and to give orders to that effect. Dr Ibrahim Rugova was a literary critic who explored (among other topics) the ambiguities and multi-layered meanings of literary texts. Dudaev, like most Chechens of his generation, spent his childhood in exile outside Chechnya and had, in his education and life in the USSR, to confront a degree of prejudice – and possibly discrimination – against the Chechens. In these circumstances, it is not surprising that his command of the Chechen language at the beginning of his new political career in Chechnya proved to be rudimentary and inadequate: until then, in his professional and public life, he had never used Chechen.

In contrast, Rugova was educated in his native language in Kosovo (and briefly studied in Paris) and, under the Communist regime, had a successful

108 *A. Pavković*

academic and political career in the sub-federal unit in which (from 1967 on) the Albanian majority and its language and culture were dominant. Since 1967, Kosovo Albanians held most of the political and managerial posts, including the top party and government positions; the same was true of the academic posts and cultural bureaucracy. Apart from being a university professor – teaching and publishing in his native language – he was the president of the official Association of the Writers of Kosovo. In Kosovo, at least until 1988, he belonged to the politically and culturally dominant group that faced no discrimination within the province.[7] In view of their professional and personal backgrounds, these two leaders were likely to have sharply different conceptions of what constitutes a political opponent or enemy and different preferences regarding the use of force. And in fact, they did hold widely different views not only about the political tactics in general, but also about the use of violence for the purpose of gaining and holding on to power. But one could also argue that these factors – the professional and personal backgrounds of the leaders – are not 'structural' features of the same kind as are those listed at the beginning of the chapter.

Be that as it may, perhaps there are other features or factors more akin to those structural ones listed at the beginning of the chapter that, in some way, determined their choices or courses of action. This chapter is not intended to close the search for such features or factors. It is intended only to point out that both secessionist leaders and their parties had political options other than the use of armed force. Why they made the choices or decisions that they did is, no doubt, a question that will continue to be the subject of further enquiry.

Notes

1 One could argue that, unlike Stalin's regime in 1944, Tito's regime had nowhere safe to deport Kosovo Albanians – wherever they were deported within Yugoslavia, they would still present a threat. Be that as it may, the Yugoslav Communist regime, unlike Stalin's, did not consider it necessary to resort to mass deportation.

2 In popular narratives of Serbian history, Kosovo and Metohija is presented as the cradle of the medieval Serbian state and Serbian Orthodoxy. This cradle was invaded in 1389 and, after a valiant defence by the Serbian Prince Lazar, occupied by the Islamic Ottomans who later settled Islamic Albanians on Serbian land, forcing Serbs out of Kosovo and Metohija. Within this narrative, Kosovo Albanians are foreign occupiers of Serbian land who were brought in by the superior military force of the Ottoman empire. A similar narrative of medieval Serbian occupation of Kosovo Albanian land – settled initially by the Albanian ancestors, Illyrians – is popular among Kosovo Albanians (Judah 2008, 18–26).

3 The LDK apparently attempted to create an armed wing but lacked access to weapons and trained personnel for this purpose.

4 The Serbian regime made no attempt to stop or suppress the elections in spite of their illegality within the Serbian legal system.

5 Gakayev in an interview with Robert Seely (2001, 105).

6 For a brief account of national liberation ideologies of secessionist movements, see Pavković with Radan (2007, 45–62).

7 The extent of discrimination against Kosovo Albanians *outside* the province of Kosovo is difficult to establish. But there is no doubt that many Serbs would have considered Kosovo Albanians – who are in popular parlance still called Sciptari – an inferior group.

References

Dunlop, J. (1998), *Russia Confronts Chechnya: Roots of a Separatist Conflict*, Cambridge, Cambridge University Press.

Fearon, J. and Laitin, D. (2003), 'Ethnicity, Insurgency and Civil War' *American Political Science Review*, 97: 75–90.

Giuliano, E. (2006), 'Secessionism from the Bottom Up: Democratization, Nationalism, and Local Accountability in the Russian Transition' *World Politics*, 58(2): 276–310.

Judah, T. (2008), *Kosovo: What Everyone Needs to Know*, Oxford, Oxford University Press.

Kubo, K. (2010), 'Why Kosovar Albanians Took Up Arms against the Serbian Regime: The Genesis and Expansion of the UÇK in Kosovo' *Europe–Asia Studies*, 62: 1135–1152.

——(2011), 'Kosovo: Secession under UN Supervision' in A. Pavković and P. Radan (eds), *Ashgate Research Companion to Secession*, Farnham, Ashgate.

Pavković, A. (2000), *The Fragmentation of Yugoslavia: Nationalism and War in the Balkans*, Houndmills, Palgrave.

Pavković, A. with P. Radan (2007), *Creating New States: Theory and Practice of Secession*, Aldershot, Ashgate.

Seely, R. (2001), *Russo-Chechen Conflict 1800–2000: A Deadly Embrace*, Abingdon, Frank Cass.

Toft, M.D. (2005), *The Geography of Ethnic Violence: Identity, Interests and the Indivisibility of Territory*, Princeton, NJ, Princeton University Press.

7 Secession and liberal democracy

The case of the Basque Country

Ferran Requejo and Marc Sanjaume i Calvet

Introduction

The academic debate about the *secession* of a territory that is part of a liberal-democratic state displays an initial contrast. On the one hand, practical secessionist movements usually legitimize their position using national lines of reasoning linked to a particular version of the principle of *national self-determination.*[1] On the other hand, philosophers, political scientists, and lawyers usually tend to leave this question basically unresolved.[2] Regarding this issue, most liberal-democratic theories have a tendency to be "conservative" in relation to empirical political borders, regardless of the historical processes of creation of current states and the empirical situation of minority nations within them. This feature is probably related to the fact that, since its inception, political liberalism has not been a theory of the nation, but of the state.[3]

As is customary in the literature, it is possible to distinguish between three types of theories of secession: just cause/remedial right;[4] choice/plebiscitarian;[5] and liberal-nationalist[6] theories. However, we would like to mention that a theory of secession for cases of plurinational liberal democracies should take into account the fact that respect, recognition, and accommodation of the rights of national minorities are also normative elements that should be added to respect for human rights and democratic procedures in the legitimizing principles of liberal-democratic states. The theoretical perspective stressed by so called Liberalism 2 (Taylor 1992) has insisted that this is a question of justice. These approaches would define national minorities in plurinational states as the subjects of the right of secession.

This question leads us to the well-known "Opinion" of the Canadian Supreme Court (Secession of Quebec 1998) regarding the case of Quebec. This juridical decision establishes several elements that any theory of secession must take into account (right of national minorities to organize a referendum, the required number of voters, etc.). The approach adopted by the Canadian Court is that of interpreting the right of national self-determination in federal rather than nationalist terms, against unilateral Canadian and Quebecker nationalisms, but opening the door to a secessionist process if certain conditions have been met.

Secession and liberal democracy 111

Bearing in mind this practical precedent, we have presented elsewhere the basis for a more multidimensional normative approach to the political recognition and constitutional accommodation of national pluralism in liberal democracies (Requejo 2005, 2011, 2012). This approach includes two philosophical elements of Hegelian philosophy: the politics of recognition (in contrast to approaches based only on the concept of individual autonomy) and an "ethical" collectivist approach (in contrast to mere "moral" approaches). These elements work together with the more individualistic, statist, and partially universal perspective usually present in political liberal theories based on a Kantian approach to moral individualism. The right of secession of national minorities in liberal democracies would be one of the institutional rules of this approach. A general framework of reference here is Isaiah Berlin's conception of value pluralism—in this case including not only a pluralism of values, but also of interests and national identities. The objective is to open the values of negative liberty and political equality to the collective dimension that characterizes nationally diverse societies. The basic normative elements of this theory are: individual and collective minority rights; the politics of recognition; constitutional accommodation through liberal group protections and partnership agreements; and the democratic vote.

In the next section, we will look at the case of the Basque Country and the institutional framework of the Spanish *Estado de las Autonomías* (the State of Autonomous Communities). This empirical case exemplifies that the political recognition and the constitutional accommodation of national pluralism are two liberal-democratic challenges for political theory and constitutionalism in the twenty-first century.

National minorities in the Spanish *Estado de las Autonomías*: a brief historical note

In contemporary times, the organization of the Spanish state has been largely based on the premises of the French model, which consisted of only two administrative levels: the central power and a politically weak municipal power. All efforts to articulate the state according to "regionalizing" premises—some of which were extremely moderate in nature—failed for different reasons. This was the case in the First Republic (1873), the *Mancomunitat de Catalunya* (at the beginning of the twentieth century), and the "integral state" of the Second Republic (1931–1939). The term "federal" continues to arouse direct opposition from the main political forces in Spain, in the name of "national" unitarianism by the traditional right—formerly linked with Catholicism and the monarchy—or in the name of a homogenizing Jacobin unitarianism that is present on the centre left—mainly in the Socialist party.

Following the Civil War (1936–1939) and the subsequent prolonged period of Francoist dictatorship (1939–1975), the territorial model that was established with the 1978 Constitution has evolved in parallel with an environment that is very different from that which existed in previous Spanish historical periods: (a) an unequivocal transition from an authoritarian state to a modern and stable liberal democracy; (b) the construction and development of a welfare state; and (c) the integration of the state into the European and international spheres (EU, NATO). In addition to these elements, there was the objective of establishing a decentralized territorial system that would result in a definitive accommodation of the minority nations, Catalonia and the Basque Country (and, to a lesser extent, Galicia) (Figure 7.1). This accommodation was something that had never been achieved throughout contemporary Spanish history. However, in contrast to other historical disputes that have now been resolved—the monarchy/republic issue, the religious question, socioeconomic development, the internationalization process, or the modernization of the state itself—more than three decades after the new constitution, the main issue that has still to be *politically* resolved is the historical dispute regarding the territorial model, which is closely linked to the plurinational character of the state.

There is no doubt that, with the new territorial model, Spain has put an end to its endemic centralism and has become a regionalized state. However, different actors pursued different objectives through the decentralization process and reflected distinct values and identities, some of which have turned out to be contradictory in practical terms. Political decentralization based on functional objectives, such as efficiency, results in different challenges from those posed by achieving *political accommodation* between different national collectivities.

It is easy to see that the Spanish *Estado de las Autonomías* represents an atypical and somewhat eclectic approach within the field of comparative politics.

Figure 7.1 Map of Spain
Source: *Estado de las Autonomías.*

Despite the fact that, in some comparative political works, Spain is often classified as a "federal" state (Elazar 1991; Watts 1999; Neremberg and Griffiths 2002/ 2005), there are many arguments that would suggest that it would be more appropriately situated in the group of "regional" states. Among the elements that distance the current Spanish model from standard federations are the following: the autonomous communities (AC) are not constituent entities; the decentralization of legislative powers is unclear;[7] judicial power remains basically that of a unitary state; the upper chamber is not linked to the federated units;[8] the *Estado de las Autonomías* is very different from any model of fiscal federalism;[9] the AC are not considered to be political actors in relation to the principal institutions of the EU (in contrast to federations of the EU, such as Belgium and Germany); and the AC do not participate in the process of constitutional reform.

The result has been the establishment of a somewhat decentralized state which, above all, shares two elements with federations: (a) a decentralization process that is designed for all the territorial subunits, and not only for some of them. That is, the total number of territories endowed with constitutionally guaranteed political autonomy—currently seventeen AC plus two cities in the north of Africa, Ceuta and Melilla (autonomous cities)—is equivalent to the whole territory of the state; and (b) the existence of a Constitutional Court as supreme arbiter of the constitutionality of laws and of conflicts between the institutions of the state (the AC have no say, however, in the appointment of the twelve magistrates of the Constitutional Court).[10] Moreover, Article 2 of the constitution distinguishes between "nationalities and regions," a distinction that is a potential source of asymmetrical rules, although it has not been developed subsequently (all the territorial units are treated as "Autonomous Communities"). The Spanish *Estado de las Autonomías* has not instituted mechanisms of coordination or cooperation between the two levels of government (there is a lack of: stable intergovernmental relations, a second "federal" chamber, real participation of the AC in European politics, the possibility of establishing horizontal relations between AC, cooperation in institutions such as the Constitutional Court, the Tax Office, the General Council of the Judicial Power, etc.).

Despite the fact that the AC enjoy a certain degree of autonomy in some areas, the basic characteristics of the model are predominantly based on a more regionalizing than a strictly federal logic.[11] However, the most important issue to be resolved by the territorial model is quite different: the political recognition and constitutional accommodation of a plurinational reality.[12]

Nationalisms, secession and the Basque case

Introduction

In this section, we will pay particular attention to Basque politics and the actors who advocate the secessionist option[13] in order to understand the specific character of Basque nationalism compared with the other forms of nationalism.[14]

The characteristic that has most differentiated the Basque case from those of Catalonia and Galicia has been support, albeit partial, for violent tactics used to express and pursue secessionist demands. There were a large number of violent acts during the 1980s and—although the position of Euskadi Ta Askatasuna or ETA is currently weaker than it has been in the past. Political violence is an element in Basque politics that must always be taken into account. Violent conflict and political conflict overlap and influence the political agendas of Vitoria and Madrid (Figure 7.2).

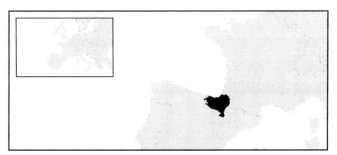

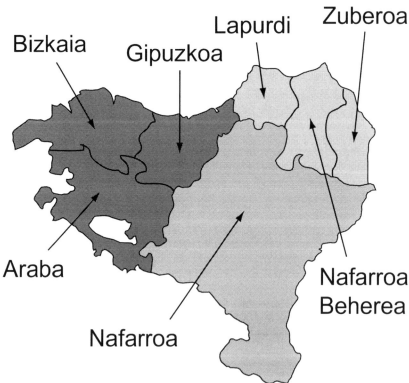

Figure 7.2 Map of the Basque Country

Secession and liberal democracy 115

Table 7.1 A summary of Basque political parties

Secessionist parties	Critical pro-autonomy/ federalist parties	Non-critical pro-autonomy parties
EA	PNV	PSE-EE
Batasuna (now illegal)	EB-B	PP
Aralar		UPyD
Bildu		

Notes: EA, Eusko Alkartasuna (Basque Solidarity); PNV, Basque Nationalist Party; PSE-EE, Socialist Party of the Basque Country; EB-B, Ezkerra Batua Berdeak (Green Unity Left); PP, Popular Party; UPyD, Union, Progress and Democracy.

Political parties

What follows is a brief description of the parties that have had seats in the Basque parliament in terms of their support, or lack of it, for secessionist demands (Table 7.1).

Secessionist parties

Eusko Alkartasuna (Basque Solidarity, EA): founded by the former *lehendakari* (president of the Basque government) Carlos Garaikoetxea in 1986 following a split from the PNV (Basque Nationalist Party). Its social orientation is social democratic. It governed the Basque Country in coalition with the PNV from 1994 to 2009. It supports secessionism and condemns the violence of ETA.

Batasuna (Unity): over the years, it has adopted many forms and different names, including Herri Batasuna (HB), Euskal Herritarrok (a coalition that included HB), and Batasuna. It has also unsuccessfully attempted to reconstitute itself in other forms for electoral purposes, such as Herritarren Zerrenda, Aukera Guztiak, or Sortu. But in 2012 the Spanish Constitutional Court legalized Sortu undermining the earlier decision of the Supreme Court that had banned this party. This organization has historically never rejected the violent strategy implemented by ETA. It has been considered illegal by the Spanish Supreme Court (Spanish Law of Political Parties 2002), although it is still legal in France. At present, some of its leaders are in prison. It supports nationalism and is extremely left wing (anti-capitalist) in orientation.

Aralar: this party was formed from a split of Herri Batasuna. It condemns ETA violence and refers to itself as the "patriotic left," in direct competition with Batasuna.

Bildu: after the last ceasefire declared by ETA (January 10, 2011) and the banning of a previous political organization (Sortu), Bildu was created by diverse political actors to run in the 2011 local elections. It includes former Batasuna members, but also EA and the far left party Alternatiba. The Supreme Court banned the coalition arguing links with ETA, but the Constitutional Court finally lifted the ban (April 2011). Its leaders declared

116 *F. Requejo and M. Sanjaume i Calvet*

their will to become a political party in the near future following the positive results obtained at local level.[15]

Autonomous/federalist parties with a critical perspective on the Spanish autonomic state

Euzko Alderdi Jeltzale—Basque Nationalist Party (PNV): it was founded in 1895 by Sabino Arana and governed the Basque Country uninterrupted from the moment that autonomy was restored in 1980 until 2009. Its position regarding sovereignty is the subject of intense debate within the party between secessionists and those who are pro-autonomy. It is centre right and Catholic in orientation.[16] It condemns violence.

Ezkerra Batua Berdeak (Green Unity Left, EB-B): it is a member of the state-level party Izquierda Unida (United Left). It is a left-wing party that advocates a "free association" as a territorial model for Spain. It has been a member of ruling coalitions with the PNV and EA and has supported the pro-sovereignty proposals of the former *lehendakari* Juan José Ibarretxe. It condemns ETA violence.

Autonomous parties without a critical perspective on the Spanish State of Autonomous Communities

Socialist Party of the Basque Country (PSE-EE):[17] its leader Patxi López is currently the president of the Basque government (*lehendakari*), leading a minority government with the parliamentary support of the Popular Party. It does not support secessionism. It is part of the state-level PSOE (Spanish Socialist Party) and maintains its Spanish nationalist trends. It was also a member of the Basque government during two previous legislatures in the 1980s and 1990s (with the PNV). It defines itself as a non-nationalist Basque party and condemns ETA violence. It is social democratic and pro-autonomy in orientation.

Popular Party (PP): it defends the status quo or a greater degree of centralization. It is conservative and Spanish nationalist in orientation. It supported a Basque socialist minority government in 2009.

Union, Progress and Democracy (UPyD): this is a recent Spanish party that has one MP in the Basque parliament. The Spanish leader is Rosa Díez, a former member of the socialist party. It proposes constitutional reform in order to find a definitive and limited autonomous model. It condemns ETA violence and maintains a strong pro-Spanish nationalist orientation.

The Basque political party system is different from the Spanish one. It has been described as a *polarized pluralist* system. Its number of "effective parties" is 4.4 (Catalonia 3.9; Spain 2.5). Competitiveness between parties is high and can be analyzed using two axes: (a) a left/right axis, common in western democracies, regarding socioeconomic issues; and (b) a territorial axis concerning national identity and demands for a greater degree of self-government, which polarizes Basque politics between those who defend the status quo or greater integration in the Spanish state and those who advocate secession or a greater degree of sovereignty.

The PNV has been the dominant party within this party system in all the legislatures until the present. Although it experienced difficulties in the 1980s when the split with EA occurred, it overcame them and continued in government until the last Basque elections (2009). The period that we would like to pay particular attention to here is that of the most recent legislatures, from 1999 to 2009, when the PNV and its partners in government, EA and EB-B, made a determined effort to achieve greater sovereignty.

ETA and peace processes

The violent strategy chosen by one part of the Basque nationalist movement has been led in recent decades by *Euskadi Ta Askatasuna* (ETA), Basque Country and Liberty. This organization, which first appeared during the Francoist dictatorship in 1959 and carried out its first violent acts during the 1960s, describes itself as secessionist, Basque nationalist, and Marxist–Leninist. During the Francoist dictatorship, it gained prominence and popularity following the Burgos Trials (1970).[18] During the 1980s, it suffered a number of splits that weakened its structure, but maintained the same ideological principles on which it was founded. To date, 828 people,[19] civilians, military personnel, and politicians have become victims of ETA; and nearly 800 people are currently detained in Spanish and French prisons.[20] The fight against ETA caused many deaths during the 1980s and included the dirty war carried out by the Spanish central government between 1982 and 1989 by the so called GAL (Autonomous Liberation Groups), which involved Spanish ministers and politicians responsible for internal affairs.

Spanish governments have attempted to negotiate with ETA on a number of occasions, but without success. One of the first attempts took place in 1988 with the so called Algiers talks, which led to a ceasefire that lasted for over 60 days and the start of negotiations by the PSOE. During the government of the Popular Party (1996–2000), negotiations also took place in 1998 following the Lizarra Pact[21] between Basque nationalist parties and the declaration of an "indefinite truce and ceasefire". Following unsuccessful negotiations in Zurich between members of the organization and the Spanish government, ETA announced its intention to resume its attacks.

The agreements between the two largest Spanish parties (PSOE and PP) with regard to anti-terrorist strategies made it possible after 2000 to gradually make illegal the "social environment of ETA," as it was called. As a result, the political arm of the organization, Batasuna, has been banned, despite the changes in name and acronyms that it has attempted. This strategy has also included the banning of *abertzale* nationalist media such as the newspaper *Egunkaria*. The law that has allowed this banning process is the Political

Parties Law (2002), which was passed in June 2002 by a majority of the lower chamber of the Spanish parliament.[22]

Between May 2003 and December 2006, ETA did not carry out any attacks despite the fact that there were numerous acts of street warfare (low-intensity terrorism) in the Basque Country. It was during this period that the *abertzale* left put forward what has come to be known as the Anoeta Proposal (November 2004).[23] This proposal expressed the commitment of the *abertzale* left to find a democratic solution to the political conflict. Moreover, it laid down a "road map" to solve the conflict, which involved the creation of two negotiating tables. The first would consist of a negotiation involving ETA and the Spanish and French governments on disarmament, the situation of ETA prisoners, and the rehabilitation of victims from both sides of the conflict. A second table would be responsible for dealing with political agreements that would have to be ratified by the Basque population. Despite the significance of this proposal, which was characterized by a commitment to opt for a democratic solution, the fact that it failed to condemn ETA violence meant that it was not put into practice. The Spanish government (PSOE) attempted to negotiate with ETA (2006), following an indefinite ceasefire that the organization itself broke once again. Finally, another peace initiative took place in November 2009 when, during a conference in Venice (Italy), leaders of Batasuna put forward a proposal inspired by the Northern Ireland peace process, which had already been mentioned in the Anoeta Proposal of 2004. Most Spanish political parties have rejected this initiative.[24]

The two proposals of President Ibarretxe and recent political developments

The issue we are concerned with, secessionist demands, was given tangible form in political proposals during the first decade of the twenty-first century. The tripartite government, (PNV, EA, and EB-B) promoted an initiative designed to obtain greater sovereignty. In 2001, the *lehendakari* Juan José Ibarretxe (PNV) put forward a proposal to the Basque parliament for a *New Political Statute for the Basque Country*. This proposal, despite being presented as a reform of the statute of autonomy, sought a new political status based on a "free association" that would have to be approved in a referendum by the Basque people. The proposal was passed by the Basque parliament in 2004 with the votes of the three governing parties and those of *Socialista Abertzaleak* (Herri Batasuna) which, despite disagreeing with the proposal, considered it opportune to support Ibarretxe's initiative.[25] However, the initiative was stopped by the lower chamber of the Spanish parliament, a majority of whom voted to reject it because of its unconstitutional nature. Both the PSOE and the PP voted against it. It was supported only by minority groups.

Subsequently, following unsuccessful negotiations with ETA held during 2006, Ibarretxe presented a second pro-sovereignty proposal to the Basque parliament that was also designed to resolve the Basque conflict. On this occasion, he presented a "road map" aimed at unblocking the negotiation, which involved conducting a plebiscite that would ratify the Basque government's negotiations with its Spanish counterpart. Ibarretxe offered the Spanish government a pact based on two ethical principles: the democratic principle (the will of Basque society) and the principle of rejection of violence.[26] In order to achieve this, the Basque government passed a Plebiscite Law[27] with the support of the PNV, EA, EB-B, Aralar, and one *abertzale* deputy; the PSE-EE and the PP voted against it. The plebiscite was to take place on October 25, 2008[28] and consisted of two questions:

> "Do you agree to support a process to achieve a negotiated end to violence, if ETA previously demonstrates its unequivocal intention to put an end to violence once and for all?"
>
> "Do you agree that the political parties of the Basque Country, without exception, initiate a process of negotiation to reach a Democratic Agreement regarding the exercising of the Basque people's right to decide for themselves, and that said Agreement be subject to a referendum before the end of the year 2010?"

The Spanish government appealed to the Constitutional Court against the law passed by the Basque parliament, which had sought protection through a number of articles of the Basque Statute and the Spanish Constitution in order to justify the legality of the plebiscite. The Constitutional Court published its ruling on September 11, 2008 (STC 103/2008) stating that the Basque law was unconstitutional, following the patterns of traditional constitutionalism and, therefore, cancelling the plebiscite announced by the Basque government and aborting Ibarretxe's "road map." The following fragment of the ruling is especially important and explicit:

> In reality, the contents of the plebiscite represent the initiation of a procedure to reconsider the established order which eventually could conclude in "a new relationship" between the State and the Autonomous Community of the Basque Country; that is, between that which, in accordance with the Constitution, is today the formal expression of a constituted order by the sovereign will of the Spanish Nation, which is unique and indivisible (Art. 2 of the Spanish Constitution), and a subject created, within the framework of the Constitution, by the constituted powers by virtue of the exercise of a right to autonomy recognised by the fundamental Law. This subject does not possess sovereign power, which is exclusive to the Nation constituted as the State. (…) The procedure that it wishes to initiate, and the repercussions that this will have, cannot fail to affect the whole of the Spanish citizenry, since said procedure would address the redefinition of the order established by the sovereign will of the Nation, whose objective is none other than the formal revision of the Constitution by means of Art. 168, that is, with the double participation of the Spanish

Parliament, as representative of the Spanish people (Art. 66.1), and the holder of sovereignty, directly, by means of the mandatory referendum of ratification (Art. 168.3).

Subsequent political events, with the end of the PNV in the Basque government after the Basque elections of 2009, have provisionally broken *institutional* pro-sovereignty demands. The new *lehendakari*, the socialist Patxi López, has expressed a wish to avoid pro-sovereignty activities and maintain the status quo.

In September 2010, the political evolution of the secessionist movement and pressure from Spanish and French security policies led ETA to declare a ceasefire. In January 2011, this ceasefire was declared permanent and verifiable by international observers. Despite the current weakness of the armed group, the reaction of the Spanish authorities has been one of cautious skepticism. Although no peace process has started, some political movements in Basque politics have proposed a new direction for the conflict. The *abertzale* secessionists have rejected violent tactics for the first time and achieved good electoral results in local elections held in May 2011 with Bildu platform. After this success, Amaiur was created to run in the Spanish elections in November 2011. Amaiur won the largest number of deputies (and the second largest number of votes) in the Basque Autonomous Community. Its leaders expressed the will to compete in the Basque elections. In spite of all these changes, at this point the Basque political conflict is still far from being solved.

Conclusion

To sum up, the Spanish state's failure over the last two centuries to accommodate the different national realities that exist within it is well known. Even in the most restricted sense, such as that embodied in expressions like the "Basque and Catalan problems," which have characterized the declarations and treatises of different political leaders and intellectuals over the last 150 years, one may at the very least detect one fact: that there is an unresolved territorial problem that mainly affects the national minorities of the state and the stability and legitimacy of the Spanish state in these territories. As has already been pointed out, the failure to resolve this issue could be described as the failure of a general process of Spanish nation-building to integrate its different internal national realities into an articulated political "union" rather than a political "unity."

In our view, as we have argued in other writings (Requejo 2005, ch. 5), the biggest design fault of the current Spanish Constitution is that it attempts to tackle two distinct issues at the same time: the decentralization of the state and the recognition/accommodation of its national pluralism (which includes the question of secession as one potential institutional element).[29] Both issues are objectives that can hardly be established through the same institutions and procedural rules as they seek to achieve very different goals. On the one hand, the Basque case shows a clash between majority and minority nationalisms and a lack of political culture capable of finding institutional formulas for the political accommodation of a nationally diverse democracy. Most political actors of both kinds of nationalism use the theory of national self-determination as their source of legitimacy, linking this theory with some elements of plebiscitary theories in the case of national minorities,[30] and with strict "legal–constitutional" considerations by Spanish nationalists. That is, political actors answer the normative questions described in the first section using elements of these two different types of theories. The final practical outcome is that the question of the "tyranny of the majority" shows an unresolved national side in Spanish plurinational democracy. Just cause theories are virtually absent from the political debate.

Furthermore, the Basque case demonstrates the limits and biases of traditional liberal and constitutional theories (Liberalism 1) when they try to deal with the national pluralism of some empirical democracies. In this sense, the three traditional kinds of theories of secession mentioned in the first section usually fail to incorporate the normative elements highlighted by Liberalism 2 associated with plurinational societies. These shortcomings affect the concepts of *individualism, universalism,* and *statism* linked to traditional liberalism and constitutionalism. In addition, in the Spanish case, these biases and shortcomings are combined with the political culture of the main Spanish political forces (PSOE and PP), which is much more unitarian than federal, and much more uninational than plurinational. It is probable that this issue will remain on the theoretical agenda of liberal-democratic theories in the near future— which should include, in our view, the aforementioned "Hegelian turn" (the fourth kind of theory of secession) in the approach to theoretical notions such as the *political recognition* and *constitutional accommodation* of national minorities in plurinational democracies (and also on the political agenda of the main political actors involved in empirical plurinational cases). These are two challenges for improving the normative and institutional quality of liberal democracies in nationally diverse societies in the twenty-first century.

Appendix

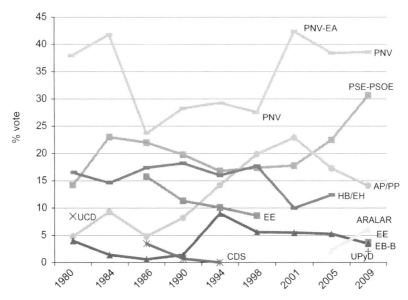

Figure 7.A1 Basque elections (1980–2009)[31]

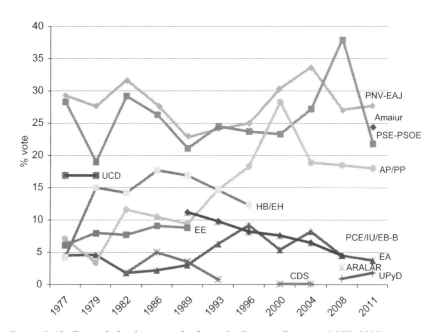

Figure 7.A2 General elections: results from the Basque Country (1977–2008)

Notes

1 The principle of national self-determination (US President Woodrow Wilson): "A free, open-minded, and absolutely impartial adjustment of all colonial claims, based upon a strict observance of the principle that in determining all such questions of sovereignty the interests of the population concerned must have equal weight with the equitable claims of the government whose title is to be determined" (Wilson 1918).

2 There is a tendency in this tradition to apply the principle of self-determination only to the states, that is to defend the status quo and the territorial integrity of existing states.

3 Political liberalism has been developed in practice in parallel with state-building and nation-building processes led by state institutions. At least to some extent, it explains the misrepresentation and marginalization of minority nations in political liberal theories until recent times.

4 These kinds of theories consider that there is no a priori right to secession, but that this right arises from the injustices suffered by a group of territorialized citizens within a state (Buchanan 1991, 2004, 2007).

5 This approach hinges on values such as freedom of association and individual autonomy, without demanding any specific cultural, linguistic, ethnic, or national characteristics of the group that wishes to secede (Beran 1984; Gauthier 1994; Philpott 1995; Wellman 1995).

6 These theories focus on an "intrinsic value" of the nation or on an instrumental "contextual sphere for individual decision" (Margalit and Raz 1990; Taylor 1992; Tamir 1993; Kymlicka 1995; Lehning 1998; Moore 1998; Nielsen 1998; Gagnon and Tully 2001; Requejo 2001, 2005, 2010a, 2010b; Tierney 2004; Norman 2006, 2011).

7 The central power maintains its hegemony through the so called *leyes de bases* and *leyes orgánicas* (base and constitutional laws), which are the same throughout the state and have been developed in a centralizing way in many areas in the post-constitutional period (education, local power, civil servants, universities, etc.).

8 The majority of the senators are elected by the "provinces," a set of administrative divisions that date back to the nineteenth century.

9 The Basque Country and Navarre are the exceptions to this rule as they enjoy an asymmetrical fiscal agreement with the central power, based on a number of "historical rights," which are regulated under terms that are more confederal than federal.

10 The twelve magistrates are elected by the lower and upper houses of the Spanish parliament, the central government, and the General Council of the Judicial Power (the judges' governing body). None of these institutions is related to the territorial model.

11 An analysis of the elements that differentiate the Spanish system from federations, in Requejo (2005, chs 5 and 6).

12 For an approach to the accommodation of nationally plural societies from the perspective of political theory, see Kymlicka (2001), Requejo (2001, 2011), and McGarry (2002).

13 The term "Basque Country" is used here to refer only to the Basque Autonomous Community (CAV), which is the administrative entity made up of the provinces of Álava, Vizcaya, and Guipúzcoa. However, Basque nationalists use the term Euskal Herria to refer to all the territory of the Basque nation which, in addition to the CAV, includes Navarre (another Spanish autonomous community) and also the provinces located within the French state: Nafarroa Beherea, Lapurdi, and Zuberoa (see Figure 7.2).

14 The current population of the CAV is 2.1 million inhabitants (Catalonia 7.3; Spain 46.1; INE July 2011). The presence of foreign immigrants is relatively low in the

Basque Country (4.6 percent) (Catalonia: 16.2 percent, Idescat 2011; Spain: 12.3 percent, Eurostat 2010). In contrast to Catalonia, the Basque Country maintained its historical legal privileges (*Fueros*) after the War of the Spanish Succession (at the beginning of the eighteenth century). These *Fueros* were also maintained in the provinces of Álava and Navarre in the Francoist period for having backed the coup against the Republican regime. This historical reference to the *Fueros* has been included in the Spanish Constitution (1978), and has become the basis for the asymmetrical fiscal agreement known as the *concierto económico* (economic agreement).

15 In the local elections of May 2011, Bildu became the second political force in the Basque Country, after the PNV, and the first in number of councilors.

16 Militants from the PNV are normally called *jeltzales*. Literally, this name means "supporters of JEL" and comes from the motto of the PNV "*Jaungoikoa Eta Lagizarrak*" (God and Old Laws).

17 In 1994, Euzkadiko Ezquerra, a Basque leftist nationalist organization, joined the socialist party, changing its official name to PSE-EE.

18 A judicial process, widely reported in the international press, in which General Franco's regime conducted a court martial involving sixteen people accused of belonging to ETA and having carried out violent acts.

19 Spanish Interior Ministry, at www.mir.es/DGRIS/Terrorismo_de_ETA/ultimas_victi mas/p12b-esp.htm.

20 Etxerat: Listado de Presos Políticos Vascos, at www.etxerat.info/orokor.php? id_saila=10&id_edukia=31&lang=es.

21 This pact was signed on September 12, 1998 by the Basque nationalist parties (PNV, EA, and Batasuna) and also EB-B. Following the Peace Agreements in Northern Ireland, it was agreed that negotiations should take place without prior conditions and in the absence of violence.

22 The law was drawn up ad hoc in order to make the *abertzale* left illegal. A number of Basque nationalist parties and Izquierda Unida expressed their disagreement with the law because they considered that it violated the civil rights of part of society. Amnesty International also expressed its concern (www.es.amnesty.org/ com/2002/com_03jun02.shtm).

23 The title of the proposal was *Orain herria, orain bakea* (Now the people, now peace). The event was held at San Sebastian and was attended by 15,000 people. The Spanish public prosecutor's office began legal actions against the organizers, considering it to be an event organized by an illegal political group.

24 The title of the document presented in Venice was *A first step towards the democratic process, principles and will of the abertzale left*. Batasuna presented this latest document as a separate proposal from ETA's strategy.

25 The result in the Basque Parliament was thirty-nine votes in favor and thirty-five against.

26 Therefore, both proposals made by Ibarretxe's government were not strictly secessionist. They combined a set of confederal and partnership rules for a new "free association" with the Spanish state. This will of establishing an "association" has been criticized by Batasuna. See IVAP (2003).

27 "Law 9/2008, of 27 June, for the official announcement and regulation of a plebiscite in order to obtain the opinion of the citizens of the Basque Autonomous Community regarding the opening of a process of negotiation to achieve peace and political normalization."

28 This was a particularly significant date as it was the anniversary of the passing of the former Statute of Autonomy (Gernika Statute, 1979).

29 An analysis of the relationship between economics and identity in the Basque Country, in Costa and Tremosa (2008). See also the collective work by Buesa (2004) (in Spanish).

30 In recent years, different political movements have favored a generic "right to decide" in Catalonia and in the Basque Country. In practice, the Spanish

Constitution prohibits the Autonomous Communities from organizing referendums. These referendums require the compulsory formal permission of the president of the Spanish government to be implemented.

31 *Euskobarómetro. Elecciones País Vasco (1977–2009)* (http://alweb.ehu.es/euskobar ometro/). Percentages achieved in the lower chamber (Congreso de los Diputados) and the Basque parliament.

References

Beran, H. (1984), 'A Liberal Theory of Secession' *Political Studies*, XXXII: 21–31.

Buchanan, A. (1991, 'Toward a Theory of Secession' *Ethics*, 101: 322–342.

——(2004), *Justice, Legitimacy, and Self-Determination: Moral Foundations for International Law*, Oxford: Oxford University Press.

——(2007), *Justice, Legitimacy and Self-Determination. Moral Foundations for International Law*, Oxford, Oxford University Press.

Buesa, M. (2004), *Economía de la secesión. El proyecto nacionalista y el País Vasco*, Madrid, Instituto de Estudios Fiscales.

Costa, J. and Tremosa, R. (2008), 'Support for State Opting Out and Stateless National Identity in the Basque Country' *The Journal of Socio-Economics*, 37: 2464–2477.

Díez Medrano, J. (1999), *Naciones Divididas. Clase, Política y Nacionalismo en el País Vasco y Cataluña*, Centro de Investigaciones Sociológicas.

Elazar, D. (1991), *Federal Systems of the World*, Harlow, Essex, Longman.

Gagnon, A. and Tully, J. (eds) (2001), *Plurinational Democracies*, Cambridge, Cambridge University Press.

Gauthier, D. (1994), 'Breaking Up: An Essay on Secession' *Canadian Journal of Philosophy*, 24: 357–372.

Hirschman, A.O. (1970), *Exit, Voice and Royalty Responses to Decline in Firms, Organizations, and States*, Cambridge, Cambridge University Press.

IVAP (2003), *Estudios sobre la propuesta política para la convivencia del Lehendakari Ibarretxe*, Oñati.

Kymlicka, W. (1995), *Multicultural Citizenship. A Liberal Theory of Minority Rights*, Oxford, Clarendon Press.

——(2001), *Politics in the Vernacular*, Oxford, Oxford University Press.

Lehning, P. (ed.) (1998), *Theories of Secession*, London, Routledge.

Margalit, A. and Raz, J. (1990), 'National Self-Determination' in J. Raz, *Ethics in the Public Domain, Essays in the Morality of Law and Politics*, Oxford, Clarendon.

McGarry, J., (2002), 'Federal Political Systems and the Accommodation of National Minorities, in K. Neremberg and A. Griffiths (eds), *Handbook of Federal Countries*, Montreal and Kingston, McGill-Queen's University Press.

Moore, M. (ed.) (1998), *National Self-Determination and Secession*, Oxford, Oxford University Press.

Nagel, J. and Requejo, F. (2007), 'El debate sobre la relación entre centro y autonomías en España' in W. Benecker and G. Maihold (eds), *España: del consenso a la polarización*, Iberoamericana/Vervuert, pp. 265–295.

Neremberg, K. and Griffiths, A. (eds) (2002), *Handbook of Federal Countries*, Montreal and Kingston, McGill-Queen's University Press (new edition 2005).

Nielsen, K. (1998), 'Liberal Nationalism and Secession' in M. Moore (ed.), *National Self-Determination and Secession*, Oxford, Oxford University Press.

126 *F. Requejo and M. Sanjaume i Calvet*

Norman, W. (2006), *Negotiating Nationalism*, Oxford, Oxford University Press.

——(2011), 'From Quid Pro Quo to Modus Vivendi: Can Legalizing Secession Strengthen the Plurinational Federation?' in Requejo-Caminal (eds), *Political Liberalism and Plurinational Democracies*, London, Routledge.

Philpott, D. (1995), 'In Defense of Self-Determination' *Ethics*, 105: 352–385.

Requejo, F. (ed.) (2001), *Democracy and National Pluralism*, London and New York, Routledge.

——(2005), *Plurinational Federalism and Value Pluralism*, London and New York, Routledge.

——(2010a), 'Federalism and Democracy. The Case of Minority Nations: a Federalist Deficit' in M. Burgess and A. Gagnon (eds), *Federal Democracies*, London, Routledge.

——(2010b), 'Revealing the Dark Side of Traditional Democracies in Plurinational Societies', *Nations and Nationalism*, London School of Economics, vol. 16, no. 1, January.

——(2011), 'The Crooked Timber of Liberal Democracies is Still Too Straight', in N. Walker, B. Shaw and S. Tierney (eds), *Europe's Constitutional Mosaic*, Oxford, Hart Publishing.

——(2012), 'Three Theories of Liberalism for Three Theories of Federalism. A Hegelian Turn' in M. Seymour (ed.), *Multinational Federalism: Problems and Prospects*, Palgrave Macmillan (forthcoming).

Requejo, F. and Caminal, M. (eds) (2011), *Political Liberalism and Plurinational Democracies*, London and New York, Routledge.

Secession of Quebec (1998), 2 S.C.R. 217, Supreme Court of Canada.

Tamir, Y. (1993), *Liberal Nationalism*, Princeton, NJ, Princeton University Press.

Taylor, Ch. (1992), 'The Politics of Recognition' in *Multiculturalism and the Politics of Recognition*, Princeton, NJ, Princeton University Press.

Tierney, S. (2004), *Constitutional Law and National Pluralism*, Oxford, Oxford University Press.

Watts, R. (1999), *Comparing Federal Systems*, Montreal and Kingston, McGill-Queen's University Press.

Wellman, C.H. (1995), 'A Defence of Secession and Political Self-Determination' *Philosophy and Public Affairs*, 24(2): 142–171.

Wilson, W. (1918), *The Fourteen Points*, The Avalon Project, Yale Law School.

8 Nationalism, unionism and secession in Scotland

Michael Keating

On 30 November 2009, the nationalist government of Scotland published a white paper providing for a referendum on independence (Scottish Government 2009c) and, 16 months later, was elected by a stunning majority. This represented the culmination of a 40-year campaign to put this issue to the forefront of the Scottish political agenda, starting with the nationalist revival of the 1960s, and might prefigure the break-up of Britain, were it not for the strange circumstance that support for independence in Scotland had actually been falling.

In a longer perspective, the question of Scotland's constitutional status has always been open. It was united with England in 1707 in a parliamentary union that guaranteed the minimum of unity required for the security of the state, but leaving large parts of Scottish civil society and administration untouched. Since then, there have been successive waves of integration and differentiation, pushing now for the creation of a unified British nation and now for a clearly plurinational union. The outcome was a compromise allowing for Scottish nationhood within a British nation and state and an elaborate series of mechanisms for managing Scottish affairs within a unitary parliament. These included the maintenance of Scottish law, the established Church (vitally important in another era) and, from the late nineteenth century, a Secretary of State and department (the Scottish Office) charged with administering British policy in Scotland. The question of sovereignty was kept open, with the dominant Westminster doctrine, elaborated by Blackstone and Dicey as being that the central parliament was omnicompetent, while a rival Scottish doctrine insisted that, the old Scottish parliament never having asserted absolute sovereignty, it could not have transferred it to the new British one. Hence, an element of popular or original sovereignty rested in Scotland (MacCormick 1999). The union may have been, as McLean and McMillan (2005) claim, 'intellectually incoherent', but it served its purpose for 300 years in keeping Scotland within the polity.

Historically, there have been three strands of constitutional opinion in Scotland: unionist; nationalist or independence-seeking; and home rule or devolutionist. Scottish (and more widely UK) unionism is a complex ideology very different from state-based or centralist ideologies elsewhere in Europe (Ward 2005; Kidd 2008). Unionists do not deny Scottish nationhood or the plurinational nature of the polity; indeed, they can be among the most enthusiastic exponents of a kind of cultural nationalism. Nor do they seek to suppress the distinct institutions of Scottish civil society and administration; rather, they see the Union as the best framework in which to maintain these. On the other hand, they have been resolutely opposed to any concession of self-government to the constituent nations, precisely because they are nations and would therefore use autonomous political institutions to assert claims to sovereignty (Dicey 1912; Wilson 1970). Another strand of unionism, associated with the Labour Party and sections of the left, opposed home rule as divisive of the working class and a threat to the unified welfare state created during the twentieth century and especially after World War Two.

Nationalists are usually identified as those in favour of independence, although the word is often used more widely and loosely. Home rulers seek self-government within some wider plurinational or federal structures; from the late twentieth century, devolution became the most common term for this, although it has rather weaker connotations than the older terminology of home rule. In constitutional theory, the distinction between independence and home rule is normally clear, as is the difference between an independent and a federated state. In the United Kingdom, however, the difference has been clear only at particular times and, for most of the last 100 years, the boundary between the two has been rather fluid. In the late nineteenth century, home rulers invariably placed their project in the context of the Empire, seeing Scotland's future as a dominion in an imperial federation, or sometimes as a second mother country alongside England. In the event, the dominions (Canada, Australia, New Zealand, South Africa and Ireland) were to evolve into independent states, especially after the Statute of Westminster in 1931, but this was not apparent earlier – we need to remember that the Irish Civil War was fought over the issue of whether Ireland would be a dominion or an independent republic. In the 1930s, when the first separate Scottish nationalist parties emerged, they were quite ambivalent on independence, and John McCormick, a leading figure in nationalist politics in the 1930s and 1940s, moved easily between nationalist and home rule politics. His son, Neil McCormick, professor of constitutional law at Edinburgh, was a Scottish National Party (SNP) activist who produced some of the most sophisticated work on divided sovereignty and was also at ease in both nationalist and home rule circles. For some nationalists (the gradualists), the question was a tactical one, with home rule seen as a staging post towards independence. Others (the fundamentalists) saw home rule as a distraction, which could undermine support for the cause, and insisted that independence would come in one step.

The campaign for a Scottish Assembly (later parliament) and subsequent Scottish Constitutional Convention during the 1980s and 1990s attracted both nationalists and home rulers, although the SNP officially stayed aloof. At one point, it even persuaded all but one of the Scottish Labour MPs to sign the Declaration of Right asserting that sovereignty lay with the Scottish people. This did not stop these same MPs later voting through the Scotland Act of 1998, which asserted the opposite (that Westminster remains supreme).

In 1997, the incoming Labour government sought to resolve this old argument by providing for Scottish devolution, after a referendum in which the proposals gained the support of some three-quarters of the voters. The triumph of the home rule option briefly seemed to clarify matters. Old unionism was dead, as all the parties accepted the new dispensation. On the nationalist side, the slogan for a short while was 'we are all fundamentalists now', united on the next stage of their journey. As we will see below, the question was not to be disposed of so easily, and there remain major ambiguities in the independence prospectus and over the differences between secession and reinforced home rule.

Becoming independent

Theories of secession pose a series of ethical, legal/constitutional and practical questions about independence. It is remarkable how few of these apply in the Scottish case. There is almost no debate about whether Scotland has the right to self-determination. Conservative Prime Minister John Major (1993) declared that no nation could be kept in a union against its will, while even Margaret Thatcher (1993, 624) conceded that, 'As a nation, they (the Scots) have an undoubted right to national self-determination; thus far they have exercised that right by joining and remaining in the Union. Should they determine on independence no English party or politician would stand in their way, however much we might regret their departure.' What Major and Thatcher, as staunch unionists, ruled out was home rule within the UK. Labour politicians have been less explicit but, in recent years, no senior representative of the party has denied Scotland's right to independence in principle.

There are no internal minorities in Scotland identifying with the host state so strongly as to demand an opt-out. English people living in Scotland have seen little need to ethnicize or minoritize themselves, even in response to independence proposals, and the Irish, previously the most visible minority, have largely been assimilated. There is no argument about the land borders and even the argument about sea borders (important because of the oil reserves) seems now to have a fairly clear solution. With the advent of the SNP government in 2007 (albeit as a minority), the legitimacy of seeking independence as a policy objective was accepted to the point that civil servants in the Scottish government, who remain part of a unified British civil service, had no qualms in helping ministers write their independence white paper and accompanying documents.

Nor are there legal or political obstacles to independence. Unionists have been hoist on their own petard in insisting on the absolute sovereignty of parliament as this must include the ability to dissolve the union itself. In the early twentieth century, the constitutional lawyer A.V. Dicey tried unconvincingly to get out of this dilemma with regard to Ireland, but nobody has suggested that a Westminster Act giving independence to Scotland would be unconstitutional. At one time, SNP policy was that winning a majority of the

Scottish seats in Westminster would give them a mandate to negotiate independence, but the advent of the Scottish parliament has changed the locus of interest. Their policy now is that a referendum, to be decided by simple majority, would give the Scottish government a mandate for independence. Although the constitution and the union between England and Scotland are clearly among the 'reserved' matters, outwith the competence of the Scottish parliament, the unionist parties have not chosen to contest the legality of a referendum. Legally, this would be merely consultative, but politically it would be binding.

Political obstacles might also be fewer than in other countries. Electors in England do not think about the Union very often but, when they do, they seem to have become rather relaxed about its future. Opinion polls have consistently shown that opinion in England on Scottish independence is close to Scottish opinion on the same question. If there is an anti-Scottish undertone in English opinion, it is not expressed in an insistence that Scots stay in the Union, but rather in a willingness to let them go. There is more resentment over the perceived prominence of Scots in London (on the make), although efforts by English politicians to get their electors exercised about the West Lothian question (the ability of Scottish MPs to vote on English matters) or the Barnett formula[1] (determining Scottish expenditure levels) have had a limited impact. Unlike electors in Spain outside the historic nationalities or those in Canada outside Quebec, English voters do not, by and large, see the retention of Scotland in the Union as essential for their own national identity or national project. There is a strong unitarist tradition in England, which sees the UK, rather confusedly, as a unitary state or greater England with which the peripheral parts have a contingent relationship. The habit of speaking of England and English instead of Britain and British, while irritating to the Scots, is revealing. So for many people in England, Scottish secession, leaving England (perhaps with Wales although they do not think much about this either) as a unitary state, would be preferable to transforming the UK into a full federation, in which the non-English parts would have an institutional role. This attitude is also extending to elite opinion, previously steeped in unionist ideology. A 2009 survey of parliamentary candidates for the Conservative Party, the quintessential party of union, showed that almost half of them (46 per cent) would not be uncomfortable were Scotland to become independent (Conservativehome 2009).

Practical difficulties, on the other hand, could loom large. The UK is an integrated welfare state, and matters such as state pensions and pensions for public sector workers would be extremely difficult to disentangle and allocate. Assets and liabilities would have to be calculated. The SNP's position is that it should not assume any share of UK debt, as Scotland's part has already been paid off in the oil revenues collected by central government since the 1980s. London will insist on a share recognizing Scotland's higher levels of public expenditure and investment. It is likely that there will be a compromise on a population-based share, just as there was in the hypothetical Quebec case (Young 1995).

The independence of Scotland 131

Independence would have to be preceded by negotiations on all this, but it is not clear just who the negotiating parties would be. A nationalist government in Scotland would face opposition in the Scottish parliament from unionist parties, themselves part of British-wide parties and presumably following a common British strategy. The UK government would (especially if it were a Labour government) include Scottish ministers. Between 2007 and 2010, the Prime Minister himself was a Scottish MP, who would have been in a poor position to negotiate for the rest of the UK. Were a Conservative government to be in power at the time, with little or no representation in Scotland (as is the case for the Conservatives since 1997), matters might be clearer, although not necessarily easier.

The economics of independence

There is endless dispute about how well Scotland has done under the Union. It appears that things went rather badly at first, but that, from the late eighteenth century, Scotland benefited from being part of the expanding British and imperial markets. By the end of the nineteenth century, Scotland's heavy industries in particular benefited from free trade and the UK's strong geo-economic position. After World War One, there was a drastic downturn, and Scotland's share of British production fell sharply in the 1920s and during the depression of the 1930s. The labour movement, hitherto favourable to home rule, turned sharply to unionism (Keating and Bleiman 1979), and the distinct Scottish industrial bourgeoisie entered into a long decline as firms were taken over by competitors from the south or from abroad. There was some recovery during World War Two but, from the 1950s, relative decline resumed, with respite coming only with the resumption of UK regional policy in the 1960s and then North Sea oil. Scottish politics came to revolve around managed dependency, with a cross-party and cross-class Scottish lobby emerging to seek favourable treatment from the British government. This included politicians and the civil servants within the Scottish Office. Home rule ideas, while not always abandoned in principle, were shunned on the grounds that they would imperil this lobby and Scotland's privileged position at the centre.

It has often been assumed (Weight 2002) that Scottish nationalism is the product of economic discontent and will flourish in hard times. In practice, the opposite is true. It is in times of relative prosperity that Scots develop enough optimism to feel that they can go it alone. In bad times, they cleave to the unionist parties, who promise to go to London for help and to use the powers and resources of the UK state. Hence, Scottish nationalism thrived in the late nineteenth century and up to World War One (in the form of the home rule movement) but fell away in the 1930s. The foundation of the first explicitly nationalist parties in those years is not a sign of strength but an indication that nationalists were getting nowhere in the political mainstream. Nationalism and home rule activity picked up during and after World War Two, but had to compete with a revived British nationalism, which was the product of the war itself. During the straitened times of the 1950s, nationalism faded away, to pick up again in the 1960s and 1970s. The recession of the 1980s took nationalism almost back to where it was before the great revival, but it picked up again in the 1990s. Figure 8.1 allows us to track this against movements in relative Scottish economic prosperity.

There are equally fraught debates about whether Scotland benefits from net fiscal transfers within the Union. Calculation is difficult but, in recent years, a data series has been available from the Scottish Office and then the Scottish government, compiled by civil servants without political control – Government Expenditure and Revenues in Scotland (GERS). These have been continually revised as the methodology has been criticized and improved. Although their interpretation is still contested, GERS generally shows that Scotland has enjoyed above-average levels of expenditure compared with the other nations in the UK. The question then is whether Scotland currently pays its way. On the income side, complications arise from the calculation of North Sea oil revenues, and GERS now provides figures without oil and with varying shares of oil revenues credited to Scotland. Even here, one can argue both ways. Oil production peaked in the mid-1980s when revenues amounted to half the non-oil gross domestic product (GDP) of Scotland, then fell away. Nationalists argue that, if all the oil revenues over the last 30 years are calculated,

Figure 8.1 Scottish GDP as a percentage of the UK figure (1924–2006)
Sources: Lythe and Majmudar (1982) GDP factor cost, 1954–1979; Office of National Statistics, GVA 1996–2004; McCrone (1965, 1969); *Regional Trends*, various years; *Abstract of Regional Statistics*

Scotland is in the black. Unionists point to current oil revenues which, until very recently, were not enough to fill the notional deficit. More sophisticated nationalists argue that an independent Scotland could have made better use of the revenues over 30 years, investing them or putting them into a future fund or legacy projects rather than using them as current expenditure to sustain a consumption boom. If the revenues had been used in this way, then they could not also be counted against Scotland's notional current budget deficit.

The calculations about how well Scotland does out of the Union have become so complex and contested that, to some degree, the two sides have cancelled each other out and, at least until the current economic crisis, the issue had ceased to drive judgements about independence. Surveys have shown that the proportion of people thinking that Scotland does badly out of the Union and wanting independence are about the same, but that there is only about a 50 per cent overlap between the two groups (Keating 2009). This leaves a hard core or less than a fifth for whom economic grievance might drive support for independence.

These considerations are all based on static analysis of how Scotland might do under independence, all else remaining the same. A dynamic analysis takes into account other changes as well as the economic policies an independent Scotland could or would pursue. But the macro-economic options for an independent Scotland closely tied to UK and European markets and monetary policies would be limited. One idea favoured by the SNP is that an independent Scotland could cut business taxes and attract inward investment, imitating the Irish success of earlier years. In practice, the scope for this is limited, and a tax-cutting strategy is not compatible with maintaining a developed welfare state such as Scotland has.

The external support system

European integration has transformed the nationalities question across the continent by providing a new level of regulation and polity-building and putting into question the old idea of national sovereignty (Keating 2004). For some nationalists, this lowers the threshold for secession, providing a new external support system and dealing with difficult matters such as market access, the currency, borders and (together with NATO) defence policy. Others draw more radical conclusions, arguing that the whole concept of sovereignty needs to be rethought so that independence itself makes little sense. For post-sovereigntists, what matters is gaining the powers and resources needed for their social and economic project, and exercising influences in those forums where decisions affecting them are taken. Post-sovereigntist ideas have often taken root where there are historical traditions or a 'usable past' of shared sovereignty and negotiated order. Scottish nationalism contains examples of both perspectives. In the nineteenth century, home rule was often placed in the context of empire and, after World War Two, there was some sympathy for the European project. During the 1960s and 1970s, the SNP campaigned against joining the European Communities, although there was some dissent in the

134   *M. Keating*

ranks during the European referendum of 1975. In 1988, however, they did an about-turn (at the same time as the Labour Party did) to accept Europe as an integral part of the independence package. Some nationalists embraced the post-sovereigntist perspective, arguing that the old independence demand was now largely irrelevant and should give way to a confederal vision in which Scotland would negotiate its status within the British, European and other unions. A usable past is available in the form of Scottish political and legal understandings, which deny the doctrine of absolute parliamentary sovereignty that underpins Westminster practice.[2] The official SNP position, however, is that Scotland will become a full member state of the European Union (EU); and generally speaking, it prefers the intergovernmental to the supra-national vision of the EU itself.

There has been some debate as to whether Scotland would automatically be admitted to the EU. Happold (1999) and Murkens (2002) consider that the remainder of the UK would be regarded as a successor state and inherit all the international obligations and privileges whereas Scotland would have to apply anew. Others, however, have argued that the UK was created by the Treaty of Union and would dissolve if it were repealed. As a practical matter, few people seriously think that the EU would effectively seek to expel part of its existing territory that is fully compliant with the *acquis communautaire*. The question rather hinges on the process of accession and whether one or both successor parts of the UK would have to re-join. What is clear is that Scotland, whether remaining in as a successor state or joining as a new member, would have to accept the *acquis*. Special dispensations and opt-outs are only available to existing members at the time of negotiating new policies. Yet the SNP proposes to pick and choose which policies it will accept, notably refusing to take on the Common Fisheries Policy. It seems to have a vision of an *à la carte* Europe that is at odds with the whole spirit of the European project (although ironically it is a very British attitude).

The SNP has now abandoned all ideas of having its own currency, but is divided over whether to adopt the euro or retain the pound sterling. Officially, the policy is to keep the pound but have a referendum at some time on the euro. In practice, however, joining the euro requires a programme of convergence over several years and is not something that can be decided in the short term. Scotland also has a dilemma over the Schengen passport-free travel zone, which the UK has opted out of. If they join Schengen, they would need to establish a border with England. If they keep the border with England open, they cannot join Schengen.

There is a strong pacifist and anti-nuclear tradition in Scottish nationalism, and SNP policy is to withdraw from NATO and expel the British nuclear bases from Scotland (the US nuclear bases have already left). This policy, however, has been weakening, and it is likely that an independent Scotland would remain in NATO; the latest party thinking even contemplates allowing the UK military to keep the (non-nuclear) bases. As the SNP government sought to build a broader consensus around its independence proposals, it has floated various other proposals for cooperating with the remaining UK, including shared embassy services and an enhanced form of common citizenship with what it calls rUK, going beyond the existing European citizenship (Scottish Government 2009a). In the same paper, it seeks to downplay the costs of establishing its own diplomatic representation, claiming that this would create valuable jobs!

The wider question of Scotland's place in its neighbourhood has not been explored systematically. Independent or not, Scotland finds itself in much the same geo-political, geo-strategic and geo-economic position as an Atlantic and European periphery caught between competing poles. There is the UK pole which, as Ireland has found, will continue to be important. There is the European pole, focused on the EU. Scotland faces the choice of following England in a semi-detached relationship or of seeking entry into the core. There is the North Atlantic pole, dominated by the US, although British governments have insisted, with ever less plausibility, on a special relationship that allows them a real influence in this sphere. There is a weaker northern European pole, expressed in the Nordic grouping, which the SNP tried to extend into the concept of the 'arc of prosperity' to encompass Ireland during its boom times.

Public opinion

From the available survey data, it appears that support for Scottish independence ran at around 20 per cent during the 1960s and 1970s and notably failed to rise much when the SNP made its first electoral breakthroughs, taking 30 per cent of the vote and eleven seats in the General Election of October 1974. From the second term of the Thatcher government, which built up huge parliamentary majorities while steadily losing support in Scotland, support for independence started to rise to around 30 per cent. It remained at this level until, strangely enough, the victory of the SNP in the Scottish elections of 2007, since when it has fallen. This is not because of disillusion with the new government. Support for independence was already falling as support for the SNP was rising and as the new administration continued to do well in the polls. It seems, rather, that respondents chose independence as their preferred option in reaction to a perceived democratic and legitimacy deficit under the Conservatives and a certain frustration with continued unionist government under Labour. Getting an SNP government committed to fighting for Scotland lessens the urgency of independence and, for some voters, may actually be a substitute. It may be that Scotland is reverting to historic form and moving back to unionism as a result of the economic recession, but the decline in support for independence in fact preceded the economic crisis.

More light is shed on the matter when we consider the wording posed in surveys about independence. Attitudes are very sensitive to the wording of the question (as they are in other stateless nations), with 'harder' options mentioning 'separate' or 'separation' gaining less support. They are also affected

136   M. Keating

by the presentation of options. For many years, a straight question about whether the respondent would vote for independence has gained substantially more support than one that compares independence with various options for devolution. Before 1999, this might be explained by some devolution voters treating independence as their second preference to direct Westminster rule. Since 1999, however, devolution has been the default option so that anyone voting against independence would in effect be voting for devolution. The anti-independence vote should thus logically be a constant. Between 1998 and 2002, ICM asked in the same survey a question about the range of constitutional options and a straight question about independence. About half of respondents consistently supported independence in the straight choice but, when a devolutionary alternative was presented, independence support fell to around a third; this was despite the fact that devolution was now the only alternative to independence. It seems that voters do not make a clear distinction between independence and more devolution but tend in their majority to want more self-government, leading them to favour change away from the status quo and towards more autonomist options. It also appears that, as elsewhere, many voters like independence as a general idea but are not so sure about it as a concrete proposition, as it has to be weighed against other considerations.

Even an apparently straight question asking about Yes or No to independence provokes different responses, depending on exactly how it is put. A question from ICM has asked:

> In a referendum on independence for Scotland, how would you vote? I agree that Scotland should be become an independent country. I do not agree that Scotland should become an independent country.

Between 1998 and 2009, this has gained the support of between 40 and 56 per cent of respondents.

After the election of the SNP government, TNS/System 3 reminded respondents of the SNP promise to hold a referendum and used the SNP's preferred question:

> I agree that the Scottish Government should negotiate a settlement with the Government of the UK so that Scotland becomes an independent state.

This is a harder question as it presents independence as an imminent prospect and mentions the word 'state'.[3] This question gained about 33–40 per cent support in 2007–2010.

YouGov has asked an even harder question, which uses the word 'separate' and reminds people that a No vote still leaves them with the Scottish parliament:

> If there were a referendum on whether to retain the Scottish Parliament and Executive in more or less their present form or to establish a completely separate state outside the United Kingdom, how would you vote?

During 2007–2008, this gained the support of between 25 and 27 per cent.

Taking polls as close together as possible suggests that the wording is indeed critical. ICM and YouGov polls were 16–20 points apart in their estimates of independence support in the spring of 2007.

A more consistent measure is provided by the Scottish Social Attitudes Survey (SSAS), which offers a 'hard' version of independence ('separate from the UK'); a Scottish Parliament with tax-raising powers; the present parliament; and no parliament:

> Which of these statements comes closest to your view? Scotland should become independent, separate from the UK and the European Union. Scotland should become independent, separate from the UK but part of the European Union. Scotland should remain part of the UK, with its own elected parliament which has some taxation powers. Scotland should remain part of the UK, with its own elected parliament which has no taxation powers. Scotland should remain part of the UK without an elected parliament.

The offer of more powerful devolution again depresses independence support. Support for independence increased slowly from 29 per cent in 1999 to 34 per cent in 2005, but fell away to 23 per cent in 2007, rising to 28 per cent in 2010 (Figure 8.2).

The last 30 years have seen a shift in national identities in Scotland, away from more British ones and towards more Scottish ones. The clearest evidence is provided in the Linz/Moreno question asked at various times since the

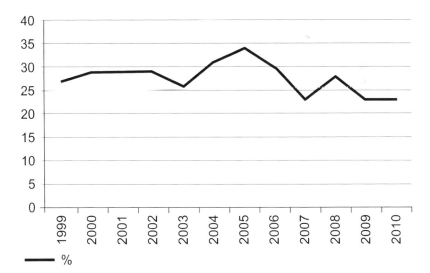

Figure 8.2 Support for independence in Scotland (1999–2010)
Source: Scottish Social Attitudes Survey.

1980s, and in the Scottish Social Attitudes Survey since 1992, in which respondents are asked about the degree to which they feel British or Scottish. The responses are shown in Figure 8.3. Given a straight choice between Scottish and British, the proportion choosing Scottish rose from 65 per cent in 1974 to peak at 80 per cent in 2000 and has since fluctuated between 72 and 80 per cent. The decline in Britishness in Scotland is not therefore linked to devolution (Heath and Roberts 2008).

Further probing reveals that these figures encompass a shifting relationship between Scottishness and other identities. Scots, particularly those identifying as Scottish, have been more likely to describe themselves as working class, irrespective of their objective occupational class (Brown et al. 1999; Surridge 2003), although most people are now reluctant to place themselves in a social class at all. Not surprisingly, SNP voters overwhelmingly prioritize their Scottish identity (that is, feeling only Scottish or more Scottish than British), but so do two-thirds of Labour voters, a majority of Liberal Democrats and nearly half of Conservatives (SSAS 2005). On the other hand, Scottishness has not displaced Britishness completely, and nearly half of even SNP supporters

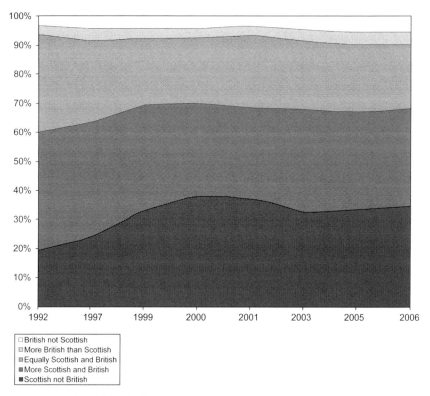

Figure 8.3 National identity in Scotland (1992–2006)
Source: Scottish Social Attitudes Survey.

retain some British identity or take pride in the British past (Bechhofer and McCrone 2007). Only at the extremes is there a real polarization, with more than half of those strongly repudiating Britain's past supporting independence against a fifth of those who were very proud, but these numbers are small, and the great majority of the population take moderate positions on both questions (SSAS 2005).

Identity, however, does not impact directly on political behaviour, or else Scots would be voting massively for the nationalist party. Most Scots are able to link Britishness and Scottishness, but a minority see them as exclusive. For some people, Scottishness is a cultural and historical identity, with no particular relevance to present-day constitutional issues. At the other extreme, some link being Scottish directly to support for independence. These identities are also linked in complex ways to class and other identities, which may undermine or reinforce the national one.

It seems, then, that there has been a shift in political identities away from the Union and towards a more Scottish perspective, but this has not created a nationalist, let alone secessionist, hegemony. The shift is not the product of increased social and economic differentiation between Scotland and England as, on almost all indicators, there has been steady convergence over recent decades. Nor does it reflect differences in values or policy preferences, as these two are remarkably similar (Rosie and Bond 2007). It is the case, rather, that Scotland is being rebuilt as a political community and a site for the realization of universal values. Opposition to Thatcherism and its continuation into the 1990s was linked to nationalism and support for constitutional change, not because England embraced Thatcherism and Scotland did not, but because in Scotland national identity was available as a vehicle for opposition, at a time when class identities no longer did the trick. This construction of Scottish nationality also explains the failure of unionists to combat nationalism by insisting on such 'British' values as democracy, fair play and social solidarity. The problem is not that of trying to build a national project on what are in fact universal values. Rather, it is in building a British national project on exactly the same values as the Scottish one, which seems to have stolen a march on it. We are thus faced with what Stéphane Dion (1991), writing about Quebec, called de Tocqueville's paradox of political divergence in the face of cultural convergence.

The best interpretation of what seem like confused data is that Scotland is increasingly salient as the primary political community for its citizens, but that they largely reject the nation-state option. Like electors in other stateless nations, they do not see a stark difference between independence and enhanced self-government in a looser federal or confederal union. They have arrived at the post-sovereigntist position ahead of most of the political parties. Closer reading of the data, where they are available, show that they do indeed want more autonomy in most domestic policy matters but are little interested in their own currency, defence policy or seat at the United Nations.

140   *M. Keating*

In the Scottish Social Attitudes data, there is some connection between attitudes to Europe and on Scottish constitutional issues, but it is rather loose. Attitudes to Europe range from the Europhile through the Eurosceptic (wanting to stay in the EU but reduce its powers) to wanting to withdraw from the EU altogether. Those few who favour Scottish independence *outwith* the EU are, of course, very Eurosceptic, as are the small number who want to reverse devolution altogether (SSAS 1999, 2000, 2003, 2005), but in neither group does a majority actually want to withdraw from the EU (although of course Scottish independence *without* Europe – the EU – entails precisely this). Supporters of Scottish independence *in* Europe are less inclined than others to want to withdraw from the EU (although oddly some 5 per cent consistently choose this option), but tend to be moderate Eurosceptics, wanting to stay in the EU but reduce its powers. Working class voters, a key part of the nationalist constituency, are less inclined to both Euroscepticism and Europhilia, whereas small businesspeople, another (albeit not numerous) pool of SNP support, are highly sceptical about Europe (McCrone 2006).

The nationalist project to shift the electorate away from supporting Scottish autonomy within a British union to a coherent project of independence within the EU has therefore had limited impact, albeit important in some sectors of the population.

The evolution of devolution

Public opinion is not favourable to independence but wants more home rule, and both nationalist and unionist parties have moved in this direction. The SNP have softened the secessionist message by talking vaguely of a continuing 'social union' and, more recently, by proposing various joint institutions and forms of cooperation. In addition to the cooperation in diplomatic representation and joint citizenship mentioned above, there are proposals to retain certain regulatory agencies, services such as the Driver and Vehicle Licensing Agency, and common standards of professional regulation and even pay (Scottish Government 2009b). In the autumn of 2010, they abandoned their plans to bring a referendum bill before the Scottish Parliament, recognizing that they did not have the majority to carry it.

The Scottish elections of 2011 did not change the constitutional position but dramatically altered the political landscape. The SNP gained an absolute majority of seats and announced that a referendum would be held towards the end of the new mandate. The UK parties did not challenge the constitutionality of the move, opting to fight on the issue. This looked like good politics as the SNP victory was not associated with any increase in support for independence in the polls. The strategy of the new SNP government was threefold. First, they would show that they were a competent governing party, indeed had replaced Labour as the 'natural governing party' of Scotland. Second, they would seek more powers, especially in fiscal matters ('the devolution max option'). Third, they would proceed to an independence referendum, probably in 2014. In this way, they sought to build on success and, if they did not go all the way to a referendum victory, would have achieved progress

It is likely that the devolution max option in some form will prevail in the form of evolutionary change. This does not mean, however, that the union will necessarily survive in the long run. Unionists have moved a long way in accepting devolution, the division of power and a stronger territorial dimension in the politics of the UK. There is very little resentment in England at Scottish self-government or its prospective extension, suggesting that some sort of confederal arrangement might be possible. On the other hand, there is some ill-feeling about Scottish influence at the centre. This has focused on the West Lothian question (the fact that Scottish MPs can vote on purely English laws in matters that are devolved in Scotland) and the financial settlement. The press has often complained about the number of Scots in Labour cabinets since 1997, although this is historically unusual. Converting the UK into some sort of federation or confederation would imply giving Scotland a formal role in policy-making and diluting the influence of English MPs who, in normal circumstances, can themselves comprise a parliamentary majority. This goes against the grain of English constitutional thinking, which remains profoundly unitarist. Another point of conflict could be the EU. At present, it is the UK government that represents the whole state in the EU Council of Ministers, although there are arrangements for an input from the devolved assemblies. Were Scottish and English interests or preferences to diverge, this arrangement could come under strain. Were Euroscepticism in England to grow, as it has been, and were pressures to mount for complete or partial withdrawal from the EU, it is likely that Scottish political opinion would opt to stay in. Similarly, there might be a preference in Scotland to opt into further forms of integration, which the UK government, especially with the Conservatives in power, would almost certainly reject. The end of the Union could then come not from Scottish demands for secession but from English unwillingness to accept the sharing of power both within the UK and across the European order.

Notes

1 Ironically, the Barnett formula provides for Scottish expenditure levels per capita (presently higher) to converge with English levels, but it is perceived south of the border as a mechanism for keeping them higher (Keating 2010).
2 In 1953, John McCormick had gone to court over the issue of the title of the Queen (who was called Elizabeth II although neither Scotland nor the UK had had an Elizabeth I). He lost this point but did get a declaration from the judge that the Westminster doctrine of parliamentary sovereignty did not apply in Scotland.
3 Voters are familiar with the term 'country' as applied to Scotland, but 'state' implies a big change.

References

Bechhofer, Frank and David McCrone (2007), 'Being British: A Crisis of Identity?' *The Political Quarterly*, 78(2): 251–260.

142   *M. Keating*

Brown, Alice, David McCrone, Lindsay Paterson and Paula Surridge (1999), *The Scottish Electorate: The 1997 General Election and Beyond*, London, Macmillan.

Conservativehome (2009), http://conservativehome.blogs.com/goldlist/2009/07.

Dicey, Albert Venn (1912), *A Leap in the Dark. A Criticism of the Principles of Home Rule as Illustrated by the Bill of 1893*, third edition, London, John Murray.

Dion, Stéphane (1991), 'Le nationalisme dans la convergence culturelle. Le Québec contemporain et le paradoxe de Tocqueville' in R. Hudon and R. Pelletier (eds), *L'engagement intellectuel. Mélanges en l'honneur de Léon Dion*, Sainte-Foy, Presses de l'Université de Laval.

Happold, Matthew (1999), *Scotland Europa: Independence in Europe?*, London, Centre for European Reform.

Heath, Anthony and Jane Roberts (2008), 'British Identity: Its Sources and Possible Implications for Civic Attitudes and Behaviour', *Citizenship Review Research*, London, Ministry of Justice.

Keating, Michael (2004), 'European Integration and the Nationalities Question' *Politics and Society*, 31(1): 367–388.

——(2009), *The Independence of Scotland. Self-Government and the Shifting Politics of Union*, Oxford, Oxford University Press.

——(2010), *The Government of Scotland. Public Policy-Making and Devolution*, second edition, Edinburgh, Edinburgh University Press.

Keating, Michael and David Bleiman (1979), *Labour and Scottish Nationalism*, London, Macmillan.

Kidd, Colin (2008), *Union and Unionisms*, Cambridge, Cambridge University Press.

Lythe, Charlotte and Madhavu Majmudar (1982), *The Renaissance of the Scottish Economy?*, London, Allen and Unwin.

MacCormick, Neil (1999), *Questioning Sovereignty. Law, State and Nation in the European Commonwealth*, Oxford, Oxford University Press.

Major, John (1993), 'Forward by the Prime Minister', in Secretary of State for Scotland, *Scotland and the Union*, Edinburgh, HMSO.

McCrone, David (2006), 'Scotland and Europe: Examining the Myths', talk given to the 6th annual conference of the Hansard Society Scotland, Edinburgh, Institute of Governance.

McCrone, Gavin (1965), *Scotland's Economic Progress, 1951–60*, London, Allen and Unwin.

——(1969), *Scotland's Future. The Economics of Nationalism*, Oxford, Blackwell.

McLean, Iain and Alistair McMillan (2005), *State of the Union. Unionism and the Alternatives in the United Kingdom since 1707*, Oxford, Oxford University Press.

Miller, David (2001), 'Nationality in Divided Societies' in Alan-G. Gagnon and James Tully (eds), *Multinational Democracies*, Cambridge, Cambridge University Press.

Murkens, Jo (2002), *Scottish Independence. A Practical Guide*, Edinburgh, Edinburgh University Press.

Rosie, Michael and Ross Bond (2007), 'Social Democratic Scotland?' in Michael Keating (ed.), *Scottish Social Democracy*, Brussels, Presses interuniversitaires européennes/Peter Lang.

Scottish Government (2009a), *Europe and Foreign Affairs: Taking Forward Our National Conversation*, Edinburgh, Scottish Government.

——(2009b), *People and Communities Taking Forward Our National Conversation*, Edinburgh, Scottish Government.

——(2009c), *Your Scotland. Your Voice. A National Conversation*, Edinburgh, Scottish Government.

Surridge, Paula (2003), 'A Classless Society? Social Attitudes and Social Class' in Catherine Bromley, John Curtice, Kerstin Hinds and Alison Park (eds), *Devolution – Scottish Answers to Scottish Questions?* Edinburgh, Edinburgh University Press.

Thatcher, Margaret (1993), *The Downing Street Years*, London, HarperCollins.

Tilley, James and Anthony Heath (2007), 'The Decline of British National Pride' *The British Journal of Sociology*, 58(4): 661–678.

Ward, Paul (2005), *Unionism in the United Kingdom*, Basingstoke, Macmillan.

Weight, Richard (2002), *Patriots. National Identity in Britain, 1940–2000*, London, Macmillan.

Wilson, Charles (1970), 'Note of Dissent', in *Scotland's Government*. Report of the Scottish Constitutional Committee, Edinburgh, Scottish Constitutional Committee.

Young, Robert A. (1995), *The Secession of Quebec and the Future of Canada*, Montreal, McGill-Queen's University Press.

Part II
Asia

9 Secessionism in independent India
Failed attempts, irredentism, and accommodation

Jean-Luc Racine

Independent India, as it has existed since 1947, is the result of a triple process engineered by opposite dynamics. The first mover has been "the freedom struggle," which ended on August 15, 1947 with independence. The Congress Party, led by charismatic leaders such as Mahatma Gandhi until the 1940s and then—in a different style—by Jawaharlal Nehru, was in the forefront of the movement, before ruling the country continuously until 1977. Unsatisfied with the Congress, a second trend emerged in 1940 when the Muslim League decided to secure a separate state for the Muslim minority of British India, which it did. Pakistan was born one day before independent India, on August 14, 1947. Although negotiated, it was a birth by forceps, stained with the blood of hundreds of thousands of victims of killings and millions of refugees. The post-colonial construction of the Indian nation has therefore been conducted to address two challenges, which are the two sides of the same coin: how to prevent the specter of secession from haunting the nation again, and how to define a polity able to accommodate unity and diversity?

To this day, the trauma of this partition is still hampering the normalization of bilateral relations between India and Pakistan, who fought four wars in 50 years, and helped separatist movements across their respective borders. However, having lost its western and eastern wings to Pakistan, India quickly started to build itself as a consolidated multicultural nation. The process was largely successful and offered a rare experiment of sustained political democracy in a post-colonial state. However, the practice of democracy failed at times, and discontent developed in areas where a mix of factors and short-sighted political expediency generated full-fledged secessionist movements. None of these, to this day, has been able to create an independent state.

The story of secessionism in post-colonial India is therefore a story of failed attempts, but it is nevertheless a significant story. First, three Indian leaders paid with their lives for the positions they had taken on secessionist issues: Gandhi in 1948, assassinated by a Hindu extremist for having allowed partition to happen; Indira Gandhi in 1984, killed for having crushed the secessionist movement for Khalistan; her son Rajiv, assassinated in 1991 by a suicide bomber from the Liberation Tigers of Tamil Eelam (LTTE), an insurgent group wishing to carve a Tamil state out of Sri Lanka. Second, among separatist

148   *J.-L. Racine*

movements, a few have not been deterred by failure: although some of the insurgents decided to join the mainstream, other factions remained on an irredentist line, sometimes for decades, such as a faction of the Naga movement. Third, the Indian state has developed a strong policy against secessionist movements. If sometimes well-thought out political accommodation contained some movements before they turned secessionist, the carrot and stick policy used against full-fledged insurgencies has not always ended opposition, and there was—and still is—a price to pay for repression: counter-insurgency and draconian special powers acts often do not offer the best face of democracy ...

On the whole, the history of independent India offers very useful materials for a comparative perspective on secessionism and separatism, and raises a number of important general questions such as how parameters ranging from identity, governance, and economy are at play in a constitutional democracy; how the principle of self-determination changed its color in post-colonial times; how large multicultural societies, in a federal framework, may address the challenge of separatism by force or by negotiation; how trans-national parameters and international relations are intertwined.

In the first section, the legacy of partition and the process of nation-building in a multicultural federation will be addressed. Recent moves to redraw regional states within the Indian Union will be looked at in the second section. Sometimes, regionalism turns to secessionism: this question will be addressed in the third section, particularly through the Punjab and Northeast crises. In the fourth section, we will analyze the most serious secessionist challenge India has to address: Kashmir. The international dimension of secessionist movements will finally be briefly addressed before offering, in conclusion, broader observations on the rationale of secessionism.

The background: partition syndrome and nation-building in a multicultural federation

Significantly, the Indian constitution adopted in January 1950 starts with these words: "We, the people of India, having solemnly resolved to constitute India as a sovereign democratic Republic ... ." The unity of the people of India (singular) is asserted in the very first line of the Preamble of the Constitution, while Article 1 declares: "India, that is Bharat (the old Sanskrit name of the land) shall be a Union of States." The union prevails therefore upon the states: the Indian Union is not born from an association of states deciding to unite themselves in an Indian Federation. If the constitution allows for the reorganization of states constituting the union, and recognizes the possibility of "acquiring" new territories (it happened with Sikkim in 1974), the right to secede is not recognized. In practice, if not in principle, the right to self-determination, which India supported when other colonized countries fought for independence, and considered a moment for Kashmir, no longer applies in the official Indian discourse, and barring a few exceptions—Timor Leste in 2002, South Sudan in 2011, Kosovo being an intricate case—this is a position adopted by most post-colonial states, strongly opposed to secessionism: a position shared by most other nation-states today, when faced with separatism, be it China with regard to Taiwan or Tibet, Russia with regard to Chechnya, or Turkey with regard to Kurdistan.

The idea of Pakistan was based upon a rationale asserting that, in the departing British Raj, two distinctive "nations" existed: one Hindu, one Muslim. The Congress Party rejected this "theory of two nations," and India became not a Hindu state, but a secular one. Furthermore, if a number of Urdu-speaking Muslims—mostly from northern India—left India for Pakistan, many other Muslims decided to stay in it and, at the turn of the century, India was inhabited by a number of Muslims (138 million in 2001) equal to the then population of Pakistan (136 million in 1998, Kashmir and Northern Territories under Islamabad control included) (Table 9.1).

In contrast to other large multilingual political entities, the Indian Union has no fully dominant language. Hindi, the most important mother tongue by far, accounts for only 41 percent of the population. Other noted languages lag far behind—Bengali, 8 percent; Telugu and Marathi, 7 percent each; Tamil 6 percent —but this low percentage, in a country of 1.2 billion people in 2011, masks a population size comparable to those of large European states. In 2001, there were 422 million Hindi speakers, 83 million Bengalis, 74 million Telugu, 72 million Marathis, and 60 million Tamils, to mention only the most important groups.

On the whole, the Indian Constitution recognizes, in an amendment of 2003, twenty-two languages as "scheduled languages." Among them, Hindi is an "official language." Outside them, English is a de facto second official language. Among other languages found in India, 234 are recognized as "mother tongue languages." Of these 234, seven had a speaker strength of one million or more in 2001, and 100 had a speaker strength of 10,000 or more.

As early as the 1950s, the Indian government had to reconsider the supremacy it wanted to give to Hindi, and had to start redrawing the boundaries of the provinces inherited from the British Raj as major linguistic groups asserted their willingness to govern themselves within the framework of the Indian Union. The so called "linguistic states" came into being mostly during the 1960s. They completely redefined the map of peninsular India, aggregating in newly established states (federal units) segments of former political entities on the basis of linguistic dominance: hence, the equations established between the Marathi language and the state of Maharashtra, Gujarati and Gujarat, Oriya and Orissa, Telugu and Andhra Pradesh, Tamil and Tamil Nadu, Kannada

Table 9.1 Religions in India (2001) as a percentage of the population and in millions[1]

Hindus	Muslims	Christians	Sikhs	Buddhists	Jains	Others
80.5%	13.4%	2.3%	1.9%	0.8%	0.4%	0.6%
827	138	24	19	7.9	4.2	6.6

Source: Census of India 2001.[1]

150   J.-L. Racine

and Karnataka, Malayalam and Kerala. The linguistic homogeneity was sometimes strong (84 percent of Tamil speakers in Tamil Nadu and the same percentage of Malayalam speakers in Kerala in 1981) and sometimes weaker, but a language always prevailed, giving these redrawn states their major identity (58 percent of Marathi speakers in Maharashtra, 54 percent of Kannada speakers in Karnataka.)

Other parameters had to be taken into account as well, including religion up to a point, despite the fact that India gave itself a secular constitution. This was particularly true when a religion, being a minority at the all-India level, happened to be dominant in a specific territory, with the propensity to religious/political dissent being stronger when this territory is also a borderland. Jammu and Kashmir has been a case in point since the late 1940s, and so was Punjab in the 1960s and, much more seriously, in the 1980s. In the 1960s, in the wake of the movement for reorganization of states on a linguistic basis, Punjab was redrawn as being limited to the space where the Punjabi language was prominent, which in fact was synonymous with the land of the Sikhs, a religious criteria not officially acknowledged. Besides language and religion, various patterns of ethnicity are important, particularly in the largely tribal Northeast, where the old province of Assam was somehow balkanized for accommodating tribal groups agitating for a state of their own within the India Union,[2] without ever granting independence to insurgents groups fighting for it, as in Nagaland. In some cases, the religious factor added to the ethnic dimensions, as some tribes in the Northeast had converted to Christianity. The sensitivity of the borders where these anti-status quo movements were active—Punjab is close to Pakistan, the Northeast close to China and Burma—added to the need to accommodate their requests, as long as they were not secessionist (Figure 9.1).

The government of India has sometimes been able to adjust its policies in order to confine assertive movements to regionalism before they turned to secession. On the eve of independence, the Dravida Kajagam, a reformist anti-Brahmin movement, toyed with the idea of an independent Dravidanad by which South India would have been freed from the supremacy of the Brahmins and Banyas (the priestly educated castes and the trader castes) from northern India. After a split in 1949, a faction of the Dravida Kajagam decided to compete for election under the flag of a new party, the Dravida Munnetra Kajagam (DMK), the Movement for the Emancipation of Dravidians. It fought for a long time for social reform and against the proposed imposition of Hindi as the *lingua franca* of India, asserted with pride the Tamil identity, and was finally elected to power in 1967 in the then Madras state, soon to be redefined as Tamil Nadu (the "Tamil Country"). Since then, the DMK or, after 1972, its breakaway faction named Anna DMK, has continuously ruled this state and has never questioned the rationale of the Indian Union.

On the other hand, when insurgencies prevailed over the failing accommodative policy of federalism, the Indian government used heavy-handed repression against resilient secessionist movements, be it in Kashmir or in the

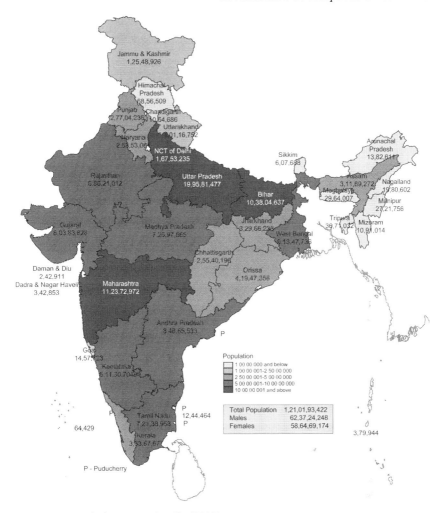

Figure 9.1 Population map of India (2011)

Northeast. But at the same time, it tried to play a political card by dividing the insurgents. It did so with unequal success, as can be seen in Kashmir where the electoral process, revived in 1996, has not been able to deter secessionist groups.

Although "secessionism" qualifies a position aiming at creating a new *independent* nation-state, "separatism" is more ambiguous. In the fluid context of the Indian Union, it may also define a movement aiming at creating a new state *within* the Union. In such cases, it seems wiser to label as "regionalist"— rather than as "separatist"—political movements or even violent groups who fight to establish a new state within the Union. "Regionalist movements," "regionalist parties," "regional parties" are part of the political lexicon, whereas secessionism is restricted to ideologies and practices aimed at breaking away from India. By implication, such true secessionist movements are confined to locations close to the borders of the Union.

This being said, we need to discriminate further. "Regional parties" may define political forces confined mostly to a state where a major political figure has been able to establish a noted stronghold based upon a party not playing mostly the ethnic card but eventually the caste card, as happens for instance in the large Hindi belt encompassing many states. However, "regionalist parties" define forces that *have* successfully played this ethno-linguistic card, such as the Dravidian parties in Tamil Nadu, the Telugu Desam Party in Andhra Pradesh, the Asom Gana Parishad in Assam. The rise of these regional forces and these regionalist parties are largely responsible for the entry of India into the era of coalition politics. This trend, often viewed as opening the door to parochialism and unprincipled electoral opportunism, is perhaps also one of the circuitous ways of strengthening the nexus between political pluralism and nation-building. If it were so, the instability brought in the short term by competitive politics would be compensated in the long term by an overarching polity which would accommodate a regional sense of belonging as well as regional forces, without negating the supremacy of the Republic of India, a "Union of States."

Regionalism and "inside" separatism: the "reorganization of states" issue today

Regionalism has often engineered active political movements, sometimes backed by violent action, but all new states established within the Union have not always resulted from political agitation. In the last "reorganization of states" which separated smaller newborn states established in hilly lands from three large and populated states in 2000, a new broad rationale was at play, suggesting that better governance requires smaller states. In the case of Jharkhand ($53,000 \text{ km}^2$; population in 2011, 33 million), which separated from Bihar, a strong political movement, the Jharkand Mukti Morcha (the Jarkhand Liberation Front), had been active for a long time before coming to power in the new state: its tribal assertiveness has developed in a context of economic change and in-migration brought by the speedy industrialization of a region rich in mineral resources. In Himalayan Uttarakhand ($53,000 \text{ km}^2$; population in 2011, 10 million), which separated from Uttar Pradesh, the movement was much less militant, whereas in Chhattisgarh ($135,000 \text{ km}^2$; population in 2011, 25 million), separated from Madhya Pradesh, the initiative came from the top rather than from the bottom. In such processes, electoral politics and political expediency are part of the game. The Bharatiya Janata Party, then in power in New Delhi for the first time, was trying to build political constituencies for itself (with unequal success) in the newly created states. How the politics of identity is intertwined with party politics is also seen today in the case of Telangana.

A part of the Telugu-speaking state of Andhra Pradesh, Telangana has a very specific history. In 1947, the Nizam of Hyderabad, the Muslim head of one the largest princely states in India, tried to preserve an independent status, despite the fact that his land was located in the heart of peninsular India. A communist insurgency in the poorer part, Telangana, in the north of his state, offered New Delhi the opportunity to "restore order" and, in the process, incorporate the state of Hyderabad, renamed later as a reorganized "linguistic state" Andhra Pradesh (275,000 km^2; population in 2011, 76 million). Decades later, the same Telangana region has reappeared as one of the hotspots of the Maoist-inspired insurgency—the Naxalite movement. Today, the Naxalites of Telangana are no more the vanguard of the insurgency, whose stronghold is in the neighboring state of Chhattisgarh, but a strong regionalist movement has resurfaced for separating Telangana (115,000 km^2; population in 2011, 35 million) from Andhra Pradesh. The movement, led by the Telangana Rashtriya Samiti (Committee for the State of Telangana, established in 2001), has been resolute enough—no insurgency, but mass agitations and a leader's hunger strike—in compelling the government of India to address an issue perturbing the political balance in a major state, which is also, with its headquarters in Hyderabad city, a focal point of the much hyped "hi-tech India." Should Telangana become a state, Andhra Pradesh would then lose more than a third of its area but also its emblematic capital city. Willing to remain a political force to reckon with in this key southern state, the Congress Party in power has also to pay attention to the regionalist Telugu Desam Party, which has ruled the state many times and had finally decided to support the Telangana bifurcation. In consequence, in 2004, the Congress decided to support Telangana as well. However, the central government's policy appears undecided. By the end of 2009, it seemed that New Delhi was ready to promote the creation of the new state—the twenty-ninth in the Indian Union. A few days later, the Srikrishna Commission set up by New Delhi recommended keeping Andhra Pradesh united while offering Telangana greater autonomy. The central government changed its line, whereas opposition parties—national and local—boycotted the consultations it organized in search of a political consensus

The Telangana agitation and the uncertainty over the issue have revived other regionalist movements in India. Some of them, particularly in the region of Darjeeling—the Himalayan part of West Bengal—have known strong political movements for decades such as the Gorkha Janamukti Morcha (Liberation Front of the Gorkha People). The latter is still unhappy with the half-measures granted long ago, a regional council with limited autonomous powers, precisely the type of autonomy that the Srikrishna report has recommended for Telangana. The new Gorkhaland Territorial Administration set up in July 2011 will clearly not solve the problem either. Other movements have revived old or more recent demands for the bifurcation of existing states. In Maharashtra (307,000 km^2; population in 2011, 112 million), the demand for a separate Vidarbha, in the eastern part of the state, has been boosted. In Uttar Pradesh, in Bihar, in Gujarat, and in Karnataka, hypothetical divisions are also contemplated locally. For the time being, the Indian government is not likely to

154 J.-L. Racine

open the Pandora's box and establish a new Commission for the Reorganization of States.

From regionalism to secessionism: Punjab and the Northeast

Most regionalist movements have developed within the confines of the Indian Union. In a number of cases, regionalist parties have not voiced specific territorial demands. They have primarily asserted the historical greatness of their respective regional identities and complained against the policy of the central government, which is supposed to be unfair to the state in question. The Telugu Desam Party, launched in Andhra Pradesh by the film star N.T. Rama Rao in 1983, perfectly illustrates this pattern. This is not always the case, however, particularly in peripheral states, where regional parties— the National Conference in Jammu and Kashmir or the Akali Dal in Punjab, for instance—have at times been ambiguous in their positions or, more often, have been overcome by secessionist forces willing to break away from India. Kashmir, a special case, will be addressed separately, after looking first at the two serious secessionist movements that have greatly shaken India in the 1980s, in Punjab and in the Northeast.

The Khalistan insurgency

When the partition of the British Raj appeared unavoidable, a section of the Sikh community[3] settled on the rich irrigated lands of Punjab and tried to carve a state for the *khalsa panth*, the "community of the pure" established in 1699 by the last Sikh guru, Gobind Singh. The project failed. Punjab, cut into two by partition, bore the brunt of massacres and migrations. Few Sikhs remained in Pakistan, while the numerous small princely states of Indian Punjab were amalgamated into a new political entity that was finally subdivided in 1966 into two states according to the principle of "linguistic states": close to the border, the state of Punjab, with a majority of Sikhs speaking Punjabi; closer to New Delhi, the state of Haryana with a majority of Hindus speaking Hindi. Chandigarh, the new capital, was finally built up as a Union Territory, the common headquarters of the two states.

This subdivision failed to satisfy the Sikhs' sense of identity and added to a sense of frustration. With the advent of the green revolution, Punjab con-tributed greatly to the food security of the country, but a number of Punjabis felt that not much was given in return: no large industrial projects (Pakistan, with which India fought wars in 1965 and 1971, was too close), no Chandigarh for Punjab alone, and part of the Indus tributaries irrigating Punjab were now diverted to irrigate Rajasthan. The old Akali Dal, a pre-independence Sikh party close to the committee managing Sikh temples, more and more raised its voice against Prime Minister Indira Gandhi.

Willing to boost her Congress Party in Punjab, Mrs. Ghandi made a major mistake. Against the Akalis, she pushed to prominence a Sikh preacher, Sant

Jarnail Singh Bhindrawale, who finally asserted himself as a charismatic fundamentalist leader, and was soon joined by a section of the student associations and by the militants of a secessionist force established in 1977, the Dal Khalsa. Abroad, part of the North American Sikh diaspora actively supported the demand for an independent Khalistan. Extremism gained strength, violence expanded, and the Akali Dal was marginalized by the rise of an insurgency abetted by Pakistan offering sanctuary to militants across the border.

In June 1984, Indira Gandhi sent the Indian Army against the Golden Temple, the most prominent Sikh temple, in Amritsar, where Bhindranwale and his cohort had entrenched themselves. The attack on this sacred place killed Bhindranwale and 100 others, but traumatized the entire Sikh community, including those condemning the insurgency. In October, Indira Gandhi was assassinated in retaliation by one of her Sikh bodyguards. An anti-Sikh pogrom followed, mostly in Delhi. In July 1985, Rajiv Gandhi, the new prime minister, signed an agreement with the Akali Dal chief Harcharan Singh Longowal, who was assassinated in August. In September, the Akali Dal won the elections in Punjab. It took years of violence and a new police strategy to suppress the remnants of the insurgency by the early 1990s.

Insurgencies in the Northeast: Assam and beyond

While Punjab was burning, the Northeast was in turmoil as well. In Assam (78,000 km^2; population in 2011, 31 million), the largest and most populous state in the region, a strong protest movement emerged against Muslim migrants coming from Bangladesh. Vocal groups called for a revision of the electoral rolls, which were supposed to be manipulated by the Congress Party. Here again, Indira Gandhi chose a dangerous line. In 1983, she refused to postpone the state elections: violence erupted mostly against Muslims, sometimes also between various communities, be they Bengalis or tribal peoples. Rajiv Gandhi signed an agreement with the protesters in 1985. Although migrants of old were to be naturalized, those settled after 1971 were to be sent back to Bangladesh. Fresh elections were organized, and a new party established by some of the leaders of the movement won: the Asom Gana Parishad (Association of the People of Assam) entered the mainstream and, to this day, has played electoral politics with its ups and downs.

Another section of the movement rejected the compromise and joined the secessionist United Liberation Front of Assam (ULFA), established in 1979. ULFA became a force to be reckoned with and launched a multifaceted insurgency combining guerrilla moves in the Brahmaputra valley, target killings, and racket against economic interests—including tea plantations. The army conducted two operations against the insurgents with some success, in 1990 and 1991, but the leaders of the guerrillas found sanctuary in Bangladesh, ironically enough. For 20 years, the movement lingered, with occasional terrorist bombings. After the insurgency, the leaders were arrested in 2009 and 2010, probably with the help of the Awami League government in power in

Bangladesh since the early 2009; ULFA's fate seems to be sealed now. Freed in January 2011, the historical leader of ULFA, Arabindo Rajkhowa, has opened the door to negotiation with New Delhi. Once again, a separatist/secessionist movement has failed.

Not that the Northeast is at peace with itself. Locked between the Himalayas and the Indo-Burmese hills, linked to India by the narrow "chicken neck" running between Bhutan and Bangladesh, the Northeast has always been a land of contact, the locus where Indian civilization meets with the confines of Tibet, Yunnan, and Southeast Asia. In a maze of hilly tracts and valleys, tribes settled long ago, and the British tried to protect them from migrant peasants and traders from mainland India by drawing an "inner line" limiting access to outsiders. The assertiveness of local movements and the sensitivity of a border crossed by Chinese troops in the 1962 war against India compelled New Delhi to grant full state status to micro-territories where, in some cases such as Nagaland, irredentist movements have fought for independence for decades. None of these movements succeeded. In Mizoram, an agreement was signed in 1987, with the separatists joining the mainstream while acceding to power after altering their agenda. In Nagaland, part of the insurgency was accommodated while a faction of the leadership of the National Socialist Council of Nagaland went into exile in Europe. This Isaac–Muivah faction entered into a discreet dialogue with New Delhi in 2002, and its leader, Tuengaling Muivah, was allowed to visit his homeland in 2010. The Naga insurgency is coming to a close, but remains a problem for greater Nagaland or Nagalim, as the Nagas would like to integrate their state with the Naga-majority districts of the neighboring state of Manipur, which opposes such a scheme.

In the intricate ethnic mosaic of the Northeast, the Nagalim issue is just one among many examples of what we may call "encased identities." In Assam, for instance, beyond the ULFA separatists, a movement for a Bodoland erupted in the 1987, separated from Assam and dedicated to the Bodos tribes established along the Brahmaputra valley, close to Bhutan. Here again, the movement divided itself between the moderates and a radical and violent force. The government of Assam tried to settle the issue by establishing a Bodoland Territorial Council in 2003—a half-measure to dissipate the specter of continuous internal fragmentation for a time. Other minor separatist movements still exist in the Northeast, such as the Liberation Front of Tripura, the Liberation Front of the People of Manipur, or the Kuki National Army dreaming of a new state for Kukis from both sides of the Indo-Burmese border.

It is hard to understand why the government of India has not yet repealed the Armed Forces (Special Powers) Act of 1958, protecting the army against accusations of excessive violence. Human rights organizations protest against this Act, which is presented by the authorities as a necessary tool in the fight against secessionist forces, although these very forces are more and more marginalized today.

The question of Kashmir

Of all the secessionist movements operating in (and against) India, by far the most resilient and the most important is the Kashmiri one. More than any other insurgent movement against Indian rule, it also has global implications on at least two counts: first, the open nuclearization of the region, after the Indian and Pakistani nuclear tests of 1998; second, the rise of jihadi forces, instrumentalized by the Pakistani Army and its Inter Services Intelligence (ISI), and radicalized by al Qaeda and by the regional consequences of 9/11, which brought US and NATO forces to Afghanistan and put pressure on Pakistan. The stakes in the Kashmiri secessionist movement are therefore extraordinarily important, not only for the Kashmiris themselves—not many great powers are interested in the Kashmiri issue *per se*—but also because of the intricate networks that link the Kashmiri insurgency to the "AfPak" imbroglio, further confused by the elimination of Osama Bin Laden in a garrison town in Pakistan in May 2011.

To cut a long story short, the Kashmir issue is the unresolved legacy of partition. The large princely state of Jammu and Kashmir (222,000 km^2) had a Muslim majority population but a Hindu maharajah who was reluctant to accede to either Pakistan or India, as was the rule with partition. A revolt by an opposition party, the Muslim Conference, provided an opportunity for newly born Pakistan to enter the game: the proxy of militias, which were supposed to be independent, was in fact under Pakistan's military control. As the militias marched upon its summer capital, Srinagar, the maharaja called for Indian help, made available only if the state decided to accede to India, which was done. The Indian army stopped the militias and the conflict turned into an open war between India and Pakistan in 1948, ended with a ceasefire on January 1, 1949, under UN mediation. In the meantime, the Indian Prime Minister, Jawaharlal Nehru, had put the case of Kashmir on the desk of the Security Council, only to discover that the UN, far from supporting New Delhi, recommended a plebiscite to settle the issue.

From the early 1950s to the late 1980s, the case remained open, with ups and downs. The UN resolutions calling for self-determination (but not for an independent state) were not implemented. Pakistan did not meet the prerequisite of withdrawing its troops. It defines Kashmir as a "disputed territory," after allowing part of it to become Azad Kashmir (Free Kashmir), a political entity in fact in the hands of Islamabad. The Northern Territories, the largest part of the Himalayan tract under Pakistan's control, have been deprived of this status. Kashmir has not been incorporated as a standard province in order to leave the dispute open. On the Indian side, south of the 1949 ceasefire line, which became a "line of control" (LOC) after the second war in 1965, New Delhi quickly rescinded the high level of autonomy promised by the act of accession. Sheikh Abdullah, the leader of the National Conference who chose India over Pakistan and took over from the maharaja in 1948, paid the price for his ambiguity and spent years under house arrest before being returned to power by Indira Gandhi in 1975 in a deal supposed to solve the issue for good.

This strategy failed, for the sense of frustration of the Kashmiris was never fully addressed by New Delhi, too prone to manipulate the political game in the state, particularly during the 1987 elections. Two years later, after the victory of the Afghan mujahideens over the Red Army, the revolt broke out in the heart of Kashmir, the Vale of Srinagar. Disproportionate repression made matters worse, and a full-fledged insurgency developed against India, albeit in confusion. The Jammu and Kashmir Liberation Front (JKLF), established in 1965, fought for an independent Kashmir. Pakistan supported it at the beginning, but soon chose to back the Hizbul Mujahideen more resolutely who are closer to the Islamist ideology and are pro-Pakistan. In 1993, Islamabad helped to regroup most of the political opponents of India in the All Parties Hurriyat Conference, which then asserted itself as "the genuine representative of the Kashmiris" but has since boycotted all elections. When the insurgency faced the brunt of the Indian forces, Islamabad decided to inject new fighters into Kashmir: the jihadist cohorts raised in Pakistani Punjab and organized in various militant groups, all backed and supported by the ISI. The most prominent among them were the Jaish e Mohammad, reorganized in 2000, and the Lashkar e Taiba, known for its terrorist-expanding agenda.

Today, after more than 20 years of insurgency and probably more than 70,000 deaths, the Kashmir issue remains unresolved. India has long denounced the "cross-border terrorism" and the "proxy war" conducted by Pakistan infiltrating its surrogates first into Indian-held Kashmir, then outside Kashmir in order to target Indian metropolises, from the Indian parliament in New Delhi in 2001 to the 3 days of mayhem in Mumbai in 2008. Pakistan and anti-Indian Kashmiris accuse India of "state-sponsored terrorism," whereas non-governmental organizations (NGOs) talk of recurrent violations of human rights.

Deadlock prevails. The open nuclearization of India and Pakistan in 1998 has not prevented the Pakistani army from testing India's resolve in the war of Kargil, on the LOC, in 1999. India did react, with restraint however. The attack on the Indian parliament was met with a major mobilization of forces, but with no action across the LOC or across the international border. And the political answer from New Delhi to the massive terrorist attack on Mumbai has been to stop the "composite dialogue" conducted with Pakistan since 2004—a dialogue that was started afresh in 2011 without any major results. Similarly, the visible fatigue and the splits among insurgents have not been conducive enough to push the Hurriyat Conference to the negotiating table: the Hurriyat does not want a dialogue with New Delhi, as it expects a tripartite dialogue between India, Pakistan, and the Kashmiris—but the organization can hardly appear to be representative of all Kashmiris. Back-door negotiations between New Delhi and Islamabad are said to have progressed during 2007, before Pakistani President Musharraf was pressed to abandon his military status and the presidency. His successor as Chief of Army Staff,

General Kayani, is obviously not interested in expanding what has been discreetly achieved in 2007, and civilian power in Pakistan is too weak to impose its views upon the army.

In fact, and despite the serious degradation of the internal situation in Pakistan as a result of the Talibanization of the tribal areas and terrorism in major cities, the army sticks to its traditional strategic paradigm: using all means available to preserve Pakistan's "strategic depth" in Afghanistan and keeping pressure on India in Kashmir—although infiltration of Pakistani jihadis in India-administered Kashmir has declined—in order to prevent a full-fledged cooperation between Kabul and New Delhi at the cost of Islamabad. As the United States has now decided to negotiate with the Taliban and withdraw its fighting forces from Afghanistan in the coming years, it will need Pakistan's support. It remains to be seen whether Islamabad will seize this opportunity to internationalize the Kashmir issue afresh in order to secure its interests against India, in both Kashmir and Afghanistan.

The trans-national dimension of secessionism

In such a context, secessionism is not just a national issue. It has trans-national connections, particularly in a region where it has won (the Muslim League in creating Pakistan, the Awami League in creating Bangladesh), has lost at huge cost (the Tamil Tigers in Sri Lanka), has survived four wars between the contesting parties (Kashmir), and has made China nervous in Tibet and Xinjiang.

Furthermore, as it unraveled in Kashmir and in Northeast India, secessionism has offered India's neighbors opportunities for action, just as India has sometimes taken sides when separatist movements emerged in her neighborhood. Separatism in eastern Pakistan, which became Bangladesh with the help of the Indian army, and separatism in Kashmir, strongly supported by jihadi movements backed by Islamabad, have become historical legacies or unresolved issues that prevent India and Pakistan from enjoying a normalized relationship. In Sri Lanka, the separatist movement of the Tamil Tigers, crushed by the Colombo government in 2009, has also had an impact on Indian politics since the 1980s. It was discreetly supported by India at the beginning in order to get the support of the Indian Tamil electorate, but the Indian Peace Keeping Force sent to Sri Lanka by Rajiv Gandhi in 1987, with Colombo's agreement, ended in disaster. The way the Tibetan movement may evolve in the future could also impact on the improving but ambiguous India–China relationship. The Chinese claim to the Northeastern Indian state of Arunachal Pradesh, labeled as southern Tibet in China, is also linked to the Tibetan question.

In other words, if secessionism has not dismantled the Indian Union, it seriously affects the overall geo-political game in the entire South Asian theatre and beyond for a number of reasons. Besides the case of "disputed territories," most countries have given sanctuary to insurgents from across borders. In all these cases, the South Asia Association for Regional Cooperation (SAARC) or the United Nations have always been unwilling or unable to contain separatist movements or to mediate in a search for an acceptable solution. Bilateral agreements have sometimes been at play, marginally, but on the most destabilizing issue, that is Kashmir, only the Great Powers have been able to interfere significantly, positively or negatively, as India accepts at best discreet "facilitation", never open mediation.

Conclusion: beyond identity, the rationale for secessionism

The standard explanation for secessionism relies on an assertion of identity. It is supposed to be so evident that, in the introduction to their book on ethnic conflict and secessionism in South and Southeast Asia, Rajat Ganguly and Ian Macduff do not immediately define the concepts of "ethnic conflict" or "ethnic insurgency" to which they refer (in a very useful comparative perspective) (Ganguly and Macduff 2003). However, no matter how strong the sense of belonging may be, ethnicity is never the sole parameter defining the rationale for insurgency. Not only are other factors at play—socioeconomic deprivation or injustice, failed or eroded political legitimacy of the ruling power, cross-border dimension of insurgency, etc. ... —but in most cases, the ethnic group involved in the insurgency is itself divided, with part of the group refusing to join the ranks of the insurgents and to acknowledge the validity of the secessionist paradigm, although it may share a sense of frustration or unease regarding the dominant power; divisions among Kashmiris are a case in point.

The field survey conducted in four hotspots in India by Neera Chandoke has underscored the ambiguity of the identity factor (Chandoke 2006).[4] Noting that the percentage of those who believe that identity is not the key factor is the same as the percentage of those holding the opposite view, she unravels other parameters of discontent pressing for separatism, be it the corruption of established governments or their inability to answer the basic needs of the people. Chandoke's analysis stands finally on three propositions:

(a) "We need to look beyond the enactment of what are euphemistically termed identity wars to see what led to the politicisation of identities in the first place."

(b) "Identities are politicised and harnessed to projects of violent resistance/secessionism when political agreements are violated, when institutions default on the promises that underpin the institutionalisation of norms (...) and when popular expectations of institutions remain unfulfilled."

(c) "None of the three factors identified by the respondents as reasons for the outbreak of conflict, i.e. corruption (the political factor), neglect of basic needs (the economic factor) and neglect of identity

Secessionism in independent India 161

(the ethnic factor), stand alone. In all four cases, conflict has resulted from the intersection of at least two out of the three factors identified above."

Beyond movements willing to redefine the status of a territory within a national political entity, secessionist movements willing to break away and to establish a new nation fit Chandoke's scheme of analysis, at least in understanding how such movements are born and how they hold on. However, additional parameters must be added to explain how such movements might last for a long time. Obviously, each separatist/secessionist movement has its own rationale, and inscribes itself in specific political and geo-political configurations. The structure of the movement eventually gives it strong resilience, as was the case with the LTTE in Sri Lanka (see also Chapter 10). Led by a dictatorial and charismatic leader, the LTTE was able to annihilate most of its more moderate Tamil opponents, and to govern the territory under its control de facto with an iron fist. The support of the diaspora (as in the case of the Khalistan movement) also added to the strength of the LTTE, and to its finances, through a "voluntary" contribution collected among the expatriate Tamil community. In comparison, the Baluchistan Liberation Army in Pakistan has not been able to hold ground as strongly in the province bordering Afghanistan and Iran, for it had to face the might of the Pakistan army for too long. On the whole, if the support of foreign forces plays an important role, as noted in Bangladesh, in most cases, the crux of the matter lies inside the territory concerned and depends on the way the government in power defines its counter-insurgency strategy. Brute repression will usually not do—albeit if it finally paid off in the case of Sri Lanka and its central government under President Rajapaksa. But in countries, such as India, unwilling fully to crush a movement by sheer force in the way that Russia did in Chechnya, the type of repression selected—harsh but conducted in what is supposed ultimately to remain a context of electoral politics—entails protracted conflicts with ups and downs.

In this general framework, Kashmir remains a case apart in a way for two connected reasons: first, the pro-independence movement led by a section of the Kashmiris inscribes itself in a context where pro-India reformist political parties and pro-Pakistan separatists are also parts of what remains an intricate game. Second, Kashmir is a "contested territory," as Pakistan would define it, and as a section of the international community sees it as well, despite India's unwillingness to accept this definition. These intricacies, still more acute with the nuclearization of India and Pakistan and the new dimension of the involvement of jihadi groups (at the beginning seen as "strategic assets" by the Pakistani services, but lately contaminated by al Qaeda's ideology), heighten the stakes attached to the Kashmir question. Despite this, India has succeeded in confining Kashmir outside the purview of the United Nations. Obviously, the way the international community looks at secessionist movements is defined by a number of factors. Three of these appear to be

162 *J.-L. Racine*

decisive: the degree of cohesion of the movement and the degree of positive visibility of its leadership; the type of answers—repressive and political— the movements draw from the established governments they are fighting; and the level of international status enjoyed by the countries affected by secessionism.

In order to make the general theory of secessionist movements more accurate and precise, be it from a political theory perspective or from an international relations point of view, comparative studies need to be carried out and to be confronted. However, I believe that the moving complexity of separatist/ secessionist movements and the configurations of their geo-political context will always challenge attempts at theorizing, which should be, by nature, an unending process.

Notes

1 At the time of finalizing this chapter, the Census of India, which conducted its last decennial survey in early 2011, had released figures on India's population but not data on religions and languages.
2 In India, "tribes" define groups who have developed in time outside the pale of the mainstream peasant/urban society, often in hilly tracts of Central and Northeast India. In 2001, the "Scheduled Tribes" accounted for 8.2 percent of the total population of India: 84.3 million people, with high concentrations in some states (94 percent of Mizoram's population is registered as "Tribes").
3 Sikhism was born in 1499 in Punjab. In India, Sikhs numbered roughly 20 million in 2001, which was less than the number of Christians and represented less than 2 percent of the total population. Some 14.5 million of them were living in Punjab.
4 From line 1, she clarifies the point: "The term ethnicity is employed as shorthand for linguistic, religious, and tribal identities, this is not to say that each of these identities are not specific." Her survey has been conducted in Punjab, Jammu and Kashmir, and two Northeastern States: Manipur and Mizoram.

References

Baruah, Sanjib (2009), *Beyond Counter-Insurgency. Breaking the Impasse in Northeast India*, New Delhi, Oxford University Press.
——(ed.) (2010), *Ethnonationalism in India. A Reader*, New York, Oxford University Press.
Bhaumik, Subir (2009), *Troubled Periphery, the Crisis in India's North East*, New Delhi, Penguin.
Chadha, Vivek (2005), *Low Intensity Conflicts in India. An Analysis*, New Delhi, Sage Publications.
Chandoke, Neera (2006), *A State of One's Own: Secessionism and Federalism in India*, London, London School of Economics, Developing Countries Research Centre Working Paper No. 80.
Ganguly, Rajat and Ian Macduff (eds) (2003), *Ethnic Conflict and Secessionism in South and Southeast Asia. Causes, Dynamics, Solutions*, New Delhi, Sage Publications.
Malik, Iffat (2002), *Kashmir. Ethnic Conflict, International Dispute*, Karachi, Oxford University Press.

Nag, Sajaj (2002), *Contesting Marginality. Ethnicity, Insurgency and Subnationalism in North-East India*, New Delhi, Manohar.

Sidhu, Waheguru Pal Singh et al. (2006), *Kashmir, New Voices, New Approaches*, Boulder, CO, and London, Lynne Reiner Publishers.

Sisson, Richard and Rose, Leo E. (1990), *War and Secession. Pakistan, India and the Creation of Bangladesh*, Berkeley, CA, University of California Press.

10 Separatism in Sri Lanka

David Feith

In May 2009, when the Sri Lankan army defeated the Liberation Tigers of Tamil Eelam (LTTE), the civil war that had lasted for some 26 years ended. The LTTE had fought to establish Eelam, a separate Tamil state in the north and east of Sri Lanka, and had succeeded in creating a de facto separate state, with borders, functioning civil administration, law courts, police, navy and air force. Many people living in Sri Lanka, and many international observers, thought that the LTTE would never be conquered militarily. However, the government of Mahinda Rajapaksa, with his brother Gotabaya Rajapaksa as Defence Minister, and with support from China and India (and other states), pursued an unrelenting military assault, over a period of many months, with thousands of civilians killed, and vanquished the LTTE. The strongly held desire for a separate Tamil state has been brutally suppressed; but an important question to consider is whether the demand for a separate Tamil state could arise again in future. This chapter will explain the growth of Tamil separatism in Sri Lanka, from the colonial period and through the post-independence period to the present, looking at the LTTE as the organization that took up arms to fight for a separate state, succeeded for some years in establishing a de facto state, but was finally defeated.

The population of Sri Lanka is approximately 20 million, made up of two main communities – the Sinhalese (some 74 per cent of the population) and the Tamils (approximately 18 per cent) (Department of Census and Statistics – Sri Lanka 2011). There are also smaller communities of Muslims (7 per cent, most of whom speak Tamil) and Burghers. For Sinhalese, the main aspects of identity are the Sinhalese language and their religion, Buddhism; for Tamils, the primary aspects of identity are the Tamil language and (for the majority of Tamils) the Hindu religion. There are a small proportion of Christians among both Sinhalese and Tamils. Among the Tamils, there are two main groups, generally referred to as Sri Lankan or Ceylon Tamils and Indian or plantation Tamils. The Sri Lankan Tamils (approximately 12.7 per cent of population) live mostly in the northern and eastern provinces, and their ancestors have lived in Sri Lanka for thousands of years (Figure 10.1). The Indian Tamils (approximately 5.5 per cent of the population) are descendants of Tamils who migrated from India during British colonial rule; they were

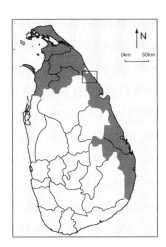

Figure 10.1 Sri Lanka – Tamil majority areas (left) and area claimed as a Tamil homeland by the LTTE (right)

recruited to work in coffee and then tea plantations in central Sri Lanka. They still live and work mainly on tea plantations in the hill country in the centre of Sri Lanka, and are generally separate, geographically, socially and politically, from the Sri Lankan Tamils living in the north and east (Peebles 2006; Feith 2009).

A strange but important aspect of Sri Lankan demography is that all the communities regard themselves, in different ways, as minorities. The Sinhalese, despite comprising over 70 per cent of Sri Lanka's population, regard themselves as a minority in relation to their giant neighbour India, and in particular the Indian state of Tamil Nadu, a very short distance across the Palk Strait, with approximately 72 million Tamils (Census of India 2011). In the South Asia region, they are a minority in terms of both language and religion – they are Buddhist, whereas the majority of Indians are Hindu, and in Pakistan, Bangladesh and the Maldives, the majority are Muslim. The Tamils in Sri Lanka are clearly a minority in relation to the Sinhalese; and the Muslims, although most speak Tamil, see themselves as a separate minority, in relation to both the Sinhalese and the Tamils.

The Tamil separatist movement in Sri Lanka arose as a consequence of colonialism. The English East India Company took control of (then) Ceylon from the Dutch in 1796, and Ceylon became a Crown Colony of Britain in 1801. The British annexed the Kandyan kingdom in 1815 and brought the whole island under their control. This was the first time the whole island had been controlled by one ruler. British documents testify that, prior to European colonization, there were three separate kingdoms on the island – Sinhalese kingdoms based around Kandy in the centre and Kotte in the southwest, and a Tamil kingdom based in Jaffna in the north (Ponnambalam 1983; Weiss

2011). The Tamil separatist movement has used British documents to support their claim for a historical separate Tamil state in Sri Lanka (Tamilnation.org 2011).

In the nineteenth century, while under British rule, there were revival movements among both Sinhalese and Tamils, looking back at their history and rediscovering their culture. Spokesmen for these revival movements attempted to define themselves as different from the English colonial rulers. Among the Sinhalese, the revival and nationalist movements stressed Buddhism and Sinhalese identity. Tamils in both south India and Sri Lanka proudly redis-covered ancient Tamil literature, Hinduism and pride in the Tamil language's antiquity. This development of Tamil identity was partly in response to British colonialism, but Tamil identity was also defined in relation to the north Indian Hindi speakers in India and the Sinhalese in Sri Lanka. These revival movements developed into nationalist movements in the twentieth century (Madura Rasaratnam 2009).

During the colonial period, schools were established in the coastal regions, particularly in the larger cities of Colombo and Jaffna. Sri Lankan Tamils saw education and government service as a means of economic and social advancement, and took up English education, and the opportunities it pro-vided in the government bureaucracy, in disproportionate numbers compared with the Sinhalese. When independence came in 1948, the fact that there was a disproportionate number of educated Sri Lankan Tamils, and Tamils in the civil service, was seen by some Sinhalese as evidence that Tamils were a privileged minority, and this was a cause of resentment.

Independence was granted in 1948 and, in the post-colonial period, separate Sinhalese and Tamil nationalist movements continued to grow. Government policies and practices had the cumulative effect of alienating Tamils from the Sinhalese-dominated state, making anti-Tamil discrimination acceptable and increasing the demands for a separate Tamil state. The Tamil separatist movement developed for a number of reasons: the growth of nationalist sen-timent among Tamils, the political and economic marginalization of Tamils after independence, the frustration with political negotiations that were not achieving anything and the outbreaks of anti-Tamil violence (Sivakumar 1984; Sivananda 1984; Sivarajah 1996; Gunasingham 1999; Wilson 2000; Taras and Ganguly 2002; DeVotta 2004; Weiss 2011).

In 1949, legislation was passed that deprived of citizenship and disen-franchised the plantation or 'Indian Tamils'. They became stateless and voteless, and the government effectively removed a large body of voters from electoral rolls. The plantation Tamils were clearly given the message that they were not wanted, and not seen as part of Sri Lankan society, despite having lived there for several generations and contributed their labour to the profits of the plantation economy. Decades later, in the 1970s, the plantation Tamils won back the right to vote, but in 1949, their disenfranchisement was an ominous sign to all Sri Lankan Tamils that the government was governing for the Sinhalese majority, not the Tamil minority.

In the early decades of the post-colonial period, Tamil political parties tried to work within the political system to improve the position of Tamils in Sri Lanka. In 1951, Chelvanayakam created the Ilangai Tamil Arasu Katchi (ITAK), commonly known as the Federal Party; this was the dominant Tamil political party throughout the 1950s, winning ten seats in the 1956 election. The four main demands of this Tamil party were: an autonomous Tamil linguistic state within a Federal Union of Ceylon; parity of Tamil and Sinhalese languages; citizenship for the plantation Tamils of Indian origin; and the end of colonization by Sinhalese in predominantly Tamil regions (Wriggins 1960; Peebles 2006).

In the 1950s, Sinhalese nationalism and patriotism grew stronger and expressed itself in a demand for '*Swabasha*' or one's own language, instead of English as the official language. In 1951, Solomon Bandaranaike formed the Sri Lanka Freedom Party (SLFP) and campaigned for Sinhalese to become the official language. This campaign grew in strength in rural areas, gaining support from Sinhalese-educated teachers, ayurvedic practitioners and Buddhist monks (*bhikkus*). The campaign was anti-western, anti-Christian and increasingly anti-Tamil (Manor 1984). In the 1956 election, this culminated in the 'Sinhala only' campaign, which brought Bandaranaike and the SLFP to power. The 'Sinhala only' campaign set the tone for Sinhalese politics that would prevail over the next 50 years, with each of the two major Sinhalese political parties competing for the Sinhalese vote by promoting Sinhalese and treating Tamils as (at best) second class citizens (de Silva 1986; Bose 2007).

The 1956 election victory by Solomon Bandaranaike proved to the Sinhalese parties that one could win elections by being anti-Tamil. The first legislation of the new SLFP government was to make Sinhalese the sole official language. DeVotta argues that this act was the decisive turning point that marked the beginning of the violent conflict between the two communities:

> The evidence suggests that the Sinhala-only movement and the Official Language Act of 1956 provided the catalyst for the numerous anti-minority policies and ethnocracy that followed, and that the institutional decay this generated over nearly two decades was what caused Tamil mobilization and the ongoing civil war. This was because the Official Language Act and the policies it inspired radically altered the rules of polyethnic existence.
>
> DeVotta (2004, 3)

Tamils felt that the government was denying them their cultural heritage and identity, and that this act would prevent Tamils from taking up government employment, because all government business was now conducted in Sinhalese. In response to the 'Sinhala-only' legislation, Tamils held a peaceful demonstration in Colombo, which was violently disrupted; the violence spread, and rioting broke out in Trincomalee and Jaffna. 'Between 20 and 200 people were killed depending on which side was doing the tallying' (Wriggins 1960, 328). This was the first serious anti-Tamil riot, with the loss of many lives.

168   *D. Feith*

Following this 1956 riot, the Prime Minister Solomon Bandaranaike held discussions with the leader of the Federal Party, Chelvanayakam, about the Tamil grievances, and the two leaders came to an agreement, known as the Bandaranaike–Chelvanayakam pact, which recognized Tamil as a national minority language and provided for Tamil to be used in administration in the northern and eastern provinces, where Tamils formed a majority of the population. However extremists, both Sinhalese and Tamil, were unhappy with the pact. Buddhist monks in the south of the island organized a campaign to boycott Tamil shops and demonstrated in front of the prime minister's house. In the north, Tamils defaced Sinhalese lettering on government buses and replaced the Sinhalese with Tamil script, following the methods adopted in south India during the anti-Hindi agitation in the 1950s and 1960s. Under pressure, Bandaranaike broke the agreement, the Tamil language was not officially recognized, and the 'Sinhalese only' policy prevailed (Weiss 2011).

This was to become a common pattern over the next decades – on numerous occasions, leaders of the Tamil and Sinhalese communities met and signed agreements, but later, the Sinhalese leaders came under pressure from Sinhalese chauvinists in the south and failed to honour the agreements. The lesson for Tamils was that non-violent and peaceful negotiations and protests did not achieve anything positive for them, and they became increasingly frustrated. The tension erupted again in June 1958 with an outbreak of communal violence. Tamils were attacked, raped, humiliated, killed, their homes ransacked and burned: 'there were lootings, burnings and savagery on such a scale as had not been known before' (Ludowyk 1967, 295). Approximately 300–400 people were killed, and thousands of Tamils fled their homes in Colombo and other parts of the south to find safety in the Tamil-majority north. This was also to form a pattern in the following decades: violent attacks on Tamils in the south, forcing them to flee to the north. This led to a growing perception, and indeed an increasing reality, that there were two separate states on the island – the Sinhalese south and the Tamil north. The government declared a state of emergency and, in 1959, Prime Minister Solomon Bandaranaike was assassinated by a Buddhist monk, 'following orders from a leading monk' (DeVotta 2004, 121), because he was perceived as giving too much away to Tamils. After elections in 1960, his wife, Mrs Sirimavo Bandaranaike, became prime minister and continued to govern without giving any significant consideration to Tamil grievances.

Relations between the Tamil and Sinhalese communities continued to deteriorate. The 'Sinhalese only' policy effectively excluded Tamils from government jobs, a major source of employment. Tamils felt increasingly frustrated as attempts at negotiating a solution to their grievances were repeatedly unsuccessful. The extremist Sinhalese-Buddhist groups in the south, including some Buddhist clergy, continued (and this still continues) to exert pressure on all governments not to make any concessions to Tamil demands. Each of the two major (Sinhalese) political parties used the extremist Sinhalese chauvinist demands for political purposes when in opposition, accusing the government of giving in to Tamil demands. This made it extremely difficult for any government to negotiate meaningfully with the Tamils, and created an environment in which discrimination against Tamils was normalized.

In the 1970s, a younger Tamil generation became increasingly disillusioned with the failed attempts at political negotiations, and many came to the conclusion that a more militant approach had to be taken for Tamil grievances to be addressed. They believed in their right to self-determination, and increasingly came to see that, for Tamils to achieve justice and equality in Sri Lanka, they would have to fight for it militarily. Militant groups began to form in the north, with the aim of establishing a separate Tamil state of Eelam. The Liberation Tigers of Tamil Eelam (LTTE), established by Velupillai Prabakaran in the 1970s, was one of a number of militant groups developing in northern Sri Lanka with the belief that the only way for Tamils to have equal rights was to take up arms. In 1975, Prabakaran carried out his first assassination, of Jaffna mayor Alfred Duraiappah, considered a traitor to Tamils because of his loyalty to Mrs Bandaranaike (DeVotta 2004). Initially, the LTTE was a small group, and its activities included robbing banks and killing policemen. External events, particularly outbreaks of violent anti-Tamil rioting, led to the growing popularity and increasing size of the LTTE and other Tamil militant groups.

By 1976, the Federal Party had been replaced by the Tamil United Liberation Front (TULF) as the main Tamil party that was trying to improve the position of Tamils by conventional political means. The TULF leader, A. Amirthalingam, was initially supportive of the newly forming Tamil militant groups, and met Prabakaran on many occasions. At a convention in Vaddukoddai, the TULF adopted a resolution calling for the restoration of Tamil Eelam (later referred to as the Vaddukoddai Resolution). In the 1977 elections, the TULF campaigned for a separate state for Tamils, and won majority support in the northern and eastern provinces, giving it an electoral mandate for a separate Tamil state. This was a significant development, because it gave Tamils a democratic claim for a separate state, as well as the historic claim (Swamy 1994; Kingsbury and Feith 2010).

Anti-Tamil rioting broke out on several more occasions, triggered by various incidents. In 1977, anti-Tamil riots 'left more than 300 people dead and many more wounded' (Swamy 1994). Then in 1981, anti-Tamil rioting broke out on a larger scale. The army and police participated in burning down the Jaffna public library, the repository of 100,000 irreplaceable rare and ancient Tamil manuscripts. This was a violent symbolic attack by government forces on Tamil language and culture. From that time on, Tamil civilians believed they could not be guaranteed safety by the government of Sri Lanka; and the Sinhalese police and army in the northern province were seen as enemy occupying forces. However, worse anti-Tamil violence was to come. The anti-Tamil riots that erupted in Colombo in July 1983 were a turning point in the conflict, and led directly to widespread increased Tamil support for the separatist movement and specifically the LTTE. In July 1983, the LTTE ambushed an army patrol in Jaffna and killed thirteen soldiers – the largest number of soldiers ever killed by a Tamil militant group in one operation. In response, the Sri Lankan army went 'on a killing spree in the Northern Peninsula in which nearly sixty Tamils died, but only the LTTE attack was made public' (DeVotta 2004, 169). When the soldiers' bodies were returned to Colombo, anti-Tamil riots erupted. 'There is no doubt that people within the government planned an attack on Tamils and were using the funeral to instigate it' (Peebles 2006, 135). Violence exploded in Colombo, where Tamil businesses and residential areas were set on fire and looted. The riots lasted for about a week and, during that time, mobs of Sinhalese systematically attacked Tamil homes and businesses, looting, destroying and murdering. The mobs had electoral rolls provided to them by people linked to the government, including government ministers, which identified Tamil properties, often next to Sinhalese homes.

Anti-Tamil violence spread during the week to Sinhalese-majority towns and to Trincomalee, where it continued for more than a month. 'The official death toll was 367, but unofficial estimates are as high as 3,000' (Peebles 2006). Tamil civilians were assaulted, raped, robbed and killed, and the police did not intervene to protect them (Manor 1984). Thousands of Tamils fled their homes in Colombo and other parts of the south, and went to the north where they believed they would be safer in Tamil-majority areas. This had the effect of increasing the Tamil majority in the northern province and reinforcing the polarization between the Tamil north and the Sinhalese south. It was as if the rioters, and the government inaction in preventing them, were driving the Tamils to a separate state. The rioters, and the government complicity in allowing the riots, gave the Tamils a clear message that they were not welcome. The message appeared to be that Tamils were second class citizens and could not expect to be protected by the laws of the country.

The 1983 riots were significant in internationalizing the conflict in Sri Lanka. Newspapers in Tamil Nadu, the neighbouring state in India, were filled with front page reports of the riots in gruesome detail. There were large street protests in Tamil Nadu against the Sri Lankan government, and the Tamil Nadu Chief Minister, M.G. Ramachandran, condemned the attacks on Tamils in Sri Lanka and led a delegation to New Delhi to raise the issue with the Indian government (Sivarajah 1996). There was widespread sympathy and support for the Sri Lankan Tamils in Tamil Nadu and, over the next few years, support and training was provided to Sri Lankan Tamil militant groups in India by the Tamil Nadu government and the Research and Analysis Wing (RAW) of the Indian government (Swamy 1994; Wilson 2000; Bose 2007).

The 1983 riots made nearly 70,000 Tamils homeless in Colombo, and more in other cities and towns. Thousands of Tamils moved to Jaffna, and many of these joined the militants, increasing the numbers in the militant groups significantly; thousands of others sought refuge overseas. This was the beginning of the exodus of Tamils from Sri Lanka to seek safety in other countries. More than 100,000 Tamil refugees fled to Tamil Nadu by boat, and several thousand others sought refuge in western countries. This led to the growth in size of Tamil communities in many countries around the world, including the UK, Canada, Germany, Switzerland, the USA, Australia, New Zealand and several other countries in Europe. According to estimates, the Tamil diaspora is currently between 800,000 and one million people. This is a significant diaspora, many of whom have continuing links to Sri Lanka through relatives, friends and the internet, and many of whom still believe in a separate Tamil state (Feith 1988; Fuglerud 1999; Wilson 2000; International Crisis Group 2010a).

After the aggressive anti-Tamil riots in 1983, there was a continuing spiral of violent attacks and counter-attacks, and a descent into civil war; an estimated 80,000 or more people have been killed and many more displaced (DeVotta 2004; Bose 2007; Weiss 2011). Each military offensive by the government armed forces led or pushed more Tamils to join the LTTE. Because of the war, there were few education or employment opportunities for Tamil youth in the northern and eastern provinces, and many turned to militancy to find meaning in their lives. The war and all the consequences of ongoing civil war increasingly strengthened a sense of Tamil nationalism and the belief in fighting for a separate Tamil state, Eelam.

In the 1980s, the LTTE emerged as the dominant militant group, in part by killing the leaders of rival Tamil militant groups. The Indian government acted as a mediator in negotiations between the Tamil militants and the Sri Lankan government in the 1980s, and sent in the Indian Peace Keeping Force (IPKF), which occupied the northern and eastern provinces from 1987 to 1990. The IPKF failed in peace-keeping and became enmeshed in a war against the LTTE. Also in the years 1987–1990, the Sri Lankan government was fighting against a Sinhalese uprising in the south, led by the Janatha Vimukthi Peramuna (JVP – People's Liberation Front), which was violently opposed to the presence of Indian troops in Sri Lanka. The Sri Lankan government fought the JVP in the south and re-armed the LTTE to fight against the IPKF in the north. When the IPKF withdrew, the LTTE claimed it had successfully defeated the world's fourth largest army and moved in to take control (Wilson 2000; Pratap 2001; Weiss 2011).

From 1990 to 1995, the LTTE controlled the Jaffna peninsula and many other parts of the northern and eastern provinces and, in that time, developed skills and experience in public administration. It ran a de facto separate Tamil state; it had a police force and law courts to maintain law and order; it regulated transport; it developed taxation and banking systems. Despite the government imposing an economic blockade on the north, the LTTE demonstrated to the Tamil people that they could effectively administer territory, as well as fight wars against the Sri Lankan and Indian armies (Feith 1992, 1995; Wilson 2000).

The 1994 parliamentary elections in Sri Lanka were won by a coalition led by Chandrika Kumaratunge, the daughter of former prime minister Bandaranaike, who agreed to a ceasefire and entered into negotiations with the LTTE. However, the negotiations broke down and war resumed in April 1995. In

October 1995, the Sri Lankan army invaded Jaffna and took control of the peninsula, which it has held since then. The LTTE and thousands of Tamil civilians fled the peninsula and moved to the Vanni region. The LTTE maintained its de facto separate state in the Vanni region, with its capital at Kilinochchi, from then until the Sri Lankan army offensive in September–October 2008, which culminated in the LTTE finally being defeated in May 2009.

During the late 1990s, the war intensified; the government and the LTTE acquired more sophisticated weaponry, and both increased the use of land-mines. The government launched several major military campaigns against the LTTE in the north, and the LTTE carried out several major attacks on army bases and on targets in Colombo. In July 2001, the LTTE attacked the airforce base next to the country's only international airport and, besides the thirteen LTTE fighters and seven Sri Lankan army soldiers dying in the attack, 'twenty-six civilian and military aircraft were either totally destroyed or damaged, at a cost to the government of nearly US $1 billion' (DeVotta 2004, 1). The tourism industry was severely affected by this, and people in the country increasingly felt the war had gone on too long. In the December 2001 parliamentary elections, Ranil Wickremesinge campaigned on a platform of peace negotiations, won and became prime minister.

After the 2001 elections, there was a cessation of hostilities by both sides and, in 2002, the government of Sri Lanka and the LTTE signed a Memorandum of Understanding (MOU) and entered into a series of negotiations, facilitated by Norway. International donors promised assistance for rehabilitation, and there was a positive sense that a peaceful settlement would be achieved. Significantly, the Sri Lankan government and the LTTE were equal partners in the nego-tiations – both controlled territory, both had armies. It was accepted by the international community that the involvement of both parties was crucial if the negotiations were to succeed in resolving the conflict. However, the peace negotiations broke down, and the ceasefire was increasingly breached. In 2005, Mahinda Rajapaksa won the presidential elections and became pre-sident of Sri Lanka. Soon after his election, he revealed that he was not interested in Norway continuing in its role as mediator between the Sri Lankan government and the LTTE. It became increasingly clear that his government was not interested in continuing peace negotiations with the LTTE and intended to pursue a military solution. The government abandoned peace negotiations, increased military expenditure and was able to secure both military and diplomatic support from China and India (Pararajasingham 2009). In 2008, it demanded that all foreign observers leave the north of Sri Lanka, so no-one would witness the final assault, and embarked on a determined effort to wipe out the LTTE militarily (Weiss 2011). During 2008–2009, the Sri Lankan government and armed forces waged a ruthless and bloody war against the LTTE. The UN estimates suggest 7,000 people were killed in the first four months of 2009 – other estimates are of up to 40,000 deaths. In this final phase of the war, no journalists were allowed in to the war zone, but significant and credible reports have emerged to confirm that it was a brutal,

Separatism in Sri Lanka 173

bloody battle, in which thousands of civilians were brutally killed (US Department of State 2009; International Crisis Group 2010b; BBC 2011; Weiss 2011).

In its struggle for an independent Eelam over a period of at least 26 years, the LTTE systematically used violence, often without discriminating between non-combatant civilians and armed opponents. The LTTE was ruthless in assassinating Tamil rivals and Tamil and Sinhalese civilians. It carried out human rights abuses, it conscripted child soldiers, and it persecuted Muslims in the north and the east. As well as being responsible for human rights abuses, the LTTE made a number of strategic mistakes, which also damaged its cause and reputation. The assassination of former Indian Prime Minister Rajiv Gandhi, carried out in 1991 by the LTTE, lost the LTTE Indian and international support. It failed to persevere with, or commit fully to, political negotiations, and instead repeatedly returned to war. The LTTE leader, Vellupillai Prabakaran, maintained tight control and was intolerant of criticism, even internal criticism, to the extent that a number of senior leaders in the organization were killed (Swamy 1994; Pratap 2001; International Crisis Group 2010b; Weiss 2011).

However, while acknowledging the above shortcomings and failures, it is important also to recognize LTTE achievements. The LTTE gave Tamils a sense of pride and self-esteem – they felt they no longer had to tolerate being treated as second class citizens. It had a reputation of being disciplined, with a strong moral code among its military cadre of no drinking, no smoking and no premarital sex. The LTTE established an efficient civil administration in the territory it controlled, including a police force, a judicial system, transport, tax, economic planning and development, rehabilitation for internally displaced people, health and welfare. It demonstrated to Tamils in Sri Lanka and in the diaspora, and to the international community, that a separate Tamil state in Sri Lanka was possible (Feith 1995, 2002; Pratap 2001; Weiss 2011).

Many Tamils, in both Sri Lanka and the diaspora, felt some ambiguity about the LTTE. They were unhappy that the LTTE killed other Tamils, and they recognized that the LTTE carried out human rights abuses and made mistakes, but they were reluctant to admit this, because they saw the LTTE as defending Tamil rights. The ambiguity felt by many Tamils is expressed clearly by Niromi de Soyza in her memoir *Tamil Tigress*: 'My heart sank. So it was true: the Tigers were eliminating their rival Tamil militant organisations. Until now, I had refused to believe the rumours as I had become so infatuated with the Tigers. They were our heroes – known for their impeccable conduct and discipline, ready to sacrifice their lives for the Tamil people' (De Soyza 2011, 48).

Prabakaran and other senior LTTE leaders were killed in May 2009 in the final days of the war, and the LTTE was defeated. The Rajapaksa government won the war, but has ignored opportunities for genuine reconciliation with the Tamil community in Sri Lanka since then. The underlying grievances that led

174   *D. Feith*

young Tamils to take up arms and join militant organizations in the 1970s and 1980s still exist. Tamils in Sri Lanka have been systematically discriminated against since independence in 1948 by successive governments. Both major Sinhalese parties have played on anti-Tamil sentiments for political purposes and to strengthen their own political position. Since independence, the minority Tamil community has been in an insecure position, and Tamils have been treated as second class citizens. During the 26-year conflict, the LTTE defended and fought for Tamils, both militarily and in several series of political negotiations, but they have now been defeated. However, the reasons why Tamils took up arms and joined the LTTE and other militant Tamil groups, and why many Tamil civilians supported the LTTE, have not been adequately addressed (Balasingham 2004; Peebles 2006).

Since the war ended, a number of significant reports have been published detailing the human rights abuses and alleged war crimes carried out by both the Sri Lankan Armed Forces and the LTTE in the final months of the war (US Department of State 2009; International Crisis Group 2010b; BBC 2011; Weiss 2011). These reports added to international pressure on the Sri Lankan government to address allegations about war crimes, and the Sri Lankan government appointed a Lessons Learnt and Reconciliation Commission, which submitted its report to the president in 2011. However, this international pressure regarding the government's alleged responsibility for war crimes and the demand for an independent investigation into these allegations has not affected the lives of the Tamil minority living in Sri Lanka.

Since the end of the war in 2009, many parts of northern and eastern Sri Lanka, the areas which were traditionally inhabited by the Tamils as their homeland and where they formed a majority for many centuries, have been under military occupation. Despite the end of the war and the defeat of the LTTE, the government has increased military spending (Perera 2011b). In November 2011, Tamil National Alliance (TNA) parliamentarian M.A. Sumanthiran tabled a report in parliament that was a serious indictment of the treatment of Tamil citizens by the military, especially those living in the north and east of the country. It detailed the heavy military presence in the north and east, the control that the military exerts over the lives of civilians and the increasing number of sexual assaults carried out against women and girls, often by government officials and the military. In response to this TNA report, the National Peace Council of Sri Lanka issued a media statement (November 2011), which read:

> As in all wars, unless work is done at the grassroots to get rid of the injustices which caused the war, unless people are treated with respect and the rule of law prevails, and unless peace with justice is made real, there is the danger of resentments spilling over into renewed conflict. There needs to be a break with the past. What happened during war has no place in a time of peace.

This is an important statement that needs to be considered by the Sri Lankan government. If Tamil grievances are not addressed, some time in the future, the demands for a separate Tamil state will be heard again.

References

Balasingham, A. (2004), *War and Peace: Armed Struggle and Peace Efforts of Liberation Tigers*, London, Fairmax.

BBC (2011), 'Sri Lanka's Killing Fields'.

Bose, S. (2007), *Contested Lands*, Cambridge, Harvard University Press.

Census of India (2011) http://censusindia.gov.in/2011-prov-results/prov_data_products_tamilnadu.html (accessed 26 November 2011).

Chatterjee, P. and P. Jeganathan (eds) (2000), *Community, Gender and Violence*, Subaltern Studies, New York, Columbia University Press.

Department of Census and Statistics – Sri Lanka (2011), www.statistics.gov.lk/ (accessed 26 November 2011).

de Silva, K.M. (1986), *Managing Ethnic Tensions in Multi-ethnic Societies: Sri Lanka 188–1985*, London, University Press of America.

De Soyza, N. (2011), *Tamil Tigress*, Sydney, Allen & Unwin.

DeVotta, N. (2004), *Blowback: Linguistic Nationalism, Institutional Decay, and Ethnic Conflict in Sri Lanka*, Stanford, CA, Stanford University Press.

Feith, D. (1986), 'Conflict in Sri Lanka' *Asia Pacific Context* 2(3).

——(1988), *Stalemate: Refugees in Asia*, Melbourne, Asian Bureau Australia.

——(1992), 'Tiger Hunters Go in for the Kill' *Modern Times* (August).

——(1993), *Human Rights in Sri Lanka*, Melbourne, Community Aid Abroad Briefing Paper.

——(1995), *Into Tiger Country: A Visit to Northern Sri Lanka*, Melbourne, Australian Volunteers International.

——(2002), *North-East Sri Lanka: Field Visit Report*, Melbourne, Australian Volunteers International.

——(2009), 'The Growth of Tamil Nationalism in Sri Lanka' in A. Pararajasingham (ed.), *Sri Lanka: 60 Years of 'Independence' and Beyond*, Switzerland, CJPD.

Fuglerud, O. (1999), *Life on the Outside: The Tamil Diaspora and Long Distance Nationalism*, London, Pluto Press.

Ghosh, P.S. (2003), *Ethnicity versus Nationalism: The Devolution Discourse in Sri Lanka*, New Delhi, Sage.

Gunasingham, M. (1999), *Sri Lankan Tamil Nationalism: A Study of Its Origins*, Sydney, M.V. Publications.

Hyndman, P. (1985), *Democracy in Peril Sri Lanka: A Country in Crisis*, Brisbane, Lawasia Human Rights Standing Committee.

International Crisis Group (2010a), 'The Sri Lankan Tamil Diaspora after the LTTE' *Asia Report* No. 186 (23 February 2010).

——(2010b), 'War Crimes in Sri Lanka' May 2010, at www.crisisgroup.be/flash/sl/sl.html (accessed 5 August 2012).

Irschick, E.F. (1969), *Politics and Social Conflict in South India: The Non-Brahman Movement and Tamil Separatism, 1916–1929*, Berkeley, CA, University of California Press.

Ismail, Q. (2005), *Abiding by Sri Lanka: On Peace, Place, and Postcoloniality*, Minneapolis, MN, University of Minnesota Press.

176   *D. Feith*

Kingsbury, D. and Feith, D. (2010), 'Tamils Have No Voice in Sri Lanka' *National Times*, 23 April 2010.

Krishna, S. (1999), *Postcolonial Insecurities: India, Sri Lanka and the Question of Nationhood*, Minneapolis, MN, University of Minnesota Press.

Ludowyk, E.F.C. (1967), *A Short History of Ceylon*, New York, Frederick A. Praeger.

Madura Rasaratnam (2009), 'Ideology of Tamil Nationalism' in A. Pararajasingham, (ed.), *Sri Lanka: 60 Years of 'Independence' and Beyond*, Switzerland, CJPD.

Manor, J. (ed.) (1984), *Sri Lanka in Change and Crisis*, London, Croom Helm.

Mendis, G.C. (1940), *The Early History of Ceylon*, Calcutta, YMCA Publishing House.

National Peace Council of Sri Lanka (2011), Media release: 'TNA statement needs to be probed and acted upon to achieve reconciliation', 1 November 2011.

Orjuela, Camilla (2010), 'Understanding Power and Change in the Context of Armed Conflict and Post-war Reconstruction' in C. Orjuela (ed.), *Power and Politics in the Shadow of Sri Lanka's Armed Conflict*, Sida Studies No. 25, SIDA.

Pandey, G. (2006), *Routine Violence: Nations, Fragments, Histories*, Stanford, CA, Stanford University Press.

Pararajasingham, A. (2009), 'The Rise, Growth and Suppression of the Tamil Armed Movement' in A. Pararajasingham (ed.), *Sri Lanka: 60 Years of 'Independence' and Beyond*, Switzerland, CJPD.

Peebles, P. (2006), *The History of Sri Lanka*, Westport, CT, Greenwood Press.

Perera, Jehan (2011a), 'TNA Report to Parliament Exposes Negative Peace' *The Island*, 31 October 2011.

——(2011b), 'Economic and Political Costs of Over-extending Military Role' *The Island*, 7 November 2011.

Pillay, K.K. (1975), *A Social History of the Tamils*, Madras, University of Madras.

Ponnambalam, S. (1983), *Sri Lanka: National Conflict and the Tamil Liberation Struggle*, London, Zed Books.

Pratap, A. (2001), *Island of Blood*, New York, Penguin Books.

Ranganathan, M. (2006), 'Nurturing Eelam on the Net: The Transmission of Nationalist Ideologies through Sri Lankan Tamil Websites', Working Papers National Centre for South Asian Studies, Monash Asia Institute, Clayton.

Sivakumar, S. (1984), 'Eelam: An Impossible Goal for the Tamils of Sri Lanka?' *Asian Studies Association of Australian Fifth National Conference*, Adelaide.

Sivananda, A. (1984), 'Sri Lanka: Racism and the Politics of Underdevelopment' *Race & Class*, 26(1).

Sivarajah, A. (1996), *Politics of Tamil Nationalism in Sri Lanka*, New Delhi, South Asian Publishers.

South Asia Terrorism Portal (2011), 'Vaddukoddai Resolution', at www.satp.org/satporgtp/countries/shrilanka/document/papers/vaddukoddai_resolution.htm (accessed 26 November 2011).

Swamy, Narayan M.R. (1994), *Tigers of Lanka: From Boys to Guerrillas*, Delhi, Konark Publishers.

Tamilnation.org (2011), 'Tamil Eelam: Right To Self Determination, Paper presented by a Working Group of the International Federation of Tamils at the London Seminar, Towards a Just Peace, February 1992, at http://tamilnation.co/selfdetermination/tamileelam/9202reversion.htm (accessed 26 November 2011).

Taras, R.C. and Ganguly, R. (2002), *Understanding Ethnic Conflict: The International Dimension*, New York, Longman.

US Department of State (2009), *Report to Congress on Incidents During the Recent Conflict in Sri Lanka*.

Weiss, G. (2011), *The Cage: The Fight for Sri Lanka and the Last Days of the Tamil Tigers*, Sydney, Pan Macmillan Australia.

Wilson, A.J. (2000), *Sri Lankan Tamil Nationalism*, London, C. Hurst & Co.

Wriggins, W.H. (1960), *Ceylon: Dilemmas of a New Nation*, Princeton, NJ, Princeton University Press.

11 Separatism, ethnocracy, and the future of ethnic politics in Burma (Myanmar)

Renaud Egreteau

Introduction[1]

Burma's protracted civil war has been raging for decades. Since independence from British rule in 1948, the country has witnessed the development of a myriad of ethnic insurgencies—Karen, Mon, Kachin, Shan, and so on. All have resisted the nation- and state-building proposed by the Burman-dominated central authorities, be they parliamentarian (1948–1962) or military-led (since 1962). Therefore, the post-1948 Burmese civil war offers a valuable, yet extremely complex, case for the study of the nexus between separatist tendencies produced by ethnic minorities and the centralizing interventions—often militarized—of an "ethnocratic" state, structured around dominant ethno-linguistic group (here, the Burmans). The underlying rationale behind Burma's everlasting democratic gridlock and a key explanation of the continuation of authoritarian rule there, the Burmese ethnic conundrum has evolved over the years. It will be argued in this chapter that it has gradually metamorphosed from forthright ethnic "secessionism" from the post-colonial state extolled by ethno-religious minorities in the early years to more conventional—yet still confrontational—"ethnic politics" within the delineation of the twenty-first century "Burmese" state—thus echoing Donald Horowitz's argument made in other places and times (Horowitz 1985, 230–232).

This chapter, after a brief overview of Burma's post-colonial ethnic land-scape and the fiery rise of separatism after 1948, intends to demonstrate that ethnic secessionism is now in decline in present-day Burma after six decades of civil war. A dramatic penetration of an ethnocratic "Burman" central state and military administration has been observed throughout the country, and this chapter will identify the reasons behind this. However, ethnic identity conflicts remain salient and unresolved despite a wide range of policies defined by the dominant Burman elite to cope with centrifugal forces, including ruthless counter-insurgency, post-1989 ceasefire strategies, and a new "federalist" constitution in 2008. If separatism has weakened in Burma, ethnic identities are constantly reshaped and re-fragmented, and one cannot rule out the violent reformulation of ethnic grievances and therefore the perpetuation of political instability in the coming decade, beyond the mere "democratic transition" stalemate the country has been experiencing since the 1950s (Figure 11.1).

Ethnic politics in Burma (Myanmar) 179

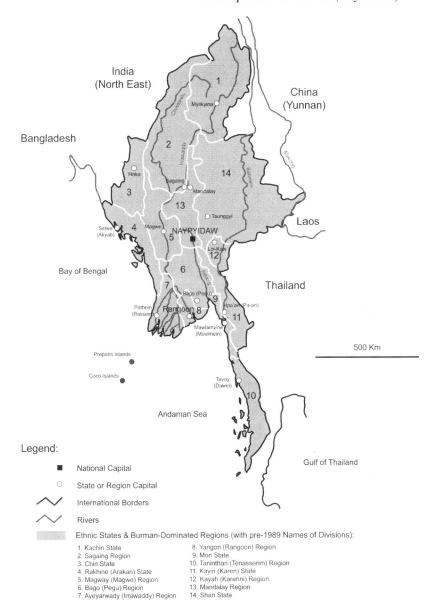

Figure 11.1 States and regions of Burma (Myanmar) since 2008

180   *R. Egreteau*

Ethnicity and civil war in post-colonial Burma

Colonial legacies: the politicization of ethnicity

British colonial rule (1826–1948) deeply altered Burma's ethno-political landscape. Before the British annexed the region during the nineteenth century—after three Anglo-Burmese wars in 1824–1826, 1852–1853, and 1885—ethnicity had little impact over the global policies defined by local kingdoms, principalities, and tribal chiefdoms there. Pre-colonial Burma's dominant cleavages were rather shaped around religious diversities and patron–client or tribute relationships among the diverse ethnic groups inhabiting the region (Lieberman 1978). However, after 1886, ethnicity became a powerful policy instrument for the colonial administration and a key element of population control. Henceforth, enacting new codes, laws, and censuses based on ethno-religious and linguistic markers, the British "categorized" Burmese people under its jurisdiction, dividing them into ethnic sub-categories, such as Indians, Karens, Kachins, or Burmans (Taylor 2007). With a clear distinction between "native" groups and "foreign" ones, and then rigorous sub-divisions of all "indigenous" groups, the colonizers therefore introduced new fractures grounded in European-conceived notions of race, border, and territoriality (Thant Myint-U 2001, 243).

The colonial politicization of a "reified" ethnicity laid the foundation for the current understanding of the Burmese ethnic conundrum. Most of the country's post-independence conflicts and its present-day territorial delineation indeed find their roots there (Taylor 2007, 75–76). Then and now, distribution of power and wealth, access to education and political influence, control of trade and warfare, all followed the politicization of local ethnicities, and the subsequent asymmetric relationship between the Burman majority and all other ethnic groups, whether indigenous or not (Taylor 1982). The British had brought along with them foreign minorities to run their Burmese colony (Indians, Chinese, and westerners), and favored newly Christianized "native" ethnic minorities, such as the Karens, Kachins, or Chins. The latter were largely incorporated into the colonial security forces and administration, and were granted favorable access to western and British Indian education. British Burma was moreover schematically divided into two administrative parts after 1886: *Ministerial Burma* (Burman-dominated central and deltaic populous zones) and the *Frontier areas* (peripheral areas scarcely inhabited by hill tribes). It became perceived by the local population and elites as a mere colonial enterprise protected by foreigners who were seconded by ethnic foreign or native minorities—as in many other parts of the colonial world (Smith 1999; Taylor 2007). Resentment and hostility grew among the dominant (and dominated) Burman Buddhist community. Burmese nationalism therefore first brewed under ethnic Burman compulsion for both anti-colonial resistance and identity pride restoration, especially once the Burmese royal family had been exiled in India in 1886 (Gravers 1999).

Ethnic politics in Burma (Myanmar) 181

World War Two and the Japanese occupation of Burma (1942–1945) shattered the country and further widened the rift among its ethnic groups. The Burman majority largely embraced the militarist and racial model offered by Japan. Picked up by Tokyo to lead the Japan-funded Burmese Independence Army, General Aung San (father of Aung San Suu Kyi) and Ne Win (future ruler of the country between 1962 and 1988) shared many of the conceptions the Japanese had brought into colonial Southeast Asia. Whereas, on the other side of the spectrum, Indian, Muslim, Karen, Chin, and Kachin ethnic groups chose to remain loyal to the British during the war. An inter-ethnic reconciliation was nonetheless attempted by Aung San at the inception of independence talks, notably through the February 1947 "Panglong Agreement," which offered a basis for a semi-federal constitution (Walton 2008). But the agreement was reached between the Burmans and only three ethnic groups (Kachin, Chin, and Shan) whereas others, such as the Karens and Arakenese (Rakhine), rejected it. Moreover, Aung San was assassinated in July 1947. Colonial wounds and war resentment therefore started off a six-decade-long civil war (Lintner 1999; Smith 1999).

"Burmanizing" Burma or how to fail at post-colonial nation-building

After Aung San's assassination, Prime Minister U Nu and a Burman-dominated elite shepherded the post-colonial state and nation-building. If most ethnic minority leaders opted tacitly to join the Federal Union of Burma created by the 1947 constitution, the Karens (Karen National Union, KNU) and Communist forces swiftly opposed it and took up arms. The transition from ethnic-dominated colonial armed forces to a Burman-dominated independent army during 1945–1949 turned mutinous, with Karen battalions rioting against the rising dominance of General Ne Win, the self-appointed (Burman) Army Chief of Staff in 1949 (Callahan 2004a, 129). As social agitation had also started in 1946–1947 in the Arakan, Naga, and Pa'O areas, centrifugal ethnic forces therefore soon threatened the country's federal unity. Through the 1950s, Burma's internal conflicts escalated into a violent struggle between ethnic *and* ideological armed groups, on the one side, against Burman-dominated central civilian and military authorities on the other. The objectives of the rebellions were as much "separatism" (for the ethnic Karens, Mons, Karennis, and so on) as "revolution," particularly for the rising Communist Party of Burma (CPB).

After 1948, the main instrument U Nu's civilian administration had at its disposal to reassert its control over Burma's territory was the armed forces, or *Tatmadaw*. "Burmanization" (*bama lumyo gyi wadda*) of the latter was fostered from the late 1940s, once the ethnic mutineers had been purged by Ne Win (Callahan 2004a). Also, foundations for the Burmanization of other state institutions were led through several policy programs the government imposed early on (education, land reform). A constant feature since the separation of Burma from British India (1937), the re-indigenization of the

182   R. Egreteau

country, its administration, society, culture, and economy, had been a key policy agenda of all Burma's post-colonial leaders. Most had indeed been trained and influenced by the Burmese nationalist movement of the pre-war era (Holmes 1967; Egreteau 2011).

While proposing a unifying rhetorical agenda based on a classical "unity in diversity" mantra that recognized and praised ethno-religious diversity, the successive post-independence Burmanization campaigns openly granted the upper hands to the Burman-Buddhist majority and its independence heroes. This pattern was only exacerbated by the military regimes that succeeded U Nu's civilian government from the late 1950s; indeed, the Ne Win-led Burmese army first took power in 1958 (caretaker military administration) and then through a proper *coup d'état* in 1962, not to leave it since. From then on, Rangoon promoted political stability through the adherence of all minority groups to the ideology, history, and objectives of the dominant group, the Burmans, of Buddhist obedience. In doing so, they followed a unitary state formation pattern as had been observed in nineteenth-century France or Italy for instance. The Burman de facto "ethnocracy" was reinforced through a state-controlled education policy, the imposition of *Bama-zaga* (Burmese) as the official language, and the development of a Burman-dominated administration nonetheless presumed to acknowledge the rights of ethnic and religious minorities (Brown 1994; Steinberg 2001; Callahan 2004b; Taylor 2009).

Drawing on the Panglong Agreement, Burma's first constitution (1947) was federalist in spirit, but in reality, it provided Burma with a Jacobinist and eth-nocratic post-colonial state structure for the first post-independence decade. Some ethnic groups (only the Shans and Karennis technically, Silverstein 1958, 43) had been guaranteed a constitutional right to self-determination 10 years after independence. But in 1958, as this right was felt to be denied, the Shans rebelled against U Nu's government, joining Karen, Karenni, Pa'O, and Mon ethnic insurgents. In 1961, the Christian-dominated Kachins (Kachin Independence Organization, KIO) and Chins (Chin Independence Army, CIA) also entered the civil war. They were primarily reacting against the willingness of the central (and democratically elected) government to impose Buddhism as the state religion (Lintner 1999, 201; Smith 1999, 192). Burma's Christian ethnic elites—albeit severely divided along communal lines (Baptists, Metho-dists, Adventists, Catholics ...)—have long used religion as a key identity marker to be defended against the Burman Buddhist majority (Rajah 2002; Fong 2008, 336–337).

Ever since, ethnic groups have perceived threats to their identities and culture (if not existence), and lambasted the successive Burman-dominated central authorities for their failure to implement a full-fledged federalist system and provide them with adequate autonomous political and cultural rights. In widening the Burmanizing post-colonial agenda after the 1960s, successive Burmese juntas under General Ne Win (1962–1988) and since 1988 have only intensified the post-independence "Burman" policies of U Nu's administration. As argued by several Burma scholars, the thorough penetration of the Burman-

Ethnic politics in Burma (Myanmar) 183

dominated post-colonial state (and along with it, Buddhism, the Burmese language, and a Burman reading of the country's history) into Burma's ethnic territories and sociopolitical systems has, since 1948, been critical to the perpetuation of the country's domestic conundrum (Smith 1999; Steinberg 2001; South 2008; Taylor 2009). Besides, the shaping and reshaping of the ethnic armed outfits and their political demands through the years, fluctuating according to the power of the Burmese Army, their access to cross-border trafficking and support networks in a Cold War context have all contributed to the failure of Burma's building as a "nation." Yet post-colonial "state"-building has not necessarily been construed as a failure; quite the opposite. The rising influence of the Burmese armed forces, incarnating the Burman dominant elite, has conferred to the state a strong instrument to deal with ethnic separatism.

State responses to ethnic separatism

Fighting separatism: militarization of the "Burmese" unitary state (1948–1988)

The pursuit of civil war since independence has been, if not exclusively, at least directly related to the increasing domination of Burman-led armed forces and the militarized response to ethnic and Communist agitation it promoted. The prestige of the anti-colonial struggle and the role of the (Burman) "Thirty Comrades" (including Aung San and Ne Win), who founded the Burmese Independence Army in 1941 and led the country to independence, facilitated the adoption of a military-defined strategy to cope with centrifugal forces after 1948. The soldiers soon projected their own views of the essentiality of the armed forces in the past, present, and future of independent Burma (Tin Maung Maung Than 1993; Steinberg 2001; Callahan 2004a). Henceforth, stability, protection of the nation, and state security had to rely on military hands. It became especially critical when the post-independence civilian political scene gradually failed to stabilize the federal union during the 1950s. Transfer of authority from civilians to soldiers during the crucial 1958–1962 period appeared logical. Yet, it was not followed by a transfer of power from an ethnic group to another—quite the contrary. Indeed, political supremacy and decision-making remained in Burman hands after 1962, and two parallel policy options were applied to consolidate the unitary state: a military one based on the pursuit of crude counter-insurgency operations by the army itself, and a political one, combining a loose recognition of Burma's multi-ethno-linguistic society and erratic peace talks with insurgent outfits proposed by Ne Win's leadership.

Since U Nu called in the armed forces to resist Communist rebels and ethnic-based mutinies in 1948–1949, counter-insurgency campaigns aimed at crushing separatist forces have become the dominant and most enduring

184 R. Egreteau

policy promoted by Rangoon. Scorched earth strategies in ethnic and border areas have been systematically conducted by *Tatmadaw* battalions, and were sophisticated in the early 1960s with the implementation of two new combined strategies: the "Four Cuts" campaigns (or *Pya Ley Pya*) and the "Home Guard" militia program (or *Ka Kwe Ye*, KKY). These were aimed at complexifying counter-insurgency warfare against a dozen increasingly strong and well-equipped armed rebellions able to sustain their struggle, notably the KNU, KIO, CPB, and the rising Shan insurgents (Smith 1999, 258–259; South 2008, 34–35). Although the "Four Cuts" policy was principally conducted by Burmese troops in ethnic areas to cut off funds, food, recruits, and intelligence from rebels, the *Ka Kwe Ye* state program allowed locally organized militias to stem larger ethnic separatist groups through smaller armed outfits formed by local warlords. Those were encouraged by the central government to run taxing and smuggling, starting with opium, in conflict areas in order to sustain their fighting. These KKY militias accepted their surrender of the separatist cause to fight as proxies for the Burmese army, being rewarded by a de facto extensive (and lucrative) local autonomy (Lintner 1999, 231; Smith 1999, 95; Egreteau 2009, 127). These brutal military strategies and the expansion of underground networks have inflamed inter-ethnic and center–periphery relations ever since.

In parallel, a more civilian-like approach to separatism has been endorsed by the post-1962 central military authorities. Gradually, the implementation of a pragmatic window-dressing of civilianization and acceptance of ethnicity (if largely assimilated to the Burman universe though) has been envisioned. Enshrined in the 1974 constitution, which replaced the 1947 one abrogated in 1962—a centralized structure colored by ethnic diversity created seven administrative "ethnic" states (Karen, Mon, Arakan, Chin, Kachin, Shan, and Karenni) and seven "Burman" divisions.[2] Yet, political power, including in ethnic states that had lost the right to self-determination granted by the 1947 constitution, remained firmly under the one-party state structure ruled by Ne Win (Steinberg 2001, 54; Taylor 2009, 306). The latter did not allow the creation of ethnic "legal" movements (or political parties) to voice their concern at the supposedly decentralized level and pursued the multi-dimensional social, economic, and cultural "Burmanization" of society (Tin Maung Maung Than 2004, 197; Egreteau 2011, 267). With the 1974 constitutional framework and then the 1982 Citizenship Law, ethnicity was accepted, but only as a cultural subordinate to the essential unifying role of the highly centralized (Burman) state. In contrast to 1947, the re-conceptualization of ethnicity in 1974 was aimed at legally preventing separatist political claims for a distinct nationhood (Taylor 1982, 19). However, most ethnic rebellions continued in the 1970s–1980s, albeit a few marginal ones chose to be co-opted by the new system. On paper, after four decades of independence, Burma could claim it had resisted disintegration, with its international borders unmoved since 1948 and ethnic secession effectively stalled. But on the ground, most separatist groups (Kachins, Karens, Shans) could praise noticeable achievements, as they had de facto gained large—if not absolute—

Ethnic politics in Burma (Myanmar)   185

political and territorial autonomy in off-limits peripheral areas where the Burman central ethnocracy had to bend its muscles.

Marginalizing separatism: the ceasefire strategies (1989–2008)

The 1988 democratic uprising changed Burma's political configuration. A new junta succeeded Ne Win's socialist administration through another military coup staged in September 1988. It then promoted a singular ethnic policy based on the negotiation of ceasefires with most historical insurgencies. This skillful, though fragile, strategy developed by the Military Intelligence Services of General Khin Nyunt led to the gradual marginalization of the once powerful ethnic secessionist groups who one after another accepted a deal with the new Burman military rulers. Contrary to *Tatmadaw* hardliners who still favored large-scale counter-insurgency to fight off ethnic rebels after 1988 (Fink 2008), Burmese Military Intelligence strategists opted for parallel appeasement processes and bargained ceasefire agreements with seventeen ethnic minorities between 1989 and 1995. The latter were consequently granted de facto autonomy, but still denied any right to secession or self-determination. In exchange, they dropped their armed rebellion against Rangoon (Steinberg 2001, 187; Zaw Oo and Win Min 2007, 30). In the late 1980s and early 1990s, it was indeed time to do (legal and illegal) business, especially along the booming Chinese and Thai borders where ethnic groups felt they could benefit from the commercial dynamism of Burma's neighbors. The ceasefire policy also freed some better equipped Burmese troops—albeit already dramatically expanded after 1989—to fight the rebels refusing to enter a ceasefire, such as the KNU, the Shans, and the Karennis. It also provided the Burmese junta with lucrative opportunities to share or tax trade resources extraction in ceasefire group-controlled areas, as with the Kachins and Was for instance. Lastly, following the KKY model of the 1960s, several ceasefire militias (such as Wa local armies) acted as Burmese state "sub-contractors," not opposing it, but beginning to fight against other non-ceasefire groups (Taylor 2009, 433).

This policy promptly weakened the most powerful secessionist voices. The historical Communist insurgents (CPB) were the first to collapse into five smaller ceasefire ethnic-based militias, as early as 1989. Then, in two successive waves (1991 and 1993–1995), new ceasefire deals were accepted by a dozen other ethnic minorities, including the Chinese-speaking Kokangs, the Palaungs, some Shan and Karen groups, the Kachin Independence Organization in 1993, and eventually the drug lord Khun Sa's Mong Tai Army in 1996. Ceasefires have survived for almost two decades, offering stability and business opportunities for every party involved, leaving only a few Karen, Karenni, Shan, Mon, Naga, and Chin armed rebellions lingering near the Thai and Indian borders (Lintner 1999; Egreteau 2009; Kramer 2010). They were efficient instruments for the semi-pacification of border areas during the 1990s. Ethnic groups were further politically weakened on the Burmese central stage, but

186   *R. Egreteau*

reinforced locally with a community-based civil society and autonomous modes of governance de facto allowed (Pedersen 2008). The way the Kachins have controlled their northern Burma territory since 1993 is illustrative of this autonomy (South 2008, 190–194). They have built up in their headquarters of Laiza (near the Chinese border) an efficient civil administration, autonomous security forces, their own education programs, and business activities, far away from the Burmese central state's hands.[3] Another KNU-opposed Karen sub-ethnic group also managed to create new political spaces for its Christian elites through a ceasefire agreement (Core 2009).

Nevertheless, the accommodation tactics chosen by the junta in the 1990s have not solved ethnic tensions. Ceasefires were mere elements of conflict management processes in which disputes are just managed to acceptable levels. But conflict resolution processes and political dialogue have never been initiated (Zaw Oo and Win Min 2007; Kramer 2010). Counter-insurgency operations have been launched against non-ceasefire groups every year since 1989. Furthermore, the policies inspired by Khin Nyunt have gradually been challenged by developments endogenous to the Burmese military institution itself. Khin Nyunt, despite being the architect of this strategy, was purged along with his Intelligence Services in October 2004. The core of the Burmese armed forces establishment under the aegis of Senior General Than Shwe then intended to take back full control of political power and sidelined the more moderate and foreign-oriented elements of their ranks during the 2000s (Zaw Oo and Win Min 2007, 55; Taylor 2009, 484–485). Above all, they aimed to control the pace and path of the gradual transition planned to cope with the inevitable generational transformation of the army and its aging post-1988 military leadership, and secure a praetorian landscape for Burma in the 2010s decade. For this, a new constitution was needed, and its drafting was the occasion to rethink center–periphery relations after 20 years of combined defensive insurgency and ceasefire deadlock.

Managing separatism: ethnicity and the 2008 constitution

This backdrop of ethno-political stalemate suited the central military state as long as its first post-1988 generation of leaders remained in power. It meant few defeats on a now limited counter-insurgency front and rising commercial opportunities in erstwhile off-limits ethnic areas. Furthermore, the ethnic conundrum was very much construed as disconnected from the pro-democratic struggle of Aung San Suu Kyi. But when the army's internal transition appeared ineluctable in the late 2000s—notably after the purge of Khin Nyunt—the foundations for a stable post-junta praetorian landscape implied the "legal" redefinition of the role of the army and its relations to the state, society, and ethnicities. The 1974 constitution had been abrogated in 1988; therefore, a National Convention purporting to draft a new constitution law was convened by the military, in two phases though (1993–1996 and 2004–2007). Ethnic minorities, despite articulating new claims within this new

Ethnic politics in Burma (Myanmar) 187

constitution-making process and being (forcibly for some) included in the second round of the National Convention in 2004, soon raised concerns about the objectives of the still military-dominated state structure and its foreseeable control of Burma's forthcoming ethno-political landscape (Pedersen 2008). The army then assertively initiated a third phase of dealing with ethnic separatist groups, purporting to make them all "return to the legal fold," including by force (Holliday 2010, 118; Smith 2010).

Since the announcement of a seven-step "Roadmap to a flourishing-discipline democracy" in 2003, the Burmese military had attempted to control the pace, modalities, and terms of the transition from direct military rule (as since 1988) to more indirect praetorian politics, under a civilian-governed political administration and a federalist state structure. Entirely controlled by the army, the process has produced a new constitution, approved through a controversial referendum in May 2008, which legalizes the dominant political role of the armed forces (Prager Nyein 2009). Yet, efforts have ostensibly been made to propose a federal state union, at least on paper. Literally, indeed, the 2008 constitutional framework offers greater advantages to ethnic minorities than the two previous constitutions. It proposed a bicameral parliament, with a 440-member House of Representatives (*Pyithu Hluttaw*) and a 224-member House of Nationalities (*Amyotha Hluttaw*, with twelve MPs for each of the fourteen states and regions). It also enshrined fourteen local parliaments and governments led by an elected "chief minister" (as in neighboring India). Each ethnic group[4] boasting more than 0.1 percent of Burma's total population was therefore to be guaranteed elected representatives. On paper, there were many reasons to satisfy the demands of secessionist groups and put an end to many rebellions. But on the ground, after the subsequent organization of the flawed November 7, 2010 elections, most scenarios converged to the renewal of a highly centralized political, civil, and financial administration (Taylor 2009, 500; Smith 2010; Steinberg 2011).

The 2010 parliamentary elections—the first of their kind since those won by the pro-democracy opposition led by Aung San Suu Kyi in May 1990, but denied by the then junta—were heavily criticized by the international community. They saw the pro-regime Union Solidarity and Development Party (USPD) wining 58 percent of the seats contested in the two national assemblies— where the Burmese armed forces had already secured 25 percent of the seats by constitutional appointment (Prager Nyein 2009, 639). Ethnic parties that were allowed to register by the military-run Election Commission won about 11 percent of the seats, whereas the Burman democratic opposition, which chose to contest the elections, won only 1 percent of the seats.[5] Worth noticing, in the seven "ethnic" local parliaments, the USDP never won a clear majority, standing for the first time with some sort of political "plurality" in ethnic areas (Steinberg 2011, 5). Early in 2011, ex-Prime Minister General Thein Sein was subsequently elected president of the union by the national parliament once the latter had convened its two USDP-dominated houses. He then controversially appointed the fourteen local chief ministers, including many former

188   R. Egreteau

members of the military administration, now officially retired from the armed forces. But as in 1962, 1974, and 1988, transfer of power and influence occurred in 2011 among the same ethno-political and military-dominated Burman circles, further asserting the Burmese state's ethnocratic proclivity and the lack of progress toward genuine democratization and ethno-political pluralism.

Beyond the shrinking room for maneuver ethnic minorities might still be granted in post-2010 parliamentary politics, grievances at the periphery have not changed much with the adoption of these post-junta institutions.[6] Ceasefire groups that have more or less accepted participation in the election process (Was, Kachins, Mons …), as well as non-ceasefire groups (Karens, Shans, Karennis …), face the very same challenges posed by the confusion of civilian and military Burman-dominated politics at the center level, and the Burmanizing inclinations of the latter (Smith 2010). The Border Guard Force (BGF) program has been a key issue antagonizing Naypyidaw and ceasefire groups after 2008. The constitution imposed the idea of an integration of "all" Burmese security forces, including insurgent and ceasefire groups, into one centrally controlled military command—an idea that appears quite logical in any modern nation-state context. This BGF scheme has, however, been vociferously opposed by most ethnic groups, starting with the Kachins and Was, still very much reluctant to surrender their arms and shift their political loyalty to a battalion commanded by Burman officers.

Although only one ceasefire had been broken in the 1990s,[7] the first cracks appeared in August 2009 when the Kokaung ceasefire militia was suddenly crushed by the Burmese Army along the Sino-Burmese borders. Forced to enter "the legal fold" and give up its arms, this local militia run by an aging drug lord trained as a KKY leader in the 1960s was swiftly replaced by a pro-Naypyidaw BGF. The Burmese state had chosen violent means for the first time to deal with one of the weakest ceasefire groups, and it raised concerns among all others. In June 2011, the 17-year-old ceasefire between the Kachin Independence Army and Tatmadaw broke down, initiating a low-intensity conflict in Kachin-controlled areas. Only two ceasefire groups (out of seventeen) had subsequently accepted Naypyidaw's BGF offer before the scheme was put on hold in late 2011 (Buddhist Karens and a dissident Kachin group). For many, dropping their weapons would mean losing their last bargaining power against the Burman-dominated center for the still powerful Kachin, Shan, and Wa armed outfits (Kramer 2010, 79–80). It would also imply losing lucrative commercial opportunities to Burman and foreign business circles close to the military and longing to get access to ethnic-controlled resources and trade routes. Yet, political and ideological divisions among ethnic groups have been more and more obvious in recent years—impeding any unified front against the center, despite the recent creation of a KIO-led United Nationalities Federal Council (UNFC), a politico-military alliance,[8] as well as the recent signing of ceasefire agreements with the Shan and Karen rebels in late 2011. Conflicting opinions expressed by ethnic leaders on the participation (or not) in the new praetorian (yet parliamentary) order proposed

Ethnic politics in Burma (Myanmar) 189

by Naypyidaw with the 2008 constitution, revival of decade-long jungle Kachin guerillas against ever-expanding Burmese armed forces (for the patterns, see Fink 2008), debated relations with the still popular democratic opposition led by Aung San Suu Kyi (a Burman), the uncertain pace and path of the praetorian transition initiated by President Thein in 2011, and contending influences of exiled ethnic leaders, all lead to the conclusion that the ethnic conundrum remains far from being solved in the post-junta context of 2011.

Continuation of separatism by other means: the salience of ethnic politics in Burma's post-2010 ethnocratic landscape

Despite a continuing center–periphery deadlock, the popularity of ethnic secessionist ideals has been declining severely during the 2000s. Political scientist Robert Taylor has argued that, if the country's multiple ethnicities can barely get along, they cannot separate either (Taylor 2005). Indeed, the idea of "Burma" as a multiethnic nation now seems well accepted, including by the once fiercest ethnic rebel leaderships. Ethnic movements for pure secession from Burma have become marginal, and only a punctual response to harsh counter-insurgency campaigns still orchestrated by the Burmese army. Rather, the search for a federal "Burmese" union recognizing ethnic differences and providing minority groups with effective power is now driving Burma's ethnic dynamics. Following Horowitz's differentiation (Horowitz 1985, 230–232), we will argue that independence is now less the primary objective of most ethnic political minorities. Rather, a far-reaching cultural, political, and above all economic autonomy, access to development and redistribution of resources to non-Burman communities within a revamped (yet democratic) "Union of Burma" is now sought.

Burma's waxing ethnic fragmentation

One of the rationales explaining the recent decline in ethnic separatism is the waxing fragmentation of Burma's myriad of ethnicities. Already a complex social, cultural, and ethno-linguistic patchwork at the time of independence, Burma's multiethnic society has become ever more complicated to read and construe with the passing of generations. Anthropologist Ananda Rajah stressed the quasi absence of rationality showed by the country's multitude of ethnic groups in defining one's belonging to a specific identity (Rajah 1998, 137). Political contradictions, inconsistencies of ethnic leaders' positioning, and the bewildering change of names of ethnically mixed people, he argues, have failed to not only unify ethnic minorities in a common front against the Burman center, but also fractionalized ethnic groups into legions of politicized sub-communities. Burma's ethno-political landscape, albeit articulated around a severe conflict between the central state and ethnic minorities, has become a complex web of inter-ethnic and intra-ethnic tensions, which has

190   R. Egreteau

diminished the potential threat that ethnic separatism posed to Rangoon in the early post-colonial days.

Ethnic identities have always been extremely malleable and conceived in flexible ways by ethnic groups themselves. The civil war has not further compartmentalized and isolated ethnicity, far from it; ethnic populations have rather mixed with one another at an increasing pace in post colonial decades, despite restrictions on people's mobility in a country torn by internecine wars. Today, a Kachin can have a Shan father, a Palaung a Chinese mother, a Christian Karen may find a Mon or Buddhist Karen wife, a Burman Muslim might very well have Bengali or Punjabi blood in his/her veins, and so on. If we scratch the surface, argues Robert Taylor, it becomes impossible to draw "racial" delineations of any of Burma's ethnic communities—including the Burmans. Ethnic identities— the outcome of colonial categorizations—have for him become an irrelevant concept in Burma's twenty-first century local landscape (Taylor 2005, 263). After all, maybe these ethnicities have indeed eventually become "Burmese," all using for instance the Burmese language as *lingua franca*—inside and outside Burma—after decades of Burmanization (Callahan 2004b; Egreteau 2011).

The Karen communities are a perfect example of this waxing fragmentation, and their case is well documented (Harriden 2002; Rajah 2002; South 2007, 2010; Fong 2008). Divided into dozens of sub-ethnic and tribal groups, which have unintelligible languages and incompatible religious practices (Buddhists, Methodists, Adventists), the Karens have set up competing armed insurgencies only unified (but not all) by their common hatred of "the Burman" (South 2007, 56). The KNU has long assumed that a Christian men-dominated elitist outfit could speak for all other Karen communities and define an unchallengeable "Karen-ness" (Harriden 2002; South 2010). Yet, this historical separatist group has been in position since the 1950s neither to efficiently challenge the Burman-dominated center nor to coalesce Karen sensibilities— including on the position that Karen leaders should adopt *vis-à-vis* the Burman democratic opposition led by Aung San Suu Kyi after 1988 or the ceasefire talks conducted in 2003 and more recently in December 2011.[9] Karen Buddhist militias and Christian-led ones are still defining contending ethno-political agendas (Core 2009). The very same patterns can be observed with the various Kachin or Shan communities and the myriad of local militias, ceasefire and non-ceasefire armed groups pretending to defend them.[10] This protracted fractionalization has therefore "balkanized" Burma's sociopolitical systems at the local and ethnic levels (Callahan 2007, 48), therefore severely dwindling unified secessionist threats away.

Ethnicization of politics in a "disciplined democracy"

The 2008 constitution seemed to have addressed for the first time some ethnic grievances, including freedom of religion and the formation of elective decentralized representation systems. But this new constitutional order and

Ethnic politics in Burma (Myanmar) 191

the subsequent policies implemented by Naypyidaw were, and still are, defined by and for the military institution and the ethnic Burman majority. The 2010 elections have created a national assembly and fourteen local parliaments, but many observers have underlined their flaws. In all, it will take considerable time before Burman-dominated praetorian rulers realize that an effective federal structure with highly decentralized powers is not a threat to the integrity of the state itself, or to the peace of its society. Most of the military establishment still in power after 2010 has indeed considered political and cultural federalism as "anathema" since the 1950s (Steinberg 2011, 7). Regional military commanders (all Burmans) still have more decision powers than the chief ministers elected in 2010.

Yet, there are few reasons to read Burma's evolving ethno-political scene with some dose of optimism after the 2010 elections. Ethnic secessionist claims are on the decline, if not simply abandoned by the most active insurgencies. The idea of "Burma" as a union of ethnicities is positively portrayed in the public discourses of inside or exiled ethnic leaders, as well as in public speeches pronounced by the post-2010 election government of President Thein Sein. It just has to be re-modeled, with its internal—not external—frontiers and administrative structures rethought (South 2008, 219). Subsequently, ethnic conflictual politics will most probably remain the nodal point of Burma's domestic affairs, without the separatist proclivity of the first post-independence decades. Secession from the Burmese state seems now less at stake; it would rather be secession from within the Burmese ethnocratic model that would be sought by the major ethnic groups, wishing nonetheless to be part of a democratic Burma. Even most of the historical KNU rebels have dropped their basic demands for a separate and independent "*Kawthoolei*" state (Fong 2008; South 2010) and reached a ceasefire agreement in January 2012. The Kachins have even proposed the creation, under a UNFC umbrella, of "Burmese federal armed forces."[11]

Rather, the aspirations of the various ethnic minorities are converging toward demands for the end of all systematic discriminations and center-led persecution based on religion and ethnicity, the guarantee of civil, cultural, and socioeconomic rights in a constitutionally enshrined federal structure with highly decentralized controls over local resources and tax collection, education, and expression of local identities (Pedersen 2008). Yet, if the majority of ethnic groups seem to agree (safe for a few marginal, but powerful, ones such as the Was or a few warlord-led local militias), all disagree as to the policy road to get there. And these federalist demands are still met with extreme suspicion and contempt by the dominant Burman military elite, wary of the separatist background of most minorities and the economic power they have gained. The Kachins, for instance, were willing to participate in the post-2008 constitutional process, but were excluded from it by Naypyidaw; the BGF issue, the KIO's overall dominance of the Kachin community (unlike KNU), and the control over resources and trade with China that the Kachin have developed since the 1990s remain strong bones of contention between

192   *R. Egreteau*

the Burmese armed forces and this peculiar ethnic group (Kramer 2010, 80–81). Nonetheless, an enduring ethnicization of Burmese politics seems to be accepted by all and might prevail in the forthcoming decade.

Conclusion

Ethnicity has been politicized by colonial rule and Burma's post-independence landscape. With the perpetuation of the political stalemate between ethnic groups and the Burman-dominated center after 1948, Burmese politics have in turn been extremely ethnicized, including outside Burma. All future scenarios for the democratization and stability of the country will necessitate a thorough addressing of this ethnic conundrum to overcome the ethnocratic proclivity of the Burman majority (Brown 1994; Holliday 2010). The creation of new sociopolitical and civil society spaces in ethnic areas, beyond what ceasefire agreements have been generating since the 1990s, is crucial. After two decades of ceasefire policies as well as savage counter-insurgency operations, extremely complex interactions between the central state and local organizations, ethnic leaderships, and other non-state actors have been developed in Burma (Callahan 2007; Pedersen 2008). Evolving ethnic identities and adaptative inter-ethnic networks have complexified relationships between competing local/national groups, which oppose, resist, co-exist with, or supplant the central (military) state in many ethnic and border areas where secession has been a fact, but not any more an objective in itself. After 2011, post-junta policy-makers will have to take into account this protracted ethnic fragmentation in order to find avenues to consolidate pluralistic politics in Burma, and definitely turn the page on ethnic centrifugal separatism. Although having been addressed by the new military-inspired "federalist" 2008 constitution, Burma's ethnic issue remains far from being solved. Centralized and military-dominated practices have all the chances of being favored by the forthcoming praetorian rulers wary of the perpetuation of separatist threats.

The latter are, however, on the decline, with the Burmese armed forces more in control of Burma's territory and central structures in 2011 than in 1988. As interestingly both the ethnic groups and the Burman majority (military or democratic) aim to build a modern Burmese polyethnic state, new foundations for inter-ethnic dialogue have to be found. The focus on ethnic areas' development could open new doors. Alleviating a balanced socio-economic development in ethnic areas plagued by poverty since colonial times could provide new opportunities for political settlements and prevent the revival of secessionist conflicts. That is what the military regime has done in Burman-dominated rural areas of central Burma where the pre-2011 junta's agricultural and infrastructure policies were met with (relative) enthusiasm, unlike in remote ethnic border areas where looting of resources, forced labor, and underground trade have boomed under military and foreign auspices since 1988. The challenge would be to address social and economic grievances before political ones, and for the international community to review its ethical approach to the Burmese deadlock and assist the Burmese in doing so.

Notes

1 For ease of linguistic simplicity and without any political connotation, the author has chosen hereafter to use the English terms "Burma," "Burmese," "Burman," and "Rangoon" instead of the vernacular terms of "Myanmar," "Bamar," or "Yangon." "Burmese" then refers to the citizenship and common language of the people inhabiting Burma, while "Burman" (Bamar) more specifically designates the ethnic majority of the country (hence the "Burmanization" processes further described), in which also dwell non-Burman ethnic minorities, such as the Karens, Kachins, Mons, … etc.
2 "Divisions" were renamed "regions" by the 2008 constitution.
3 Author's interview with KIO leadership, Laiza, August 2011.
4 Out of the 135 recognized by Naypyidaw, therefore excluding the Rohingyas for instance.
5 Aung San Suu Kyi's party, the National League for Democracy (NLD, officially illegal since May 2010) boycotted the elections. For the complete results, see Burma Fund, *Burma's 2010 Elections: A Comprehensive Report*, New York, The Burma Fund UN Office, January 2011.
6 The military-run State Peace and Development Council (SPDC), which in 1997 succeeded the State Law and Order Restoration Council (SLORC) formed in 1988, was indeed dissolved in March 2011, opening up a new civilian phase.
7 In 1995, by the Karenni National Progressive Party (KNPP); author's interview with KNPP Joint Secretary, September 2008.
8 Author's interview with KIO leadership, Laiza, August 2011.
9 Author's interview with David Thackarbaw, KNU Joint General Secretary, September 2008.
10 Author's interview with Colonel Yawd Serk, SSA-S commander-in-chief, September 2008, and with General Gun Maw, with KIA Vice-Chief of Staff, Laiza, August 2011.
11 Author's interview with General Gun Maw, Laiza, August 2011.

References

Brown, David (1994), *The State and Ethnic Politics in Southeast Asia*, London, Routledge.
Callahan, Mary (2004a), *Making Enemies – War and State-Building in Burma*, Ithaca, NY, Cornell University Press.
——(2004b), 'Making Myanmars: Language, Territory and Belonging in Post-Socialist Burma' in J.S. Migdal (ed.), *Boundaries and Belonging: States and Societies in the Struggle to Shape Identities and Local Practices*, Cambridge, Cambridge University Press, pp. 99–120.
——(2007), *Political Authority in Burma's Ethnic Minority States: Devolution, Occupation, and Coexistence*, Washington, DC, East–West Center Policy Studies, No. 31.
Core, Paul (2009), 'Burma/Myanmar: Challenges of a Ceasefire Accord in Karen State' *Journal of Current Southeast Asian Affairs*, 28(3): 95–105.

194   *R. Egreteau*

Egreteau, Renaud (2009), 'Burma's Militias: Between Insurgency and Maintaining Order' in L. Gayer and C. Jaffrelot (eds), *Armed Militias of South Asia: Fundamentalists, Maoists, and Separatists*, London, Hurst & Co, pp. 112–133.

——(2011), 'Birmanie: "Birmanisation"' in J. Medeiros (ed.), *Le Mondial des Nations*, Paris, Editions Choiseul, pp. 260–282.

Fink, Christina (2008), 'Militarization in Burma's Ethnic States: Causes and Consequences' *Contemporary Politics*, 14(4): 447–462.

Fong, Jack (2008), 'Revisiting the Ethnodevelopment Model: Addressing Karen Self-determination within the Context of the Failed Ethnocratic State of Military-ruled Burma' *Ethnic and Racial Studies*, 31(2): 327–357.

Gravers, Mikael (1999), *Nationalism as Political Paranoia in Burma: An Essay on the Historical Practice of Power*, Richmond, Curzon.

Harriden, Jessica (2002), 'Making a Name for Themselves: Karen Identity and the Politicization of Ethnicity in Burma' *The Journal of Burma Studies*, 7: 84–144.

Holliday, Ian (2010), 'Ethnicity and Democratization in Myanmar' *Asian Journal of Political Science*, 18(2): 111–128.

Holmes, Robert (1967), 'Burmese Domestic Policy: The Politics of Burmanization' *Asian Survey*, 7(3): 188–197.

Horowitz, Donald (1985), *Ethnic Groups in Conflict*, Berkeley, CA, University of Berkeley Press.

Kramer, Tom (2010), 'Ethnic Conflict in Burma: The Challenge of Unity in a Divided Country' in L. Dittmer (ed.), *Burma or Myanmar? The Struggle for National Identity*, Singapore, World Scientific, pp. 51–82.

Lieberman, Victor (1978), 'Ethnic Politics in Eighteenth Century Burma' *Modern Asian Studies*, 12(3): 455–482.

Lintner, Bertil (1999), *Burma in Revolt: Opium and Insurgency since 1948*, Chiang Mai, Silkworm Books.

Pedersen, Morten (2008), 'Burma's Ethnic Minorities: Charting Their Own Path to Peace' *Critical Asian Studies*, 40(1): 45–66.

Prager Nyein, Susanne (2009), 'Expanding Military, Shrinking Citizenry, and the New Constitution in Burma' *Journal of Contemporary Asia*, 39(4): 638–648.

Rajah, Ananda (1998), 'Ethnicity and Civil War in Burma: Where Is the Rationality?' in R. Rotberg (ed.), *Burma: Prospects for a Democratic Future*, Washington, DC, Brookings Institution Press, pp. 135–150.

——(2002), 'A "Nation of Intent" in Burma: Karen Ethno-nationalism, Nationalism, and Narrations of Nation' *The Pacific Review*, 15(4): 517–537.

Silverstein, Josef (1958), 'Politics in the Shan State: The Question of Secession from the Union of Burma' *The Journal of Asian Studies*, 18(1): 43–57.

Smith, Martin (1999), *Burma: Insurgency and the Politics of Ethnicity*, Bangkok, White Lotus.

——(2010), 'Ethnic Politics in Myanmar: A Year of Tension and Anticipation' *Southeast Asian Affairs*, 1: 214–234.

South, Ashley (2007), 'Karen Nationalist Communities: The "Problem" of Diversity' *Contemporary Southeast Asia*, 29(1): 55–76.

——(2008), *Ethnic Politics in Burma: States of Conflict*, London, Routledge.

——(2010), 'Governance and Legitimacy in Karen State' in N. Cheesman, M. Skidmore and T. Wilson (eds), *Ruling Myanmar: from Cyclone Nargis to National Elections*, Singapore, ISEAS Publications, pp. 63–89.

Steinberg, David (2001), *Burma: The State of Myanmar*, Washington, DC, Georgetown University Press.

——(2011), 'Myanmar's Perpetual Dilemma: Ethnicity in a "Discipline-Flourishing Democracy"' Washington, DC, East–West Center Working Paper, No. 22.

Taylor, Robert (1982), 'Perceptions of Ethnicity in the Politics of Burma' *Southeast Asian Journal of Social Sciences*, 10(1): 7–22.

——(2005), 'Do States Make Nations? The Politics of Identity in Myanmar Revisited' *South East Asia Research*, 13(3): 261–286.

——(2007), 'British Policy towards Myanmar and the Creation of the "Burma Problem"' in N. Ganesan and Kyaw Yin Hlaing (eds), *Myanmar: State, Society and Ethnicity*, Singapore, ISEAS Publications, pp. 70–95.

——(2009), *The State in Myanmar*, Singapore, NUS Press.

Thant Myint-U (2001), *The Making of Modern Burma*, Cambridge, Cambridge University Press.

Tin Maung Maung Than (1993), 'Neither Inheritance nor Legacy: Leading the Myanmar State since Independence' *Contemporary Southeast Asia*, 15(1): 24–63.

——(2004), 'The Essential Tension. Democratization and the Unitary State in Myanmar (Burma)' *South East Asia Research*, 12(2): 187–212.

Walton, Matthew (2008), 'Ethnicity, Conflict, and History in Burma: The Myths of Panglong' *Asian Survey*, 48(6): 889–910.

Zaw Oo and Win Min (2007), *Assessing Burma's Ceasefire Accords*, Washington, DC, East–West Center Policy Studies, No. 39.

12 Language practices and protracted conflict

The Tibet–China dispute

Robert Barnett

Why are disputes between nation-states and subsidiary groups difficult to resolve even when one side is willing to make major concessions? In this chapter, I look at the ongoing talks process between the Chinese government and the exiled Tibetan leadership, and argue that the positions of the two sides, at least in terms of a political resolution, are in many ways quite close. I ask why their differences have nevertheless remained so divisive and resistant to resolution, and look at the role of rhetoric in delaying any settlement of the issue.

The Tibet–China dispute is acutely asymmetrical, between what is broadly recognized as the second largest military and economic force in the world, with a population of 1.3 billion people, and a small group of some 150,000 exiles with minimal economic power and no military resources, who aim to represent another 5.9 million or so Tibetans inside Tibet.[1] The dispute came to a climax with the decision in 1950 of the newly constituted People's Republic of China to send an army of some 30,000 men to "liberate" the Tibetans and to enforce its claim that Tibet has long been a part of Chinese territory. It easily defeated the Tibetan army, leading the Dalai Lama and his government to accept a surrender agreement, known as "the 17 Point Agreement," in 1951, in which the Tibetans stated for the first time that Tibet was part of China and in return were promised effective self-rule. The arrangement collapsed following widespread resistance in eastern Tibet, which culminated in an armed uprising in Lhasa, the Tibetan capital, in 1959, the failure of which led the Tibetan leaders and some 80,000 other Tibetans to flee to India. Once there, they declared that the 17 Point Agreement had been forced on them, had anyway not been adhered to by the Chinese side, and under the leadership of the fourteenth Dalai Lama, established an administration in India that, although never formally recognized by other states as a government-in-exile, appears to have since gained wide support among the Tibetans still living in Tibet.

In terms of their demands, both sides moved dramatically toward moderation in the late 1970s: the Tibetan side abandoned violence and gave up calling for independence, opting for some kind of increased self-rule within China.[2] The Chinese state stopped proactive military attacks and mass cultural destruction and instead promised local autonomy for Tibetans, promoted rapid economic development, and allowed a limited measure of cultural tolerance (PRC 2000). The two sides began informal talks in 1978 and, since then, have been involved in numerous forms of dialogue or contact up to the present day, with ten rounds of talks between 2002 and 2010. These talks have seen little progress, and have brought the two sides increasingly close to deadlock.[3] Despite this dialogue process, the situation has continuously deteriorated, with nationalism growing on both sides. A factor in this has been the decision by the Tibetan exile leaders in 1987, after the first series of talks collapsed, to seek high-profile international support. This was followed by a series of major pro-independence protests in Tibet from 1987 onward, which led to martial law being imposed in Lhasa for 13 months from March 1989 (Goldstein 1997). As for the Chinese authorities, their policies in Tibet hardened somewhat in 1986 and again, much more sharply, in 1994 (Barnett and Spiegel 1996), leading eventually to a wave of unrest that spread across the Tibetan plateau in March 2008. This in turn led to a sharp increase in the Chinese military presence there.

The number of deaths of Chinese caused by Tibetan protestors since talks began three decades ago remains small—an estimated twenty-three people killed over 30 years—but nineteen of those deaths occurred in a single protest in 2008 (Barnett 2008b), indicating an abrupt increase in the level of violence by Tibetans. The number of Tibetans killed by the Chinese security forces in suppression of protests or through maltreatment of political detainees in prisons since the 1980s is hotly contested but runs into the hundreds. These casualty figures are minute compared with major conflicts such as Kosovo, Darfur, or the Congo, but the Tibet dispute has achieved a prominent position in regional and even world affairs. This is striking given that, 20 years ago, it was seen by almost all observers as a peripheral aspect of Chinese local politics, of no consequence internationally, and of interest in the west only among eccentrics and exoticists. Just how wrong that view was became clear in 2007, when the Tibet issue was formally acknowledged by China as a "core national issue" and declared to be an even more serious concern than its relations with Taiwan. A conflict that had been viewed as a marginal dispute over relatively moderate demands had become acute and significant without a change in the demands.

Convergence with limitations

Since the 1980s, the two sides have converged on some key issues besides agreeing to hold talks and giving up violence (on the Tibetan side) and tolerating a limited measure of religion and culture (on the Chinese side). For some years, the Tibetans proposed various arrangements for the Tibetan region or regions within China, notably "a peace zone" or "buffer region" (1987), "association" (1988), and "federation" (1991–1995); they also mooted less formal suggestions, such as "one country, two systems" (mentioned briefly in 1982–1984 and again in 1994 and 1998), and occasionally a return to the terms of the 17 Point Agreement. But since at least the late 1990s, the exiled leadership has sought only a form of autonomy, which it has described variously as "genuine," "meaningful," or as having "a high degree."[4] In theory, this is not so far from the approach of the Chinese government, which had promised autonomy for Tibet in 1951 and, by 1965, had formally accorded it to the areas it considers Tibetan (PRC 2000; Lundberg and Zhou 2009). So, since at least the late 1990s if not longer, on paper, the two sides have been arguing over the same issue: what kind of autonomy the Tibetans should be given. They of course have different conceptions of its form and features, but both say that independence is not required and that autonomy has been or should be delivered.

This is true in other general areas of policy as well, despite differences over specificities. Beijing's strategy of boosting infrastructure, modernization, and wealth creation through state subsidies (Fischer 2009) is in essence not opposed by the Tibetan side, despite concerns about implementation and motivation. Since the late 1970s, both sides have concurred on the importance of modernization, development, and an end to poverty. They even both support democratization, although this is viewed in a very limited way on the Chinese side. Both claim a commitment to maintaining the distinctiveness and vitality of Tibetan culture. Since 2004, China's leaders have recognized religion as having a beneficial role in society and have described it as playing an important role in the creation of social "harmony," currently their central policy objective. Both sides say that they have no racial or ethnic antagonism toward members of the other group. They agree about the importance of environmental and water source protection and, despite popular disapproval among many Tibetans, the two leaderships even agreed on the building of the railway to Lhasa, completed in 2006. None of this is very obvious in the public debates that we see, nor should we expect otherwise. But, in terms of broad objectives and negotiating points, both sides are within the same conceptual domain, at least on paper, and have been for many years.

Efforts at bipartite resolution of the dispute have been tried repeatedly. There was an early round of negotiations in 1982–1984 which failed, perhaps because the Tibetans avoided presenting specific proposals or because their aims were over-ambitious (Goldstein 1997, 72), and the formal "talks about talks" held from 2002 to 2010 have not proceeded beyond the pre-negotiation stage. This deadlock is because the Chinese side says that the Tibetans have not yet met the preconditions that they have set— primarily, that they give up the claim to independence. The Tibetan leadership has repeatedly stated that it has already done this. The two sides have now been involved in dispute for over 50 years, making this twice as drawn out as the average conflict, which is said to last 25 years, according to Gurr (1995, 52; cited in Miall et al. 1999, 32). Urgency and frustration have spread among Tibetans as a result, deepened by a widespread view that a negotiated settlement will not be feasible once the Dalai Lama, born in 1935, dies or becomes infirm.

Thus, the Tibet–China issue has become more tense and liable to collapse even though it has not involved military conflict or significant levels of violence since the 1970s, it has not been a "secessionist" dispute since at least the early 1990s, and no other state has offered support for it to seek independence for decades. It is thus not like Quebec or Scotland, which sought independence through peaceful means, or Kosovo or Palestine, which used largely forceful means to seek statehood. It does not claim colonial status and the rights that go with that, and the support it has had from foreign powers has been largely limited to rhetoric since the 1970s. Yet the dispute, which the weaker side insists is not separatist, insoluble, or even ethnic, is treated by the more powerful side as all these things.

Is language the issue?

Both sides have been criticized by commentators, scholars, and participants for the failure of the talks. China has been accused of forcing concessions from the other side without giving any of its own, whereas the Tibetan side has been accused of equivocating about its own concessions. The Tibetan side has responded to pressure over the years by giving steadily more emphatic assurances that it does not seek independence, and eventually gave explicit assurances after 2008 that it does not seek to challenge China's constitution or to change its political system (TGiE 2010).[5] The decision by the Chinese side not to respond with concessions is typical of asymmetrical negotiations (see Pfetsch 2008). Müller (2004) refers to this as the "hyperstrategist" approach—the more obdurate and insulting the negotiating behavior of the stronger party, the more it can put the weaker party under pressure to give further concessions in advance of any formal negotiations taking place, a tactic that has worked with the Tibetans. Müller argues that such an approach is irrational and counterproductive because it alienates other players and damages reputations.[6] But concern about reputation is not of consequence for China as there are no other parties to the China–Tibet dispute, which it sees as an internal matter, and which concerns paramount issues of sovereignty and territory.

Outside academic circles, one hears polemical, culturalist, or essentialist explanations for China's decision not to make concessions, such as that the Chinese or Communist character is capable only of zero-sum negotiations, a Cold War view not borne out by academic research.[7] An extreme view, found widely among Tibetan exiles, that the Chinese side secretly wants to wipe out Tibetan culture, has had little or no evidence to support it since the late 1970s and can be set aside. On the contrary, political scientists and historians have shown multiple times why China's pursuit of its interests is rational from its perspective (see, for example, Azar 1990, on protracted social conflict). This does not, however, explain why it has not resolved this conflict, given that a solution is within its grasp and in its interests, and given the strategic importance of the area, which covers over a quarter of China's territory and holds much of its water supplies. Certainly, any settlement would involve difficulties for Chinese officials, such as having to deal with a figure, the Dalai Lama, whom they mistrust. But such factors are largely incidental: they apply in any conflict resolution and do not explain why policy-makers in Beijing seem to be avoiding a settlement in this issue.

Rather than seeking evidence of some competing interest or cultural trait to explain the protracted nature of this dispute, I focus here on some of the linguistic practices and practical mechanisms in the discussions between officials. From a positivist point of view, the dispute remains protracted because the two sides have starkly different views of autonomy and what it means; inevitably, the Tibetans want a version that would give more local control than the Chinese side considers acceptable. Clearly, the Tibetan leaders began in 1979 with ambitious demands in this respect and, over time, have been forced to accept greatly reduced expectations; as we have seen, they once spoke of "association" and "two systems," but now call for a Tibet that would be not only within China, but would be non-democratic, socialist, and under the leadership of the Communist Party—a major shift. But I argue that the gulf between the two sides concerning the meaning of autonomy was widened by linguistic practices, and could have been narrowed far earlier if those practices had been more transparent to each side; many of the differences are explicable as negotiating maneuvers. In this view, the 30 years it took to go from one position to another result not so much from substantial disagreements but to linguistic difficulties in conveying them to the other side.

The role of language in negotiations has been extensively discussed in many fields, including court procedures in the US (Maynard 1984), business negotiations, classroom situations, various areas of sociolinguistics (Sidner 1994), and conflict resolution (Cohen 2001), particularly since the 1980s. The debate over these issues in international relations is discussed in Müller (2004), based on discussions that stem from Habermas's *Theory of Communicative Action*. Related approaches can be found in pragmatics—the study of "the way communicative interaction develops meanings beyond the explicit semantic or denotative content of linguistic forms" (Light 2007, 50)—as well as in the writings of Bakhtin on the social life of language and of Austin on performativity. My interest here, however, is not to discuss negotiations in general, but to describe the main linguistic strategies that have figured in this dispute and the way in which they have contributed to its continuance.

This involves distinguishing between what causes the continuance and what causes the origination of the dispute: what makes a conflict last may not be the same as that which led it to begin, or made it last at an earlier stage. The natures of conflicts change constantly, as do the means required to resolve them, a process explored in theories of conflict dynamics (see Miall et al. 1999, 16; Kriegsberg 2005, 77). In this case, initially incidental factors of discourse seem to have turned into causes rather than embellishments of the systemic failure of a process, and a conflict originally produced by an independence movement seems to be prevented from transitioning into a discussion over terms of autonomy because of linguistic habits among the main disputants. The mechanics of discussion have thus created their own effects

The Tibet–China dispute   201

and appear to have replaced the rational pursuit of self-interest. As Keiichi Kubo put it, when describing the real-world impact of discursive practices by NATO and other Western governments in their dealings with Kosovo, "It was a terrible mistake for the Western countries to call the KLA 'terrorists', since this excluded negotiation" (Kubo, Ch. 5, this volume). In such cases, the linguistic and discursive practices of disputants become determinative factors in themselves.

Equating difference with intractability

A certain intellectual framework among academics, policy-makers, and others generates a normative, neo-Freudian presumption that conflicts over deep-seated differences can only be resolved or reduced by ending those differences. But in fact, many communities find ways for effective coexistence despite such differences. These successes rely in part on social and linguistic practices, basically forms of etiquette, that are favorable for dispute settlement. The Tibet–China dispute is widely seen as a conflict between peoples or nationalities that are wholly different in history, culture, religiosity, and character. Even within China, officials and writers emphasize the distinctiveness of Tibetans in architecture, language, music, culture, and religion (see Gladney 1994), even though in political statements, they emphasize political and even genetic unity. More broadly, the dispute is seen as a Huntingdonian clash between animist and Confucian civilizations, between mountain nomads and lowland agriculturists, between religion and atheism, and so on. Such visions have fueled a presumption that the China–Tibet dispute is deep-seated and long-running, and it is often grouped among "ethnic" disputes and "separatist" conflicts that are seen as deeply fueled by irrational factors and as inherently difficult to resolve. In the Tibet–China case, it has been rare to find challenges among intellectuals to the concept of deep-seated difference, in part because the contrasts between the two sides are so readily apparent.

In other contexts, views of this type have been frequently critiqued, as with discussions in the 1990s about "intractable" disputes in the Balkans (Glenny 2000). They reflect a rationalist approach typical of modern nation-states, in which officials and allied intellectuals see themselves as not influenced by ethnic emotion or cultural factors and thus able to resolve conflicts in unbiased ways, while often in fact resolving them by force. Others have argued that such "intractability" arguments are generated purposively by the lesser parties to establish primordial or ancient claims, or by a state to argue that the weaker party is emotional, pre-rational, and prone to violence (see Kriegsberg 2005, 70). But the core critique of intractable difference is not that there are no significant differences between communities, but that differences do not prevent a solution (see Crocker et al. 2005). The semantic elision within the word "difference" of "distinctiveness" and "disagreement" is misleading: it does not follow that being distinctive leads to conflict, or that the China–Tibet issue is inimical to resolution. In fact, in the Tibetan case, it is not evident that deep cultural or historical differences, important and emotive though they are, are blocking a resolution. This does not mean that the two peoples will ever like each other, that they have similar cultures or ideologies, or that they do not have hidden aims, but it does suggest they have or had shared interests.

In fact, the Dalai Lama and his officials have repeatedly remarked upon these common interests—but, demonstrating how a linguistic practice can conceal and neutralize underlying convergence, in their public speeches, as we shall see, they tend to emphasize the differences. In general, the presentation of the Tibet–China dispute is so concentrated on the prominent cultural and historical differences between the two sides that it is difficult to keep in mind the closeness between them in terms of their main political demands. Historically, the Tibetans had a history of cooperating with powerful neighbors, to a degree often lampooned by those neighbors as slavish and opportunistic (Barnett 2007). From at least the mid-thirteenth century until 1910, there was little or no conflict between Tibetans and Chinese; they found ways to resolve their differences amicably and productively without visible conflict, let alone war. Those mechanisms were in essence linguistic. For example, from the mid-seventeenth century, the Chinese or, rather, the Manchus recognized the Tibetan leader as their spiritual teacher or preceptor, and the Tibetans recognized the Manchu emperor as an emanation of the Bodhisattva Manjusri, and therefore as spiritually equivalent to the Dalai Lama. This created what was politely referred to by Tibetans at the time as the "priest-patron" (*mchod–g.yon*) system of relations (Seyfort Ruegg 1991), which was particular to the Tibetan Buddhist cultural sphere.

These forms of linguistic resolution collapsed when the nation-state concept took hold in late Qing China, provoked by a challenge from another late imperial power, the British, who had briefly invaded Tibet in 1903. The Qing decided to establish their status as the sovereign authority in Tibet and, in 1910, sent a Chinese army to turn Tibet into a province of China. The collapse of the Qing or Manchu dynasty the following year allowed the Tibetans to repel the Chinese soldiers and declare their independence, but it also ended a long history of coexistence, leading to a series of small wars between the Tibetans and the Chinese until 1950. Since then, relations between the Tibetan government and China have been characterized by conflict, war, military occupation, uprisings, or popular unrest.

It is often argued that pre-twentieth century international relations in Inner Asia were of a sort that facilitated consensual forms of political relations, whereas the modern nation-state system tolerates only highly defined and bounded relations of very limited kinds. The China–Tibet case is an important instance of this thesis: the nation-state system could not replicate the complex nature of the Tibet–China relationship as found in the imperial system, insisting on describing it with rigid terms such as sovereignty, ownership, and territory or their opposite—an example of a dispute over language leading to war. Unlike the cases of, say, British recognition of the status of India or Nigeria at the end of its empire, or Russian and later Soviet recognition of

Mongolia's independence after the collapse of the Qing, for diplomatic and strategic reasons, no major outside power would declare its opinion as to which modern term to use to describe Tibet's status after 1911.[8] Without linguistic consensus internationally, war was more or less inevitable.

The Tibet–China dispute was thus initially about how to define—or, more precisely, about who gets to define—an imperial dominion in a post-imperial age.[9] But as the Tibetan leadership has recently sought only "genuine" or "meaningful autonomy," terms that are part of accepted nation-state discourse, the dispute is now over such issues as what defines autonomy, what constitutes the Tibetan area within China, and whether Chinese policies since the 1980s in some ways threaten traditional Tibetan culture and identity, as they had done explicitly in the 1960s and 1970s. On paper at least, these are relatively non-contentious, and we can say that the Tibet–China dispute has moved from a military conflict to a linguistic one. Clearly, this shift was because of the successful deployment of overwhelming force by the Chinese side and the absence of international support for Tibetan independence: it does not mean that language is the only important issue of disagreement, nor does it deny that the issue has involved deeply felt suffering for the participants in the past and still does so today. But, as we have seen, that is not in itself a bar to settlement and, whether out of desperation, guile, manipulation, or good will, the leading parties to this issue, and many ordinary Tibetans too, have for some decades committed themselves to a negotiated settlement that aims to agree on mutually acceptable language as a basis for a resolution.

That linguistic turn here is important not because language is the only effective mechanism for negotiating settlements, but because it is constitutive: in important ways, the nature of the dispute has changed into one that is largely about terminology and concepts, and thus in theory could be resolved by terminological niceties much as it was in Manchu times. But in the China–Tibet case, this reconstituting of the issue as linguistic is so far failing to achieve an imperial-era solution based on etiquette or to fulfill modern expectations of language as a rationalist conduit for resolution. Instead, the linguistic turn—or, rather, the particular practices of interpretation being used around it—is producing new forms of obstruction and intractability.

Interpretative practices

In its current form, the formal dispute between the two leaderships is over what constitutes proper autonomy for Tibetans within contemporary China,[10] and the two sides use particular interpretative maneuvers to articulate their disagreement with each formulation presented by the other side. These maneuvers are not just tools in a debate among negotiators across a table, but are distributed widely through the mass media and political organizations to entire populations where they rapidly become normative and can then be used by political leaders and negotiators to justify and maintain a particular position. This use of the mass media to replicate a single interpretative practice

204   *R. Barnett*

throughout a population is exceptionally consistent and coordinated in China, as all media there are controlled by the state and are thus univocal, with only a few isolated exceptions. The creation of a domestic echo chamber strengthens popular support for political leaders and for the nation which is seen as under attack or as not shown respect (Kriegsberg 2005, 80ff). But, as Kubo and others have noted, these practices also limit the range of options open to leaders and negotiators, particularly when it comes to compromise with political critics and opponents. They are not the root causes of the conflict or of the distrust, but they magnify and sustain the potential of any talks for failure.

The Tibetans' linguistic practices in their discussions can be characterized as loose, rhetorical, or emotive in style, with considerable inconsistency and a range of views, but they also suggest a relative openness to rational argument and change. This approach belongs broadly to what scholars of international relations term "communicative action," a mode of speech that "aims at producing consensus with the presumption that both speaker and listener enter the communication with a readiness to submit to the better argument" (Müller 2004, 397). The Chinese practices are highly disciplined and consistent, with almost military uniformity among their officials and public commentators. As is normal with the stronger party in acutely asymmetrical negotiations, their practices are "strategic," a mode that aims at "making one's own preferences prevail, using all instruments available for achieving this objective." As "communicative" practices are typically responsive to "better arguments," "strategic" practices are more relevant to the failure of resolution efforts.

I give three examples of interpretative practices found in this dispute, which I call reverse interpretation, cumulative stacking, and dogmatic literalism. In reverse interpretation, one side argues that a key term used by the other side actually means the opposite. This is done by parsing its statements to find a contrary or deviant meaning and then accusing that side of hypocrisy. Its principal function is to denounce and discard any concession offered by the other side. If one views this practice as strategic, it is a device to extract further concessions. The key example of this is the reading by the Chinese side of the word "autonomy" when used by the Dalai Lama as a concealed sign for "independence." This reading generates almost all the official rhetoric used by the Chinese side which, especially since 1994, has focused on representing exiled Tibetans officials as users of deceptive language.[11] Thus, we find the Dalai Lama described repeatedly in official statements from China as a "hypocrite" who is wearing "a mask," using religion "as a veil," having policies that are "in disguise," and, in one instance, being "a wolf in monk's clothing."[12] These repeated accusations of hypocrisy demonstrate what Müller describes as the impossibility of any party guaranteeing that any concession is genuine, no matter how much it engages in "costly signalling" (Müller 2004, 400). They can again be explained in terms of rational interests or historical causes—as a reaction by Chinese officials to mixed signals from the Dalai Lama, to historical memory of Tibetans' previous reversals and reassertions of their independence, to internal weakness within the Chinese leadership, or to some in-built tendency within Chinese political culture in dealings with perceived "minorities" and religious figures. Alternatively, as we have seen, it can be explained as a cynical device to prevent progress or extract further concessions.

But, again, these are analytical explanations rather than descriptions of the functional mechanics of deadlock: in the actuality of discourse and exchange, whatever the reasons for it, it is this practice by the stronger side that ensures the continuing failure of talks. In terms of resolving deadlocks, recognizing the practice that creates it may be as important as guessing the reason for its use as, if the powerful side does not in fact want a resolution, all other explanations and practices are moot or irrelevant, whereas if it does want a resolution, those explanations will be secondary and, instead, it will be the interpretative practice that needs to change, irrespective of its original cause.

Cumulative stacking

A second interpretative practice that is central to the China–Tibet discussion treats all statements as valid, irrespective of time or subsequent correction. I use the term "cumulative stacking" to describe this, to capture the unstated norm in most negotiations that allows a participant to replace an earlier position with a later one, provided their credibility is accepted. In effect, each side places a pile of items on the table, representing previous positions, demands, and declared interests and, in successful negotiation, is allowed by the other side to remove conflictual ones from the stack and replace them with more congenial ones or put them to one side. Negotiation is impossible without this practice; it is the essence of conflict resolution. But in cumulative stacking, every former contentious position is treated by the other side as remaining on the table, however much effort is made to remove it by the weaker side in order to reduce conflict. This rhetorical strategy is central to all polemical critiques of the Tibetan position, whether by Chinese officials, Stalinists, or rationalist critics such as Sautman (2010) and Parenti (2003); they tend to treat all statements and positions taken by Tibetans at any time as an inventory to which Tibetans can add but from which they cannot subtract.

One example of this is the effort of the Tibetan leaders to renounce the use of violence, which they had practiced in the 1950s and had continued until 1974, if the secret guerrilla movement is included. But Chinese officials will sometimes refer to the conflicts of the 1950s, particularly the uprising of 1959, as if the Tibetan side is still involved in that violence and has never changed its policy on this issue. The same device is used not just for declared positions or past statements but also for actions or qualities, real or imagined, ascribed to one's opponent in the past. Thus, accusations that the exiles collaborated with the Central Intelligence Agency (CIA) in the 1960s are not modified by subsequent evidence that the CIA stopped that collaboration in 1969 (Knaus 2000). Similarly, because some exiled Tibetan leaders or their predecessors in Tibet were born with feudal entitlements and had once inherited land and laborers, they are referred to by Chinese officials as still being feudal landlords and serf-owners. Because of a strongly held and conscientiously propagated Chinese claim that, in pre-1959 Tibetan society, landlords and officials inflicted extensive brutality on peasants (or "serfs" in official Chinese terminology), all current Tibetan leaders are routinely accused of having being inclined to brutality toward their laborers in the past and as likely to repeat this in the future. This is not varied by the facts that very few of the current Tibetan leaders were more than teenagers when the Chinese arrived in 1950, that exiled Tibetans created a democratic system in exile, that most former aristocrats and landlords left the exiled administration after about 1962, that there are few if any reports of brutality by officials or landlords in exile, or that similar arguments of past abuse could be applied to almost any government or party.

These attacks are derived from class or anti-imperialist analysis and similar intellectual framings, which were of course routine and required in China until at least the 1980s. Chinese discussions of Tibetan issues are nowadays generally framed in non-class terms (Tuttle 1998), and the Tibetan elite is now described as a religious theocracy, which Chinese officials say secretly aims to regain power for itself in Tibet in order to reintroduce feudalism and mass exploitation there. Ahistorical analysis of this kind is common in a structuralist view, as for example in Marxism, where many changes are contingent exteriorities that conceal an unvarying class relationship. But in a negotiation process, they are deal-breakers: progress cannot be made if all past statements and accusations are kept on the table as valid reasons for attack.[13]

Sometimes, when the intended audience is the international community, this practice is used in a more sophisticated and less combative way. Chinese officials and official scholars have often made the argument that China cannot make concessions to the Tibetans in case it leads to a domino effect in other areas of China, which also have actual or nascent pro-independence claims and would demand similar concessions, fragmenting the country. This argument is inherently reasonable and not polemical. But it incorporates a hidden "stacking" practice: it includes the assumption that Tibetans are still asking for substantive changes. That was indeed the case until the 1980s but, as we have seen, Tibetans then replaced these with demands that requested, at least on paper, only administrative adjustments to China's autonomy system in Tibetan areas, which would make little difference to China's unity if replicated widely.

This technique, of taking all statements or actions by one's negotiating partner as happening at the same time and independent of context or history, is as legitimate as any other rhetorical device used by political opponents and is effective as a tool for demonizing one's opponent and continually applying pressure to them. It agglomerates the stages and layers of a dispute as it mutates over time and then selects the worst or most controversial as the defining feature of the process. But this means that the weaker party is always treated in terms of the strongest demand it ever made or is accused of, and cannot replace it. This is complicated by the inevitable need of the weaker side to avoid its concessions being seen by its own followers as signs of weakness. Effective conflict resolution requires each party to allow the other to make statements that maintain its domestic standing and its claims to strength and consistency within its own constituency, especially when it is making concessions to the other side. Unless both sides are able to allow the other to make concessions and compensatory, face-saving tactical demands in public, a dialogue process is unable to proceed. In the Tibet–China case, it is increasingly likely that the Chinese use of this "scorched earth" tactic will force the Tibetan side to withdraw from the talks as it increasingly loses domestic support for giving major concessions with no returns.

Reading popular context

A third interpretative practice, which I call dogmatic or exclusive literalism, has a similar function, but in terms of meanings rather than time: instead of taking history as having no changes, it treats statements as having no context. For example, a Tibetan who says they want independence will be treated by the state as having called for secession at all costs, and therefore will have committed a serious crime. But "wanting independence" might not describe the pursuit of a single, exclusivist political demand; language can be seen as a practice, "an activity, a mode of doing things, and not just a vehicle of 'communication'" (Maynard 1984, 18). It could be aspirational, with no particular action or time specified, much like wishing to be a good person or to achieve enlightenment; it could be idealistic, with no external implications for the present world; it could be nostalgic, an expression of loss for a past condition, without any implication of pursuit or ambition to re-establish it; it could be exploratory, a move to open a discussion. The reduction of a statement to its most extreme interpretation is a strategy used by all revolutionary movements and states at war, but is almost certain to produce intractability.

The meaningful context of a statement is often to be found in the views of the ordinary people represented by the delegates in a dispute, as it is the community as a whole that will decide if an agreement will hold. Reading popular views in context suggests that, among many Tibetans, the practical meanings of a phrase such as "I want independence" may be more varied and moderate than among, say, ordinary Chinese or some Tibetan exiles. Direct research into such questions cannot be undertaken safely inside Tibet but, as Light shows with his study of joking by Uighur musicians (Light 2007), one can identify some opinions from casual remarks. During the 18 months or so I was allowed in Tibet between 2000 and 2007, the most obvious instances were whispered jokes about history and about television films. According to one, it would have been much better if the British had never left Tibet after their 1903–1904 invasion (because, implicitly, then the Chinese could not have invaded) and, according to another, the best films to watch are World War Two films made by the Americans or the British (because one could imagine that the Germans they defeated were Chinese). In another instance, a Tibetan scholar told my students ironically that he was unable to remember the text on a certain stone column in Lhasa, thus drawing attention to its importance: it records a ninth-century agreement that Tibetans should live to the west and Chinese to the east. These remarks certainly implied that Tibet had been independent in the past and that it had been invaded.

Within the social groups that I lived with, practical opinions about the current situation showed considerable nuance, however. These were rarely expressed openly, but there was clearly acute disapproval of policies that had called for greatly increased propaganda attacks on the Dalai Lama since 1994, had limited religious practice, or had encouraged Chinese migration into Tibet. However, I did not encounter suggestions that all Chinese should be made to leave Tibet; the concern was about their numbers, roles, and attitudes. Such opinions were indicated most frequently by omission—some Tibetans pointedly ignored certain official buildings while guiding visitors around, skipped certain passages in official texts that they were reading aloud to others, conspicuously declined to listen to governmental statements and news broadcasts on television, or apologized for including Chinese words within Tibetan-language conversations. These comments indicated disdain for official bodies and the competence of people who ran them. Where there were jokes against officials, they were mainly about Tibetans who work with the Chinese in running Tibet. The immediate problem seemed to be the excessive behavior of the Chinese state, its institutions, and its policies, rather than a wish to expel all Chinese or a demand that China abandon any role within Tibet.

The situation thus differed from what are usually termed "ethnic" or "separatist" conflicts, making the terms inappropriate for any general description of the China–Tibet dispute. This supports Darby's observations on the way in which ethnicity in conflicts is "often situationally determined and may wax and wane according to circumstances" (Darby 1997, 3–4, cited in Miall et al. 1999, 32). The implicit criticisms by those speakers that I met of the dominant role of Chinese people and language in Tibetan governance and culture suggested that, for them, the immediate, functional meaning of "wanting independence" was the need for pragmatic social and political reforms, such as allowing Tibetans to regulate migration and manage their own affairs. Such concerns match the political aim for Tibetans to have effective autonomy,[14] a pragmatic rather than an exclusivist approach (this view may be quite widespread, judging from the fact that at most protests participants display photographs, slogans, or banners proclaiming support for the Dalai Lama, presumably indicating outline support for his autonomy proposals).[15] This does not mean that the Tibetans I met would not prefer independence if it were freely available, or that they might not call for it at some time in the future: Chinese officials are thus right to recognize that they might one day face such demands following any settlement. But that is true with any issue and is not a reason for refusing an offered settlement; in fact, it should make one more urgent.

Framing implications

Replacing literalist with practice- or context-based interpretation thus provides potential ways to ease deadlock. It also allows the elements of a dispute to be disaggregated and different levels or areas of concern to be identified. In the Tibetan case, the primary or base level consists of historical questions about Tibet's status, which are long standing matters, emotionally laden and difficult to resolve, but often dormant if immediate conditions are satisfactory. The secondary level concerns current policies in Tibet and the practical implications of autonomy, such as the Chinese government's encouragement of non-Tibetan migration, limitations on religion, and so on. Flexible interpretation practices allow differentiation between these levels and can allow reframing—adjusting the linguistic or conceptual organization of the issues—in ways that can reduce antagonism. The Chinese framing strategy, by interpreting all Tibetan demands for greater autonomy as a hidden demand for independence, treats all Tibetan concerns as equally contentious, making impossible the two-tier option for resolving deadlock. Separating issues in this way is a long recognized method of overcoming blockages in talks and negotiations, and has been used with some success by the Indian and Chinese sides since 1988, when they agreed to divide their border dispute from other aspects of their relationship. Short-term success on practical issues can improve conditions for the discussion of historical ones—as Azar wrote of social conflicts in underdeveloped countries, "conflict resolution can truly occur and last if satisfactory amelioration of underdevelopment occurs as well" (Azar 1990, 155). Kriegsberg too notes that "conflict de-escalation and transformation" in intractable conflicts are "often associated with grievance reduction" (Kriegsberg 2005, 75).

From this perspective, much of the difficulty in resolving the Tibet–China dispute lies in the framing strategies used to present concerns: all issues are treated as challenges to China's claims to sovereignty and its historical relationship with Tibet. The Dalai Lama has shown awareness of this difficulty by suggesting that the historical question be put to one side.[16] This is unlikely to be accepted, partly because the framing that he uses is also contentious: although his current demands are relatively pragmatic and are much reduced compared with earlier positions, they are still expressed in terms of a wish to change the current system—to replace "regional nationality autonomy" in Tibet with "genuine autonomy." This can be seen as a category error: it invites the Chinese side to see all his concerns as an attempt to reopen the question of Tibet's status. It thus attracts and re-stimulates the linguistic practices that lead to protracted delay and irresolution. Many of the minor elements of disagreement are framed by the exiles and their leadership as issues of status, historical relations, or political power, for understandable historical reasons, but they could more effectively be presented as practical issues to do with immediate local policies, as is done by at least some Tibetans in Tibet, as we have seen.

210   *R. Barnett*

As Azar put it, protracted social conflicts are aggravated in many cases by "grievances resulting from need deprivation [and] failure to redress these needs by the authority" (Azar 1990, 9). The approach taken on the ground by the Chinese authorities in Tibet reflects the same analysis: it has tried to pacify local needs by rapidly inflating the size of the economy. This strategy has failed so far because of its own framing practices: it interprets "needs" and "development" as largely economic and as color blind—any beneficiary is equally worthy, including non-Tibetan migrants, and so it draws in more Chinese work-seekers to the area. The Tibetan side has attempted to communicate a view that its essential needs are not limited to the economy. Azar made the same point in his study, where he defined "needs" in such conflicts as including not just development, but also security, political access, and identity (Azar 1990, 9), with the last term referring to cultural and religious expression (Miall et al. 1999, 73). The interpretative practice maintained by the Chinese side in the 1990s in its definition of "needs" and "development" is at the core of the secondary dispute, that over practical issues and current policies. These have no immediate connection to issues of status, do not threaten China's national interests or claims, and could be modified relatively easily. For example, migration is already regulated for areas such as Hong Kong and Macau, less confrontational ways to manage monasteries could be developed, bans on the worship of the Dalai Lama could be quietly dropped, and the Tibetan language could be reconsidered for use as a teaching medium in middle schools.

Chinese framing practices that conflate almost all levels of critical discourse among Tibetans with separatism have increased markedly since 1994 (Barnett and Spiegel 1996). The opposite practice—interpreting such statements as contextually driven, as symbolic, as legitimate negotiating strategies, or as non-threatening to the state—has been rare since that time in Tibetan cases,[17] and has reinforced perceptions among Tibetans that even practical issues can only be solved by achieving independence. Tibetan activists inside and outside Tibet thus increasingly come to consider formal independence rather than Chinese presence as the key issue; this is evident in exiled Tibetan rhetoric and may explain the escalation of protest inside Tibet since 2008 and the increase in the level of violence there.

An important example of the effect of framing is seen in the classification by either side of the dispute as internal or as international. Chinese officials treat it as internal, as it would otherwise imply that Tibet is not part of China. Tibetan exiles, on the other hand (unlike many Tibetan intellectuals within Tibet), speak of the dispute as if it were a form of international relations, as do most exiled and foreign commentators, which must seem provocative to the Chinese side. This "blurred demarcation between internal and external sources and agents" is typical of protracted social conflicts in "underdeveloped areas of the world" (Azar 1990, 6, cited in Miall et al. 1999, 72). This has practical consequences—for example, the talks with Tibetan exiles are not handled by Chinese diplomats or officials involved in foreign affairs, but by officials from the United Front Department (*Tongzhanbu*), the agency within the Communist Party that is in charge of all issues to do with nationalities and religion within China. As a result, the exiled delegates face what we might call "gladiatorial combat," where a complainant is forced by a powerful leader to deliver his or her complaint directly to the perpetrator: the officials whom the Tibetan delegates face in the China–Tibet talks are those who have designed and implemented the policies that are the subject of the Tibetans' criticisms. Thus, the Tibetans are put in the position of asking these officials in effect to encourage their leaders to repudiate their own work and by implication to dismiss them. Obviously, the officials are highly motivated to fight energetically any such approach from the exiles. Like its literalist interpretative practices, China's framing of the issue as domestic can be seen cynically as a negotiating tactic, but it is also a legitimate defense of its interests. This is another factor in the continuing deadlock, adding yet more pressure on the Tibetans to moderate or abandon their demands.

Interpreting exile rhetoric

Exiled Tibetan leaders have, as we have seen, a rhetorical style marked by looseness and wide variation, even contradiction. Before 1980 or so, they had a single, consistent, and absolute accusation against China, namely that it was an invader guilty of genocidal practices. But since 1980, as a more nuanced approach developed, exiled leaders have sometimes expressed muted praise of China and, at other times, strong condemnation. Some of this is more or less a matter of personal style, as when the Dalai Lama describes himself as a "simple Buddhist monk" while clearly having a major role in Tibetan if not world affairs. He likes to present personal views that are counter-intuitive, such as his admiration for Mao in the early 1950s and for Marxism's approach to socioeconomic issues, but at the same he denounces the Communist Party and advocates multi-party democracy. Similarly, he says that he seeks only autonomy within the Chinese state, but at the same time that Tibet was independent in the past: not in fact a contradiction, but a move that encourages surprise if not distrust. In addition, he often pairs concessional statements about seeking autonomy within China with strong attacks on China's record in Tibet, including the extreme accusation of "cultural genocide." Other exiled leaders similarly declare their commitment to autonomy but at the same time refer to Tibet as a country and describe their objective as Tibetan "freedom."[18]

This kind of rhetorical style has led to accusations of duplicity, especially from literalist commentators (Sautman 2000; Roemer 2006). Some of these accusations are polemical, such as denouncing the Dalai Lama for not being a vegetarian, a view that reveals little knowledge of Buddhism, but others suggest a reluctance to consider utterances in context. The Dalai Lama's speaking practices are loose in part because he almost always improvises his public remarks, because he chooses to speak to foreigners as if in a normal conversation with a friend, and because he addresses different audiences in line with issues of mutual concern to him and them. With his domestic constituency, he tries to reassure them of his respect for Tibet's past history as a country and of his recognition of the abuses they have suffered as a result of China's past policies. With potential western allies, he emphasizes his political moderation by accentuating his aspiration for autonomy. In some contexts, he appears to want to show consistency with demands made in the past and so discusses Tibet's historic independence. When considering the Chinese public, he needs both to reassure them of his reasonableness and remind them of his respect for some of their institutions, at least in the past. This highly informal adjustment of his discourse to audience and place is probably a major factor in his international success, and can be understood from context, but it is a fluid, undisciplined style of discourse and puts progress in the talks at risk.

Foreign commentators on Tibetan issues also get caught up in framing problems. In 2008, when the Tibetan side said that, in a future settlement, the thirteen Tibetan autonomous areas in China should be made into a single autonomous administrative entity, some foreign observers condemned it as aggressively as did China. But for outsiders to attack this was a framing error: it clearly could be read not literally but as a negotiating position. It met the minimum expectations of the domestic constituency, did not contest China's claims to sovereignty, and could easily be addressed by the Chinese side, if it wished, through a face-saving compromise involving some kind of adjusted administrative arrangement far short of the actual demand. Indeed, in 2010, the Chinese side instituted such an adjustment, which was welcomed by the exiles.[19] The Tibetans need to have strong demands in place before negotiations begin so that they have some concessions still to yield; otherwise, they have nothing with which to negotiate; this is fundamental to any contextual reading of their statements.

Conclusion

The Tibet–China dispute is an acutely asymmetrical dispute in which the formal demands of the two sides are relatively close whereas the styles of their negotiating behavior are directly opposite. As is usual in such situations, the weaker party has made major concessions while the stronger party has given very few, probably as part of a strategy to force yet more concessions from the weaker side or to damage it irretrievably. In order to avoid potentially crippling loss of standing among its domestic audience in exile, the weaker side compensates for its concessions by a rhetorical practice which is loose, as in normal speech behavior, thus winning popular support and international sympathy for its humanistic style, but making it increasingly vulnerable to accusations of hypocrisy by its critics, which the stronger side then can use as a reason for stalling talks. The stronger side capitalizes on its advantages by interpretative strategies that either treat all statements by its opponent as devious concealments of their opposite, or dogmatically in an ultra-literal sense, without allowing for contextual variability. It also interprets its opponents' statements ahistorically by treating any former utterance or supposed attribute as still valid even if withdrawn, qualified, or disproved decades ago. Each concession offered by the weaker side is dismissed as a deception, labeled an act of provocation and contempt for talks, and deployed to extract further concessions. At the same time, this increasingly erodes the long-term credibility of the weaker side and weakens its support base.

In a narrow sense, these practices can be seen as normal negotiating strategies, although as Ogura Kazuo argued in his discussion of similar "scorched earth" practices in the Chinese–Japanese negotiations of the 1970s, they seem to be adhered to by Chinese negotiators with unusual rigidity (Kazuo 1979). When Kazuo was facing Chinese negotiators, they could be explained as due to totalitarian ideological adherence, but in contemporary conditions, these practices are harder to justify. However, because the Tibet–China talks are domestic, the costs for China of using tactics of attrition or forcing the other side to withdraw are much lower. As the process has been protracted and has not even reached a negotiating stage, it is particularly vulnerable to the weaker side being forced by its base to pull out of talks. In addition, it is played out through the media, thus amplifying any attacks and involving vast national audiences in opportunistic interpretations of statements by the other side, arousing strong nationalist feelings. This generates deep-seated negative perceptions of one side by the other among entire populations and pushes the issue closer to becoming an ethnic or hate-driven conflict.

Some practical implications arise from the analysis suggested in this chapter. If some Tibetan concerns are a response to recent policies on the ground, then these could be disaggregated from questions of history and status. Such reframing could allow the talks to be split into two processes that would proceed at different rates. If the amplification effect of megaphone negotiations is damaging to their progress, then avoiding public statements by both sides could reduce some of that damage; this alone could make a significant difference to the process. And enabling participants to recognize each others' interpretative practices and demonstrating alternatives could lead to more productive forms of discussion (see Cohen 2001, 50). Study of language practices in the China–Tibet dispute can thus help identify significant factors that have delayed a resolution.

Deep understanding of the underlying causes and competing emotions in a conflict is necessary for any study of such an issue, but—assuming that both sides actually want a settlement—neither embedded distrust nor entrenched differences in culture, history, or outlook make a conflict irresolvable. Neither are they necessary reasons for a resolution process to fail once the fundamentals have been conceded by both sides. In such cases, detailed understanding of the way in which language works in exchanges between the two sides can be productive, as it was with Tibet–China relations for centuries before the 1910 invasion. Appropriate linguistic practices can offer methods for effective coexistence despite such differences, whereas aggressive interpretative practices, positivist

214   R. Barnett

linguistic practices, and inappropriate framing can prolong deadlock, and can come themselves to be constituents and drivers of conflict, even in situations in which, in fact, despite strong emotions and distinct histories, there is relatively little technical difference between the parties on their negotiating points.

Notes

1 The term Tibet is used in official Chinese documents and in Chinese language ("Xizang") to refer only to the central and western areas of the Tibetan plateau, which were the areas ruled directly by the Dalai Lama and his government prior to 1950. However, a majority of Tibetans live in the eastern part of the plateau, and I therefore use the term Tibet here in its very loosest sense to refer to the whole plateau, or all the Tibetan-inhabited areas of China. I use the terms "Tibet–China" and "China–Tibet" interchangeably to describe the dispute, rather than "Tibetan–Chinese," as I do not see it as an ethnic dispute, but with the realization that all these phrases are contentious and inexact.

2 I use the term "sides" or "parties," or "Tibetans" and "Chinese" in this chapter to refer to the leadership of each side, as certainly not all Tibetans or Chinese agree with their leaders or their stated aims. However, in a referendum among exiles organized by the exiled Tibetan government in 1995 (criticized by some as not being neutral), about 66 percent agreed with the "Middle Way," meaning a negotiated settlement with China (Roemer 2006, 84–86).

3 In late 2011, after eleven incidents of self-immolation by Tibetans in Tibet in the previous 9 months, the leader of the exiled delegation responsible for talks, Lodi Gyari Gyaltsen, wrote that "the present tragic situation in Tibet and the most repressive policies of the Chinese authorities makes one wonder if it is even worth making any efforts for the dialogue" (Gyari 2011).

4 The Tibetan side appears to have decided to renounce the claim to independence by 1979, according to Van Walt, who later said that the 1988 call for "association" was understood as "an autonomous Tibet *within* the PRC" (van Walt 2001, [81], emphasis in the original). But the exiles seem to have avoided clear statements on this, did not use the term "autonomy" until perhaps 1990, and only used it consistently from the late 1990s. Sautman (2000) argues that their references to "association" or "federation" justify the PRC's denunciation of all their proposals as the veiled pursuit of independence. Another complication arises from the fact that the exiles have retained their claim to having been independent in the past; what they have agreed to abandon since 1979 is any claim to *continuing* independence. In addition, the exiles have said that they *will* accept China's sovereignty claims when an agreement is concluded, not that they have already done so—another nuance used by their critics to denounce them. In 2008, the exiled government formally clarified its position as, "We remain firmly committed not to seek separation or independence. We are seeking a solution to the Tibetan problem through genuine autonomy, which is compatible with the principles on autonomy in the Constitution of the People's Republic of China" (TGiE 2008).

5 "The form and degree of autonomy proposed in the Memorandum is consistent with the principles on autonomy in the Chinese Constitution … the position of His Holiness the Dalai Lama, as presented in the Memorandum, in no way challenges or brings into question the leadership of the Chinese Communist Party … the Memorandum also does not challenge the socialist system of the PRC. Nothing in it suggests a demand for a change to this system or for its exclusion from Tibetan areas" (Gyari 2010b; see also Gyari 2010a; TGiE 2010). This was a significant change from the Tibetan position 10 or so years earlier.

The Tibet–China dispute 215

6 "Like other rhetorical actors, they [hyperstrategists] risk being outlawed by the rest of the negotiators, who are frustrated because of their refusal to reciprocate if actors behave in a communicative mode. ... Even within the bonds of rationalism, then, the hyperstrategist violates the rule that reputation is an asset for bargaining in repeated rounds of negotiations; this, however, is non-rational behaviour" (Müller 2004, 406).

7 China's attitudes in international negotiations in recent decades have been seen by some scholars as broadly cooperative and concessional (see Nathan and Ross 1997).

8 The British reached a formal description of Tibet's status during treaty talks with Tibet in 1913–14, in which they (the British) recognized China's "suzerainty" over Tibet. This was a more nuanced and informative description than others that have been proposed, but the term had little currency in twentieth-century international relations. China rejected the British term, which was finally repudiated by the British in 2008. The Tibetans had declared independence jointly with Mongolia in 1913 but, after their failure to get the British to accept this, they were not proactive in establishing their independence claim internationally until the mid-1940s. In the thirteenth Dalai Lama's 1913 proclamation of Tibet's independence, he describes Tibet as a former "colony" of the Qing, perhaps in an informal sense, but otherwise the Tibetans seem not to have described themselves as a former "colony" or "protectorate."

9 A similar point was made by the Chinese political scientist, Da Wei, a member of a leading official think tank in Beijing: "Was Tibet part of China? There is no easy answer to this question since there was no nation state as we call 'China' in history." This is rare in Chinese writing. Da argued that Tibet was part of China anyway because of "close historical links" (Da Wei 2008).

10 The Chinese side has said since at least 1985 that it will only discuss the personal status of the Dalai Lama (Zhu Weiqun 2009), meaning whether he will return to China, and that it will only meet his personal representatives. In practice, however, it allows discussion of the autonomy question. Zhu's 2009 interview is an important source for the current Chinese position on the talks and for the interpretative mechanisms described in this chapter. For a brief history of the talks process, see Rabgey and Sharlo (2004).

11 As noted above, Chinese suspicions about the Dalai Lama's renunciation of independence may be based on the call in the Strasbourg Proposal (1988) for Tibet to be recognized as "in association with" China, as association is a form of independence in law. Sautman (2000) and Roemer (2006) cite other remarks and actions that they say indicate a continuing pursuit of independence.

12 Tibetan practices of this kind treat Chinese references to "autonomy" as actually meaning control by ethnic Chinese with a veneer of local participation. They also often argue that Chinese support for Tibetan culture and economy in fact represents a hidden intention to destroy or weaken them. It can be argued that the Tibetan statements are "communicative," rather than intrinsic or fundamental to their position; they seem to be added to give color or intensity to their arguments.

13 One sees similar practices by Tibetans who describe China as if it were still involved in the Cultural Revolution and pursuing policies designed to eradicate religion or Tibetan culture. This is relatively rare among the Tibetan delegates to the talks, but prevalent elsewhere in the community.

14 The fact that autonomy as currently offered in Tibet is purely token and without substance is regarded as self-evident within Tibet and was explicitly stated by Ngapo Ngawang Jigme, an important Tibetan leader within China, in a famous essay in 1989, before a policy shift in 1992 made it too dangerous for even major leaders to make such comments (Barnett 2008a).

15 Pro-independence supporters among the exiles, such as the essayist Jamyang Norbu, who opposes the Dalai Lama's strategy, have argued that these protestors

216 *R. Barnett*

must be demanding Tibet's independence, partly because in some cases they also show the former Tibetan national flag. But that requires one to believe either that these Tibetans are unaware that the Dalai Lama gave up independence 30 years ago, or that they are using him as their figurehead while not agreeing with his views.

16 "History is a past event and it cannot be altered. However, His Holiness the Dalai Lama's position is forward-looking, not backward grasping. He does not wish to make this difference on history an obstacle in seeking a mutually beneficial common future within the People's Republic of China" (TGiE 2010).

17 The opposite framing is often used by Chinese officials with non-Tibetan protests, and was even applied to a protest in Inner Mongolia in 2011, when an official newspaper editorial declared that "some of their requests are reasonable, and should be responded to by the local government. Anger of local Mongolians toward the Han driver is understandable. The anger is also partly a result of their anxiety over a wave of industrialization, and how the mining industry might affect their lives. We believe the majority of Chinese sympathize with their reasonable requests ... The incidents there should not be exaggerated or over-interpreted. The key is to understand the reason behind, face it, and find the solution" (Global Times 2011). In Maoist terminology, this would be termed treating the event as a "non-antagonistic contradiction" that is "among the people."

18 Referring to Tibet as a country while claiming to seek autonomy can be explained by context, as the exile position takes for granted that they will formally declare their recognition of Tibet as part of China only once negotiations over autonomy are completed.

19 The Fifth National Forum on Tibet Work, held in Beijing from January 18 to 20, 2010, announced that policies would be standardized across the various Tibetan areas. It is probably unlikely that this was a response to exile demands, but the Tibetan side nevertheless responded: "We welcome the fact that the Fifth Tibet Work Forum has looked into the issues of development in all Tibetan areas – The Tibet Autonomous Region as well as other Tibetan areas. It is our strong belief that all the Tibetan areas must be under a uniform policy and a single administration. If we take away the political slogans, many of the issues that have been prioritized by the Forum are similar to the basic needs of the Tibetan people outlined in our Memorandum" (Gyari 2010a).

References

Azar, Edward E. (1990), *The Management of Protracted Social Conflict. Theory and Cases*, Aldershot, Dartmouth.

Barnett, Robert (1997), 'The Babas are Dead: Street Talk and Contemporary Views of Leaders in Tibet' in Elliot Sperling (ed.), *Proceedings of the International Association of Tibetan Studies*, University of Indiana, Bloomington; at http://www.columbia.edu/itc/ealac/barnett/pdfs/link7-babas.pdf (accessed 8 August 2012).

——(2007), 'Tsogt Taij and the Disappearance of the Overlord: Triangular Relations in Three Inner Asian Films' *Inner Asia*, 9(1): 41–76.

——(2008a), 'Language and Ethnicity: Cadre-Speak in Contemporary Tibet' *Inner Asia*, 10(1): 171–205.

——(2008b), 'The Tibet Protests of Spring, 2008: Conflict between the Nation and the State' *China Perspectives* (guest editor: Françoise Robin), Hong Kong (July), 2009 (3): 6–23.

Barnett, Robert and Mickey Spiegel (1996), *Cutting Off the Serpent's Head: Tightening Control in Tibet, 1994–95*, London, TIN, and New York, Human Rights Watch.

The Tibet–China dispute   217

Cohen, R. (2001), 'Language and Conflict Resolution: The Limits of English' *International Studies Review*, 3: 25–51.

Crocker, Chester A., Fen Osler Hampson and Pamela R. Aall (2005), *Grasping the Nettle: Analyzing Cases of Intractable Conflict*, Arlington, VA, US Institute of Peace Press.

Darby, J. (1997), *Scorpions in a Bottle: Conflicting Cultures in Northern Ireland*, London, Minority Rights Publications.

Da Wei (2008), 'China's Pride versus Western Prejudice' *Asia Times*, 2 May, at www.atimes.com/atimes/China/JE02Ad01.html (accessed 12 November 2011).

Fischer, Andrew Martin (2009), 'The Political Economy of Boomerang Aid in China's Tibet' *China Perspectives* (guest editor: Françoise Robin), Hong Kong (July), 2009(3): 38–54.

Gladney, Dru (1994), 'Representing Nationality in China: Refiguring Majority/Minority Identities' *Journal of Asian Studies*, 53(1): 92–123.

Glenny, Misha (2000), *The Balkans: Nationalism, War, and the Great Powers, 1804–1999*, New York, Viking.

Global Times (2011), 'Putting Mongolian Protests into Context' *Global Times*, May 31, at http://opinion.globaltimes.cn/editorial/2011-05/660386.html (accessed 14 November 2011).

Goldstein, Melvyn (1997), *The Snow Lion and the Dragon: China, Tibet, and the Dalai Lama*, Berkeley, CA, University of California Press.

Gurr, T. (1995), 'Transforming Ethnopolitical Conflicts: Exit, Autonomy or Access?' in K. Rupesinghe (ed.), *Conflict Transformation*, London, Macmillan, pp. 1–30.

Gurr, T.R. (1995), *Minorities at Risk – a Global View of Ethnopolitical Conflicts*, Arlington, VA, United States Institute of Peace Press.

Gyari, Lodi Gyaltsen (2010a), 'Statement by Special Envoy of His Holiness The Dalai Lama, Kasur Lodi Gyari, Head of the Delegation which Visited China in January 2010', February 2, at www.tibet.net/en/print.php?id=96& articletype=press (accessed 12 November 2011).

——(2010b), 'The Way Forward on Tibet: The Status of Discussions Between His Holiness the Dalai Lama and the Government of the People's Republic of China', Remarks delivered at the Center for Strategic and International Studies, Washington, DC, March 5, at www.savetibet.org/files/documents/lgg_csis_05_march_2010.pdf (accessed 12 November 2011).

——(2011), 'Message from Special Envoy of H.H. the Dalai Lama, Lodi Gyari, Washington, DC, 11 November 2011', at www.savetibet.org/resource-center/message-special-envoy-hh-dalai-lama-lodi-gyari (accessed 11 November 2011).

Kazuo, Ogura (1979), 'How the "Inscrutables" Negotiate with the "Inscrutables": Chinese Negotiating Tactics vis-à-vis the Japanese' *The China Quarterly*, 79 (September): 529–552.

Knaus, John Kenneth (2000), *Orphans of the Cold War: America and the Tibetan Struggle for Survival*, New York, Public Affairs.

Kriegsberg, Louis (2005), 'Nature, Dynamics and Phases of Intractability' in Chester A. Crocker et al. (eds), *Grasping the Nettle: Analyzing Cases of Intractable Conflict*, Arlington, VA, United States Institute of Peace Press, pp. 65–98.

Light, Nathan (2007), 'Cultural Politics and the Pragmatics of Resistance: Reflexive Discourses on Culture and History' in Ildikó Bellér-Hann, M. Cristina Cesaro, Rachel Harris and Joanne Smith Finley (eds), *Situating the Uyghurs Between China and Central Asia*, Aldershot, UK, Ashgate, pp. 49–68.

218 R. Barnett

Lundberg, Maria and Yong Zhou (2009), 'Regional National Autonomy under Challenge: Law, Practice and Recommendations' *International Journal on Minority and Group Rights*, 16: 269–327.

Maynard, Douglas W. (1984), *Inside Plea Bargaining: The Language of Negotiation*, New York, Plenum Press.

Miall, Hugh, Oliver Ramsbotham and Tom Woodhouse (1999), *Contemporary Conflict Resolution: The Prevention, Management and Transformation of Deadly Conflicts*, Malden, MA, Blackwell.

Müller, Harald (2004), 'Arguing, Bargaining and All That: Communicative Action, Rationalist Theory and the Logic of Appropriateness in International Relations' *European Journal of International Relations*, 10(3) (September): 395–435.

Nathan, Andrew J. and Robert S. Ross (1997), *The Great Wall and the Empty Fortress: China's Search for Security*, New York, W.W. Norton.

Parenti, Michael (2003), 'Friendly Feudalism: The Tibet Myth', *New Political Science*, 25(4): 579–590.

Pfetsch, (2008), 'Bargaining and Arguing as Communicative Modes of Strategic, Social, Economic, Political Interaction' in Judith Schueller, Andreas Fickers and Anique Hommels (eds), *Bargaining Norms, Arguing Standards*, The Hague, SIT, pp. 52–65.

PRC (People's Republic of China, 2000), 'National Minorities Policy and Its Practice in China, Information Office of the State Council of the PRC', Beijing, June, Government White Paper, at www.china.org.cn/e-white/4/index.htm (accessed 12 November 2011).

Rabgey, Tashi and Tseten Wangchuk Sharlo (2004), *Sino-Tibetan Dialogue in the Post-Mao Era: Lessons and Prospects*, Washington, DC, East–West Center.

Roemer, Stephanie (2006), *The Tibetan Government-in-exile: Politics at Large*, New York, Routledge.

Sautman, Barry (2000), 'Association, Federation and "Genuine" Autonomy: The Dalai Lama's Proposals and Tibet Independence' *China Information*, 14(2): 31–91.

——(2010), '"Vegetarian between Meals": The Dalai Lama, War, and Violence' *Positions: East Asia Cultures Critique*, 18(1) Spring: 89–144.

Seyfort Ruegg, D. (1991), '*Mchod-yon, yon-mchod* and *mchod-gnas/yon-gnas*: On the Historiography and Semantics of a Tibetan Religio-social and Religio-political Concept' in E. Steinkellner (ed.), *Tibetan History and Language, Studies Dedicated to Uray Géza on His Seventieth Birthday*, Wiener Studien zur Tibetologie und Buddhismuskunde, heft 26. Wien, Arbeitskreis für Tibetische und Buddhistische Studien, Universität Wien, pp. 441–453.

Sidner, Candace L. (1994), 'An Artificial Discourse Language for Collaborative Negotiation' in *AAAI-94: Proceedings of the Twelfth National Conference on Artificial Intelligence*, Menlo Park, CA, AAAI Press; and Cambridge, MA, The MIT Press, pp. 814–819.

TGiE ('Tibetan Government in Exile' or 'Central Tibetan Administration') (2008), 'The Memorandum on Genuine Autonomy for the Tibetan People', Note formally presented by the Envoys of His Holiness the Dalai Lama to their Chinese counterparts during the eighth round of dialogue in Beijing, November 4–5, at www.tibet.net/en/print.php?id=589& articletype=flash (accessed 12 November 2011).

——(2010), 'Note relating to the Memorandum on Genuine Autonomy for the Tibetan People', Note formally presented by the Envoys of His Holiness the Dalai Lama to their Chinese counterparts during the ninth round of dialogue in Beijing, January 26–31, at www.tibet.net/en/print.php?id=1368&articletype=flash (accessed 12 November 2011).

Tuttle, Gray (1998), 'Modern Tibetan Historiography', *Papers on Chinese History* (Spring). Cambridge, MA, Harvard University, pp. 85–108.

Van Walt, Michael van Praag (2001), 'The Relevance of the 17-Point Agreement Today' in *Facts about the 17-Point 'Agreement' Between Tibet and China*, Dharamsala, Department of Information and International Relations, 22 May (no page numbers).

Zhu Weiqun (2009), 'Official: The Chinese People Never Allow Other Countries to Interfere with Internal Affairs', 17 October, China Tibet Information Center/Xinhua, at http://english.peopledaily.com.cn/90001/90776/6785850.html# (accessed 12 November 2011).

13 Separatism in China

The case of the Xinjiang Uyghur Autonomous Region

Dru C. Gladney

In this chapter, I will argue that the continuing incidents of violence that have occurred in the region known as the Uyghur Autonomous Region of Xinjiang, or Eastern Turkestan, are best understood as incidents of civil unrest in the public sphere, and can rarely be described as "secessionism" (*fenliezhuyi*) in the traditional sense of the term (which I take to mean coordinated acts of violence against the government and civilian populations for the purpose of establishing an independent state).[1] The struggles of the Uyghur people with the Chinese nation-state that have taken place since its incorporation in 1949 are best understood in the context of efforts to attain sovereignty, not as a religious or Islam-inspired campaign. Except for the fact that the Uyghur are a Muslim people, their concerns and issues resemble those of Tibet, and the occasional violence that takes place in the Tibetan Autonomous Region in China and protests against Chinese rule are rarely if ever described as "terrorist," although they are often lumped together with the Uyghur incidents as "secessionist" (*fenliezhuyi*). At the same time, in this chapter, an attempt will be made to show that the region of Xinjiang, which had been extremely peaceful since the late 1990s, but then erupted in the last few years, has been caught up in an economic boom that would be the envy of any of its surrounding Central Asian states. Indeed, China should be congratulated for the enormous economic and social transformation of the region over the past two decades, but at the same time should be encouraged to find ways to preserve and promote the vibrant and extraordinary Central Asian civilization that Uyghur culture represents.

By paying attention to Uyghur engagement in the public sphere, especially domestically in the urban spaces of Urumqi and other Uyghur centers, such as Kashgar and Khotan, as well as examining further Uyghur participation in the virtual public sphere through new forms of social media and the internet, in this chapter, it will be argued that a new virtual community of Uyghur has begun to counter the hegemonic discourse of the Chinese state regarding Uyghur unrest and aspirations in the region. Sites of contestation, it will be argued, have thus been translocated through these new forms of social media, leading to a re-territorialization of public space, not only virtually on the internet, but with real implications for actions on the ground. Arjun Appadurai (1990, 2) seminally argued that "deterritorialization" is a prominent condition of modernity at large in the new public sphere, yet I am suggesting that we are witnessing the increasing role of the internet in *re-territorializing* homeland spaces lost to subject peoples, often displaced by authoritarian regimes. In an earlier article (Gladney 2007, 95–97), I argued that growing Uyghur "cyber-secessionism" and "cyber-separatism" did not really pose a threat to the Chinese state at that time, as it was supported by a disembodied mix of competing international diasporic groups who had little chance of mounting any organized resistance that could possibly challenge Chinese sovereignty within Xinjiang. In his masterful survey, Yitzhak Shichor similarly argued that contradictions and competing agendas among the diaspora kept the Uyghur from forming a unified agenda (Shichor 2003, 283–284). However, given the dramatic rise in Uyghur connectivity and recent events in the Middle East among the various Arab Springs and Jasmine Revolutions of 2011, in this chapter, I shall argue that a new virtual Uyghur community has begun to emerge in the diaspora that has indeed given Beijing much greater cause for concern. In short, this chapter suggests that cyber-separatism is becoming more than just virtual for the Uyghur diaspora and, not unlike events in the Middle East, has begun to have real impacts on the colonized space that was once known as Eastern Turkestan leading, indeed, to a possible future re-territorialization. To some extent then, Uyghur cyber-secessionism/separatism could lead to the establishment of a virtual nation, but one that for the distant future will remain outside China, existing virtually in the diaspora and on the internet.

Rumblings from the west

After nearly 10 years of relative peace in the Xinjiang Uyghur Autonomous Region, sporadic incidents of violence in 2008 presaged a huge urban uprising in Urumqi in 2009 that nearly overwhelmed local authorities, leading to the highest death toll from civil violence in the history of the People's Republic of China.[2] Previously, in 1997, bombs exploded in a city park in Beijing on May 13 (killing one) and on two buses on March 7 (killing two), as well as in the northwestern border city of Urumqi, the capital of Xinjiang Uyghur Auton-omous Region, on February 25 (killing nine), with over thirty other bombings in 1998, and six in Tibet that year as well. Most of these are thought to have been related to demands by Muslim and Tibetan secessionists. Numerous members of the Uyghur Muslim minority have been executed since those events of the late 1990s, with hundreds arrested on suspicion of taking part in ethnic riots and engaging in secessionist activities. Although sporadically reported since the early 1980s, such incidents were rather frequent in the late 1990s, and harsh treatment of suspects involved in those incidents was docu-mented in a scathing report of Chinese government policy in the region by Amnesty International (Amnesty International 1999). As far as we know, these incidents from the late 1990s represent the only documented incidents of violence that appeared to be well-coordinated, taking place at the same time across urban and national spaces. Nothing since has matched the level of sophistication or coordination of these late 1990s events. The *Wall Street Journal* (1999) reported the arrest on August 11, 1999 of Rebiya Kadeer, a well-known Uyghur businesswoman once sent to represent the Xinjiang region at the International Women's Conference in Beijing (1995), during a visit by the United States Congressional Research Service (USCRS) delegation to the region, indicating China's strong response to these tensions. Amnesty International labeled Rebiya a "prisoner of conscience" as her only tangible offense was an unsuccessful attempt to meet with the USCRS (Amnesty International 2000). Her release to the US in 2005 and her active role in promoting a "World Uyghur Congress" have led to her assuming a prominent position among the Uyghur exile community both in the US and abroad, and to her being labeled as a "terrorist" and "secessionist" by the Chinese government.[3] Her leadership has helped galvanize the Uyghur diaspora as never before and, lacking a Dalai Lama, some analysts have started referring to her as the "Dalai Mama" for the Uyghur diaspora. Skillful use of the public media and international news outlets have helped bring her message about the "plight" of her people to the greater public to an unprecedented degree.

It is important to note that the Uyghur protests and subsequent crackdowns of the 1990s and mid-2000s have rarely been connected to freedom of religion issues, but rather to a range of "indigenous rights" issues, of which religion is only one concern. Chinese officials argue that "splittists" (that is, secessionists) violate the law and that full freedom of religion is allowed under Article 36 of the constitution.[4] An earlier White Paper on nationalities policy in China published just prior to the Fiftieth Anniversary of the PRC in October 1999 argued that religious freedom was guaranteed for all minorities, but acknowledged continuing problems in minority regions, especially vast economic inequities (China State Council 1999).

Despite ongoing tensions and frequent reports of isolated terrorist acts, there has been no evidence that any of these actions has been aimed at disrupting the economic development of the region. Not a single documented incident has targeted infrastructure (railways, bridges, power stations, airports), which one would expect if there were a well-organized terrorist or secessionist conspiracy. Most confirmed incidents have been directed against Han Chinese security forces, recent Han Chinese émigrés to the region, and even Uyghur Muslims perceived to be collaborating with the Chinese government too closely. Even those who claim that there is active Taliban and al Qaeda coordination of Uyghur violence in the region have a hard time pointing to violent incidents that resemble al Qaeda techniques, such as sophisticated weaponry, roadside bombs, or even suicide bombings.[5] There has been no confirmed evidence of such violence in the Xinjiang region, with almost all incidents evidencing low-grade weaponry (knives, stones, public buses) and public security targets (police stations, checkpoints, etc.). Most analysts agree that China is not

Xinjiang: a "new region" rooted in the past

Chinese histories notwithstanding, every Uyghur firmly believes that their ancestors were the indigenous people of the Tarim Basin, which did not become known in Chinese as "Xinjiang" ("new dominion") until the eighteenth century. Nevertheless, the identity of the present people known as Uyghur is a rather recent phenomenon related to Great Game rivalries, Sino-Soviet geopolitical maneuverings, and Chinese nation-building. Although a collection of nomadic steppe peoples known as the "Uyghur" have existed since before the eighth century, this identity was lost from the fifteenth to the twentieth century. It is one of the world's least subtle ironies that Chinese histories resolutely assert the long-term dominance of the region by Chinese rulers, yet continue to officially promote the term "Xinjiang" ("New Region") as the territory's appellation. This irony is certainly not lost on the Uyghurs, who continue to regard themselves as an internal colony of China, and a rather recent one at that (Gladney 1998d, 20–21).

The idea of a Uyghur nation, and as an independent state that has roots back to the seventh-century Uyghur empire, has been further aided by the internet, which regularly refers to this romanticized, territorialized past.[6] The Uyghur culture and its people's genetic make-up reflect the fact that they migrated from an area that is now in Mongolia to the region now known as Xinjiang or Eastern Turkistan. The region had always been at the center of a "civilizational cross-roads," involving long-distance travel and intermixing by speakers of Iranian, Indian, Chinese, Tibetan, Turkic, Mongolian, and even European tongues. Until their rather belated conversion to Islam (compared with the rather rapid conversion of other Central Asian peoples), the Uyghurs were shamanists, Buddhists, Manichaeans, and even Nestorian Christians. The Uyghur-dominated oases of the region, on account of their superior agricultural and mercantile economies, were frequently over-run by nomadic powers from the steppes of Mongolia and Central Asia, and even intermittently Chinese dynasties who showed interest in controlling the lucrative trade routes across Eurasia. According to Morris Rossabi, it was not until 1760, and after their defeat of the Mongolian Zungars, that the Manchu Qing dynasty exerted full and formal control over the region, establishing it as their "new dominions" (*Xinjiang*), an administration that had lasted barely 100 years, when it fell to the Yakub Beg rebellion (1864–1877) and expanding Russian influence (Rossabi 1979). Until major migrations of Han Chinese were encouraged in the mid-nineteenth century, the Qing were mainly interested in

224   *D.C. Gladney*

pacifying the region by setting up military outposts that supported a vassal state relationship. Colonization had begun with the migrations of the Han in the mid-nineteenth century, but was cut short by the Yakub Beg rebellion, the fall of the Qing empire in 1911, and the ensuing warlord era that dismembered the region until its incorporation as part of the People's Republic in 1949. Competition for the loyalties of the peoples of the oases in the Great Game played between China, Russia, and Britain further contributed to divisions among the Uyghur along political, religious, and military lines. The peoples of the oases in this region lacked any coherent sense of identity until the challenge of nation-state incorporation.

Thus, the incorporation of Xinjiang into a nation-state for the first time required unprecedented delineation of the so called nations involved. Before its recent reemergence, the label "Uyghur" was last used 500 years ago to describe the largely Buddhist population of the Turfan Basin. In spite of this, this label has been in use in the last 80 years as the appellation for the settled Turkic-speaking Muslim oasis dwellers. Its use has never been disputed by the people themselves or the states involved. There is too much at stake for the people labeled as such to wish to challenge that identification. For Uyghur nationalists today, the direct lineal descent from the Uyghur Kingdom in seventh-century Mongolia is accepted as fact, despite overwhelming historical and archeological evidence to the contrary.[7]

The end of the Qing dynasty and the rise of Great Game rivalries between China, Russia, and Britain saw the region torn by competing loyalties and marked by two short-lived and drastically different attempts at independence: the proclamations of an "East Turkestan Republic" in Kashgar in 1933 and another in Yining (Ghulje) in 1944.[8] As Linda Benson (1990) has extensively documented, these rebellions and attempts at self-rule did little to bridge competing political, religious, and regional differences within the Turkic Muslim people who became known officially as the Uyghur in 1934 under successive Chinese Kuomintang (KMT) warlord administrations. Andrew Forbes (1986) describes, in exhaustive detail, the great ethnic, religious, and political cleavages during the period from 1911 to 1949 that pitted Muslim against Chinese, Muslim against Muslim, Uyghur against Uyghur, Hui against Uyghur, Uyghur against Kazak, warlord against commoner, and Nationalist against Communist. There was short-lived independent Uyghur rule during two important periods, which the Uyghur today claim provide indisputable evidence of self-governance and even secular-inspired democratic rule. Uyghurs, Uzbeks, and other Central Asian Turkic peoples formed an "Eastern Turkestan Republic" (ETR) in Kashgar for less than a year in 1933, which was inspired by religious, Islamic ideals.

A decade later, the Soviet Union supported another attempt at independent Uyghur rule, establishing a more secular nationalist state, another "Eastern Turkestan Republic" in the northern part of Xinjiang, around the town now known as Yining (where there was a Russian consulate in recognition of this newly formed nation-state). During 1944–1945, the ETR fought against the

Chinese Nationalists (KMT) who were holding southern Xinjiang. Owing to a wartime alliance between the KMT and the Soviets, the Russians eventually pressured the ETR to cooperate with the Chinese, and they formed an uneasy alliance, until the Chinese communists defeated the KMT and occupied the region in 1949, in what they described as a "peaceful liberation" (due to Sino-Soviet cooperation at that time). Uyghur nationalists had then hoped to achieve a semi-independent republic along the Soviet lines of Uzbekistan and Kazakhstan, but they had to settle for recognition as a Chinese "minority nationality" with an Autonomous Region of Xinjiang (with much less juridical authority than the Soviet "union republics"). The extraordinary factionalism and civil disunion during this period, which caused large-scale depletion of lives and resources in the region, still lives in the minds of the population. Indeed, it is this memory that many argue keeps the region together, a deep-seated fear of widespread social disorder.[9]

Today, despite continued regional differences among three, and perhaps four, macro-regions, including the northwestern Zungaria plateau, the southern Tarim Basin, the southwest Pamir region, and the eastern Kumul–Turpan–Hami corridor, there are nearly 10 million people spread throughout this vast region who regard themselves as Uyghur, among a total population of 17 million (Chen 1977, 57; Gladney 1990, 1–28; Rudelson 1998, 8). Many of them dream of, and some agitate for, an independent "Uyghuristan." The "nationality" policy under the KMT identified five peoples of China, with the Han in the majority. The Uyghur were included at that time under the general rubric of "Hui Muslims," which then included all Muslim groups in China. This policy was continued under the Communists, eventually recognizing fifty-six nationalities, the Uyghur and eight other Muslim groups split out from the general category "Hui" (which was confined to mainly Chinese-speaking Muslims).

The separate nationality designation awarded to the Uyghurs in China continued to mask very considerable regional and linguistic diversity, with the designation also applied to many "non-Uyghur" groups such as the Loplyk and Dolans who had very little to do with the oasis-based Turkic Muslims who became known as the Uyghur. At the same time, contemporary Uyghur secessionists look back to the brief periods of independent self-rule under Yakub Beg and the Eastern Turkestan Republics, in addition to the earlier glories of the Uyghur kingdoms in Turpan and Karabalghasan, as evidence of their rightful claims to the region. Contemporary Uyghur secessionist organizations based in Istanbul, Ankara, Almaty, Munich, Amsterdam, Melbourne, and Washington may differ in their political goals and strategies for the region, but they all share a common vision of a continuous Uyghur claim on the region, disrupted by Chinese and Soviet intervention. The independence of the former Soviet Central Asian Republics in 1991 has done much to encourage these Uyghur organizations in their hopes for an independent "Uyghuristan," despite the fact that the new, mainly Muslim, Central Asian governments all signed protocols with China in Shanghai in the spring of 1996 that they would not harbor or support secessionist groups. These

226   D.C. Gladney

protocols were reaffirmed in the August 25, 1999 meeting between Boris Yeltsin and Jiang Zemin, committing the "Shanghai Five" nations (China, Russia, Kazakhstan, Kyrgyzstan, Tajikistan) to respecting border security and suppressing terrorism, drug smuggling, and secessionism (CNN News Service 1999). The policy was enforced on June 15, 1999, when three alleged Uyghur secessionists (Hammit Muhammed, Ilyan Zurdin, Khasim Makpur) were deported from Kazakhstan to China, with several others in Kyrgyzstan and Kazakhstan awaiting extradition (Eastern Turkistan Information Center 1999). The Shanghai Cooperation Organization (SCO) has evolved from what was originally a trade and border settlement alliance to become an increasingly powerful multi-lateral organization with a strong focus on anti-terrorism security cooperation.

That Islam became an important, but not exclusive, cultural marker of Uyghur identity is not surprising given the sociopolitical oppositions with which the Uyghur were confronted. In terms of religion, the Uyghurs are Sunni Muslims, practicing Islamic traditions similar to their co-religionists in the region. In addition, many of them are Sufi, adhering to branches of *Naqshbandiyya* Central Asian Sufism. Uyghurs are powerfully attached to their musical traditions, colorful dress, and patronage of saintly tomb complexes (*mazar*).[10] These practices are anathema to the strict Wahhabi-inspired Islamist codes of the Taliban and al Qaeda who severely persecute many Sufis and folk artists.

However, it is also important to note that Islam was only one of several unifying markers for Uyghur identity, depending on those with whom they cooperating at the time. This suggests that Islamic fundamentalist groups such as the Taliban in Afghanistan will have only limited appeal among the Uyghurs. For example, to the Hui Muslim Chinese in Xinjiang, numbering over 600,000, the Uyghur distinguish themselves as the legitimate autochthonous minority, as both share a belief in Sunni Islam. In contrast to the formerly nomadic Muslim peoples, such as the Kazakh, numbering more than one million, the Uyghur might stress their attachment to the land and oasis of origin. Most profoundly, modern Uyghurs, especially those living in larger towns and urban areas, are marked by their reaction to Chinese influence and incorporation. It is often Islamic traditions that become the focal point for Uyghur efforts to preserve their culture and history. One such popular tradition that has resurfaced in recent years is that of the *Mashrap*, where generally young Uyghurs gather to recite poetry and sing songs (often of folk or religious content), dance, and share traditional foods. These evening events have often become foci for Uyghur resistance to Chinese rule in past years. However, although within the region many portray the Uyghur as united around secessionist or Islamist causes, the Uyghur continue to be divided from within by religious conflicts, in this case competing Sufi and non-Sufi factions, territorial loyalties (whether they be oases or places of origin), linguistic discrepancies, commoner–elite alienation, and competing political loyalties. These divided loyalties were evidenced by the attack in May 1996 on the Imam of the Idgah Mosque in Kashgar by other Uyghurs, as well as the assassination of at least six Uyghur officials in September 1997. It is this contested understanding of history that continues to influence much of the current debate over secessionist and Chinese claims to the region. That many of these divided loyalties are beginning to be overcome in the diaspora marks an important development in global Uyghur identity. As Kristian Petersen (2006, 66) has noted, the internet has played an increasingly important role in uniting Uyghur sectarianism and factionalism.

Han nationalism and the Uyghur

The Uyghur are an official minority nationality of China, identified as the second largest of ten Muslim peoples in China, primarily inhabiting the Xinjiang Uyghur Autonomous Region. Many Uyghur with whom I have spoken in Turfan and Kashgar argue persuasively that they are the autochthonous people of this region. The fact that over 99.8 percent of the Uyghur population are located in Xinjiang, whereas other Muslim peoples of China have significant populations in other provinces (e.g., the Hui) and outside the country (e.g., the Kazak) contributes to this important sense of belonging to the land. The Uyghur continue to conceive of their ancestors as originating in Xinjiang, claiming to outsiders that "it is our land, our territory," despite the fact that the early Uyghur kingdom was based in what is now Outer Mongolia and the present region of Xinjiang is under the control of the Chinese state.

Unprecedented sociopolitical integration of Xinjiang into the Chinese nation-state has taken place in the last 60 years. Although Xinjiang has been under Chinese political domination since the defeat of the Zungar in 1754, until the middle of the twentieth century, it was but loosely incorporated into China proper. The extent of the incorporation of the Xinjiang Region into China is indicated by Chinese policies encouraging Han migration, communication, education, and occupational shifts since the 1940s. Han migration into Xinjiang increased their local population by a massive 2,500 percent between 1940 and 1982, representing an average annual growth of 8.1 percent, and they have maintained an average growth of nearly 5 percent ever since, with a current population of nearly 45 percent. Indeed, many conclude that China's primary program for assimilating its border regions is a policy of integration through immigration.[11] This was certainly the case for Inner Mongolia, where the Mongol population now stands at a mere 17 percent (rather than 12 percent, according to more recent data) and, given the following figures, may well be the case for Xinjiang. The former Party Secretary of Xinjiang from 1994 to 2010, Wang Lequan, also known as the "stability secretary" for his role in ruthlessly suppressing dissent and fervently executing Beijing's "strike hard campaign," masterminded the unparalleled flooding of Xinjiang with Han migrants from the interior. A native and former vice-governor of Shandong province, many suspect Chairman Wang lost his position as Party Secretary

228   *D.C. Gladney*

of Xinjiang for his poor handling of the July 2009 riots, although he retained his position in the central Politburo of the CCP (elevated in 2004).[12]

Meager Uyghur efforts at cultural survival

Integration with China has not been smooth for the Uyghur. Many Uyghur resent the threats to their cultural survival and have resorted to violence. After denying the existence of conflicts for decades and stressing instead China's "national unity," official reports have detailed Tibetan and Muslim conflict activities in the border regions of Tibet, Yunnan, Xinjiang, Ningxia, and Inner Mongolia. With the March 1997 bus bombings in Beijing, widely attributed (although this has never been verified) to Uyghur secessionists, coupled with the Urumqi bus bombings on the day of Deng Xiaoping's 1997 memorial on February 25, Beijing can no longer keep them secret. The Yining uprising on February 7, 1997, which left at least nine dead and hundreds injured, with seven Uyghur suspects arrested and most probably slated for execution, was widely covered by the world's media. This distinguishes these last few events from ongoing problems in the region in the mid-1980s that met with little media coverage. In 1996, the *Xinjiang Daily* reported five serious incidents since February 1996, with a crackdown that rounded up 2,773 terrorist suspects, 6,000 lbs of explosives, and 31,000 rounds of ammunition. Overseas Uyghur groups have claimed that over 10,000 were arrested in the round-up, with over 1,000 killed. The largest protest, which took place from February 2 to 8 1996, was sparked by a Chinese raid on an evening *Mashrap* cultural meeting. Protests against the arrests made during the meeting led to 120 deaths and over 2,500 arrests. On March 2, 1996, the pro-government *mullah* of Kashgar's Idgah mosque and his son were stabbed by knife-wielding Uyghur militants, on May 27, there was another attack on a senior government official, and in September of the same year, six Uyghur government officials were killed by other Uyghurs in Yecheng.

The government responded severely in the late 1990s with widespread arrests and new policy announcements. In spring 1998, the National People's Congress passed a New Criminal Law that redefined "counter-revolutionary" crimes to be "crimes against the state," liable to severe prison terms and even execution. Included in "crimes against the state" were any actions considered to involve "ethnic discrimination" or "stirring up anti-ethnic sentiment." Many human rights activists have argued that this is a thinly veiled attempt to criminalize "political" actions and to make them appear as illegal as traffic violations, supporting China's claims that it holds "no political prisoners." As any minority activity could be regarded as stirring "anti-ethnic feeling," many ethnic activists are concerned that the New Criminal Law will be easily turned against them.

The Chinese authorities are correct that increasing international attention on the plight of indigenous border peoples has put pressure on the regions. Notably, the formerly elected chair of the Unrepresented Nations and

People's Organization (UNPO) based in The Hague was the Uyghur, Erkin Alptekin, son of the Uyghur nationalist leader, Isa Yusuf Alptekin, who died in Istanbul in December 1995 where there is now a park dedicated to his memory. There are numerous international organizations working for the independence of Xinjiang (under the name of Eastern Turkestan), based in Amsterdam, Munich, Istanbul, Melbourne, Washington, DC, and New York. An organization that seeks to coordinate these disparate movements is the World Uyghur Congress, formed in 2004 with Erkin Alptekin as president. In its Washington, DC, meeting from May 21 to 25, 2006, the Congress elected Madam Rebiya Kadeer as president (www.uighurcongress.org). Although, as Chung (2006, 7) has noted, the WUC is merely an umbrella organization uniting a large number of Uyghur diaspora organizations in a democratic format for the first time, the Chinese government has nevertheless labeled the WUC a "terrorist organization" (Mackerras 2007, 101). The official position of the WUC, which is growing in influence among Uyghur communities and organizations across the globe, is to push for real autonomy and not demand independence or secession at this time, along the same lines as the Tibetan government-in-exile.[13]

Clearly, as Xinjiang is the last Muslim region under Communism, the international support for the WUC and Uyghur independence is of more concern to the Chinese authorities than the international support for Tibetan independence.

The important question is: why do the Chinese authorities call such attention to these Tibetan and Muslim activities and external organizations? From 1998 to 2008, there was a decade without a single incident of Uyghur-related violence. The Istanbul-based groups have existed since the 1950s, and the Dalai Lama has been active since his exile in 1959. Secessionist actions have taken place on a small but regular basis since the expansion of market and trade policies in China and, with the opening of overland gateways to Xinjiang in addition to the trans-Eurasian railway since 1991, there seems to be no chance of closing up shop. In his 1994 visit to the newly independent nations of Central Asia, Li Peng called for the opening of a "new Silk Road." This was a clear attempt to calm fears in the newly established Central Asian states over Chinese expansionism, as was the April 1996 Shanghai communiqué that solidified the existing Sino-Central Asian borders. Documented separatist and violent incidents in Xinjiang had dropped off dramatically since the late 1990s. In a July 14, 2002 *Washington Post* (2002) interview, Philip Pan reported that local Xinjiang security officials were only able to cite three relatively small occurrences. Beijing's official publication of the secessionist issue may have more to do with domestic politics than any real internal or external threat. Recent moves, such as evidenced in the 2008 Olympics, suggest efforts to promote Chinese nationalism as a "unifying ideology" that will prove more attractive than Communism and more manageable than capitalism. By highlighting secessionist threats and external intervention, China can divert attention away from its own domestic challenges of natural disasters

230 *D.C. Gladney*

(especially the 2008 Sichuan earthquake), economic crises (such as the Asian economic downturn's drag on China's currency), rising inflation, increased income disparity, displaced "floating populations," Taiwan reunification, and the many other internal and external problems facing the Chinese Communist Party leadership. Perhaps nationalism will be the only "unifying ideology" left to a Chinese nation that has begun to distance itself from Communism, as it has from Confucianism, Buddhism, and Daoism in the past. This is perhaps why religiously based nationalisms, such as Islamic fundamentalism and Tibetan Buddhism, are targeted by Beijing, whereas the rise of shamanism and popular religion goes nearly unchecked. At the same time, a firm lid on Muslim activism in China sends a message to foreign Muslim militant organizations to stay out of China's internal affairs, and to the Taliban to stay well within their Afghan borders. Although it is hard to gauge the extent of support for Uyghur secessionism and separatism among the broader population, it is clear that cultural survival is a critical concern for many, and a significant attempt to preserve Uyghur culture is taking place, assisted to some extent by international tourism and the state's attempts to demonstrate its goodwill toward its restive Muslim population.

Territorializing the Uyghur future

To an extent never seen before, the continued incorporation of Xinjiang into China has become inexorable, and perhaps irreversible. The need for the oil and mineral resources of the region since China became an oil-importing nation in 1993 means that Chinese influence will only grow. To be sure, the Uyghur are still oriented culturally and historically toward Central Asia in terms of religion, language, and ethnic custom, and interaction has increased in recent years as a result of the opening of the roads to Pakistan and Almaty. China has also recently discussed opening the border between Afghanistan and Xinjiang via the ancient Wakhan Corridor, where there is no road but only an ancient donkey trail used since Silk Road days.[14] Certainly, pan-Turkism was appealing to some, but not all, Uyghurs during the early part of this century. Historical ties to Central Asia are strong. Turkey's late Prime Minister Turgut Ozal espoused a popular Turkish belief when, on his first state visit to Beijing in 1985, which sought to open a consulate there, he commented that the Turkish nation originated in what is now China. Yet separatist notions, given the current political incorporation of Xinjiang into China, while perhaps present, are not practicable. They remain visions of a virtual community, but a community that is nevertheless becoming better organized and more audible in its message broadcast to those inside and outside China. In his prescient article, Dale Eickelman (2005, 39) noted that the new social media were beginning to transform the heretofore isolated authoritarian and reform-resistant regimes of the Middle East. Why should China be immune to these global trends? As noted above, much of what is written about China is predicated on the assumption that China holds together as a nation. But, if China should fail at the center, or the "Great Wall" of information control should be breached, the peripheries will certainly destabilize, with Xinjiang and Tibet having the strongest prospects for secession given their cultural unity and attempts at government-in-exile, as substantially augmented by the networking and community-building power of the internet and social networks.

The problems facing Xinjiang, however, are much greater than those of Tibet if it were to become independent. Not only is Xinjiang more integrated into the rest of China, but the Uyghur part of the population is less than half the total and primarily located in the south, where there is less industry and fewer natural resources, except for oil. As noted above, however, unless significant investment is found, Tarim oil and energy resources will never be a viable source of independent wealth. Poor past relations between the three main Muslim groups, Uyghur, Kazakh, and Hui, suggest that conflicts among Muslims would be as great as those between Muslims and Han Chinese. Most local residents believe that independence would lead to significant conflicts between these groups, along ethnic, religious, urban–rural, and territorial lines. Given the harsh climate and poor resources in the region, those caught in the middle would have few places to which to flee. Xinjiang Han would naturally seek to return to the interior of China, as Russia and Mongolia would be in no position to receive them. Yet given the premise that only a complete collapse of the state could precipitate a viable independence movement and internal civil war in Xinjiang, there would be few places the Han would be able to go. Certainly, the bordering provinces of Gansu and Qinghai would be just as disrupted, and Tibet would not be an option. Uyghur refugees would most likely seek to move south, as the north would be dominated by the Han and the western routes would be closed off by Kazakhstan and Kyrgyzstan. That leaves only the southern routes and, with the exception of Pakistan, no nation in the region would probably be equipped to receive them. Certainly, they would not be better off in present-day Tajikistan and Afghanistan. Given the ongoing conflicts in Kashmir, even Pakistan, the most likely recipient of Uyghur refugees, would probably not wish further destabilization of the region. Note also that the main southern route to India and Pakistan, along the Karakorum Highway through the Torghurat Pass, is generally passable for less than 6 months out of the year. India, despite its poor relations with China, would probably not want to add to its Muslim population. During many conversations in Xinjiang with local residents, Muslim and Han alike, it became clear that this is a well-known fact. Most think that, in such a worst-case scenario, there would be nothing to do but stay and fight.

In terms of religious freedom, as with many other policies, the Chinese constitution is laudable when honored. However, in a country where the rule of law often gives way to local and national politics, it is often only honored in the breach. As long as religion is perceived by Chinese officials as a threat to Chinese sovereignty, mosques and religious practice will be closely

232   *D.C. Gladney*

monitored and in some cases restricted. In light of international Islamic interest, however, Chinese officials have to be careful regarding any oppressive treatment of religious practice—especially if casting it as "splittist" or seditious, as in the February 1997 incident in Ili.

The history of Chinese–Muslim relations in Xinjiang, as Millward's (2007) book documented, has been one of relative peace and quiet, broken by enormous social and political disruptions, fostered by both internal and external crises. The opposition to Chinese rule in Xinjiang has not reached the level of Syria, Yemen, Chechnya, or the Intifada, but similar to the Basque separatists of the ETA in Spain, or the former IRA in Ireland and England, it is one that may erupt in limited, violent moments of terror and resistance. And just as these conflicts have not been resolved in the Middle East, North Africa, or Europe, the Uyghur problem in Xinjiang does not appear to be one that will readily go away. Nor are Uyghur in the diaspora able to engage with the region and participate regularly in its reform or development. To paraphrase Sean Roberts, unlike many Middle Easterners who regularly visit their homelands, Uyghur who are "waiting for Uyghuristan" must do their waiting and imagining on the internet, as expatriates are not allowed to visit the region. The admitted problem of Uyghur terrorism and dissent, even in the diaspora, is thus problematic for a government that wants to encourage integration and development in a region where the majority population is not only ethnically different, but also devoutly Muslim. How does a government integrate a strongly religious minority (be it Muslim, Tibetan, Christian, or Buddhist) into a "market–Leninist" system? China's policy of intolerance toward dissent and economic stimulus does not seem to have resolved this issue. Given events at the western end of the Eurasian continent, China should find ways to open dialogue with representative Uyghur individuals and groups to better cooperate in finding solutions to this ongoing problem. There has been much progress and relatively peaceful development of this important region. Surely a dialogue can be opened up in order to help insure a more prosperous and peaceful future, for both Uyghur and Han alike.

Notes

1 For the sake of coherence (cf. the Introduction to this volume), we decided to translate *fenliezhuyi* as "secessionism" instead of "separatism." Although the Chinese translation of "secession" is *tuoli*, "*tuolizhuyi*" is never used and what the Chinese authorities derogatively qualify as *fenliezhuyi* can cover, on purpose and in order to dismiss them, both the movements that fight for independence and those that only demand meaningful political autonomy.

2 Estimates range from 140 to 1,000+ deaths, two-thirds Han Chinese, which led to unprecedented coverage and criticism in the Chinese media. See "Xinjiang riot hits regional anti-terror nerve," *Xinhua*, July 7, 2009, at http://news.xinhuanet.com/english/2009-07/18/content_11727782.htm; also Minxin Pei, "Uighur riots show need for re-think in Beijing," *Financial Times*, July 9, 2009; "China says 140 die in riot, Uighur separatists blamed," July 6, 2009, at www.bloomberg.com/apps/news?pid=newsarchive& sid = aBWP2E9DJPlU. An extensive report by the Uyghur

Human Rights Project of the Uyghur American Association was released on July 5, 2011, "A city ruled by fear and silence: Urumchi, two years on," at http://docs.uyghuramerican.org/July5-report.pdf.

3 Although she has yet to be received by the Obama administration, Ms. Kadeer presented testimony to the US Committee on Foreign Affairs, Congressional Sub-committee on International Organizations, Human Rights, and Oversight, on June 10, 2009, entitled: "The Uyghurs: a history of persecution," at http://foreignaffairs.house.gov/111/kad061009.pdf.

4 Freedom of Religion Law, Article 36 of the December 1982 PRC Constitution: "Citizens of the People's Republic of China enjoy freedom of religious belief. No state organ, public organization or individual may compel citizens to believe in, or not to believe in, any religion; nor may they discriminate against citizens who believe in, or do not believe in, any religion. The state protects normal religious activities. No one may make use of religion to engage in activities that disrupt public order, impair the health of citizens or interfere with the educational system of the state. Religious bodies and religious affairs are not subject to any foreign domination."

5 Rohan Gunaratna, as cited in "Xinjiang riot hits regional anti-terror nerve," *Xinhua. China Daily*, July 18, 2009, at http://www.chinadaily.com.cn/china/2009-07/18/content_8445811.htm. Although Gunaratna, a self-styled terrorism expert with no research experience in China, has claimed direct links between ETIM and al Qaeda, he has yet to offer independent confirmation that the group is still active, or that any of the violence in Xinjiang is connected to global jihadism, other than Chinese sources (Gunaratna 2002).

6 One of the best examples of this is the website maintained by the ethnomusicologist, Dr. Nathan Light, at http://homepages.utoledo.edu/nlight/uyghpg.htm.

7 The best "Uighur nationalist" retelling of this unbroken descent from Karakorum is in the document from the Eastern Turkestani Union in Europe (n.d.). For a review and critique, including historical evidence for the multiethnic background of the contemporary Uighur, see Gladney (1998c); for a discussion of the recent archeological evidence derived from DNA dating of the desiccated corpses of Xinjiang, see Mair (1998).

8 The best discussion of the politics and importance of Xinjiang during this period is that of an eyewitness and participant, Owen Lattimore (Lattimore 1950).

9 James Millward's history is the best overview of this tumultuous period (Millward 2007).

10 See the important article by Rahile Dawut, a female Uyghur ethno-historian, on Uyghur tomb complexes and grave veneration with beautiful color photographs (Dawut 2009, 56–67), at www.silkroadfoundation.org/newsletter/vol6num2/srjournal_v6n2.pdf.

11 For China's minority integration program, see Mackerras (1994).

12 Edward Wong and Jonathan Ansfield, "China replaces leader of the restive Xinjiang Region," *New York Times*, May 15, 2010: A10; Michael Wines, "A strongman is China's rock in ethnic strife," *New York Times*, July 10, 2009: A11; Gladney (2004, 378–385).

13 See the position of the World Uyghur Congress, at www.uyghurcongress.org/en/?cat=1. The Globalsecurity.org report on "Uyghur militants" states unequivocally that, with regard to the World Uyghur Congress, it is "a nonviolent and peaceful opposition movement against Chinese occupation of East Turkestan … " with an "unconditional rejection of totalitarianism, religious intolerance and terrorism as an instrument of policy," at www.globalsecurity.org/military/world/para/uighur.htm.

14 See the Stratfor paper documenting the Afghan Prime Minister's request for China to open the Wakhan corridor, June 11, 2009, "China: Afghan FM seeks Wakhan Corridor supply route," www.stratfor.com/sitrep/20090611_china_afghan_fm_seeks_wakhan_corridor_supply_route.

234   *D.C. Gladney*

References

Amnesty International (1999), *Peoples Republic of China: Gross Violations of Human Rights in the Xinjiang Uighur Autonomous Region*, London, 21 April.

——(2000), 'China: Uighur Businesswoman Rebiya Kadeer Sentenced to Eight Years after Secret Trial' News Service 47/00, AI Index: ASA 17/10/00, 10 March.

Appadurai, Arjun (1990), 'Disjuncture and Difference in the Global Cultural Economy' *Public Culture*, 2(2): 1–24.

Banister, Judith (1987), *China's Changing Population*, Stanford, CA, Stanford University Press.

Benson, Linda (1990), *The Ili Rebellion: The Moslem Challenge to Chinese Authority in Xinjiang, 1944–1949*, New York, M.E. Sharpe.

Chen, Jack (1977), *The Sinkiang Story*, New York, Macmillan.

China State Council (1999), 'National Minorities Policy and Its Practice in China', Beijing, Information Office of the State Council of the People's Republic of China, September.

Chung, Chien-peng (2006), 'Confronting Terrorism and Other Evils in China: All Quiet on the Western Front?' *China and Eurasia Forum Quarterly*, 4 (2): 75–87.

CNN News Service (1999), Rym Brahimi, 'Russia, China, and Central Asian Leaders Pledge to Fight Terrorism, Drug Smuggling', 25 August, at www.uygur.org/enorg/wunn99/990825e.html.

Dawut, Rahile (2009), 'Shrine Pilgrimage among the Uighurs' *The Silk Road Journal*, Winter/Spring 6(2): 56–67, at www.silkroadfoundation.org/newsletter/vol6num2/srjournal_v6n2.pdf.

Dorian, James P., Wigdortz, Brett and Gladney, Dru (1997), 'Central Asia and Xinjiang, China: Emerging Energy, Economic, and Ethnic Relations' *Central Asian Survey*, 16(4): 461–486.

Eastern Turkistan Information Center (1999), 'Kazakhstan Government Deport Political Refugees to China', Munich, 15 June, at www.uygur.org/enorg/reports99/990615.html.

——(n.d.), 'Population of Eastern Turkistan: The Population in Local Records', Munich, at www.uygur.org/enorg/turkistan/nopus.html.

Eastern Turkestani Union in Europe (n.d.), 'Brief History of the Uyghers', at www.geocities.com/CapitolHill/1730/buh.html.

Eickelman, Dale F. (2005), 'New Media in the Arab Middle East and the Emergence of Open Societies' in Robert Hefner (ed.), *Remaking Muslim Politics: Pluralism, Contestation, Democratization*, Princeton, NJ, Princeton University Press, pp. 37–59.

Forbes, Andrew (1986), *Warlords and Muslims in Chinese Central Asia*, Cambridge, Cambridge University Press.

Franke, Herbert and Twitchett, Denis (1994), *Cambridge History of China: Volume 6: Alien Regimes and Border States (907–1368)*, Cambridge, Cambridge University Press.

Gladney, Dru C. (1990), 'The Ethnogenesis of the Uighur' *Central Asian Survey*, 9(1): 1–28.

——(1996), *Muslim Chinese: Ethnic Nationalism in the People's Republic of China*, second edition, Cambridge, MA, Harvard University Press.

——(1998a), *Ethnic Identity in China*, Fort Worth, Harcourt Brace.

——(ed.) (1998b), *Making Majorities: Constituting the Nation in Japan, Korea, China, Malaysia, Fiji, Turkey, and the United States*, Stanford, CA, Stanford University Press.

——(1998c), 'Ethnogenesis and Ethnic Identity in China: Considering the Uygurs and Kazakhs' in Victor Mair (ed.), *The Bronze Age and Early Iron Age People of*

Eastern Central Asia: Volume II, Washington, DC, Institute for the Study of Man, pp. 812–834.

——(1998d), 'Internal Colonialism and China's Uyghur Muslim Minority' *International Institute for the Study of Islam in the Modern World Newsletter*, October, 1: 20–21, at http://isim.leidenuniv.nl/newsletter/1/regional/01AC23.html.

——(1999), 'Making Muslims in China: Education, Islamicization, and Representation' in Gerard A. Postiglione (ed.), *China's National Minority Education: Culture, State Schooling and Development*, New York, Garland Press.

——(2004), *Dislocating China: Muslims, Minorities, and Other Subaltern Subjects*, Chicago, University of Chicago Press.

——(2007), 'Cyber-Separatism, Islam, and the State in China' in J. Craig Jenkins and Esther E. Gottlieb (eds), *Identity Conflicts: Can Violence be Regulated?* New Brunswick, Transaction Publishers, pp. 95–97.

Gunaratna, Rohan (2002), *Inside Al Qaeda: Global Network of Terror*. New York: Columbia University Press.

International Taklamakan Human Rights Association (ITHRA) (n.d.), 'How Has the Population Distribution Changed in Eastern Turkestan since 1949', at www.taklamakan.org/uighur-L/et_faq_pl.html.

Lattimore, Owen (1950), *Pivot of Asia: Sinkiang and the Inner Asian Frontiers of China and Russia*, Boston, Little, Brown.

Mackerras, Colin (1994), *China's Minorities: Integration and Modernization in the Twentieth Century*, Hong Kong, Oxford University Press.

——(2007), 'Xinjiang and the War against Terror' in Simon Shen (ed.), *China and Antiterrorism*, New York, Nova Science Publishers, pp. 91–112.

Mair, Victor (1998), 'Introduction' in Victor Mair (ed.), *The Bronze Age and Early Iron Age People of Eastern Central Asia: Volume II*, Washington, DC, Institute for the Study of Man, pp. 1–40.

Millward, James A. (2007), *Eurasian Crossroads: A History of Xinjiang*, New York, Columbia University Press.

Moseley, George (1966). *The Party and the National Question in China*. Cambridge MA: MIT Press.

People's Republic of China (1987), *Population Atlas of China*, National Population Census Office, Hong Kong, Oxford University Press.

——(1991), *Major Figures of the Fourth National Population Census: Vol. 4*, National Population Census Office, Beijing, China Statistical Publishing House.

——(1994), *Population of China's Nationality (Data of 1990 Population Census) [Zhongguo Minzu Renkou Ziliao (1990 nian Renkou Pucha Shuju)]*, Department of Population Statistics of State Statistical Bureau and Economic Department of State Nationalities Affairs Commission, Beijing, China Statistical Publishing House.

Petersen, Kristian (2006), 'Usurping the Nation: Cyber-Leadership in the Uighur Nationalist Movement' *Journal of Muslim Minority Affairs*, 26(1): 63–73.

Renmin Ribao (1991) 'Guanyu 1990 nian renkou pucha zhuyao de gongbao [Report regarding the 1990 population census primary statistics]', 14 November, Beijing.

Roberts, Sean R. (1996), *Waiting for Uighurstan*, Los Angeles, University of Southern California, Center for Visual Anthropology (video documentary).

Rossabi, Morris (1979), 'Muslim and Central Asian Revolts' in Jonathan D. Spence and John E. Wills Jr. (eds), *From Ming to Ch'ing*, New Haven, CT, Yale University Press.

Rudelson, Justin Jon (1998), *Oasis Identities: Uighur Nationalism along China's Silk Road*, New York, Columbia University Press.

236 D.C. Gladney

Shichor, Yitzhak (2003), 'Virtual Transnationalism: Uyghur Communities in Europe and the Quest for East Turkestan Independence' in Stefano Allievi and Jorgen Nielsen (eds), *Muslim Networks and Transnational Communities in and across Europe*, Leiden, E.J. Brill, pp. 283–284.

Starr, Frederick S. (ed.) (2004), *Xinjiang: China's Muslim Borderland*, Armonk, NY, M.E. Sharpe.

Todd, Reed J. and Raschke, Diana (2010), *The ETIM: China's Islamic Militants and the Global Terrorist Threat*, Westport, CT, Praeger.

Turkistan News and Information Network (1999), 'Press Release', June 8.

Wall Street Journal (1999), 'China Arrests Noted Businesswoman in Crackdown in Muslim Region', Ian Johnson, August 18.

Washington Post (2002), 'In China's West, Ethnic Strife Becomes "Terrorism"', Philip Pan, July 14, A4.

14 The case of Taiwan

Independence without secession?

Jean-Pierre Cabestan

Taiwan, under the official name of Republic of China (ROC), is a de facto, yet ill-recognized independent nation-state whose security remains guaranteed by the United States but whose long-term future is uncertain. The reason is that, since its establishment in October 1949, the People's Republic of China (PRC) has both claimed Taiwan as part of its territory and tried to reunify with it. In other words, although at the end of the Chinese civil war, the official authorities of the ROC took refuge on Taiwan where they perpetuated their political regime formally based in Nanjing, the Chinese Communist Party (CCP) has always pretended that the PRC was the only legitimate representative of China and as a consequence the ROC had ceased to exist in 1949. Conversely, while dreaming, at least until the early 1960s, to re-conquer what it still calls today the Chinese mainland (*Zhongguo dalu*), the ROC claimed, until the beginning of its democratization in the mid-1980s, to be the only legal Chinese government, considering the PRC authorities to be "Communist bandits" (*gongfei*). As a consequence, there has always been only one China seat in the United Nations (UN), occupied from 1945 to 1971 by the ROC and, since then, by the PRC.

The PRC's initial aim was to "liberate" Taiwan by military means. It has failed (and actually never tried) to do this, primarily because of the United States 1952 security agreement with the ROC. Since 1979, the PRC has embarked on a peaceful reunification and economic integration strategy aimed at gradually bringing the island back into the "womb of the motherland." Concomitantly and linked to US–China (PRC) normalization, this new strategy has not put an end to American support for the island's security; this support has just become more ambiguous. At the same time, China's rise and Taiwan's growing economic dependence upon the Chinese market have been powerful drivers of détente, reconciliation, and even "rapprochement" between two Chinese states which, however, do not recognize each other. This politico-legal complexity underscores the ambiguity of Taiwan's international status, the formidable difficulties for the Beijing and Taipei governments in fully normalizing their relationship as well as the uniqueness of the Taiwan situation among all the secession and separatist cases discussed in this volume. As Taiwan has never been part of the PRC, it cannot be assimilated

238   *J.-P. Cabestan*

to the secession or autonomous claims made by large segments of the autochthon population in Xinjiang or in Tibet. At the same time, because most Taiwanese do not wish to reunify with the PRC and some still want to move to a permanent and, if possible, de jure independence, contrary to Beijing's hope and in spite of its threats, Taiwan's situation does not totally fit the divided nation model, which was epitomized by Germany during the Cold War era (1949–1990) and is still represented today by the two Koreas (Metzler 2001).

Yet, since the outbreak of the Korean War in 1950, the US has been a constant and crucial factor in relations across the Taiwan Strait. Perceived by the PRC as a key obstacle to reunification and, conversely, by some Taiwanese as a barrier against de jure independence, the US administration has played a stabilizing role that has allowed the status quo to perpetuate up to now. From a security viewpoint—and this is also unique—the US has since 1979 and even since 1950 been the de facto guarantor of Taiwan's independence from the PRC as well as non-secession from the Chinese nation, and actually the ROC framework. To our knowledge, no other "secession" or "separatist" cause has received this type of support. Although, owing to China's growing military power, some Americans today have some doubt about their country's capability to commit itself to the island's security in the long term, as we will see, it is hard for the US to disengage itself from its strategic role and responsibilities in East Asia. For all these reasons, Taiwan's case of *independence without secession*, as it was qualified in the title of this chapter, can be regarded as *sui generis*. For how long?

A rich but complex history

Taiwan's past to a large extent explains the present situation as well as its likely futures. Taiwan's history is of course the object of conflicting narratives, motivated by irreconcilable political objectives. For the PRC authorities, the island has been part of China since "ancient times." On the contrary, for Taiwanese nationalists, its history has been a 400-year quest for freedom and independence from China. The historical truth is probably halfway between these two extreme discourses: although Taiwan's Chinese heritage and integration in the Manchu Empire are hard to deny, its specific trajectory since the end of the nineteenth century, its long separation from the Chinese mainland, and its democratization have contributed to the building of a distinct nation or "community of citizens" (Wachman 1994; Schnapper 1998; Le Pesant 2011).

Until the early seventeenth century, Taiwan was an island exclusively inhabited by Austronasian populations, located outside the Chinese Empire and visited from time to time by Chinese fishermen. At the end of the sixteenth century, it was spotted by some Portuguese navigators who found it "beautiful" (*formosa*), hence its traditional name in the west. Then, it was colonized by the Dutch in the south (1624) and, for a short period of time, by the Spanish in the north (1626–1642), who were later to be kicked out by the former. In need of a labor force, the Dutch colonizers encouraged small-scale

Chinese migration to Taiwan. However, in 1661, they were themselves expelled by General Zheng Chenggong (Koxinga), a Ming dynasty loyalist who had decided to take refuge on the island with his army in order to prepare a counter-offensive against the Manchu who had just conquered China (1644). Zheng failed, but ironically was the first ruler to "sinicize" Taiwan in establishing a Ming-type government there. Seen as a challenge by the Manchu Court based in Beijing, Zheng's regime was toppled by Admiral Shi Lang who took control of the island in 1683. In the following two centuries, Taiwan remained a border region of the Manchu Empire (Shepherd 1993). Operating under the authority of the Fujian provincial government, Manchu and Han administrators ruled its western half, leaving in de facto independence the aborigines who lived in the mountainous eastern parts. In order to preserve social peace and dissolve land disputes between Chinese migrants and plain Austronasians, Beijing regulated migrations, originated mostly from southern Fujian (Minnan) and, to a lesser extent, from eastern Guangdong (Hakka). Today, Minnan (or Hokkien, 70 percent of the population) and Hakka (or Kejia, 15 percent) are the two major Taiwanese communities as well as dialects spoken on the island. The fourteen surviving Austronasian tribes just represent 2 percent of the population. The other 13 percent of Taiwanese are "mainlanders" (or "province outsiders" as they are called in Chinese, *waishengren*) who arrived on the island after its return to China in 1945.

As maritime powers (particularly Britain, France, and Japan) started to covet Taiwan in the middle of the nineteenth century, the Manchu government decided to modernize the island and, in 1885, to give it full provincial status. However, 10 years later, in 1895, after Beijing's military defeat by the Japanese over the control of Korea, and the signing of the Shimonoseki Treaty, Taiwan was annexed by Japan. The 50 years of Japanese occupation had a huge impact on Taiwanese society and its post-World War Two elites, including personalities such as Lee Teng-hui or Peng Min-ming. Although Japan's colonization imposed a tough and globally uncompromising rule, it directly contributed to modernizing Taiwan and educating (in Japanese) large segments of its society. In the Taisho and early Showa eras, and in particular between 1919 and 1936, the Japanese colonizers granted more autonomy to the island, promoting some of its elites through local elections or access to the university. In those years, neither Sun Yat-sen's, then Chiang Kai-shek's Kuomintang (KMT, Nationalist Party) nor Mao Zedong's Chinese Communist Party demanded Taiwan's return to China (Rubinstein 1997).

The ROC government's first formal claim was made by Chiang at the Cairo Conference in 1943, in the middle of World War Two. Endorsed by the Allied powers, it was confirmed 2 years later by the Potsdam Declaration (August 1945), according to which all territories that Japan has stolen from China (including also Manchuria) "shall be restored to the ROC." As a result, in October 1945, ROC troops took over Taiwan and the Pescadores (Penghu) Islands situated in the middle of the strait. Although most Taiwanese welcomed this change, tension between the newly established but incompetent,

240   *J.-P. Cabestan*

penniless, and greedy KMT administration and the local population grew rapidly, triggering the well-known February 28, 1947 incident and the bloody repression that followed (around 10,000 deaths). Considered as a watershed and a defining moment in the formation of Taiwanese consciousness (*Taiwan yishi*) and identity (*Taiwan rentong*), this crisis fed both long-entrenched resentment against mainland Chinese rulers and a small Japan-based pro-independence movement that would gradually expand after 1949 (Lai et al. 1991; Rubinstein 1995).

It is clear that, in 1947, most Taiwanese did not support or even conceive of any independence option. What the local elites wanted was a genuine political and democratically represented autonomy within the Chinese Republic. However, the unexpected arrival on Taiwan in 1949 of Nanjing-based central ROC and KMT-dominated authorities—1.5 million civilian and military refugees, who today constitute the bulk of the "mainlander" community—created an unprecedented situation. On the one hand, Chiang Kai-shek, who still considered himself as the president of the only legitimate Chinese regime, presented this transfer as provisional and, until his death in 1975, kept alive the hope—which in the 1960s became an illusion—of a military reconquest of the mainland. Supported and protected by the US, which moved its 7th Fleet into the Taiwan Strait after the outbreak of the Korean War in June 1950 but opposed any military adventure against "Communist China," the ROC managed to keep China's seat in the UN until 1971 and its diplomatic relations with Washington until December 1978. On the other hand, the ROC gradually settled down on the island and had no other choice but to start integrating local Taiwanese into the political system. The unfinished civil war with the mainland and the martial law regime declared on Taiwan in 1950 imposed many restrictions on the implementation of the politically liberal 1947 ROC Constitution. Intellectuals who tried to set up an independent political party, such as Lei Chen in 1960, and pushed for democratization and two Chinas representation in the UN, such as Peng Min-ming in 1965, were sentenced to long prison terms. Yet, although the central institutions of the ROC remained controlled by representatives elected on the mainland in 1947–1948 in a context of civil war and an already divided country, local governments and assemblies were opened to elections. Until the lifting of martial law in 1987, the KMT remained the only authorized party; after the mid-1960s, more independent—called *Dangwai* (outside of the party)—candidates were allowed to run for election. In the same period of time, the KMT was slowly "Taiwanized," an evolution that speeded up after Chiang Ching-kuo formally succeeded his father in 1978.

Taiwan's rapid economic modernization, growing diplomatic isolation, and profound social changes intensified pressure on the KMT to initiate political change. However, the democratization process was neither easy nor fast (Cheng and Haggard 1992; Chu 1992; Tien 1996). Shortly after the US "de-recognition," the American Congress voted on the Taiwan Relations Act (TRA) in April 1979, a very important piece of legislation that organized the development of non-official relations with "the people of Taiwan" and has perpetuated up to now, although in vaguer terms, as a strong US security guarantee—including the sale of "defensive arms"—to the island.

Immediately denounced by Beijing, the TRA has not weakened the Taiwanese political opposition—or what then became the *Dangwai* movement—and its pressure on their government, triggering a major political riot in Kaohsiung in December 1979, remembered as the *Formosa* (*Meilidao*) incident.

Earlier that year, when normalizing its relations with the US, the PRC had adopted a peaceful reunification policy that challenged the KMT's old policy banning any contact with the Chinese Communists. In the following years, Deng Xiaoping made several propositions regarding Taiwan's reintegration, the most famous of them being the "one country, two systems" formula, which would later be successfully applied to Hong Kong in 1997 and Macau in 1999, turning these two territories into "special administrative regions" of the PRC. But Deng was ready to grant more autonomy to Taiwan, promising in particular that, in contrast to these two former colonies, it would be allowed to keep "part of its military." In the same period of time, in August 1982, although it secretly gave a series of important guarantees to Taiwan a month earlier—the so called "six assurances"—Washington signed a third communiqué with Beijing, according to which the US accepted to gradually reduce the numbers of weapons delivered to Taipei.[1] This new, although vague, commitment—no termination date was indicated in the communiqué—led the ROC government to try to acquire a nuclear military capability for the second time in a decade, an attempt that was (again) abruptly aborted under US pressure in 1988. This episode shows how isolated and insecure Taiwan felt as the PRC was opening to the outside and speeding up its economic development.

In Chiang's eyes, only democratization could help Taiwan break this diplomatic isolation and improve its security. In 1984, he took the unprecedented decision to promote a local Taiwanese, Lee Teng-hui, to the position of ROC vice-president. Then, in 1986, he personally tolerated the establishment of the first opposition grouping, the Democratic Progressive Party (DPP); a year later, he lifted martial law and restored many civil liberties. Simultaneously, he decided to carefully open up Taiwan to the PRC, allowing ROC citizens to travel to and trade with mainland China through a third place.

After Chiang Ching-kuo's death in January 1988, Lee Teng-hui accelerated Taiwan's political reforms. In 1990, he started to introduce the necessary constitutional amendments to allow democratic elections in and full representation of the "free areas" of the ROC, in other words the portions of the country under Taipei's jurisdiction (Taiwan, Penghu, as well as Kinmen and Matsu, two groups of small islands located off the Fujian coast). The following year, he officially and unilaterally announced the end of the civil war—or "the communist rebellion"—with the mainland, making possible non-official contacts with the PRC (see below). In 1992, for the first time, the Legislative Yuan, the ROC parliament, only represented Taiwanese voters. In 1996, after another series of amendments, Lee organized the first democratic presidential

242   *J.-P. Cabestan*

election in a Chinese society, which he won handsomely. Four years later, the DPP candidate Chen Shui-bian managed to get elected ahead of two other contenders, KMT's Lien Chan and KMT maverick James Soong Chu-yu, although the parliament remained controlled by the opposition. He was reelected 4 years later. But in 2008, Ma Ying-jeou, the KMT candidate, comfortably won the presidential election and, 4 years later in January 2012, was re-elected, underscoring, after two smooth transfers of power and in spite of persisting weaknesses (e.g., corruption or incomplete rule of law), the steady consolidation of Taiwan's democracy.

The crucial impact of democratization on cross-strait relations and Taiwan's future

Taiwan's democratization has dramatically changed the equation in the strait as well as in the Beijing–Washington–Taipei triangle (Garver 1997). Although it has directly contributed to strengthening Taiwan's identity, it has also allowed a rapid, though bumpy development of cross-strait relations and increased rather than weakened the role of the US in the future of Taiwan as a democratic entity, if not a fully recognized nation-state.

The rise of Taiwan's identity

First of all, Taiwan's democratization has consolidated Taiwan's identity and turned the island or the "ROC on Taiwan," as it was often referred to in the 1990s, into a real "community of citizens" and a genuine although ill-recognized nation-state (Wachman 1994; Hughes 1997). Although identity has remained a highly debated and contested issue in Taiwan, most island citizens see themselves as Taiwanese (52 percent in 2011) or, to a lesser degree, as Taiwanese and Chinese (43 percent); only a minority still regards themselves as exclusively Chinese (5 percent). Whereas a majority of Taiwanese would not deny that they are culturally Chinese, the long domination of the mainlanders' elite, a domination closely associated with the martial law era and the obligation to use Mandarin (*guoyu*), the strong identity developed by the Minnan majority with the support of their dialect and, more generally, by the three communities or "sub-ethnic groups" (*zuqun*) that constitute the local Taiwanese population (Minnan, Hakka, and Austronasians or *benshengren* in Chinese) have directly led not only the "Taiwanese consciousness" or the Taiwanese identity mentioned earlier but to a new Taiwanese nationalism (Chen et al. 1994; Chang 2000; Corcuff 2002). Nurtured and capitalized by the DPP and, more widely, the independence-leaning "green camp" (green is the color of Taiwan island on the DPP flag), in the first two decades after democratization, advocates of this nationalism were tempted to ostracize mainlanders and only trust and promote local Taiwanese.

However, several factors have gradually changed the nature of Taiwanese nationalism and made it more inclusive and also more ambiguous (Cabestan

2005). As the mainlanders' first generation is disappearing and mixed marriages are increasing, the distinction between mainlanders and local Taiwanese is becoming less relevant. All ROC citizens born in Taiwan (or who hold an ROC identity card) are entitled to and enjoy the same political rights. Although originally—especially in the 1970s and 1980s—Taiwanese identity was regarded by its promoters as both cultural and political and often exclusive, today this identity has become much more a political than a cultural catalyst. True, Taiwan's cultural identity remains a divisive topic: although the KMT or "blue camp" (blue is the color of the KMT flag) elites still emphasize the true Chinese nature of Taiwan's culture and insist that the ROC has protected Chinese traditions better than the PRC, DPP or green-leaning Taiwanese argue that Taiwan's cultural identity, in spite of its Chinese foundation and because of its Minnan, Hakka, and aborigine dimensions and its successive strong Japanese and American influences, has developed differently and distinctively.

However, Taiwan's political identity matters more as it is the one that all politicians—blue as well as green—feel compelled to refer to in their discourse, especially during electoral campaigns. This identity is based on shared political values centered on the principles of democracy and self-determination, in the sense that Taiwan's future can only be decided by the Taiwanese themselves. Put differently, in political terms, Taiwan, under its official ROC name, has witnessed, by default since 1949 and by design since its democratization, an undeniable nation-building process. Although it is the heir of the 1911 ROC, the ROC on Taiwan has initiated a "second Republic of China," as Taipei's political scientist Hu Fo once wrote, or a new nation-state whose political boundaries are those of Taiwan, Penghu, Jinmen, and Matsu.

Can the unprecedented development of economic and people-to-people relations across the Taiwan Strait reverse this trend? Most studies have so far demonstrated that this has not been the case. Although younger Taiwanese are often attracted by a job or career on the mainland and are inclined more frequently to use Mandarin than Minnan or other local dialects, and thus tend to adopt a more flexible and relaxed attitude toward the PRC, their Taiwanese identity and nationalism have continued to consolidate: the main differences from the older generation are that younger Taiwanese associate their identity more closely with democracy and tend to be more open-ended regarding the long-term solution of the cross-strait differences (independence or unification) (Cabestan and Le Pesant 2009). But like their parents, they are keen to protect Taiwan's sovereignty under the current name of the ROC and to keep in their hands the power to choose the island's future themselves. That is what I have called Taiwan's "sovereignist consensus" (Cabestan 2005).

Taiwan's increasing but difficult interactions with China

Taiwan's democratization has allowed Taipei and Beijing to put into place a pragmatic channel of communication, develop unprecedented economic and people-to-people relations, and stabilize the relations across the Taiwan Strait

244   J.-P. Cabestan

to some extent. Although at the same time strengthening Taiwan's "sovereignist consensus" as well as its willingness to be considered as a "normal country," democratization has complicated the Beijing–Washington–Taipei triangle. Having said that, as we will see, the main obstacle to any solution to the deep political differences on both sides of the strait is not Taiwan's democratization: it is the inability of the PRC regime to free itself from authoritarianism and to recognize the "other," the ROC on Taiwan, as a sovereign nation-state, before any final and mutually acceptable solution can be found.

In 1991, in order to reassure the right wing of the Nationalist Party, Lee Teng-hui set up a KMT-dominated and unelected National Unification Council that adopted some national unification guidelines (*tongyi gangling*). Although immediately denounced by the DPP, these guidelines just paid lip service to unification, presented as a very long-term objective that can only be achieved after the mainland regime democratizes, and emphasized the political arrangements to be put into place by both sides in the meantime. These guidelines actually gave the necessary freedom to Lee Teng-hui and his government to adopt an overall strategy aimed at both improving Taiwan's international status and normalizing Taiwan's relations with the mainland. In order to succeed, this strategy had to be based on a widening disconnection— and contradiction—between the legal definition of the ROC (the whole of China) and its political definition (the ROC on Taiwan or ROCOT).

On the one hand, the KMT stuck to the legal fiction that the ROC claimed sovereignty over the whole of China; as a result, the ROC could not formally recognize the PRC as an independent nation-state: for the KMT, the "Chinese Communists" (*Zhonggong*) only exert jurisdiction on the mainland part of the country, now considered as a "political entity" (*zhengzhi shiti*). Conversely, the CCP considers Taiwan as "a sacred part of the PRC" (1982 PRC constitution), a political entity (*zhengquan*) only administered by undefined "Taiwan authorities" (*Taiwan dangju*), which should eventually be reunified according to the "one country, two system" formula. In order to circumvent this typical and rather unique case of overlapping sovereignty, and allow both sides to communicate without formally recognizing each other, Taipei and Beijing had to establish non-governmental or, to be more accurate, semi-governmental organizations. In early 1991, Taipei set up the Strait Exchange Foundation (SEF) and, a few months later, Beijing created the Association for the Relations Across the Taiwan Strait (ARATS). However, both organizations report to a ministerial level organ, the Mainland Affairs Council and the Taiwan Affairs Office of the State Council respectively. Similarly, in 1992, Taipei enacted a law on the relations between the peoples on both sides of the strait (*liang'an renmin guanxi tiaoli*), which organizes exchanges between the Taiwan area and the mainland area of the ROC; although amended many times, this legislation is still enforced today. Disagreement between Beijing and Taipei on the "one China" principle also postponed talks. In November 1992, the SEF and the ARATS eventually reached a "verbal" understanding on this delicate issue that would later appear much more important than it was at the time: for the PRC, there is one China but both sides do not get into its definition to conduct "functional talks," whereas for the ROC, there is one China but each side has a different interpretation of this principle (*yige Zhongguo, gezi biaoshi*). This awkward compromise allowed the SEF and the ARATS to hold their first summit in 1993 in Singapore and then open technical negotiations on a number of issues (such as fishing disputes and the return of criminals).

On the other hand, around the same time, Lee embarked on pragmatic diplomacy (*wushi waijiao*) whose clear objective was to enhance Taiwan's international status and promote a de facto two China or one China, one Taiwan formula. He actively tried and managed somewhat to increase the number of Taiwan's diplomatic allies (from twenty-two in 1979 to thirty-one in 1996). In 1993, he launched an attempt to reintegrate Taiwan into the United Nations (under the name of the ROC). And he succeeded in making private or informal visits to several Southeast Asia countries and in 1995 to the USA.

Carried out by a freshly democratized Taiwan, this double policy—de facto normalization with the PRC and an ambition to transform the ROC into a normal state—could only clash with Beijing's unification policy. In the wake of Lee's unexpected June 1995 visit to the US (the Clinton Administration had initially promised Beijing not to give him a visa) and his *alma mater* Cornell University, the PRC president Jiang Zemin initiated a more threatening strategy aimed at reining in Taiwan's "separatist forces" and speeding up reunification. In 1995–1996, the People's Liberation Army (PLA) launched two series of missile tests across the Taiwan Strait, a move that forced Washington in March 1996 to move out of its reserve and dispatch two aircraft carriers to the Taiwan area in order to make sure that the island's first democratic presidential election took place in a peaceful and reassuring environment.

Jiang's strategy failed. Although in 1998–1999, under US pressure, SEF–ARATS talks resumed for a short while, they rapidly stumbled on the divisive question of expanding them to political issues. In order to prevent a development that he perceived as dangerous, in July 1999, Lee Teng-hui decided to qualify the relations across the Taiwan Strait "as state to state" or "quasi state to state relations," triggering another (but smaller) crisis with Beijing and forcing the Clinton Administration to distance itself from this initiative. Although facing growing pressure from China and the US, at the end of his second term, Lee had clearly given priority to consolidating Taiwan's statehood over normalizing relations with the mainland and, in so doing, prepared the ground for DPP candidate Chen Shui-bian's victory in the March 2000 presidential election.

The election of an independence-leaning president for the first time in Taiwan was a new challenge for both Beijing and Washington. Again, the US exerted strong pressure on Taiwan and compelled Chen to accept the ROC institutional framework and stick to the status quo in the strait ("the four no's, one not").[2] Although cross-strait relations deteriorated, communication did not collapse and cooperation proceeded to develop to some extent.

246   *J.-P. Cabestan*

After some hesitation, Chen refused to recognize the so called "1992 consensus" (*jiu'er gongshi*), a reinterpretation of the compromise reached by the SEF and the ARATS in November 1992 on the question of the "one China" principle, which was proposed in 2000 by the freshly defeated and more conservative KMT (Lee was then expelled from the party) and immediately endorsed by Beijing. As a result, under Chen, no SEF–ARATS summit could take place. However, everyday exchanges and negotiations between these two semi-governmental organizations were never interrupted. Using professional organizations as front negotiators, Taipei and Beijing even managed to open shipping links between Kinmen and Xiamen (Fujian), the so called three small links (*xiao santong*), and start direct charter flights between Taiwan and a few mainland cities in 2003.

More importantly, perhaps, although Chen was able to postpone the opening of full direct air and sea links with the PRC, in spite of the KMT and the Taiwanese business community's pressure, he could not slow down the increasing economic integration between both sides of the strait. Between 2000 and 2008, the Taiwanese economy actually became much more dependent on the mainland: bilateral trade and Taiwan's investments in the PRC grew very rapidly; in 2004, Beijing became Taipei's first trade partner ahead of Washington; and the Taiwanese business community on the mainland reached one million, and probably more.

Yet, in spite of the US administration's initial strong political and strategic support (in April 2001, George W. Bush made a huge and unprecedented weapons offer to Taiwan, including submarines), Chen became rapidly frustrated by China's adamant strategy of intensifying military threats and diplomatic isolation. In August 2002, he reactivated Lee's two state approach, proclaiming that there was "one state on each side of the Strait" (*yibian yiguo*). And in December 2003, in order to increase his chances of being re-elected, Chen decided to organize a referendum on the PLA missile threat on the day of the presidential election in March 2004. This populist initiative triggered an angry response from President Bush who asked Chen not to question the status quo and forced him to tone down the questions asked of the voters, underscoring US concern with the deepening gap and increasing tension in the strait.[3]

Upset by Chen's razor-thin and contested re-election, the KMT and its then chairman Lien Chan decided to resume party to party relations with the Chinese Communist Party in April 2005. This "reconciliation" took place just one month after the National People's Congress, the PRC parliament, had adopted an anti-secession law (*fan fenlie fa*), which threatens Taiwan with the use of "non-peaceful" means if the island shows signs of moving toward independence or procrastinating *sine die* unification. Although the KMT objected to this new law, its criticism was much milder than the Chen government's or the American administration's, highlighting the widening divergences of view within Taiwan about its relations with the PRC. The KMT's priority was clearly to propose and test an alternative mainland policy, more in tune with the demands of Taiwan's business community and an overall economic environment in which China had become the main growth engine. Turning its back on both Lee and Chen's mainland policies, the KMT was hoping that a return to a more legalistic approach to the ROC–PRC conundrum would help Taipei not only gradually normalize with Beijing but also improve its security and international status.

The easy election of the popular KMT candidate Ma Ying-jeou as ROC president in 2008 did not yield the expected results. True, as promised by Beijing, in exchange for a return to the so called "1992 consensus," high-level SEF–ARATS talks were able to resume; in less than 4 years, both sides concluded sixteen economic and technical agreements, including a symbolic Economic Cooperation Framework Agreement (ECFA) in June 2010 and bilateral trade has reached US $ 160 billion in 2011. In 2009, Taiwan joined the Assembly of the World Health Organization (WHO) as an observer, the first UN-affiliated body that Taiwan had been able to reintegrate with since 1971. A diplomatic truce was tacitly implemented by Beijing, allowing Taipei to keep the twenty-three diplomatic allies it still had by the end of Chen Shui-bian's term. And in 2008, large groups of PRC tourists started to visit the island (6 million to January 2012).

Nevertheless, what has been qualified by the KMT and Ma as a full cross-strait "rapprochement" has deepened Taiwan's economic and political dependence upon mainland China without in any way overcoming its diplomatic and security challenges (Cabestan 2010). Bilateral trade reached US$140 billion in 2010; Taiwan's exports to the PRC represent 40 percent of its overall sales; and although around 60 percent of its foreign direct investments (FDI) are made on the mainland every year, its accumulated FDI to the mainland are estimated at US$150 billion. As a result, Taiwanese constituencies whose well-being depends upon China—business people, unemployed or ill-paid Taiwanese youth, the tourist and service industries, the housing sector—are increasing, and they are more and more interested in maintaining a stable relationship with Beijing. These expanding vested interests contributed directly to Ma's re-election and DPP candidate Tsai Ying-wen's defeat in 2012.

Simultaneously, Taiwan's international status has not improved: in the WHO, it appears as "Taiwan, province of China," a clear downgrading compared with other international organizations, such as the Olympic Committee (Chinese Taipei) or the Asian Development Bank (Taipei, China). And Taiwan's security and capacity to protect its de facto sovereignty have deteriorated. In spite of the "détente" that Ma Ying-jeou's election has facilitated in the strait, the PLA has continued to increase its deployment of conventional missiles (around 1,200 in 2011), aircrafts, and ships based in the Nanjing and Guangzhou military regions that can be used in an attack against Taiwan (Shlapak et al. 2009).[4] On its side, in spite of Ma electoral promises, Taiwan is putting less money into its defense at a time when its military is going through a delicate and costly transition to an all-volunteer force, relying more than ever on the strong albeit vague US security guarantee against any unprovoked aggression.

248   *J.-P. Cabestan*

Worried about the dangerous implications in terms of the sovereignty of any political or security talks, the KMT has been reluctant to open negotiations on military confidence-building measures, let alone on a peace treaty. And while political discussions may start in Ma's second term, it is unlikely that they will lead to the conclusion of any meaningful accord.

The "green" (pro-independence) opposition and the DPP's strong criticism of what they perceive as Ma's too accommodating, if not "capitulationist," mainland policy have also contributed to this relative caution and impasse. As we have seen, as there is no consensus in Taiwan on the status and the boundaries of the ROC—for the DPP, the ROC = Taiwan—its long-term future and, as a result, its relation with the PRC, it is hard for any Taiwanese government to embark on substantial security or political negotiations with the latter. At the same time, because of Taiwan's growing dependence upon mainland China, no Taiwanese politician can totally dismiss the signed agreements and the benefits of creeping normalization that have been taking shape in the Taiwan Strait since 2008. For these reasons, the status quo, as we presented it at the beginning—de facto independence without formal secession—is likely to prevail in the future. However, as we have also seen, it is not a static but a dynamic status quo, the preservation of which depends not only upon Taiwan's willingness to remain, under the ROC framework, a sovereign entity separated from the PRC. The perpetuation of the status quo also depends upon China's perception that its current unification policy is working and, perhaps more critically, upon the US's ability and willingness to protect it.

An unsolvable quandary

For all these reasons, it is clear that Taiwan's de jure independence appears less and less feasible. But, spurred by a dynamic local cultural and political identity and a rapid democratization process, Taiwan's nation-building process cannot be ignored either, putting the three actors involved, Taipei, Beijing, and Washington, into an unsolvable quandary.

PRC's adamant claims and objectives

For its part, the PRC has no reason to put an end to its claim to Taiwan. True, since 2007, after having resumed relations with the KMT, Hu Jintao's CCP has given priority to "the peaceful development of cross-strait relations" over "peaceful reunification" and, in so doing, quietly accepted the status quo in the strait. Nevertheless, simultaneously, the PRC has, on the one hand, continued to promote policies that multiply cross-strait business and human links and make Taiwan more and more dependent upon China. And, on the other hand, it has kept accumulating an increasingly credible military force able to be projected across the strait. As the PRC is getting more powerful, self-confident, and assertive, it has no incentive to compromise on the "one China principle," let alone contemplate giving the ROC full international status even within the Chinese nation. For several reasons—semantic (*guojia* means both state and country) but also the large geographical and demographic discrepancy between the mainland and Taiwan and the existence of a pro-independence force on the island—the past German (one nation, two states) or the present Korean (one people, one nation, two governments, and two republics represented in the UN) formulas cannot be accepted by the PRC in the foreseeable future. In the last few years, some Chinese scholars have been toying with a "one country, two governments" formula close to the Korean model and reminiscent of KMT ideas initiated at the end of Chiang Ching-kuo's era (Chu 2011). But it is doubtful whether Beijing is ready to test a long-term solution that is still far from certain to be accepted both by the majority of the CCP leadership and the independence-leaning Taiwanese, especially the DPP.

A more dependent, still divided, but anti-unification Taiwan

As we have seen, Ma Ying-jeou is having difficulties convincing the Taiwanese voters that the "rapprochement" with the PRC he has been promoting since 2008 will help the ROC to be more secure and eventually reintegrate with the international community. The PRC's lack of flexibility, its military threat, and its authoritarian polity have become both the main obstacles to any further reconciliation and the principal feeders of Taiwan's nation-building process. In other words, the Taiwanese may be divided about their relationship with the Chinese mainland and the island's long-term future. Yet, they are united around the following constraints and beliefs: legally, Taiwan has always remained part of the Chinese nation under the official name of the ROC but, politically, the ROC on Taiwan is a new nation-state; consequently, most Taiwanese refuse to identify with the PRC; and according to opinion polls, while preferring the status quo, they are open to any solution that would respect the ROC and Taiwan's dignity, sovereignty, and de facto independent democratic polity. Beijing, on its side, although excluding any de jure independence, arguing that most Chinese on the mainland oppose such an option, is aware that no solution to the differences across the Taiwan Strait can be solved without the support not only of the KMT but also of the DPP (representing 45 percent of the electorate in 2012); in other words, a large majority of the island's voters. The PRC authorities, therefore, do not offer short-term solutions to what it calls the "Taiwan issue."

The US factor and its long-term uncertainties

The US has always claimed to be "agnostic" about Taiwan's future as long as both sides find a peaceful agreement (Goldstein and Schriver 2001). And, as we have seen, Washington has remained much more ambiguous than many think, including in the US and the PRC, about Taiwan's sovereignty (Tucker 2009). Nevertheless, China's more assertive foreign policy as well as stronger military units will probably force Taiwan's unique protector to play a bigger,

250   *J.-P. Cabestan*

yet stabilizing role in the coming years. Since Ma Ying-jeou's election in 2008, a debate among US experts and politicians has taken shape about not only the usefulness of arms sales to a Taiwanese military that is less willing to fight and more porous to PRC espionage, but also the long-term sustainability of the TRA and the security guarantees given to Taiwan's separation from the mainland. It is obvious that, since 2009, Beijing has intensified its pressure on Washington to stop selling weapons to Taiwan and abide by the long-for-gotten (because inapplicable) 1982 communiqué, complicating a bilateral relationship that the US administration needs to keep stable more than before, especially in view of America's huge accumulated debt and increasing economic interdependence with China. It is also clear that the PLA has the means not only to win a war against Taiwan (massive missile attack, naval blockade or landing are the most probable scenarios), but also to cause great damage to any US naval and air task force that might intervene. However, in the case of an unprovoked PLA attack against Taiwan, can the US remain outside the conflict? Although it is hard to imagine the likelihood of a war between two nuclear powers, the US's role, alliance systems, and responsibilities in the Asia-Pacific region and particularly the East Asia theater would probably compel it to get involved in one way or another. The US willingness expressed in 2011–12 to "rebalance" its strategy and military deployment in favour of this region can only increase the likelihood of such a reaction.

As cross-strait relations are improving and the capacity of any elected DPP president to question the agreements signed since 2008 is diminishing, Washington's security preoccupations are actually moving elsewhere: Taiwan's inability to keep a credible asymmetrical defense and risk of moving too close to the PRC has become one of the main security challenges, if not the main security challenge to US international interests—and to the interests of the US Asia-Pacific allies such as Japan.

Conclusion

Given such a role for the US, unless the PRC democratizes, the anti-unification forces on Taiwan will continue to dominate even if the growing economic integration and the intensifying people to people contacts across the strait push Taipei and also, to some extent, Beijing toward additional moderation rather than confrontation. In the final analysis, the main challenge that both Taiwan and China are facing is their respective present or potential internal divisions. In Taiwan, there is a real danger of Hongkongization of not only the dark blue elements of the KMT but also larger segments of the business community. By calling for increasing accommodation, this process may eventually lead to the compromises with the Beijing authorities that may threaten the island's security and the ROC's survival. If they become too powerful, these accommodating forces may trigger a backlash and deeper divisions and tensions in Taiwan. In China, economic slowdown and political instability could have a hard to predict impact on cross-strait relations, probably consolidating Taiwan's willingness to remain separate and distant from the mainland. Although a longer term risk, China's democratization may dramatically change the equation, perhaps opening the way to a more acceptable solution for both sides, but also forcing the KMT and its allies to seriously contemplate unification between the ROC and the new polity established on the mainland and, in so doing, creating unpredictable divisions on the island.

In the foreseeable future, however, Taiwan's "sovereignist consensus" is stronger than many estimate and should not be dismissed: it is likely to remain centered on the ROC's long-term survival and an ambition to be considered as a normal state, yet characterized or handicapped by a special relationship with the PRC and vaguely but surely protected by the US. For all these reasons, Taiwan is likely to remain a *sui generis* case of de facto and so far peaceful coexistence of two states that do not recognize each other, an unusual example of (de facto) independence without secession.

Notes

1 The first two US–China communiqués were the Shanghai communiqué signed in Shanghai in February 1972 and the normalization communiqué made public on December 15–16, 1978. The six assurances include promises not to set a date for the termination of arms sales to Taiwan, not to alter the terms of the TRA, not to consult the PRC about the level and nature of weapons sold to Taiwan, not to mediate between China and Taiwan, not to alter the US position about the sovereignty of Taiwan, which is that the question is to be decided peacefully by the Chinese themselves, and not to formally recognize China's sovereignty over Taiwan.

2 The "four no's and one not" (*sibu yimeiyou*) were stated in the following extract from Chen's speech of May 20, 2000: "As long as the CCP regime has no intention of using military force against Taiwan, I pledge that during my term in office, I will not declare independence, I will not change the national title, I will not push for the inclusion of the so-called 'state-to-state' description in the Constitution, and I will not promote a referendum to change the status quo with regard to the question of independence or unification. Furthermore, the abolition of the National Reunification Council or the National Reunification Guidelines will not be an issue."

3 Eventually, the referendum asked the Taiwanese voters whether they wanted to buy anti-missile weapons, presumably from the US, in order to better counter the growing PLA missile threat and open "peace negotiations" with China. These questions were regarded as useless by the US.

4 The Taiwanese military tends to include in its calculations both short-range and mid-range missiles and expects their number to reach nearly 2,000 (1,960) before the end of 2010, cf. *Taipei Times*, July 19, 2010. The US only refers to the former, evaluated at 1,000–1,200 at the end of 2010. The PLA mid-range missiles (such as some of the CSS-5 and the DH-10) also target Japan and US bases and ships in Asia (Annual Report to Congress 2011, 2, 51, 78).

References

Annual Report to Congress (2011), *Military and Security Developments Involving the People's Republic of China 2011*, Washington, DC, Office of the Secretary of Defense, August.

252   J.-P. Cabestan

Cabestan, Jean-Pierre (2002), 'Integration without Reunification' *The Cambridge Review of International Affairs*, XV(1): 95–103.

——(2005), 'Specificities and Limits of Taiwanese Nationalism' *China Perspectives*, 62, Nov–Dec: 32–43.

——(2010), 'The New Détente in the Taiwan Strait and Its Impact on Taiwan's Security and Future: More Questions than Answers' *China Perspectives*, 3: 22–33.

Cabestan, Jean-Pierre and Le Pesant, Tanguy (2009), *L'esprit de défense de Taiwan face à la Chine. La jeunesse taiwanaise face à la tentation de la Chine* (Taiwan's Will to Fight and China. The Taiwanese Youth and the Temptation of China), Paris, L'Harmattan.

Chang, Mau-kuei (2000), 'On the Origins and Transformation of Taiwan National Identity' *China Perspectives*, 28, Mar–Apr: 51–70.

Chen, Chung-ming, Ying-chang, Chuang and Huang, Shu-min (eds) (1994), *Ethnicity in Taiwan: Social, Historical and Cultural Perspectives*, Taipei, Institute of Ethnology, Academia Sinica.

Cheng, Tun-jen and Haggard, Stephan (eds) (1992) *Political Change in Taiwan*, Boulder, CO, Lynne Rienner.

Chu, Shulong (2011), 'Communication for Better Understanding and Improvement of Cross-Strait Relations', *Brookings Northeast Asia Commentary*, 50, June, at www.brookings.edu/articles/2011/06_cross_strait_shulong.aspx (accessed 10 August 2012).

Chu, Yun-han (1992), *Crafting Democracy in Taiwan*, Taipei, Institute for National Policy Research.

Corcuff, Stéphane (ed.) (2002), *Memories of the Future, National Identity Issues and the Search for a New Taiwan*, New York, M.E. Sharpe.

Garver, John W. (1997), *Face Off. China, the United States and Taiwan's Democratization*, Seattle and London, University of Washington Press.

Goldstein, Steven M. and Schriver, Randal (2001), 'An Uncertain Relationship: The United States, Taiwan and the Taiwan Relations Act' *The China Quarterly*, 165, Mar: 147–172.

Hughes, Christopher (1997), *Taiwan and Chinese Nationalism—National Identity and Status in International Society*, London, Routledge.

Lai, Tse-han, Myers, Ramon H. and Wei, Wou (1991), *A Tragic Beginning: The Taiwan Uprising of February 28, 1947*, Stanford, CA, Stanford University Press.

Le Pesant, Tanguy (2011), 'Generational Change and Ethnicity among 1980s-born Taiwanese' *Journal of Current Chinese Affairs*, 40(1): 133–157.

Metzler, John J. (2001), *Divided Dynamism. The Diplomacy of Separated Nations: Germany, Korea, China*, Lanham, MD, University Press of America.

Rubinstein, Murray A. (1995), *The Other Taiwan: 1945 to the Present*, Armonk, NY, M.E. Sharpe.

——(ed.) (1997), *Taiwan: A History (Taiwan in the Modern World)*, Armonk, NY, M.E. Sharpe.

Schnapper, Dominique (1998), *Community of Citizens: On the Modern Idea of Nationality*, Piscataway, NJ, Transaction Publishers.

Shepherd, John Robert (1993), *Statecraft and Political Economy on the Taiwan Frontier, 1600–1800*, Stanford, CA, Stanford University Press.

Shlapak, David A., Orletsky, David T., Reid, Toy I., Tanner, Murray Scot and Wilson, Barry (2009), *A Question of Balance: Political Context and Military Aspects of the China–Taiwan Dispute*, Washington, DC, Rand.

Tien, Hung-mao (ed.) (1996), *Taiwan's Electoral Politics and Democratic Transition: Riding the Third Wave*, New York, M.E. Sharpe.

Tucker, Nancy Bernkopf (2009), *Strait Talk: United States–Taiwan Relations and the Crisis with China*, Cambridge, MA, Harvard University Press.

Wachman, Alain M. (1994), *Taiwan National Identity and Democratization*, Armonk, NY, M.E. Sharpe.

Index

Page numbers in italic (*274*) refer to a table. Page numbers followed by 'n' (19n) refer to a note at the bottom of the page.

17 Point Agreement 196, 198, 219

Abdullah, Sheikh 157
Abkhazia 6, 43, 45, 46–49, 53, 61, 64; and Georgia 5, 23, 43, 45, 46, 55, 61, 62; recognition of statehood 28, 44, 62; and Russia 53, 61
Aceh 2,16
Adjara 5, 43, 45–46
affirmation model 5, 59
Afghanistan 12, 31, 37, 167, 159, 161, 226, 230, 231
Africa 17, 24, 34, 113, 232,
Agenda for Peace 26, 33
aggression 248
agreement(s) 16, 17, 26, 29, 31, 33, 56, 74, 78, 93, 94, 103, 119, 123, 124, 155, 156, 159, 168, 181, 186, 191, 196, 207, 208, 209, 214, 328, 247, 249
Al Qaeda 157, 222, 226, 233, 235
Alaska 21
Albanians Albanians in Kosovo 7, 74, 75, 86, 87, 91, 92, 95n, 101–6, 108–9n; Albanians in Macedonia 75, 76, 86, 87, 90–93
annexation 55
Arbitration Commission (Badinter Commission) 67, 73, 76
Armenia 44, 47, 51, 53, 55, 56, 63
Australia 44, 128, 171
Austria 71
Austro-Hungarian Empire 3
authoritarianism 244
autonomy x, xiv, 34–35, 10, 12, 14–15, 26, 33, 37, 38–49, 50, 51, 62, 68, 71, 100, 111, 113, 116, 118, 119, 124, 139,

140, 153, 157, 184, 185, 189, 196, 198, 200, 203, 204, 206, 208, 209, 211, 212, 214, 215, 229, 233, 240
Azerbaijan 6, 28, 47, 53, 55, 57, 63; and Nagorno-Karabakh 6, 53, 55, 63

Badinter Commission. *See* Arbitration Commission
Balkanization 25
Baltic republics 5, 53–57, 59, 99
Bangladesh 1, 4, 25, 31, 155, 156, 159, 165
Basque Autonomous Community 9, 120, 123, 124
Basque Country 2, 9, 10, 110, 112, 115–18, 199, 122–23, 125
Basque Nationalist Part (PVN) 115, 116
Batasuna party (formerly Herri Batasuna) 115, 117, 118, 121, 124
Belarus 6, 55, 56, 60
Belgium 37, 113
Beran, Harry 23, 33, 124, 125
Berlin Conference 24
Berlin, Isiah 111
Biafra 25, 33
borders 3, 11, 21, 25, 18, 29, 34, 49, 63, 66, 79, 110, 129, 133, 147, 150, 151, 159, 164, 184, 185, 188, 229, 230
Bosnia and Herzegovina 6, 7, 68, 72–74, 79, 80
Britain (see also UK) 127, 130, 139, 143, 165, 224, 239
Buddhism 14, 164, 166, 183, 211, 230
Bush, George W. 246

Index 255

Cabestan, Jean-Pierre 15, 18n
Canada 4, 9, 128, 130, 171; and Quebec
  111, 126, 140, 139, 143, 199
capitalism 60, 69, 229
Catalonia 29, 112, 114, 116, 123, 124
Catholicism 111
Caucasus 2, 37, 40, 44–45, 48–49, 52,
  53, 55, 58, 61, 64
centralization 5, 48, 61, 116;
  decentralization 5, 10, 37, 38, 51, 52,
  112, 113; recentralization 68
Chechnya 6, 8, 9, 18, 28, 43, 44, 57, 61,
  62, 99–101, 104–07, 109, 149, 161, 232
Chen, Shui-bian 242, 245–47, 251
Chiang, Ching-kuo 240, 242, 249
Chiang, Kai-shek 239, 240
China 4, 13, 14–16, 18, 20, 28–30, 31,
  32, 37, 39, 150, 159, 164, 172, 191
  220, 233, 234; and Taiwan 2, 149,
  237–51, 252, 253; and Tibet 2, 14, 24,
  149, 159, 196–212, 214–19; and
  Xinjiang 220–32, 233, 234
Chinese people 29, 208
citizenship 21, 135, 140, 166, 167, 184, 192
civil rights 83, 124
civil wars 7, 51
clan 8, 32, 55, 60, 85, 102
Cold War 4, 21, 24–27, 29, 31, 32, 66,
  67, 69, 77, 78, 94, 183, 199, 217, 238
colonization/decolonization 1, 3, 5, 24–
  25, 27, 28, 58, 62, 165, 167, 224, 239
Commonwealth of Independent States
  (CIS) 57
Communism 32, 229–30
community 7, 15, 65, 66, 78, 139, 154,
  55, 161, 173, 174, 180, 185, 191, 207,
  215, 220, 221, 222, 230, 238, 240, 242
community, international *see*
  international community
conflict, ethnic (or inter-ethnic) 54, 67,
  59, 82, 93, 160, 213
conflict, secessionist 43–46, 47
conflict, violent (or armed) 7, 8, 17, 38,
  46, 47, 48, 74, 79, 86, 87, 91, 92, 93,
  102, 103, 114, 157, 161, 188, 202, 203
conquest 3, 20, 23, 24, 54, 101
consent 1, 4, 22, 32, 75
constitutionalism 30, 62, 111, 119, 121
corruption 46, 60, 64, 160, 242
Corsica 12
Crawford, James 1, 18, 33
Croatia 6, 68, 69, 70–75, 79, 100;
  secession of, 69–72, 74–75, 100; culture
  8, 12, 18, 22, 77–79, 108, 121, 166, 169,

181, 182, 197–99, 201, 201, 203, 205,
  208, 213, 215, 220, 223, 230, 243
Cyprus 53
Czechoslovakia 1, 4, 6, 11, 29, 37, 53, 77

Dalai Lama 14, 196, 198, 199, 202, 209,
  210–11, 214–16, 222, 229
Dayton agreements (or treaty) 73–74
debt 6, 11, 68, 130, 250
decentralization. *See* centralization
defence 16, 58, 108, 133, 139
democracy 16, 24, 29, 30, 31, 32, 43, 76,
  83, 111–12, 121, 139, 147, 148, 187,
  190, 211, 242, 243; and secession 16,
  29, 30, 32, 111
Democratic League of Kosovo. *See*
  League of Democratic Kosovo (LDK)
demonstrations, peaceful 74, 88, 106
Deng Xiaoping 228, 241
devolution 10, 11, 17, 18, 29, 37, 127–
  29, 136–38, 140–41. *See also* Scotland
diasporas 155, 161, 171, 173, 221, 222,
  227, 229, 232; Tamil diaspora 161,
  171, 173; Uyghur diaspora 221, 222,
  227, 229, 232
discrimination 8,47,62, 74, 107–9,166
  169 191, 228
dissolution 1, 3, 6, 7, 11, 17, 29, 46, 54,
  55, 73, 74, 78; *see also*
  Czechoslovakia; Soviet Union;
  Yugoslavia
domination 11, 13, 15, 102, 183, 227,
  233, 242
Dudaev, Dzohkhar (alternative spelling
  "Johar") 9, 57, 100, 101, 103, 105–7
Đukanović, Milan ("Milo") 76, 88

East Timor 16, 24, 27, 29, 30, 33
economic development 18, 48, 83, 87,
  89, 112, 192, 197, 222, 241
education 9, 60, 101, 107, 123, 166, 171,
  180–82, 185, 191, 227
elections 6, 46, 61, 68, 71, 72, 74, 84,
  88–92, 104–5, 108, 115, 117, 120, 122,
  124, 135, 140, 155, 158, 167, 169, 171,
  172, 187, 190, 191, 193, 239, 240–42
Eritrea 27, 33, 36
Estonia 5, 43, 54, 56, 59, 63
ethnic cleansing 63, 73, 79, 84
ethnicity 44, 61, 150, 160, 162, 180, 184,
  186, 189, 191, 208; *see also* culture;
  minority communities
Europe 2–4, 6, 11,12, 16, 17, 18, 11, 24,
  25, 28–33, 39, 40, 48, 66–69, 72, 78,

256 *Index*

92, 127, 134, 140, 149, 156, 171, 232–33

European Community(Communities)/ European Union (EU) 6, 8, 9, 11, 16, 66, 67, 70, 74–77, 92, 93, 100, 112, 113, 134, 135, 127, 140, 141

ETA (Euskadi Ta Askatasuna) 10, 114–20, 124, 232

exploitation 59, 206

federalism 10, 27, 42, 54, 58, 60–62, 68, 113, 150, 190; ethno-federalism 54

force, use of 2, 6, 23, 66, 77, 92, 100, 104–8

France 2, 21, 25, 74, 115, 182, 239

freedom 211, 238, 244; of religion 12, 190, 222, 231, 233; of association 123; struggle for 148

French Revolution 3, 21, 23

Galicia Ukraine 58; Spain 112, 114

Gellner, Ernst 23, 33

genocide 60, 211

Georgia 5, 6, 23, 28, 43, 45–47, 49, 54–59, 62, 63

Germany 15, 43, 69, 92, 73, 79, 90, 113, 471, 238

Ghandi, Mrs 154

globalization 18, 21, 22, 32

Goa 24

Gorbachev, Mikhail 54, 57–59, 101, 104, 105

governance 38, 54, 58, 148, 152, 185, 208, 224

Greece and Macedonia 76

grievance 10, 101, 102, 133, 209

heros/heroic 88, 101, 173, 182

homogenization 71

Horowitz, Donald 38, 50

host state 2–4, 8, 22, 53, 54, 82, 99–102, 129

human rights 26, 30, 110, 156, 158, 173, 174, 228

Hyderabad 24, 152, 153

ideology 28, 78, 102, 105, 107, 127, 130, 158, 161, 182, 229, 230

income distribution 49, 58, 199

independence 2, 4, 10–16, 20, 24, 24–30, 33, 37, 43–46, 53, 55, 57, 61–63, 69–71, 73–77, 100, 102–6, 127–30, 133–36, 140, 148, 150, 166, 174, 178, 180–84, 188, 189, 196–99, 200, 202–4,

107–10, 212–16, 223, 225, 229, 231, 232, 238–40, 242, 243, 245, 246, 248, 249, 251

India 2. 4. 12–14, 7, 24, 25, 28, 30, 31, 43, 83, 147–62, 164–67, 170–73, 180, 181, 185, 187, 197, 202, 2–9, 126, 231

indigenous groups/people 180, 222, 223, 228

indivisibility 10, 109

Indonesia 2, 16, 24; and East Timor 16, 27, 29, 33

industrialization 152, 216

injustice 26, 40, 62, 123, 160, 174

insurgency /counter-insurgency 7, 11, 99, 100, 103, 104, 148, 153, 154–58, 160–62, 178,183, 186, 189, 192

international community 4, 26, 31, 62, 84, 92, 93, 161, 172, 173, 187, 192, 205, 249

International Court of Justice (ICJ) 27, 29

International Criminal Tribunal for Yugoslavia (ICTY) 73, 79, 94

international law 22, 27, 29, 33, 75; and International Court of Justice (ICJ) opinion on Kosovo 27, 29

international relations 2, 23, 148, 162, 200, 201, 204, 210, 215

intervention military 7, 28, 29, 31, 72, 74, 75, 77, 84, 90, 101, 179, 225; humanitarian 30; UN 16

Iraq 31, 38

Ireland/Northern Ireland 30, 118, 124, 128, 129, 135, 232

irredentism 147

Israel 84

Italy 5, 44, 90, 94, 118, 182

Jammu and Kashmir Liberation Front 158

Japan 13, 21, 22, 32, 181, 181, 213; and Taiwan 239, 240, 243, 250, 252

Jashari, Adem 7, 8, 85, 103

Javakheti 5, 45, 47

justice 6, 18, 21, 111, 169, 174

Kachin 178, 181, 184, 188–91

Kachin Independence Organizatin (KIO) 182, 185, 188

Karen 13, 178, 181, 182, 184, 185, 188–90

Karen National Union 181

Karenni 182, 184, 185, 193

Index 257

Kashmir 12, 30, 148–51, 154, 157–62, 223, 231
Kazakhstan 55, 101, 225, 226, 231
Korea 238–40, 249
Kosovo (or Kosovo and Metohija) 5–9, 18, 27–31, 53, 63, 68, 69, 73, 74, 79, 84–89, 92, 94, 99–109, 197, 199, 201; and declaration of independence of Kosovo 27, 53, 75; and NATO (North Atlantic Treaty Organization) intervention 7, 18, 73–75, 90, 94, 103
Kosovo Liberation Army (KLA) 7, 74, 75, 85, 89, 90, 103–7, 201
Kuomintang (KMT) 13, 14, 16, 224, 225, 239–44, 246–51
Kurdistan 149
Kyrgyzstan 55, 60, 226, 231

Labour government 10, 129, 131, 136, 141
Labour Party 128, 134, 138
Laiza 186, 193n
language 8, 9, 18, 46, 59, 60, 63, 79n, 103, 107, 149, 150, 162n, 164, 196, 208, 214n; and culture 78n, 230; and ethnicity 63, 165, 168, 182, 190, 192n, 199, 202, 203, 207, 210
Latin America 25
Latvia 5, 54, 56, 59
law. See constitutional law; international law
Lazar, Serbian Prince 108n
LDK. See League of Democratic Kosovo.
leadership 39, 57, 104–5, 192, 198, 214n
League of Democratic Kosovo (LDK) 103–7, 108n
Lee Teng-hui 239, 241, 244–47
legitimacy. See right of secession
Leninist 101, 117, 232
Lessons Learnt and Reconciliation Commission 174
Leviathan 32
Lhasa 196–98, 208
liberalism 121, 123n; neo-liberalism 69
Liberation Front of Tripura 156
Liberation Front of the People of Manipur 156
Liberation Tigers of Tamil Eelam 13, 83, 147, 161, 164–65, 169–74
Lien, Chan 242, 246
"line of control" (LOC) 157–58
Ljubljana 70
LOC. See "line of control"

loyalties, divided 22, 102, 224, 226, 227
LTTE. See Liberation Tigers of Tamil Eelam
Lukashenko, Alexander 60

Ma Ying-jeou 247, 250
Macedonia 7, 75, 76, 82, 86–87, 91, 93, 95n; and Albanians 7, 91, 93; recognition of statehood 75–76; and Yugoslavia/Serbia 75–76, 83
Macedonia Albanian National Liberation Army (NLA) 7–8, 86, 92
Madeira 44
Madrid 114
Madhya Pradesh 151–52
Maharashtra 149–50, 151
Mainland Affairs Council (MAC) 244
mainlanders 239, 242–43
Major, John 129
Malayalam 150, 151
Malaysia 29, 58
Maldives 21, 165
Maleski, Denko 93
Manchu dynasty (Empire) 17, 202, 238–39. See also Qing dynasty (Empire)
Manchuria 239
Madarin language 242–43
Manichaeans 223
Manipur 151, 162n
Mao Zedong 211, 239
Marathi 149, 150
Mari El 44
Marxist, Marxism 85, 94n, 211
Marxist-Leninist 117
Mayall, James 3–4
Mboya, Tom 25
McCormick, John 141n
media 76, 203, 204, 221–22, 228, 232n
mediation 26, 27, 30, 70, 157, 160, 251n
Meghalaya 151
Melbourne 225
Melilla 113
Methodists 95n, 182, 190
Metohija 108n
Mexico 43
migration 208, 227, 239; forced 74
Miko, Jason 91, 95n
Milcev, Robert 91, 95n
Mill, John Sturat 32
Millward, James 232, 233n
Milošević, Slobodan 7, 70, 74, 76, 87–90, 92, 94n, 100, 106
Milton, John 49n
Ming dynasty 13–14, 239

258 Index

Ministerial Burma 180
Minnan people 239, 242, 243
minorities 8, 13, 14, 16, 29, 37, 63, 71, 75, 111, 129, 148, 165, 167, 174, 180, 185, 191, 193n, 222, 227, 233n. *See also* Albania; China; Croatia; ethnicity; India; Serbs; Sri Lanka; Uighurs human rights 63, 111
Minorities at Risk (MAR) 40, 94n
Mizoram 151, 156, 162n
Moldova 5, 55, 56; and Transdniestria 55
Mon 178, 181–82, 184, 185, 190
Mong Tai Army (MTA) 185
Mongol Empire 530
Mongolia 14, 203, 215n, 216n, 223, 224, 227. *See* Inner Mongolia
Montenegro 76
Mordovia 44
Morocco 20
MTA. *See* Mong Tai Army
Muivah, Tuengaling 156
Müller, Harald 199, 200, 204
Munich 229
Muslims 12, 73, 147, 149, 152, 165, 224–27, 229–32
Muslim League 147
Myanmar/Burma 2, 178–79, 192n
myth 22, 56, 62

Naga (region, movement) 148, 156, 181, 185
Nagaland 150, 151, 156
Nagalim. *See* Nagaland
Nagorno-Karabakh 6, 53, 55, 63
Nakarada, Nadmila 6–7
Nanjing 237, 247
Nasheed, Mohammed 21
National Conference party (Kashmir) 154, 157
National League for Democracy (NLD) 193n
National Peace Council of Sri Lanka 174
National People's Congress (NPC) 225, 246
nationalism 3, 5, 6, 17, 22–24, 28, 32, 45, 58, 61, 70, 71, 83, 88, 111, 113, 115, 120, 121, 127, 128, 131–34, 139, 167, 181, 197, 227, 229, 230, 242, 243; and conflict, violent 92; and culture 128; and democracy 32; and economics 63; and ethnicity 83, 181; Basque 113, 115, 120–21, 123n, 124n; Burmese 181; Chinese (Han) 15, 17,

227, 229–30; Kurdish 83; nationalist ideology 230; Russian 59–61; Scottish 127–34, 139; Sinhalese 167; Soviet Union 5–6, 55, 58; stateless nations 135, 139, 166; Tamil 171; Taiwanese 242–43; Yugoslavia 6, 69–71, 88
nationalist parties 7, 15, 71, 88, 111, 115–17, 128, 130, 139, 225, 239, 244
NATO (North Atlantic Treaty Organization) 7, 9, 18, 31, 112, 133–34, 157, 201; and Yugoslavia 18, 72–75, 84, 90, 92, 93, 94n, 103, 201
natural resources 100, 231
Navarre 123n, 124n
Naxalite movement 153
Naypyidaw 179, 190–91, 193n
Ne Win, General 181–85
negotiation 8, 10, 30, 55, 70, 74–75, 86, 91–93, 102, 105, 117–19, 124n, 131, 148, 158, 166, 168–69, 171–74, 185, 198–201, 204–6, 209, 212–13, 215n, 216n, 245–46, 248, 251n; asymmetrical negotiations 199, 204
Nehru, Jawaharlal 147, 157
Nenets Autonomous Okrug 44
Nestorians 223
New Delhi 12, 151–54, 156–59, 170
New York City 229
New Zealand 128, 171
Nigeria 25,43, 58, 202. *See also* Biafra
Ningxia 228
NLA. *See* Macedonia Albanian National Liberation Army
non-governmental organizations (NGOs) 79n, 158, 244
Normans 21, 123n
North Africa 113, 232
North America 4, 29, 40
North Bukovina 54
North Caucasia 101. *See also* Caucasia
North Ossetia-Alania 44. *See also* Ossetia-Alania
North Sea oil 132
Northern Cyprus 54. *See also* Cyprus
Northern Ireland. *See* Ireland
Northeast, the (India) 148, 150–51, 154–56, 159, 162n
Northern Territories (Pakistan) 149, 157
Norway 29, 172
Nova Revija 69–70

Obama Administration 233n
Oberg, Jan 68

occupation 16, 59, 108n, 174, 180, 202, 234n, 239
Ohrid Agreement 8, 86, 92–93
oil industry 27
OKChN. *See* All-National Congress of Chechen Peoples
Okinawa 20, 32n
Operation Storm 72
opinion polls 11, 88, 130, 249
opportunism 20, 152
oppression 11, 102,
Organization for Security and Cooperation in Europe (OSCE) 75, 92
Orissa 149, 151
Oriya 149, 151
Orthodox Church 91, 102, 108n
Ottoman Empire 3, 17, 22, 46, 58, 102, 108n
Outer Mongolia. *See* Mongolia
Owen, Lord David, 88
Owen-Stoltenberg Plan 92
Ozal, Turgut 230

Pakistan 12, 25, 31, 147, 149–50, 166, 230–31. *See also* Bangladesh and India 25, 31, 147, 149–50, 154–55, 159–61; and Kashmir 12, 157–59, 161
Palaung 185, 190
Palestine 84, 199
Palk Strait 165
Pa'O 181–82
Papua New Guinea 26, 33n
parallel systems of government 46, 71, 74, 106
Paris 9, 107
Paris, Treaty of (1763) 21
partition 1, 12, 24, 32, 147–48, 154, 157
patriotism 167
Pavković, Aleksandar 7–9, 18n, 49n
Pax Africana 25
peace-keeping 30–31, 72, 171
peasants 156, 162n, 206
Peng Min-min 239
Penghu. See Pescadores.
People's Liberation Army (PLA) 245–47, 250, 251n
People's Republic of China (PRC) 16, 197–98, 214n, 216n, 222, 233n, 237, 245–51, 251n. *See also* China
perestroika 54
Pescadores 239, 243
PLA. *See* People's Liberation Army

PNV. *See* Basque National Party.
Poland 56
Police 46, 100, 103–4, 155, 164, 169–71, 173, 222
police, Serbian 7, 71–72, 74, 82–83, 85–87, 89, 103–6
political power 102, 184, 186, 209; and minorities 102, 184, 209
political recognition 111, 113, 121
political rights 243
political violence 114,
Popular Party (PP) 116–18, 121
population 1, 2, 3, 8, 15, 21, 22, 32, 58, 83, 88, 100–101, 130, 139–40, 149–50, 152–53, 155, 157, 162n, 164–65, 180, 187, 213, 225, 242; and religious communities 8, 102, 149–50, 164, 224–25, 230–32; Kosovo 68, 74, 101, 103, 105; and minority communities 7, 15, 25, 30, 59, 83, 118, 123n, 164–65, 168, 187, 189, 196, 204, 221, 225, 227, 230–32, 238–40; Soviet Union 60, 63; Yugoslavia 70–72
Portugal 5, 44, 239
Portuguese colony. *See* East Timor
Postdam Declaration 239
poverty 18, 102, 192, 198
power-sharing 7
Prekaz massacre 85, 90
prestige 183
privilege 28, 44, 77, 124n, 131, 134
protection of minorities 9, 44, 63, 111, 119
protest marches 74, 106, 170, 197, 208, 210, 215n, 216n, 222, 228
Protestants 91
Provisional Council (Chechen Supreme Soviet) 104
Provisional Irish Republican Army (PIRA) 30
PSOE party (Partido Socialista Obrero Español, Spanish Socialist Worker's Party) 116–18, 121
Punjab 30, 148, 150, 154–55, 158, 162n, 190
purchase, of territory 3, 21, 48
Putin, Vladimir 61

Qing dynasty (Empire) 202–3, 215, 223–24. *See also* Manchu dynasty (Empire)
Qinghai 15, 231
Quebec 4, 9, 16, 21, 26, 110, 130, 139, 199

260 *Index*

race 180, 190. *See also* ethnicity
racial antagonism 198
Racine, Jean-Luc 12
Radan, Peter 1
radicalization 55, 71, 83–84, 91, 94n
Rajapaksa, Gotabaya 164
Rajapaksa, Minhanda 161, 164–65, 172
Rajkhowa, Arabindo 156
Ramachandran, M. G. 170
Rangoon 16, 183, 185, 190, 192n
Rao, N. T. Rama 154
Ratner, Stephen 25
recognition of statehood 4, 9, 23, 29;
    Abkhazia 62; Bangladesh 4; Biafra
    25, 33n; Croatia 72, 79n; Kosovo 29,
    75; Macedonia 76; South Ossetia 62
referendums 10–11, 23, 26, 29–30, 33n,
    73, 246, 251n; Basque Country 118–
    20, 125; Bosnia 73; Macedonia 75;
    Montenegro 77; Papua New Guinea
    and Bougainville 26, 33n; Quebec
    110; Scotland 10–11, 29, 127, 129–30,
    134, 136, 140–41; Slovenia 70; Soviet
    Union 56–57; Sudan 30, 33n; Taiwan
    246, 251n; Tibet 214n
refugees 147, 170, 231, 240
religion 8, 12, 60, 77, 78n, 91, 95n, 102,
    112, 149–50, 162, 164–65, 178, 180–
    82, 190–91, 197–98, 201, 204–6, 208–
    10, 211n, 22, 224, 226, 230–31, 233n
religious movements 73, 220,
religious rights 14, 222, 226, 230, 233n
remedial theories. *See* justice theories
    (remedial theories, just cause
    theories)
repression, state 59, 82–83, 87, 94n; and
    India 148–49, 158, 161; and Kosovo
    7–8, 12; and Taiwan 240
Republic of China (ROC) 16, 237–38,
    240–51. *See also* Taiwan
Republic of China on Taiwan (ROCOT)
    242, 244
Republic of India. *See* India
Republic of Mongolia. *See* Mongolia
Republic of Srpska Krajina 73
Republika Srpska 44, 73–74
Requejo, Ferran 9–10
respect 110, 171, 204, 212, 249
responsibility 84, 91, 174
revolution 46, 61, 221
right of secession 23, 25. *See also*
    constitutional law; territorial rights,
    secession and China 37n, 334; and
    human rights 385, 413–23, 428, 429–

31, 447–48; and international law 39,
    136–37, 301–2, 321–30, 354–55, 391,
    399, 408, 423–25; and secession,
    unilateral 136, 138, 139–40, 142–43,
    258, 321–30, 333; political 84, 341,
    354–55, 382, 391–93, 401–2; and
    United Nations 39, 439
Roberton, George 92
Romania 55, 63
Rossabi, Morris 223
Rugova, Dr Ibrahim 9, 12, 103, 105–7
rule of law 174, 231, 242
Russia 5, 6, 8, 17–18, 21, 27–28, 43, 56–
    62, 202, 224–25, 231; and Abkhazia
    28, 62; and Chechnya 8, 18, 28, 57,
    100–102, 104–6, 161; constitutional
    law 54, 61; and Estonia 63; and
    Georgia 53; and Kosovo 27, 74, 90,
    94n; and South Ossetia 28, 62; and
    Soviet Union 6, 43, 53, 58; and
    Ukraine 43, 63
Russian Federation 28, 44
Russian Soviet Federative Socialist
    Republic (RSFSR) 53–54
Russian language 46, 60
Russian nationalism 61
Ryukyu kingdom 32n

SAARC. *See* South Asia Association for
    Regional Cooperation
Sakwa, Richard 5–7
Sanjaume y Calvet, Marc 9–10
Sardinia 44
Satsuma clan 32n
Scotland 2, 4, 10–11, 18, 127–41
Scottish Assembly. *See* Scottish
    Parliament
Scottish National Party (SNP) 10–11,
    29, 128–30, 133–36, 138, 140
Scottish Parliament 11, 127–28, 136–37,
    140
secession 2, 4, 5, 7, 10, 12, 16–18, 20–33,
    38, 47, 53, 55, 62–63, 67–68, 127,
    237–38, 246–48; secession, by default
    4, 17; secession, colonial 5. *See also*
    colonization/decolonization secession,
    consensual 4, 7, 27. *See also* Soviet
    Union; Yugoslavia secession,
    dissolving 4, 62–63, 67. *See also*
    Soviet Union; Yugoslavia secession,
    non-consensual. *See* secession,
    unilateral secession, peaceful 9, 67,
    76. *See* Iceland; Norway; Slovakia
    secession, right of 23, 123n; *See* right

of secession secession, theory 9, 121;
secession, unilateral 4, 62–63, 74–75,
101, 103–6, 110, 113; *See also* Bosnia
and Herzegovina; Bougainville;
Kosovo; Montenegro; Quebec; Sudan
secessionism/secessionist movement 2, 7,
9, 12, 31, 33n, 43–45, 47, 55, 99, 108,
115, 120, 147–62, 189, 191, 221–22,
225–26, 229, 232n
security 26, 83, 155, 226, 238, 241, 247–
50
security forces 94n, 180, 183, 185, 188,
222, 229
self-determination, internal 1, 21, 25–26,
30, 33, 69, 157, 169
self-interest 32, 201
separatism 1–2, 4, 9, 11, 13–14, 17, 21,
37–38, 40–45, 48, 57, 61, 148, 151–52,
159–60, 164, 178, 181–84, 189, 192,
210, 220–21, 230, 232n; definition 1–2
Serb Krajina 72
Serbia 2, 4, 6–8, 12, 17, 27, 29, 44, 67–
70, 73–77, 79n, 80, 82–93, 94n, 99–
104, 106, 108n; and Croatia 6, 70–72;
and Kosovo 7, 27, 68, 89–90, 94n, 99–
106, 108n; and Macedonia 8, 82, 84,
90–93; and Montenegro 27, 29, 68,
76–77, 87; and Yugoslavia 7
Serbian Academy of Arts and Sciences
69
Serbian Democratic Party (SDP) 72
Serbian National Council 71–72
Serbian nationalism 70–71
Serbs in Bosnia and Herzegovina 73, 84;
in Croatia 70–72; in Kosovo 73–75,
85–86, 87–89; in Montenegro 76–77
Šešelj, Vojislav 88
SFRY. *See* Socialist Federative Republic
of Yugoslavia
Shamanism 223, 230
Shan 13, 178, 181–82, 184–85,
188–90
Shanghai 14, 39, 225
Shanghai communiqué 229, 250n
Shanghai Five 226, 229, 251n
Shanghai Cooperation Organization
(SCO) 226
Shevardnatze, Eduard 45
Shi Lang 239
Shichor, Yitzhak, 221
Siberia 47, 60
Sikh 149, 154–55, 162n
Sikkim 30, 148
Silk Road 229, 230

Singh, Gobind 154
Singapore 29, 245
Sinhalese 13, 164–70
Siroky, David 4–5
Skopje 92–93, 95n
Slavonia 72
Slovakia 4, 11, 18, 99; peaceful secession
4
Slovenia 6, 67–76, 78n, 99, 100
SNP. *See* Scottish National Party
social class 138
Socialist Federative Republic of
Yugoslavia (SFRY) 66–75, 78n, 99–
100, 103. *See* Yugoslavia
Socialist Party of the Basque Country
115, 116, 124n
Solana, Javier 92, 95n
Solzhenitsyn, Alexander 59
Somalia 25
Song dynasty 13
South Africa 128
South Asia Association for Regional
Cooperation (SAARC) 160
South Caucasus 37, 44–45, 53, 55, 58.
See also Caucasus
South Ossetia 5, 6, 23, 28, 43–47, 54–55,
61–62; recognition of statehood 28,
53, 62
Southern Sudan 26–27, 30–31, 33n, 148.
See also Sudan
"sovereignist consensus" 243–44
sovereignty 1, 6, 10, 16, 26, 31–32, 54,
57, 59, 61, 68, 70–72, 75, 102, 116–18,
120, 123n, 127–29, 133–34, 141n, 202,
209, 220–21, 231, 243–44, 247–49,
251n; dynastic 202, 209, 214n;
popular 3, 22; territorial 199
Soviet Socialist Republic (SSR) 28, 44
Soviet Union 2, 5, 6–7, 17, 24, 27, 37,
42–46, 53–61, 66, 77, 101, 223, 225;
and federal republics 6, 43–45, 53, 56,
59; and Russia 6, 58–59;
disintegration 5–6, 27, 44, 46, 55
Spain 2, 4, 9–10, 12, 21, 30, 37, 43,
124n, 130, 232, 238; and Basque
Country 10, 30, 111–13, 116, 123n,
124n; colonization/decolonization 21
Sri Lanka 2, 4, 12–13, 17, 21, 30–31, 99,
161, 164–75; and Tamils 30, 83, 147,
159, 161, 164–75
Srinagar 157–58
stability 57, 59, 91, 120, 182–83, 185,
192, 227
Stalin, Joseph 55, 63, 101

262 *Index*

state. *See also* nation state. state
behaviour, towards ethnic minority
groups 1, 54, 82–87, 93, 94n, 99–102,
117, 119–20, 122, 123n, 124n, 129,
136, 140, 141n, 147–49, 165–75, 181–
83, 207–8, 224–27; state formation 56,
61–62, 72–76; state disintegration 58,
78n; state institutional arrangements
62, 66–67, 106, 108n, 110–13, 116,
123n, 127, 134, 152–59, 165–75, 183–
85, 187; state theory 28, 78n; state to
state relations 245–46, 251n
stateless nations 135, 139, 166
statist theory 111
Statute of Westminster 128
Straits Exchange Foundation (SEF)
244–47
Sudan 26–27, 31, 33n. *See also* Southern
Sudan.
Sufis, suficism 226
suicide bomb attacks 147, 222
Sumanthiran, M. A. 174
Sun, Yat-sen, 13, 239
Supreme Court of Canada 9, 110
Supreme Soviet 43, 59, 104
suzerainty 215n
Sweden 29, 55
Switzerland 33n, 43, 171
Syria 232

Tbilisi 45–47
Taipei 237, 241–43, 246–50
Taiwan 2, 15–16, 149, 230, 237–51; and
China 241–45; and Japan 239–40,
250, 251n; and the US. *See* Taiwan
Relations Act, United States.
international status 237, 247; history
238–42
Taiwanese consciousness 240, 242
Taiwanese identity 242–43
Taiwanese nationalism 242–43
Taiwan Relations Act (TRA) 240–41,
250, 251n
Tajikistan 55, 223, 226, 231
Taliban 159, 222, 226, 230
Tamils (Hindu) 13, 30, 83, 147, 149–50,
159, 161, 164–75
Tamil diaspora 171
Tamil identity 150, 164–66
Tamil kingdom 165
Tamil Nadu 13, 149–52, 159, 165,
170
Tamil National Alliance (TNA) 174
Tamil nationalism 166, 171

Tamil state (in Sri Lanka) 147, 164, 166,
169, 171, 173, 175
Tamil Tigers 30, 159
Tamil United Liberation Front (TULF)
169
Tang dynasty 13
Tanzania 33
Tatarstan 57, 61
Tatmadaw 181, 188
Taylor, Robert 189
taxation 113, 133, 137, 171, 173, 185,
191
Telangana 152–53
Telugu 150–54
Telugu Desam Party 152–54
territorial autonomy 113, 161
territorial conquest 54
territorial integrity 3, 12, 123n
territorial loyalties 227
territorial secession 4, 20, 54, 111, 171
territory 1, 3, 4, 72, 75, 113, 123n, 134;
purchase 3, 21
terrorism 8, 89–90, 92, 155, 158–59, 220,
222, 226, 228–29, 232, 233n
Than Swee 186
Thatcher, Margaret, 129, 135
The Hague 94n, 229
Thein Sein 187, 189, 191
Tibet 2, 5, 14–15, 18, 24, 149, 156, 159,
196–216, 220, 231, 238; political
autonomy 14, 29, 198, 200, 209;
history 14, 24, 202–3, 212, 215n;
migration to 208, 210; renunciation to
violence 196–97, 205; renunciation of
independence 14, 211, 215n
Tibetan Autonomous Region 29
Tibetan in exile 14, 196–99, 210, 214n
Tibetan identity 203
timing 5
Timor-Leste 16, 24, 27, 30, 33, 148. *See
also* East Timor.
Tito, President (Josip Broz) 67, 71, 101,
108n
Tongzhanbu. See United Front
Department
Torghurat Pass 231
TRA. *See* Taiwan Relations Act
trade 78n, 131, 180, 185, 188, 223, 229,
241, 247
Trajkovski, Boris 8, 86–87, 91–92, 95n
Transcaucasian Federation 55
transition 21, 57, 78n,
Transnistria 6, 43–44, 55, 63
Trentino-Alto-Adige Sudtirol 44

Trincomalee 167, 170
Tsai, Ying-wen 247
Tskhinvali, Micheil 46
Tudjman, Franjo 71
TULF. *See* Tamil United Liberation Front
Turfan 224, 227
Turkestan. *See* East(ern) Turkestan
Turkey 47, 53, 83, 149, 230
Turkic language/people 223–24
Turkish Republic of Northern Cyprus (TRNC) 53. *See also* Cyprus
Turkmenistan 56
tributary relationship 32n
Tripura 151
"tyranny of majority" 10

U Nu 181–83
UÇK. *See* Kosovo Liberation Army (KLA)
Udmurtia 44
Ukraine 5, 43, 53, 55–56, 58–60, 63
ULFA. *See* United Liberation Front of Assam
UN General Assembly 28
Uniates 60
unification 16, 244–45, 248
"Union of States" 148, 152
Union of Sovereign States (USS) 56
Union of Soviet Socialist Republics (USSR). *See* Soviet Union
Union, Progress and Democracy (UPyD) 115–16
Union Treaties 64n
United Front Department (*Tongzhanbu*) 211
United Kingdom 2, 3, 9–12, 90, 92, 127, 129–37, 140–41, 171; and Scotland 129–37, 140–41
United Liberation Front of Assam 155–56
United Nations 26, 31; and Kashmir 157; and Kosovo 104; and Republic of China, Taiwan 238, 240, 245, 247, 249; and Serbia 72, 75, 90, 100, 103; and Sri Lanka 172; Charter 24; peacekeeping 31, 73
United Nations Protected Area (UNPA) 72
United States (US) 8, 12, 16, 24, 27, 31, 33n, 123n, 134–35, 157, 159, 171, 200, 222, 237; and Bosnia and Herzegovina 73–74; and Croatia 39, 101, 165, 168, 524; and Kosovo 75,

89–91; and Serbia 76, 88–91; and Taiwan 16, 237–38, 240–42, 245–50, 251n; and Xinjiang 222, 233n
United States Congressional Research Service (USCRS) 222
unity, national 10, 78, 86–87, 148, 181, 201, 206, 228, 231
universalism 32
Unrepresented Nations and People's Organization (UNPO) 228–29
USSR. *See* Soviet Union
Ustasha 71
Uttar Pradesh 151–52
Uttarakhand 151–52
uti possidetis juris 3, 25, 27–28, 33n, 66
Uyghur 29, 220–33; Uyghur culture 220, 223; Uyghur diaspora 221–22, 228–29; Uyghur identity 223; Uyghur nationalism 223
Uyghur American Association 233n
Uyghur Autonomous Region of Xinjiang 220–21, 227. *See also* Xinjiang
Uyghur Empire/kingdom 223, 225
Uyghuristan 225, 232
Uzbekistan 43

Vance Plan 72
Vance-Owen Plan 73
Veliu, Fazli 86
Venice 118, 124n
Vikh 47
Vojvodina 44, 79n
vote 9, 23, 29, 45, 56, 77, 84, 91, 111, 128, 130, 135–36, 139, 166–67. *See also* elections

Wakhan Corridor 230, 233n
Wang Lequan 227–28
Was 188, 191
Washington DC 229, 241, 242, 244–45
water resources 27, 198–99
wealth 21, 180, 198, 231
welfare 112, 128, 130, 133, 173
West Bengal 151, 153
West Lothian question 130, 141
West Irian 24
Westminster doctrine 127, 141n
Westphalian International Order 24
Wickremesinge, Ranil 172
Wilson, Woodrow 123n
Wilsonian vision 23
Wolff, Stephan 90

264   *Index*

Wood, John 1, 2
Woodward, Susan 69
women 7, 22, 85, 103, 174
World Health Organization (WHO) 247
World War I 17, 22, 24, 77, 101, 131, 180
World War II 5, 13, 22, 31, 49n, 54, 63, 66, 71, 77, 78n, 128, 131, 133, 239
World Uyghur Congress (WUC) 15, 222, 229, 233n

Xhaferi, Arben 91, 95n
Xiamen 246
Xinjiang 5, 15, 18, 220–33

Yangon. *See* Rangoon.
Yecheng 228
Yeltsin, Boris 6, 59, 94n, 104–5, 226
Yemen 232
Yining 224 Yining uprising 228
Yuan dynasty 14
Yugoslav Communist Party 101, 108n
Yugoslav People's Army (YPA) 70, 72–73, 76

Yugoslavia 6, 30, 66–79, 99, 101, 103, 108n. *See also* Bosnia and Herzegovina; Croatia; Kosovo; Macedonia; Montenegro; Serbia; SFRY; Slovenia constitutional reform 68; dissolution 6, 71–78; and ethnicity 2, 313, 322–23; Federal Republic of Yugoslavia (FRY) 103; and foreign intervention and European Community/European Union 66–67, 70; and NATO (North Atlantic Treaty Organization) 72–75, 84, 90, 92–93, 94n, 103; and United Nations 1, 27–28, 71–72, 75, 90, 100, 103–4; and United States 8, 72–73, 75–76, 79n, 88–91, 100
Yunnan 156, 228

Zajedno 88
Zambia 33n
Zheng Chenggong 239
Zimmermann, Warren 88
Zhuang 15
Zungars 223, 227
Zungaria plateau 224